Hedgewar

Hedgewar

A DEFINITIVE BIOGRAPHY

SACHIN NANDHA

VINTAGE
An imprint of Penguin Random House

VINTAGE

Vintage is an imprint of the Penguin Random House group of companies whose addresses can be found at global.penguinrandomhouse.com

Published by Penguin Random House India Pvt. Ltd
4th Floor, Capital Tower 1, MG Road,
Gurugram 122 002, Haryana, India

First published in Vintage by Penguin Random House India 2025

10 9 8 7 6 5 4 3 2 1

ISBN 9780143467663

Typeset in Minion Pro by MAP Systems, Bengaluru, India
Printed at Thomson Press India Ltd, New Delhi

www.penguin.co.in

To all those who dare to challenge the status quo

Contents

Introduction

At 9.15 a.m., on 21 June 1940, Dr Keshav Baliram Hedgewar passed away after enduring severe fever and chronic back pain. He was fifty-one years old. He remained unmarried all his life, practised celibacy, was a teetotaller and a fervid revolutionary who had chosen a life of poverty. Thousands attended his cremation at Reshimbagh in Nagpur, but none of those who attended could have foreseen how his legacy would go on to shape India in the decades to come.

Much of the history of India in the twentieth century, and even more so the early twenty-first century, is Hedgewar's legacy. Prof. Madhav Golwalkar, Madhukar Deoras, Prof. Rajendra Singh, K.S. Sudarshan and the current incumbent Dr Mohan Bhagwat—icons to millions and monsters to others—are his heirs. These men lead the socio-cultural grassroots organization started by Hedgewar in 1925, which became known as the Rashtriya Swayamsevak Sangh, or the RSS in its better-known form.

In less than a century, the RSS has become the largest voluntary organization in the world, boasting some 60,000 centres across India, where men from all walks of life gather every morning to train, play and get organized. RSS training camps are attended by tens of thousands of volunteers and have produced two Indian prime ministers—Atal Bihari Vajpayee and the present incumbent Narendra Modi, who won the general elections in 2014, 2019 and 2024, with the largest mandate in thirty years. Modi is the leader of the Bharatiya Janata Party (BJP), widely known as the Hindu nationalist party, and an organization deeply influenced by men who belong to the RSS. Indeed, there is something to be said about the fact that Modi, and Vajpayee before him, were both *prachaaraks*[1] of the RSS before entering politics. At any given time, thousands of prachaaraks dedicate their lives to realizing the vision Hedgewar sculpted—that of a vibrant Hindu nation. Not since Jesus Christ has an obscure pauper inspired such devotion or been so calamitously misinterpreted.

It is time to strip away the mythology and try to rediscover Keshav the man. Hundreds of books have been written about the RSS, but almost all are by academics who have naively tried to make sense of the movement by framing it in Eurocentric constructs, and against the backdrop of twentieth-century European nationalism. The RSS was quickly dubbed as 'Hindu nationalist', and therefore, bigoted, orthodox, conservative, militant and, ultimately, dangerous for secular Indian society. To counter this, there have been many books written by supporters of the RSS for whom it is near blasphemy to treat Hedgewar as a man of flesh and blood. Consequently, they have further exacerbated the caricatures of the RSS by using similar rhetoric as the academics, albeit to mean something very different.

Hedgewar, an orphan by the age of twelve, found himself at a nationalist university in Calcutta in imperial India. He was tasked to collect firearms by bribing British soldiers. These would be collected by day and smuggled out by night through a secret countrywide network of revolutionaries determined to end British rule. He was an angry agitator in the eyes of the British authorities, and someone who spent much of his time in scholarly silence; to then becoming a political activist for the Indian National Congress, believing that India's independence was nigh, only to have an epiphany that Indians, and in particular the Hindus, were unfit to govern themselves due to an inner civilizational weakness that had to be remedied. He foresaw the inevitable tragic outcomes that would tear the country apart on religious lines as a direct consequence of Gandhi's leadership seven years after his own death; a gregarious and convivial man who went on to create, in the eyes of his opponents, the world's largest fascist organization; a deeply earnest philosopher who wrote very little and remained understated. One who had the audacity to dream of a nation served by upright citizens underpinned by that most nebulous of terms—*dharma*.

For large portions of the Muslim community in India, and all those who saw India as a strictly non-Hindu nation to be built on the socialist principles of the 1950s, Hedgewar was the demonic begetter of all evil, the founder of an awesomely sinister cult, the man whose baleful influence must be suppressed. In the western imagination, the RSS was an Indian version of the nationalist movements of the twentieth century in Europe with a topsoil of Indianness.[2] A version that looked to build a nation-state on the lines of caste and religion. Western academics, albeit earnestly, played into the caricaturing of the RSS as a danger to minorities in India and potentially an antithesis of what the West wanted to manifest in India. The RSS was caricatured as an anti-capitalist, fascist, para-military organization bent on creating a 'pure fatherland', by fashioning a Hindu hegemony.[3]

But why was it caricatured in this way? Certainly, western commentators have had very little direct access to the RSS or its inner workings, and the Indian academy was simply citing western academics and vice versa. Each fuelling the other until the RSS had become Hedgewar's brahmanical monster unleashed upon the vulnerable and ill-educated Indians. While state power was firmly in the hands of Indian elites, including the English-speaking media, socialists and communists, the RSS, with its millions of active volunteers, continued to work relentlessly at the grassroots. The organization became increasingly admired by those that it touched through its educational institutions, labour unions, students' unions, farmer's union, charities and hospitals. In all, RSS-trained men have started and run thousands of organizations across the entire spectrum of Indian society. In every nook and cranny of daily Indian life, the RSS has its influence, and with it, a little bit of Hedgewar's militant genius.

Like Marx, Hedgewar is not as he appears at first glance. Marx—ever the ardent critic of capitalism, understood capitalism better than anyone, and to this day, his critique is arguably the best there is. In much the same way, Hedgewar, the militant Hindu, was penetratingly critical of Hindu society-at-large and foresaw much of the chaos that was to ensue post-Independence. Unlike his contemporaries who blamed colonialism for all of India's ills, Hedgewar put the blame squarely on the Hindu majority. Just as Marx cannot be read earnestly if the reader carries the deforming mental lens of Lenin, Stalin and Mao—his so-called heirs—Hedgewar cannot be understood with the pre-conditioned mindset formed by academics who label him as ultra-Hindu and a hater of minorities.

To understand Hedgewar, one must understand his critique of Hindu society. It is his critique that is imbued into millions of RSS volunteers; that channels the life force of so many to reform Indian society. In Hedgewar's imagination, India had to be rebuilt on its own terms and not in line with some pseudo-western idea of how society ought to be organized. For Hedgewar, India had to be something that is equally modern and, as in the words of Erich Fromm, 'authentically' Indian. Sadly, Marx was a victim of his own disciples, something which Rudyard Kipling, as so often, rightly captured:

He that has a Gospel
To loose upon Mankind,
Though he serve it utterly –
Body, soul and mind –
Though he go to Calvary
Daily for its gain –
It is his Disciple
Shall make his labour vain.[4]

Hedgewar must have learnt this lesson well. He set out to build an organization not around himself, or his ideas, but upon systems and processes. His was an organization made to last with the single-minded aim of building men with a nationalist fervour that could shape a modern India in sync with its rich civilizational heritage spanning several millennia. Eighty-nine years later, RSS-trained men and women (through its sister organization, the Rashtra Sevika Samiti), having quietly transformed the grassroots of Indian society, saw one of their own become prime minister with the largest majority in three decades, ending the monopoly of power held by old Indian elites. Even though the RSS is a cultural organization, one must not be under any illusion that if India is to become a global power, as many predict, Hedgewar's legacy is going to shape, in one way or another, all of our lives at some point in the near future.

Only a fool could ignore Hedgewar all these years; but there is, alas, a ready supply of fools. I, not wanting to be a fool any longer, decided to start researching this biography, while many friends looked at me with incredulity. Why, they wondered, would anyone wish to write about—still less read about—such a discredited, outmoded and irrelevant figure? I carried on regardless; and the more I discovered Hedgewar, the more astoundingly topical he seemed to be. Modern-day pundits and commentators in India and abroad seldom, if at all, talk about the RSS, or Hedgewar, in any meaningful way. Indeed, all talk of the RSS is seen through the myopic narrative surrounding the BJP—its political creation, in their lame attempt to construct a rationale of the forces that have opposed the status quo, the hegemony of the Indian elite and minority interest groups.

The narrative goes something like this: if the Indian National Congress stood for liberty, development, secularism and modernity, then its opposing force must be authoritarian, backward, communal and orthodox; and the BJP being the 'political wing' of the RSS closes the matter once and for all on what the organization must stand for, and furthermore, its founder who is best forgotten and erased out of history books. The persistent myopia of pundits and commentators in modern India—who never paused to question whether the Indian elite and their political wing, the Indian National Congress, still upheld the ideals they once professed—ultimately led to a self-reinforcing, post-truth reality and biased news reporting. In other words, everything was framed in simplistic constructs where the Indian establishment, or as Marx would say, the Indian bourgeoisie, stood for a progressive India, despite the failed reality on the ground; while those who opposed them were labelled regressive, regardless of the dynamism and progress they showed at the grassroots level. Everything in academia and the English-speaking media was employed to reaffirm this false, myopic reality. Charles Spurgeon, the quintessential English Baptist minister, once quipped, 'A lie can travel halfway around the world, while the truth is still putting on his shoes', and in the case of Hedgewar, the truth has just come out the front door.

Hedgewar's legacy cannot be ignored. Policymakers, journalists, politicians and international investors around the world will need to grapple with what the RSS is and how it shapes Indian society. Without a new understanding, Indian society will remain a riddle wrapped in a mystery inside an enigma to outsiders, fostering uncertainty that in turn creates a collective psychology of needless fear.[5] Hedgewar and his creation could be an ally; an ally against global terrorism; an ally to fight global poverty; an ally to shape a global world order built on liberty and pluralism, all of which, I believe, is at the heart of Hedgewar. I will go further and contest that the RSS, at its core, is a pluralistic organization, with a caveat, being within a construct of the wider Indian civilizational narrative. For the world to make sense of India, it must make sense of the RSS, and an earnest starting point would be to become familiar with its founder.

Not bad for a man who was orphaned, lived in poverty, died relatively young and was only known in the wider freedom struggle as a sidekick to all the major players, including Gandhi. People have always viewed India through the prism of Gandhi, which may have served well in understanding India's struggle for freedom, but it has grossly misconstrued the reality that is India in the twenty-first century. It is now imperative that, in order to understand modern India, we must view it through the legacy of Hedgewar. For indeed, I contest that it is Hedgewar who has become the father of the Indian nation, which ironically would have been a title he and the RSS would abhor.

ONE: 1889–1902

Roots

'It's 1889, in Imperial India. Can anyone name which famous person was born in this year?' A couple of hands rocket upwards, trying to be acknowledged as the first to know the answer, itching to be picked by the teacher. 'Erm, I think Rohit's hand went up first. Rohit, who am I thinking of?' she asked, a good teacher by all accounts.

'Nehru chacha,' the boy sweetly tells the teacher, with glee in his eyes.

'You're absolutely right. Well done. Our first Prime minister was born in that year. Can anyone tell me his full name?' More hands shoot-up. Clearly, this answer is known by many more seven-year-olds in this school for India's privileged classes. 'Oh-so many hands to choose from, let me see, who shall I pick?'

'Me. Me. Me,' the classroom is filled with the sound of tweeting birds.

'Ok, Ok, Meera, can you tell me the answer?'

With her hand, still straight in the air, and head tilted, she answered 'Jawaharlal Nehru' with a flash of pride woven into her innocent tone.

'That's right. Well done. You can now lower your hand, Meera,' with a suggestive sign to calm down.

'At this point, seated at the back of the class, I felt compelled to chime in with a question of my own,' he says with a nostalgic smile, and radiant white eyes gleaming through his thick spectacles, 'Who else was born in the same year, and is a little older than Nehru chacha? There was silence. Even the teacher, a little surprised, was trying to look around the class to encourage the children to answer the question, while she herself was trying her dandiest to come up with a name. 'The person I am thinking

> of,' I continued, to break the awkward silence, 'was the founder of the largest voluntary organization in the world.' Nothing. The kids looked distinctly unimpressed. The teacher, a little flustered asks me, 'Can you tell us, as we may not have covered this in their lessons?' 'Dr Keshav Baliram Hedgewar,' I reveal with as much enthusiasm as I could muster. He was the founder of the RSS, the Rashtriya Swayamsevak Sangh. 'He was born on the 1 April 1889.' Silence. A disinterested silence filled the room. Even the teacher had a blank look about her. The teacher had some recollection of hearing about the RSS in the news, but often in disparaging ways, and she had certainly never heard of Doctor ji, and she stressed to remind me that she was a history major'. He broke into a child-like chuckle as he ended his story.

This was the experience as recollected jovially by an old RSS *swayamsevak* on his first visit to one of the elite schools in Delhi.

Hedgewar's influence is everywhere in modern India and nowhere in India's collective memory. He has been systematically removed from history textbooks and erased out of India's struggle for freedom. Apart from those who attend one of the 60,000 daily centres and 25,000 weekly centres, called *shakhas* (branches), of the RSS, who are actively, albeit informally, educated about the life and values of Hedgewar, seldom will you find people who can accurately articulate anything meaningful about the man. At best, one will find poor caricatures, either unrealistic impressions of a godlike character, the saviour of the Hindus or downright extremist, a hater of minorities and the Hitler of India. None of these extremes are remotely accurate or meaningful.

In 1928, Hedgewar echoed the sentiments of another global figure, Rabindranath Tagore, lamenting that 'the mental composition of our people is not suited for an orderly society. They do not pursue even the most elementary day-to-day tasks to their successful conclusion but work with one eye on loud and vulgar publicity'.[1] Hedgewar was by no means the first to articulate the problem with Indian society, but he was the first to offer a way out of the fly bottle. From thinkers and social reformers such as Tagore, Aurobindo, Tilak, Gandhi and Nehru, to countless others who saw the problem all too clearly, but alas, failed to offer a lasting solution. Hedgewar would have agreed with Marx, in that individuals reflect the world they inhabit. He was not a messiah descended from heaven, but rather a product of his unique set of circumstances and his own latent genius. He died relatively young, aged fifty-one, and had a sickly constitution by the time he was in his mid-forties, something which was probably caused by the life he chose—one of asceticism.

Keshav was one of six children—two brothers and three sisters, born to parents who lived in relative poverty. Fifth in the pecking order. He was a Deshastha Brahmin, who were those that came from the Deccan region. He was born, lived most of his life and died in Nagpur, a thriving city even then. Around 4 per cent of Nagpur's population were Brahmins, of whom 60 per cent were Deshastha.[2] Keshav would have been born into an established community, relatively stable and in all likelihood, he would not have noticed his poverty, disguised as it was by his notable lineage.

The Hedgewar family came from a small village on the border of modern-day Maharashtra and Telangana called Kandakurthi. Today, it has a mere population of 4500, and in the mid-nineteenth century, it would have been half of that. Three locally important rivers meet nearby, the Godavari, Vanjra and Haridra. As you walk along the banks of this confluence, you would see a mere trickle of water flow by with all three rivers dammed upstream to create the Sriramsagar reservoir. For most of the year, it is an arid landscape, both in terms of the amount of rainfall it receives and its relative insignificance. It is now a small village in nowhere significant, with nothing much happening. The monsoon rains seldom reach the Deccan plains, blocked by the Nilgiri mountain range in the west.

At the time of the Hedgewars living here, this area would have been a place of pilgrimage for local Hindus who always personified rivers into goddesses. All three rivers would have merged in a confluence with vast amounts of water passing by in a steady but strong current. It would have been an important resting point for traders and travellers. At the point where the village is located, the rivers would have been 450 metres wide. It would have been quite a sight, with temples on both banks, and with devotees offering salutations at sunrise to the rising sun, and again at dusk. Constant activity throughout the day would have lined the banks with an equal measure of ritual and trade. As a result, Kandakurthi acted as a gateway for Hindus in the region, and as such became home to many Brahmin families. Thus, becoming a centre of learning. It was a centre point, literally, of ideas from east and west, as well as north and south. It would have enjoyed the distinction that all deeply religious places hold, composed of magnificent views across a vast river, the rising sun in the east, with temple bells and incantations of mantras being recited throughout the day, traders and travellers looking to rest.

The Hedgewars lived around Kandakurthi as far back as the eighth century, where local folklore suggests that Shankaracharya, the famous Advaitin scholar and *rishi* (seer), would nominate a member of the Hedgewar family to teach and preserve the authentic verses from the Rig Veda, the source of modern Hindu culture and civilization written down around 1800 BCE. Over hundreds of years, the Hedgewars, father to son, carried on a tradition which was to learn verbatim the Vedic verses and to teach others in the local area. Like many respected Brahmin families, the Hedgewars would have had a continuous *havan* burning in their house, just as how ancient Zoroastrians personified the fire as the ultimate reality.

In Hedgewar folklore, learning to wrestle and achieving mastery in some form of self-defence was a must for every young man. Hedgewars were known equally for their physique as much as for their knowledge. They would have lived mostly through the patronage of the kings in one shape or another, as well as by means of small stipends from local villagers and landlords. Their life would have been simple, but highly ordered and disciplined. Learning, teaching, performing daily rituals and providing pastoral care for those around them. The Hedgewars, and Brahmins like them, were the storehouses of ancient Indian civilization. It was through these vessels that Indian customs, traditions, religious thought, philosophy, mathematics and the like were transferred, iteratively evolving, generation by generation.

Keshav was born in the bustling city of Nagpur on 1 April 1889. A poignant day to be born on, and one that the literature of the RSS never fails to point out whenever the Hedgewar story is recited. It was the Hindu New Year. A little ironic then that this 'man of men' would be an ardent critic of Hindu society throughout his life. So much so that he would expend his entire life force in trying to reform it. The RSS literature is always highly suggestive as this being so significant that it must be some sign from the divine of what was to come, appealing to the superstitious and hero-worshipping Indian mind.

Nagpur is a six-hour drive on modern Indian roads from Kandakurthi and located right in the centre of modern India. It was Keshav's grandfather, Narhar Shastri Hedgewar, who relocated the family to Nagpur some two hundred years ago.[3] It seems that irony followed the Hedgewars as much as divinity did. Keshav's grandfather would have been gently forced from his ancestral home due to the changing socio-economic climate of the time. The Hedgewars, and Brahmins like them, would have had the patronage of the rulers and could rely on the powerful to ensure that their way of life could be preserved without having to 'sell knowledge', nor abandon it, for the sake of making a livelihood.

All that had changed when Tipu Sultan took over the reins of Srirangapatnam from his father Hyder Ali in 1782. He revoked any subsidies enjoyed by the Brahmins and his atrocities against Hindus, who comprised most of his subjects, began to mount up. Historians have written extensively about the piety of Tipu Sultan as a Muslim first and foremost.[4] One can also speculate that it was his 'Muslim first' policy that led him to forcefully convert and circumcise some forty thousand Hindu captives.[5] On one occasion, he is reported to have ordered the mutilation of the breasts of thousands of Hindu Lingayat women for having a custom dating back millennia of not covering their breasts.[6] This act had its desired effect, and Hindu women in this region cover themselves with long garments even today.[7] Incidents such as this would have been well reported to families, such as the Hedgewars, who were also pastoral carers of the local Hindu population. It is little wonder then that Tipu Sultan was eventually defeated by the (East India) Company in 1799, as one can be quite certain that the loyalty of most of his Hindu subjects would have waned during his reign.

The East India Company divided his kingdom into three parts. The northern part was given to the Bhosale rulers, where Kundakurthi was located. For some time, there would have been hope that things will return to the good old days, and indeed they may well have done, but then a new foreign power was ruling over the land of the Hedgewars. Things probably went from bad to worse, and Narhar Shastri decided to finally leave his ancestral home and move to Nagpur, a four-day journey. Hopes of prospering under a Hindu kingdom were short-lived. In 1817, the third Anglo-Maratha war took place, and Nagpur too fell into the hands of the Company in all but name. Officially, Nagpur was taken over in 1854.

The Hedgewars prospered in Nagpur, at least for the first few years. But eventually, the shadow of colonial rule caught up with them. The British saw no value in being patrons of an 'exceedingly depraved religion'.[8] The general, simplistic narrative given in RSS renderings is that the British were exploiters, and systematically wanted to deconstruct the Hindu culture and subjugate the minds of the Indians. This is by no means some off the wall anti-British slandering, Lord Macaulay's minute to the Supreme Council of India in February 1835 is worth citing in full:

> I have no knowledge of either Sanscrit or Arabic. But I have done what I could to form a correct estimate of their value. I have read translations of the most celebrated Arabic and Sanscrit works. I have conversed both here and at home with men distinguished by their proficiency in the Eastern tongues. I am quite ready to take the Oriental learning at the valuation of the Orientalists themselves. I have never found one among them who could deny that a single shelf of a good European library was worth the whole native literature of India and Arabia. It will hardly be disputed, I suppose, that the department of literature in which the Eastern writers stand highest is poetry. And I certainly never met with any orientalist who ventured to maintain that the Arabic and Sanscrit poetry could be compared to that of the great European nations. But when we pass from works of imagination to works in which facts are recorded and general principles investigated, the superiority of the Europeans becomes absolutely immeasurable. It is, I believe, no exaggeration to say that all the historical information which has been collected from all the books written in the Sanscrit language is less valuable than what may be found in the most paltry abridgments used at preparatory schools in England. In every branch of physical or moral philosophy, the relative position of the two nations is nearly the same. I feel... that it is impossible for us, with our limited means, to attempt to educate the body of the people. We must at present do our best to form a class who may be interpreters between us and the millions whom we govern, – a class of persons Indian in blood and colour, but English in tastes, in opinions, in morals and in intellect. To that class we may leave it to refine the vernacular dialects of the country, to enrich those dialects with terms of science borrowed from the Western nomenclature, and to render them by degrees fit vehicles for conveying knowledge to the great mass of the population.[9]

The Hedgewars and families like theirs—the repositories of ancient Hindu culture, would need to be removed from positions of influence and patronage. In the mid-nineteenth century, the family fell on hard times. With no patronage for the arts, philosophy or ritual, many Brahmin families fell into destitution. Several Brahmin boys ended up giving up their ancestral professions as teachers, philosophers, mathematicians,

Ayurveda practitioners and such-like, to learn English, and the 'lucky' few would land jobs in the Indian civil service. As a last resort, many Brahmins joined the British military to avoid falling into destitution.[10] The British took on the boys from these learned families all too readily. They were capable of learning, literate, disciplined, moral and loyal.[11] Until 1931, there was a Brahmin-only regiment in the British Indian Army. Interestingly, during both World Wars, Brahmin boys were actively encouraged to join the war struggle, and in some instances, the British forced Brahmins into military service.

Whether the British knew it or not, but by the Brahmins joining the army, it legitimized British rule, and in Bengal, it even made the army as an aspirational career for many sections of the Hindu community. Those Brahmin boys who could not join the army or the civil service had to rely on ritual to earn their living. It is not surprising that ritualism rampantly took hold on the Hindu *samaj* (community). Since Brahmins had to now scrape out a living from ritual, they began to create ever more elaborate routines purporting to some belief or another, in order to then charge for their service. The ritualism often associated with Hindu culture in popular European imagination stems from two sources. The first from Christian missionaries who 'studied' the Hindu culture and naturally applied a fuzzy logic to their interpretations in order to raise funds back in England for the Christian mission. Their sole aim was to 'harvest' the souls of the natives and bring them to the love of Christ; and the second a more legitimate source from the increasing ritualism preached by the Brahmins in order to make a living.[12]

Brahmin women were not spared from the long dark shadow cast by colonialism. The British systematized prostitution and introduced state control. Across the British Indian Army, in every regiment consisting of a thousand soldiers, a *chakla* would be created consisting of twelve to fifteen young girls who were selected to 'service' the soldiers and officers. Families that fell into destitution often had little choice but to sell themselves into sex work to provide for themselves.[13] Many Brahmin women would become housemaids and nannies for British officers. The hours were long, and the demands put upon them made certain that raising their own children became a reluctant secondary activity. Brahmin parents were unable to effectively teach their children all the knowledge accumulated by their forebears, and soon that great storehouse of Hindu learning was diminished within a generation or two, often replaced by an unconscious self-loathing, just as Macaulay had prescribed.

By the time of Keshav's birth, around 11 per cent of the population would have lived in urban centres, and the young Keshav would not have been overtly aware that India was effectively colonized.[14] The British ruled much of India through an efficient civil service ordered by them but run by Indian clerks and soldiers. Often laws were made in the name of the rulers who sat on the throne as proxies. The British were an invisible power for the ordinary Indian at the time. They would have known that a formidable foreign power was in control over their lives and that they were subjects to it, but the subjugation would have felt like some bad dream, difficult to conceptualize, decipher or remedy, but its effects could be felt to the core of one's being. In the 1891 census of British India, 2,41,000 people registered English as their mother tongue, in a population of around 300 million. Of the British population, 66,000 were officers in the Army. So few ruled so many, clandestinely. It had to be that way.[15]

In all likelihood, Keshav would have never seen a white British person in his early years. Yet, he would have known the hardships endured by his people due to the rule of a foreign power. He would have the weight of dead generations upon his shoulders from a young age. His grandfather and father, along with uncles and older siblings, would have passed down not only gifts of language, philosophy, ritual and custom, but also the family folklores relaying his lineage, the 'Golden' age of Hindu India, tales of great rishis and sages, as well as great Hindu kings such as Chandra Gupta Maurya, who famously repelled Alexander of Macedon in 326 BCE with the help of that wily teacher called Kautilya. Mixed in with this would have been dark tales of atrocities dished out by invaders who wanted to do nothing more than exploit his people. An 'us' identity would have been quite a natural phenomenon to have taken place in forming young Keshav's character. But of course, with an 'us' comes a 'them'. Keshav would have been aware that many of his friends aspired to join the civil service or the army, and prioritized English over Sanskrit. He would have seen that his parents struggled to make ends meet. But this later point he would have seen throughout society, and so he would have seen it as a matter of fact, and when everyone is poor, no one is poor!

Keshav's father, Baliram, was a burly man. Often a suffix 'pant' denoting a mark of respect would be added by locals due to his prestigious lineage. He was a short-tempered man, a disciplinarian and stern taskmaster at home.[16] He was nevertheless equally liked and respected by family and friends. He provided immense pastoral care for the hundreds of families in Nagpur that were struggling to cope with their new reality under an invisible tyranny. He was a man not seduced by the prospects of his children joining the military or any state apparatus inadvertently designed to subvert the Hindu culture. He instilled the same patriotism in all six of his children.[17] A certain degree of self-pride in oneself and one's culture, with a topsoil of awareness of the leviathan that confronted them, was created through osmosis.

Revati Hedgewar, Keshav's mother, on the other hand, was different. She was the *ying* to Baliram's *yang*. Revati too was born in Nagpur, but her family came from modern-day Telangana. She was a Paithankar, another Brahmin family name with an old lineage. Like the Hedgewars, the Paithankars would have come on hard times first under Tipu Sultan, and then under the British, and would have come to Nagpur to seek shelter from the troubles brewing all around them. We know little about her. There are no letters and no accounts, except Keshav's own description of her to his friends. All we can discern is that she was the quietly strong type who was in complete control of the household finances, as were many women in traditional Hindu homes. She ensured that the family always had enough and would have held her husband to account if pennies were squandered.[18]

They had six children together. Not uncommon for those days. Infant mortality was staggering; at 521 out of every 1000 born and getting worse throughout the 1800s.[19] The eldest was Mahadev. He was a hothead. A wrestler taking after his grandfather and father. He built a gymnasium in the house and used to bring friends home to wrestle with. He was bright too. From what little we do know about Mahadev, he was gregarious, studious and was quite the model Brahmin boy for those times. Two girls, Raju and Sharayu, followed in relatively quick succession, followed by another boy named Sitaram. Then came young Keshav, followed by his younger sister Rangu. We know practically nothing of any of the girls except they married into 'good' families in what today we would consider to be child marriages, but quite the norm in nineteenth century India. In a patriarchal society, where male lineage matters, and women were on the whole revered as mothers and wives, their memories, if any at all, come through their sons and husbands.

As far as we can tell, young Keshav led an ordinary life for a boy from his background. We know that his father, who was making a living out of performing rituals and pujas, taught him these tools from an early age. He enjoyed his local playschool, and competitive sports drew him in early. He was competitive but quiet. He was particularly attached to the household cow. Many working families would have had their own cow and would literally live with them as a member of the family.[20]

Cows have always held a confusing significance in the Hindu psyche. To those not rooted within the Hindu culture, it sounds cute at best, and downright backward at worst—some hang-up of a bygone age. In some sense, this is quite right. And yet, like all things ancient, there is far more than meets the eye. Indeed, this issue of cows plays at the heart of politics in twenty-first century India. Western commentators have often utilized caricatures and overly simplified models to explain the relationship Hindus have with cows.

The RSS promotes the protection of cows and has been lobbying assertively on bringing in anti-slaughter legislation. At times, news reports have suggested that *swayamsevaks* (those that attend RSS *shakhas*) have taken the law into their own hands and become vigilantes dishing out corporal punishment on individuals that harm cows—often, but not always, Muslims are at the receiving end. In his adult years, Hedgewar confronted anyone, whether Hindu or not, whom he saw mistreating cows or taking them to slaughter. There could only be two outcomes, they either sell him the cow there and then, or face a beating, and he would take the cow anyway, leaving behind some money for the poor fool who didn't heed his earlier warning. In RSS *bauddhiks*, that is imparting titbits of knowledge and inspiration through storytelling, there are several tales of Hedgewar 'bravely' protecting *gaumata* (cow personified as a mother). These stories would surely go some way in explaining the deep-rooted love the RSS has with cow protection. But this is not all.

Cows have always been treated with deference in most ancient cultures.[21] All the Hindu sects, including Buddhism, hold the cow in immense veneration. As did the Persians, Greeks and Romans. The latter three cultures are now extinct by all accounts, and so the West suffers a collective amnesia regarding the relationship our ancestors would have had with their animals, especially the cow. The Hindu still recalls this memory from a deep past. It is deep-rooted and hardwired into the culture. It is quite well documented that cows in ancient cultures were integral to the economy. Cows provided milk, a plethora of dairy products, fertilizer and dung as fuel.[22] The Vedas emphasize the need to protect cows, which means that this notion of protecting the cow certainly was not modern. Keshav would have been taught the Vedic texts by his father through an oral tradition, and the practice of looking after the cow would have been learnt from watching and helping his mother. It would have seemed completely natural to Keshav that the cow should not only be regarded as an extended member of the family but maybe more, it too must be revered, as one would do one's own parents. By the second century CE, the entire Hindu culture, including Jainism and Buddhism, preached that ahimsa (non-harming) was the highest virtue one can live by. We shouldn't be dulled into thinking that ahimsa is some obscure religious tenant. It is what drove Gandhi, Dr Martin Luther King and Mandela in the twentieth century, and you will find Hindu students across the West discussing ahimsa and its application in modern life. This is a concept that is central to being Hindu. Furthermore, the cow is just the tip of the iceberg. Ahimsa is a concept that applies to all life —not just cows. The cow has become a totem pole, a thing of veneration, but one must see beyond it. So, when the RSS says it is protecting the cow, it is merely protecting the totem pole. Once it has secured that, it will move on to protect all life forms, including rivers, something which has already begun to happen in India. When seen through this prism, the whole cow issue in modern India should be an animal rights campaigners wet dream.

Keshav was an active kid. Early mornings consisted of a quick prayer in front of the mandir (temple) in the house, something which every Hindu home has even today, and then he ran outside with his neighbourhood friends playing a game now lost called *chakori*[23]. Keshav would have learnt yoga as part of his education being a good Brahmin, and his older brother Mahadev taught him some introductory gymnastics, something which he would have learnt through his wrestling teacher.[24] Kids from Keshav's background didn't have the opportunity to learn sports as we do today. Rather it would have been unstructured ruffian games, where boys were encouraged to be active and take it upon themselves to build a physique. Keshav, being well endowed from his father and mother, was not a small timid specimen. Coupled with coaching and mentoring from his equally tough elder brother Mahadev, he would have been the antithesis of what the popular image in the West had been of scrawny looking poor Indian boys running around the street.

It is certainly true that during the 1900s, the size of the average Indian became diminutive compared to their Caucasian European cousins. Malnutrition was rife. Food was in relative scarcity. And what food there was, was often not wholesome. Beggars couldn't be choosers. In 1930, the young American historian Will Durant visited India for the first time. Durant wrote in his short, but compassionate book, *The Case for India*:

> 'The British conquest of India was the invasion and destruction of a high civilisation by a trading company utterly without scruple, or principle, careless of art and greedy for gain, over-running with fire and sword a country temporarily disordered and helpless, bribing and murdering, annexing and stealing, and beginning that career of illegal and 'legal' plunder which has now [1930] gone on ruthlessly for one hundred and seventy-three years.'[25]

India suffered from twelve major famines between 1769 to 1944. In total, historians have estimated that almost fifty million people died from starvation during these famines.[26] The economic, social and psychological impact this would have had on a culture is quite unimaginable. India during this time was also systematically de-industrialized, Shashi Tharoor writes in his book *An Era Of Darkness* that India went from contributing 23 per cent to the world economy to 3 per cent by the time Keshav was in his early adolescence.[27] Keshav's society had reached the inglorious bottom. Given the situation, for Hedgewar to be close to six feet tall, would have made him a relative giant amongst his own people, and many Europeans.[28]

Whereas Mahadev and Sitaram were enrolled in a Hindi medium school, Baliram was convinced by friends to enrol the young Keshav into an English medium school. It took Baliram a long time before his resolve broke, and he made his youngest son join a school where a foreign language would the medium of education. It was everything he stood against. And yet, no matter how strong-headed or stubborn a person is, and Revati knew exactly how unyielding Baliram could be, the sheer weight of acknowledging the difficult position one finds themselves in is often the only way to bring about a change. The Hedgewars were struggling. Baliram would not have wanted his sons to suffer likewise, and so he finally admitted Keshav to learn English, in the hope of giving him better opportunities in a fast-changing world, which he was quickly falling out of step with. Even though Baliram would have made this decision with a heavy heart, we know that Keshav delighted in it. He wanted to learn English. He was eager to read, learn and absorb what he could from this new world they all found themselves in. Ironic really, a theme I will keep bringing up in this tale, that a man who in modern circles is seen as an icon for conservatism, orthodoxy and backwardness, was keen to break with tradition in his youth and became the first one in his family to receive an English education. He was enrolled at the Neil City High School in Mahal, Nagpur.[29]

There is something to be said about the fact that Baliram chose this school for the young Keshav. Neil City High School is a deceiving name. It was not a British institution in any sense. It was run by the Nagpur Shikshan Mandal, which at best can be rendered as Nagpur Education Society. The school was named after a British commissioner of Nagpur, a gentleman named Neil, who assisted the society in procuring land. Unlike Keshav's father who came to terms with his reality rather late in the day, the society had started teaching English in 1869, twenty years before Keshav was born. The society was a collection of well-educated men who came together to build schools for the community. It would have been created during Bhosale rule, before the Anglo-Maratha wars of 1817. In 1881, some eight years before Keshav's birth, the society had started a school for girls called the Morris Girls School. Once again, the name of the school can be misleading, as to assume that the British had anything to do with it, except allow the Mandal (Committee) to procure land that it had won through the end of a bayonet. Interestingly, the Nagpur Shikshan Mandal still exists and runs Mathurdasji Mohota College of Science, which was founded in 1949.

Along with a classical Sanskrit education, Keshav now had access to western knowledge. He became an avid reader, absorbing the writings of many European philosophers, from Nietzsche's nihilism to Mazzini's call for patriotism. English also opened his world to international news, and in some real sense come to terms with the decrepit state of his people. The *Kesari*, a pro-free India daily run by another great name in Indian history—Bal Gangadhar Tilak—whetted his appetite for politics.[30] It would not have been missed by his father that Keshav was developing in a different direction to the rest of his children. Baliram would have known access to the English language meant that he could no longer keep an ever-watchful eye on his son and would have to trust in the young man's own reason. Around this time, Keshav started exploring what had happened to his country before the British had arrived. He eagerly read the life and deeds of the great Maratha king, Shiva Bhonsle, better known as Shivaji.[31] The life and times of Shivaji, above all others, had played a formative role in shaping what a Hindu polity might look like.

Shivaji became the epitome of Hindu achievement at a time when the population at large was in a rather decrepit state. In modern India, and especially in the RSS, Shivaji has taken on Churchillian significance, where questioning the moral fibre of this great king would, in a psychological sense, be tantamount to treason. Just as the figure of Churchill has become embedded in the British psyche as the ultimate British wartime leader, a man who somehow epitomizes British resilience and determination, so Shivaji's life embodies the ultimate Hindu king who upheld the values espousing dharma. He is the emblem of Hindus, and especially the RSS. The Churchillian comparison goes further. In the same way that British culture has whitewashed Churchill's less than perfect character, and has overlooked his alcoholism, bouts of depression, racism, bigotry, sexism and callousness towards British subjects in the popular narrative, Shivaji, too, is remembered in a eulogized form.[32] It is this form that Keshav would have read. Shivaji is the king who symbolized Indian revivalism in the late nineteenth century.

By the time Keshav was in his adolescence, the Bhosale rulers of Nagpur had been reduced to little more than decorative props for British rule. The Bhosale family kept up appearances, signed legal decrees and passed laws, but only in name. They held great street pageantries once a year in Nagpur where beautifully draped elephants, uniformed soldiers on horseback and great big cannons for good measure were rolled out to entertain the Indian mob. A show of strength, albeit British strength, masquerading as Bhosale military prowess. Thousands would line the streets to cheer and clap the soldiers as they rode by in all their military splendour. Keshav was one of those cheering kids who was taken in by the circus until he began to piece together that something was not quite as it seemed. The free-India newspaper called *Kesari*, published out of Pune, coupled with the influence of his father, would have been the source of Keshav's realization that he and his people were being colonized. His English education would have given him access to literature that most Indian children would not have had. His early realization that his people were under the rule of a foreign power, coupled with exposure to Hindu heroes like Shivaji, and the weight of his lineage, which remembered the golden age of India through stories, scripture and folklore, all would have culminated in building the foundational character traits that served him, for better or ill, for the rest of his life. These were the seeds that were planted in young Hedgewar that would later germinate through a rainfall of tragedy.

The storm clouds of history were gathering in 1896, a year before the sixtieth anniversary of Queen Victoria's coronation. The crown had decided that across the empire, celebrations were to be held and public displays of loyalty from all British subjects were on the menu for popular public consumption. And lest one was to forget, 'this vast empire on which the sun never sets' to which a century later the Indian writer and politician Shashi Tharoor quipped, 'even God couldn't trust the British in the dark', was beginning to creak by the end of the nineteenth century.[33,34] The looming coronation was the moment that separated those Indian communities that were jockeying for political capital, and those nationalists who wanted to see a free India, often described as radicals in Eurocentric readings of modern Indian history. However, these nationalists came in many different shapes and sizes and often were deeply critical of one another. But on this occasion, many were put in a dilemma—how best to balance congratulatory messages with political protests? Ultimately, this question helped widen fissures between those loyal to the crown, and the nationalists. By the time the jubilee festivities ended in late 1897, the nationalists had proven themselves to be a force with which to be reckoned.[35] Keshav was eight years old, only just learning to read English newspapers, and he would have begun to map out some of the forces that were shaping his world. By reading newspapers, listening to public announcements, conversations between adults, and the sheer act of living consciously would have been enough for his sympathies to have formed towards the nationalist agenda. On all counts, Keshav was a brilliant boy growing up in turbulent times. But it is no surprise at all that he was moulded by his early years to be a nationalist for the rest of his life, especially in light of what happened in 1897.

That year he would have seen and read about a large number of loyal Indians tripping over themselves to pay homage to the Crown. The British were inviting delegations from across the Indian subcontinent to Shimla, at the foothills of the Himalayas, where the Viceroy lived during the summer months. The Hindus of Lahore, Khojas of Bombay, Awadhi Taluqdars and Muslim Bengali women[36] all flooded into the Viceroy's home one after another to give their congratulations. Other Indians lost no opportunity for lavish and oftentimes servile demonstrations of their loyalty to the crown. Princes held *darbars*, fed thousands of poor people and laid foundation stones for new hospitals, schools and churches to be named after the Queen, or some Christian saint. Prayer meetings were organized in mosques and temples. Keshav would have noticed that even some of his father's friends, devout Brahmins from his community, were arranging prayers for the distant Queen of England. Newspaper articles were making frontline news about statues of the Queen being erected across many cities. In Nagpur, Keshav would have walked by two Queen Victoria statues, made of white stone, which were located outside Vidhan Bhavan and the Victoria Technical College, which is today the location of Maharaj Bagh Zoo.[37] Both statues would have been less than an hour's walk from Keshav's home located at Mahal. Interestingly, the Jain community of Calcutta made the most of their congratulatory note by requesting Victoria to ban all animal slaughter on the day of her jubilee. Of course, it goes without saying that this was swiftly ignored. These memorials, durbars and festivals were all enthusiastically reported on by the British and European press for domestic consumption, often to reinforce the common European narrative that the only thing that united a diverse India was British imperialism.[38]

The young Keshav would have contrasted this show of flowery servility with those that chose to make themselves heard loud and clear to the world that Indian political consciousness was rising. The year 1897 was, and still is, considered to be pivotal in the Indian freedom struggle. Across India, the plague had been raging since 1896. According to official British records, it was probably imported from Hong Kong where an epidemic had spread three years earlier. This was the first official acceptance that the bubonic plague had entered India. Historians now believe that the British had brought it with them as early as the late 1700s.[39] It was largely confined to small areas, and never acknowledged by the British authorities. The plague of 1896 came to port cities such as Bombay (now Mumbai), Karachi, Calcutta (now Kolkata), and later to Pune. In all, over 12.5 million Indians would lose their lives over the next decade. It would soon directly touch Keshav, but alas, these were still the years where the storm clouds were gathering. As if things were not bad enough, a famine had struck North-west India, to which the British authorities responded in their own laissez-faire manner by preaching the gospel of free markets at the end of sharpened bayonets. The famine had affected some 69 million people, of which a million had lost their lives by 1897.[40] It was against this backdrop that the nationalists were agitating against imperialism. A tipping point had arrived.

Leaders of the Indian National Congress, an organization to represent that Indian voice to the authorities that was barely twelve years old, were at loggerheads as to how to balance loyalty to the crown with public agitation against British exploitation. According to Dinyar Patel, a Harvard historian, the Congress held a meeting in 1896 in Calcutta, where they passed a feeble resolution congratulating the Queen.[41] This sent Henry Hyndman, the British writer and politician, who became a leading socialist figure after 1880 having read Marx's *Communist Manifesto*, into a fit of rage. 'Congratulations for what?' he asked his friend, Dadabhai Naoroji, in January 1897. 'For having ruined India for two or three generations to come? It is pitiful.'[42] Hyndman's relationship with the leader of the Indian National Congress forms an important part of the story of India's response to the jubilee, which, in turn, affects Keshav's weltanschauung.[43] Naoroji was living in London at this time, where he was agitating for Indian political reform. Mounting pressure coming from the motherland by way of news stories and personal accounts of death, starvation and in equal proportions stories of British brutality and indifference, led Naoroji to throw in his lot with Hyndman's Social Democratic Federation (SDF)[44]. They began to launch a series of protests and public meetings across Britain. Both men agreed that the massive drain of wealth and resources by the British were the root cause of India's poverty and misery. They had by now spent several decades lobbying for more Indian representation in the Imperial government. On one occasion at a public meeting, he thunderously told the crowd 'that the silver jubilee should be celebrated in a manner befitting a monarch who had been the empress of famine and the Queen of black death.'[45] In the same month, Naoroji wrote directly to the Queen, accusing the British government of inflicting upon the Indians 'all the scourges of the world war, pestilence and famine.'[46] Another British sympathizer was William Wedderburn, an aristocratic Scotsman who had joined the Indian civil service in 1860 and later became a politician, who advised the Congress that there should also be mass agitations in India by the public-at-large if they were to avoid being labelled as mischievous opportunists. Wedderburn's advice fell on deaf ears and Naoroji's campaign came to a grinding halt. The irony is that an Indian found a British white man's rhetoric, that of Hyndman, for his call on the Indian masses to agitate, too extreme and decided to distance himself.

However, others in Pune, on 22 June 1897, were thinking along the same lines as Hyndman, albeit their thoughts were much darker in nature. On that night, as carriages departed jubilee celebrations held at Ganeshkhind, the Governor of Bombay's official residence, two men leapt out of the dark and fatally shot the hated local plague commissioner, WC. Rand, and his young guard, Lieutenant Charles Ayerst. Rand carried an infamy all over Maharashtra. He had granted soldiers the right to force entry into private homes and strip residents down to their skins in public to search for signs of contamination of the plague. Women were not spared this humiliation. Petitions from locals had been ignored by Rand.[47] The actions of Damodar, Balkrishna and Vasu Hari Chapekar, known as the Chapekar brothers, bolstered the prominence of an emerging band of revolutionary nationalists The two men, along with their third brother, became the early heroes of the freedom struggle. All three were hanged the following year. The British authorities immediately set upon Bal Gangadhar Tilak, the editor of *Kesari* and a senior member of the Congress. He was imprisoned for eighteen months after being found guilty of sedition. It was only after his stint in prison that he became famous nationwide and was given the honorary title *Lokmanya*, meaning 'accepted by the people', or 'trusted by the people'. Keshav, as we now know, was an avid reader of *Kesari* and would have been following all these events with an ever-growing despondency with the life his countrymen were forced to live. A distinct sense of an unjust world, where innocence is exploited, the strong prey on the weak and the weak remain so because of their inability to organize themselves, took root in his mind.

On 22 June, Keshav carried out his first act of dissidence along with a small group of local boys at his school. He was eight years old. The British wanted to make sure that there was a mood of celebration and that every child should pledge their allegiance to the Crown. On this day, boxes of sweets were donated by local businessmen and were to be handed out to all school children. Keshav, sitting where he did, usually at the back of the class, saw his classmates revelling in the occasion, perhaps not quite understanding the significance of the day. However, Keshav and a handful of other boys felt otherwise. Hedgewar, in later years, recollected this incident to his friend Palkar, who went on to write the first biography of Hedgewar in Marathi. He writes that Keshav could 'only see and smell slavery in the boxes'.[48] Keshav refused to eat the sweets to the embarrassment of the teacher and the local dignitary. Having returned home with a heavy heart, recollected Hedgewar, 'I threw the damned sweets in the bin to the amazement of my brother Mahadev. When he asked why I had thrown the sweets away, I retorted by asking him what was there to celebrate in losing the Bhosale kingdom?'[49] Palkar recalls in his book that Keshav found no joy in the festivities, seeing them as celebrations marking the fall of one's own nation.[50] Keshav had made quite an impression on his family with this act, and certainly as far as we can tell, his relationship with Mahadev went from being one of a big brother pushing around his little brother, to one of mutual respect, where Mahadev took extra effort in teaching Keshav how to wrestle, while he took to listening when Keshav read out articles from Kesari.

By the age of twelve, Keshav, the loveable rogue, was becoming an adolescent Hedgewar. Only in adolescence, when a boy is midway to becoming a man; when testosterone floods the bloodstream; when clothes are outgrown far too quickly and reasonableness escapes leaving behind raw energy, which can easily mislead one into mischief, even if the intentions were noble. Only such an explanation can be given for some of the stunts Keshav tried to pull off with some of his equally naïve comrades. In 1901, the old 'Queen of the Black Death' had died and her son, the 'uncle of Europe' ascended to the throne. To mark the occasion, the Tata family, which was already well known as one of the great beneficiaries of British patronage, chose their largest mill, not surprisingly called Empress Mills, to be the place for a large and spectacular fireworks display. Crowds lined the streets around Sitabauldi Fort. At the top of the fort flew the Union Jack. Keshav had convinced his friends that it was their Dharmic duty to one way or another remove the Union Jack and replace it with the *Bhagwa dhwaj*.

The *Bhagwa dhwaj* is the saffron flag on top of Arjun's chariot in the great epic, the Mahabharata. It was the flag chosen by Shivaji. It is the flag that represents *Dharma*. A flag that evokes something deep, almost from a primordial past, a 'something' that stirs in the Hindu heart. It represents history, the golden age of Hindu civilization. It represents the heroic deeds of Rama, Sita, Lakshman and the great Hanuman from the *Ramayana*. It represents the great avatar Krishna, Arjun's valour and truth. It is uprightness, and the highest human virtue(s). It is no surprise then that the RSS hold the *Bhagwa dhwaj* to be the symbol that best represents perfection and something that they can pay homage to; a symbol that all Hindus can rally under.

Of course, at twelve, for Keshav, this was the flag of Shivaji, and that was enough for it to be flying at full mast on top of the fort. The fort was a restricted area. The public could not enter. The boys, in their testosterone highs, decided that if they could dig a tunnel from their tutor's house, which was a few kilometres away from the six-metre-high walls of the fort, into an area inside, then in the dead of night they would sneak up to the mast and replace the flag. They must have imagined the shock and awe they would create by such an audacious, yet dastardly act. So, a few days before the firework display, the boys, in their charade for learning, turned up at Mr Vazey's house.[51] He was their tutor. He had kept a room on the ground floor as a place of study for the boys during extra tutorials. He was a kindly man, and all too keen to support eager young minds. For three successive days, the boys turned up at the house by mid-morning and would studiously work behind closed doors until late into the evening. On the third day, Mr Vazey became a little curious to see what was driving the boys to study so hard, and so without forewarning entered the room only to find a gaping hole where his floor once had been.

He recalled many years later, retelling this story to Palkar. When seeing the hole and one of the little rascals covered from head to toe in dirt with a shovel in his hand looking up with the eyes of a wild animal having just been caught, he could not hold his nerve and he bellowed 'What is the meaning of this?.[52] He remembers turning towards Keshav without hesitation as he knew that only he would have the audacity to do something like this, and the other boys were mere hacks following his supreme command. 'Keshav', he says, 'immediately confessed, and began to tell me the whole story and their intention behind their vandalism of his home. They were immediately apologetic, and I could see no malice in any of them'. Mr Vazey confessed to Palkar 'that seeing no malice in the boys and upon hearing their intentions, and witnessing their audaciousness and commitment, how could I remain angry with them?'[53] He gave the boys a verbal slap on the wrist and reported it to Baliram. One need only imagine that he may not have taken it so sympathetically. This is a story that was never narrated by Hedgewar himself, but by Mr Vazey in later years. It is a story now in RSS folklore, rendered in many ways, and often to evoke the patriotism of the young Hedgewar and his brothers in arms.

Keshav was studious. He devoured literature, particularly in English. He was consuming the news and was politically aware. He was beginning to realize the vastness of India, the diversity of its people and increasingly becoming familiar with the names of the most prominent nationalists. He appeared to be a rather domesticated child too, helping his mother in household chores and practising daily morning rituals. He was clearly loved by his mother, had two older brothers and Mahadev most certainly spent time with him in the *akhada* (gymnasium). His two elder sisters were already married by this time. We know that Keshav internally began to challenge the customs of his father and the treatment of women. All around him he could see that he lived in a male-dominated culture and that there were other role models apart from his mother that he had seen, albeit through books. He would have been aware that women were capable of equally great feats as men. He read extensively about Jijabai, who was the nurturing, and later political strength of Shivaji. He would have read about the exploits of Queen Lakshmi better known as *Jhansi ki Rani* in the first Indian war of independence of 1857. He would have also been somewhat knowledgeable about women like Marie Curie from his science classes at school. Even though the inner churnings of discontent about the inequality he saw all around him had begun, it would be many years before this would culminate into something radical.

In 1902, the Black Death had arrived in Nagpur. It would be this that would turn, once and for all, Keshav into Hedgewar. The Bubonic plague had arrived in India in 1896 from its coastal cities. It had been causing widespread devastation across the country. But it took a full six years before making it inland to the centre of India where it would kill 300 people every day at its height. Half of the population of Nagpur had evacuated to surrounding villages, thereby further spreading the disease. Around 2,00,000 people died in the Central Provinces alone between 1902 and 1903. Across India, almost 7,50,000 people died in less than a year.[54] First-hand accounts and official governmental records describe how families were literally cremating bodies one after another. Some people volunteered, and the army was brought in to stop people leaving the city and keep people under quarantine. To make things worse, it seemed that the British reaction was completely draconian and heavy-handed. People, even if they were mildly unwell were sent off to 'death camps' where they were left to die. Many doctors in the city without conducting any examination were sending patients off to the camps to die.[55] Law and order was difficult to maintain with rampant looting across the city. The Hedgewars stayed put in their family home. Baliram was a volunteer, delivering the final rites to hundreds of mourning families. The winter months were the most terrible. The contagion seemed to spread most during December and March, and it was only inevitable that Baliram would contract the disease by constantly putting himself in harm's way to aid others.[56] At the end of 1902, Baliram decided to move his children from Mahal to his son-in-law's house in Badkas Square in Nagpur. A few weeks later in February 1903, the news came that the disease spread to both Baliram and Revati, killing them both. The situation was so desperate that both were cremated together on the same funeral pyre.

Keshav would have seen first-hand death on an epic scale. It would have felt like the apocalypse. He would have noted the people who got up and left; those that stayed to loot; those soldiers that carried out orders blindly, causing great harm and humiliation to a desperate people; he would have seen the callousness of the British authorities and he would have seen the countless people who volunteered to serve others by way of delivering food, medicines, water and offering final rites as did his father. This experience above all else would go on to shape his personality to become a medical doctor; to live an ordered and clean life; his emphasis on voluntary service; and even to this day the RSS may be criticized for a great many things, but it is universally accepted that the RSS is first in line during all national calamities. That regimented discipline, commitment and expertise harboured by the Sangh has been well documented. There hasn't been a national calamity, whether political like the partition, or natural disasters like the earthquakes that have ravaged India, where the RSS hasn't been first on the scene to support and help recovery efforts.

Nietzsche, the maladjusted German philosopher, once said, 'I wish great pain and suffering to befall on all those I respect'.[57] He made this remark because he said that those that endure have the greatest chances of becoming the Übermensch. Keshav from this point onwards slowly becomes Hedgewar, a man who through great endurance becomes Nietzsche's Superman.

TWO: 1902–1907

Fire and Famine

The last book of the New Testament, the Book of Revelation, talks about the Four Horsemen of the Apocalypse who would bring forth the final judgement upon the world.To any devout Christian of Hedgewar's time, it would have looked as if the Indian world was coming to an end—a final judgement was at hand. India had faced conquest, now she was facing pestilence, famine, war and death.

Keshav witnessed first-hand that even the apocalypse is not fair in its selection. The poor, often rural, and those on the bottom rung of Indian society, were its principal victims. It is hard to imagine the utter tragedy that was unfolding in colonial India between the 1890s and the early part of the twentieth century. India was economically bled dry by the time Keshav was orphaned.[1] She had been completely and thoroughly de-industrialized.[2] The plague killed millions. Keshav and thousands of children like him witnessed the malice death could yield. They saw how people quite literally could rot while still alive. The fingers and toes are the first to blacken, and smell, before pus-filled boils called buboes begin to appear around the groin, armpits and neck. Keshav saw how a perfectly healthy neighbour was fine one day, and dead the next. A simple headache or stomach pain would have been enough for everyone to panic, and for the authorities to send them to their deaths by quarantining them in large warehouses—hot, humid, dirty and full of sickly people who were sent there to perish.

India was not only being ravaged but also starved. Her people were literally starving to death in their millions. Yet, India never had an aggregate shortage of grain. Crop yields often fell during poor rains, or severe monsoon rains resulting in flooding destroying crops, but these were regional, and India, on the whole, had harvests to meet the demand. In ancient India, the people ensured, through trade and relief measures, that poor harvests never became famines. Under the British, things were very different, with free-market economics being applied at the tips of bayonets on a hapless people, while unscrupulously taking vast amounts of surplus grain out of India to feed the rest of the empire, especially the army[3,4]. This meant that regional shortages, which could have been easily dealt with through open trade coupled with relief work between regions, became historic catastrophes killing tens of millions.

Keshav had become fluent in English and read enthusiastically. He read about the havoc British policies were causing in certain parts of the country, especially in the countryside. Leading lights of the Indian resistance, through newspapers, were making it plain what they thought. Bal Gangadhar Tilak, for example, wrote uncompromising articles in his English paper called *The Mahratta*, with inflammatory titles like 'Has the government gone mad?' and 'The country's misfortune'.[5] These articles resulted in Tilak facing a prison sentence as he was calling for mass public uprisings and civil unrest. Keshav would have read both articles. He would have also known through social interaction, and by just living in those times, that there were inherent social customs which exacerbated the problems, and it wasn't just all down to the 'white Mughals'.

The fragility of Indian society was cultural and socio-economic in nature. Namely, the scourge on Indian society, what the Portuguese named, and then the British popularized as the 'caste system'. During Keshav's time, a social system later dubbed as the *Jajmani* system in its various forms ran across the country.[6] It was a system of barter between high-class land-owning families and the 50 per cent rural peasant classes who worked the land. The poor worked and toiled on the land, and in turn, they were offered grain. The small craftspeople and labourers too—washermen and women, cleaners, artisans, blacksmiths, carpenters and the like—were paid partly in cash and partly in grain. Consequently, this meant that for the vast majority in this agrarian arrangement, the food supply depended on their employment entitlements or their class in society.[7] A crop failure could create a famine, not because it led to an aggregate shortage of food, but because it deprived a significant proportion of the population of the means to acquire food.[8] In the urban centres, people were cushioned from these agricultural shocks because they were paid in cash, and therefore, the worst they had to deal with was inflated food prices during bad times.

Keshav heard elders talk endlessly about what was happening in the countryside, and how grain prices fluctuated so sporadically.

At such an impressionable age, Keshav asked 'Why?' Why was it that the labourers, artisans and petit merchants around the city struggled to survive while those who were landowners from specific segments of society, who, although they complained about the situation, were on the whole living relatively comfortable lives? This inequality of opportunity would haunt Keshav throughout his adulthood, and he would spend the rest of his life working to eradicate all notions of 'caste' and with it the Jajmani system.

The plague epidemic subsided in the summer of 1903 and people began to return to their homes to try to pick up the pieces and carry on. We know little, and there are no surviving records as to the welfare of Keshav's sisters. We know from Palkar's biography that the older two, Raju and Sharayu, were married before the onset of the plague, but his younger sister, Rangu, is not spoken of after this.

Mahadev, Sitaram and Keshav returned to an empty home. Keshav would have just turned fourteen, with Sitaram no more than eighteen years old and Mahadev barely in his twenties. These were young men, now left without guidance. Our modern understanding of human development, especially attachment theory, makes it abundantly clear that to lose both parents relatively young would have a shattering impact on most children of Keshav's age. According to Dr Romeo Vitelli, children who suffer from parental loss through suicide or some other form of violence, have a far greater propensity to struggle to build lasting intimate relationships of their own in adulthood.[9] Could this explain the absence of sexual desire or a private life in Hedgewar's later years? Maybe. But this would be a shallow dive at best in understanding the formative years.

Children who have lost their parents also grieve inwardly rather than outwardly. Keshav may well have suffered from increased anxiety, something which may have followed him to his death. He may also have suffered from increased levels of stress caused by focusing on the very basic things of life, such as finding wood chippings to burn, thinking about where the next meal would come from, maintaining cleanliness and earning money for necessities. Research suggests that the sudden death of both parents would cause some form of psychiatric disorder in one-fifth of teens today.[10] Disorders such as self-isolation, depression or post-traumatic stress disorder are quite common. But would this have been the case with young Keshav, in 1903, in a plague-ridden Indian society?

The only plausible stand to take is one best expressed by Jane Hirshfield, in her poem of 1953, 'I wake, doubt, besides you, like a curtain half-open.'[11] In other words, we simply do not know and can never fully be content with any answer we are likely to formulate. Nevertheless, like a 'curtain half-open', we can claim some certainties and can then bring our courage to simmer while gazing into the openness of what could have been the case. Parental loss was not an isolated phenomenon tragically met by the Hedgewar children, but was rather a footnote to the collective trauma of the entire society. Thousands were left orphaned. Many families became single-parent units, struggling to carve out a living. The Indian society, even today, is known for its collective spirit and extended family living arrangements. In modern Britain (2019), it is still quite common to see three generations living together under the same roof. The full force of Keshav's personal tragedy may well have been somewhat cushioned by being part of an integrated community where his fathers' and mothers' side of the family, who were local, would have rallied around the children as best as they could. The kind of social isolation and loneliness we are always prone to in our modern community structures didn't exist, and the Indian society formed of cousins, maternal and paternal uncles and aunts, as well as elders, would have lessened the trauma, at least in some sense, for those who were orphaned. Relief ashrams were set up, food rations were handed out and the three boys, now living together, often had to rely on these 'food banks' to survive. Rangu, Keshav's younger sister, may well have been adopted by one of their paternal uncles or aunts.

Regardless of what help was available, the situation could only have been described as ominous. The three boys were still alone. With no income, it fell on Mahadev to earn whatever little he could to feed himself and his two younger brothers. The stress, anxiety and self-loathing that would have run through Mahadev's mind must have been dire. He was proud and tough, but still unaccustomed to trials and tubulations, he would have struggled with the lot life had given him. To ask for money, for food and for help would have dented his alpha-male pride. We do have some clues as to the effects of the trauma of parental loss on Mahadev. He became irritable and even aggressive towards his two younger brothers, becoming increasingly controlling. He also turned to drinking.[12]

Hedgewar recalled in his later years that Mahadev would insist on him making bhang at home, something which he abhorred. Nevertheless, mostly out of fear, and not wanting to displease his menacing older and bigger brother, Keshav made this intoxicating drink at home, at least for a while. Bhang has been made across greater India for at least three millennia. It is a cannabis-based drink. Using a pestle and mortar, young Keshav would have crushed the cannabis leaves into a paste, before mixing it with milk, sugar and some spices. With the right concoction, this can be a very intoxicating drink. A drink that is often used in religious rituals, especially when evoking the ancient deity, Shiva. Eventually, Keshav, with the support of Sitaram, refused to make bhang at home. Mahadev, who by now must have been somewhat of a shadow of his once confident self, could not tolerate this 'rejection' from his own. It was too much for his already devastated ego to bear, and he soon deployed violence on his brothers. Regular fighting and scuffles became the norm. Relations between Mahadev and the younger two became increasingly strained. As their differences with Mahadev grew, Sitaram and Keshav became closer.

On alternate days, Sitaram and Keshav would walk a short distance to eat at the house of their late father's friend. Tatya Fadnavis and his family ensured that the Hedgewar boys at least managed to get one square meal whenever they came. Like Fadanvis, many families would have felt a duty of care towards those worse off. Keshav continued with his education, the money for school fees being pooled together by relatives and family friends. It was clear from the off that Keshav was bright, and the best care one could give him was to ensure that his studies were not disturbed. In turn, Keshav never ignored his studies. He attended school regularly. He studied and passed his exams. Overall, he was amiable and pleasant toward his teachers, earning popularity among his peers.

The only names we have of his friends during these years are Moru Abhyankar, Ganesh Joshi and Hanumant Naidu.[13] All three, apart from leaving us their names, have passed out of history.

After school, his friends and he would go on long walks and make their way to Telang-khedi to swim in Futala lake. Today, the lake is completely walled up and has become a local hangout spot for young couples at dusk seeking a quiet spot away from peering eyes to stoke the flames of their passions. At dawn, locals in their fifties gather to walk around the lake, inhaling the fresh, moist and dew-filled morning air. Many practice yoga while basking in the first rays of the morning sun. During Keshav's childhood, the lake had unrestricted access and was a regular space for adolescent boys to swim in during the dry heat of summer. From here the boys often hiked the short distance up to Seminary Hills where stood a Hanuman mandir in the midst of a British colony. Seminary Hills was a place where the British built their homes and offices so as to be a little higher up to enjoy the fresher air and take refuge under the shade of teaks. The boys could enjoy the views from this height and play on fields overlooking the city down below. Today, these hills are protected by the forestry department and the winding roads leading up the hills are paved with splendid amaltaas trees, better known as the 'golden rain tree'. Hours would seamlessly float by without a care. Here, in moments such as these, young Keshav would have found a little sense of joy in his childhood. He would have known that the amaltaas trees are native to the land. He delighted in them, especially when the trees shed their leaves only to burst into a mass of long, grape-like bunches of yellow-golden flowers.

Somewhere near the Hanuman mandir, Palkar describes a mound that Keshav and his young friends would play 'protect the flag' with a certain amount of militancy hatched by their vivid imaginations. The theme was always the same, to save the *Bhagwa dhwaj* from the invading Islamic forces. No prizes for guessing which side the young Keshav always played for. The *Bhagwa dhwaj* is a unique symbol, something which all Hindus can relate with. Yet, in Keshav's time, he would not have had the widest possible connotation, that of a great united and strong India, which the RSS today champions. This would come much later in his life.

At fourteen, Keshav's world began in Nagpur and the coastline of his knowledge ended at the borders of Maharashtra. He would have morsels of knowledge about the rest of India and the world at large through books and newspapers. What he did know was the life of Shivaji, the great Hindu king who died in 1690 having planted the seeds of 'Hindavi', or rule based on Hindu culture across the country. History, and especially Indian history, is a nuanced maiden. A naked damsel that takes on the clothing of the writer and is enjoyed or loathed by the reader.

Shivaji as a national character comes to the fore around the first war of Independence in the mid-1850s. He was projected as the ultimate symbol of freedom. He was a gift from a near past to those Hindus who wanted to liberate India from British occupation and Islamic aggression, who wanted to build a nation that would serve the interests of the majority and not the chosen few. Shivaji was a timely reminder that Hindus too could govern themselves. What is often not popularized is that Shivaji was a true ruler, and a ruler if he is to be successful, must be pragmatic. Shivaji allied with the British, the Mughals, the French and the Portuguese when it suited him and fought with all of them when required. One example of his pragmatism is that he plundered the wealthy port city of Surat in 1664, having defeated the Mughal captain Inayat Khan, and ransacked the city for six days, taking all the plunder to Raigadh Fort. According to the British captain James Grant Duff, a 'partial' observer, two-thirds of the city was burnt down. And yet, we know that Shivaji targeted the Portuguese, French and British warehouses, as well as wealthy merchants who supported the Mughals. According to the historian Govind Sardesai, four people were executed, and a further twenty-four had their hands cut off for hiding their wealth.[14] On the whole, however, the working poor and the majority of Hindus supported the Marathas who restored the prestige of Sanskrit and re-instated scholarship and learning across their territory. It was with this latter connotation that Keshav and his friends would have played 'protect the flag', emulating the courage and fierceness of Shivaji and his band of warriors, many of whom were Muslim.[15]

By this time, Keshav had also read and re-read the works of Shivaji's guru, a man that has almost passed out of history and is little known in the West, and not much better known in modern India. He was a wandering monk who established temples dedicated to Hanuman, the warrior disciple of Rama, from the ancient epic the *Ramayana*, in the seventeenth century. Swami Samarth Ramdas, born as Narayana Thosar, was a *bhakt* of Rama, who taught Advaita Vedanta. Better known as the non-dual school in Western parlance. It is prudent to spend a little time understanding the profound influence the works of Ramdas had on Keshav around this time. Keshav's metaphysical ideas, taken from Ramdas, became the substratum upon which his later physical, emotional, moral and political life would be built. Writers and commentators have often completely ignored the influence of Ramdas on Hedgewar and subsequently the RSS.

Ramdas wandered around Maharashtra and visited many parts of India in his day. He was a sadhu (mendicant). He was a man who had renounced the material world to pursue the study of, and, as is customary in Hindu tradition, to experience different states of consciousness. He was a forest hermit, who travelled into urban centres for food and to teach. He wrote prolifically and produced substantial works of poetry and literature. His works and teachings have gone on to influence many subsequent, and better-known, philosophers and sadhus in the Hindu tradition. But his most famous disciple was Shivaji. He was not only taught philosophy but also matters of statecraft by Ramdas.

Keshav, through the deeds of Shivaji, came to know the writings of Ramdas. It is not surprising that the guru of the hero becomes quite naturally the guru of the boy. According to Sinha, Keshav had memorized the *shlokas* (aphorisms and pithy statements) of Ramdas's most famous work, the *Manobodh*, a work of simple syntax, made easily memorable. The *Manobodh*, through a combination of eloquent poetry and unequivocal aphorisms, teaches matters of the mind, behaviour, virtue and conduct in society.[16] It is a work of virtue ethics as much as a work of psychology. He writes with the flair of Gibran, and with the uncompromising directness of Nietzsche. And yet, when rendered into English it loses Gibran's wings and Nietzsche's pointedness, and what we are left with is a somewhat tasteless and mediocre sounding verse:

> Let us not indulge in futile debates. Let us spread happiness through meaningful discussions. Let us shun sadness and irritation. Let us shun futile debates and make fruitful discussion.
>
> We should make discussion to end the ongoing debates. We should dissolve our ego under the influence of conscience. Whatever we tell others to do, let us do so first. Let us change our action and follow the path of devotion.[17]

No matter how bland this verse might sound in English, it had a profound influence on Keshav. Hedgewar, for all his uncompromising demeanour, never liked to debate. He, like the verse says, shunned debates. Debates are simply a tussle of two or more egos, each convinced they have a handle on the truth. While a discussion is an open-minded conversation without the gladiatorial machismo. It is a forum to learn and teach. This attitude has carried on into the RSS through its *pracharaks*. The organization does not debate—period! This has often been received in the public sphere, and most certainly in mainstream Indian media, as 'guilt' or acknowledgement of whichever heinous crime it was accused of. Consequently, it is somewhat understandable that the RSS has been labelled as 'mysterious' and Machiavellian in nature. As far as we can tell, the 'RSS way' is to have private discussions with those whom they can learn from, and equally influence. This is the 'Hedgewarian' approach to dealing with diverse and opposing ideas.

The young Keshav, unknowingly at the time, had memorized verses that would go on to not only shape his inner life but significantly shape the workings of the RSS and the millions of people that it touched. Verses such as, 'Let us have great patience. Let us bear the evil words spoken to us. Let us always speak politely. Let us always understand others.'[18] This is another example of the devastatingly poor rendering into English of another wise majestic verse from the original text. Once again, we must not be fooled by its sheer boringness, for this verse describes the Hedgewarian way to tackle those that oppose one's progress. There is a saying one hears from *pracharaks* and senior administrators, '*sab ko sath lekar chalna*', which means 'We must take everyone with us'. In order to achieve this task, the RSS is mind-numbingly patient (as the verse suggests) and infuriatingly passive when it wants to be. Misinformation, insults, accusations, charges, slurs and caricatures just slide off its back. It bides its time. It seeks the right opportunity to engage, and when it does, it does so with a single-mindedness, a relentlessness to understand one's opponent. After wearing down its opponents by doing absolutely nothing, and when everyone is looking the other way, the organization suddenly engages and through a combination of action and *sampark* (making contact), it has won over many hardnosed adversaries. People who once loathed the RSS, today actively support it and some even work for it as dedicated *swayam sevaks*.

By now, Keshav had devoured many biographies of Shivaji and had known all too well of his pragmatism, and his use of mercenaries to combat the Mughal empire, many of whom were Muslim. Couple this with his memorization of Ramdas's *Manobodh*, and it is fairly safe to conjecture that Keshav would have developed a nuanced understanding of history. That which was percolating deep within his being, probably unknown to him at the time, was the germination of what Veer Savarkar would later dub as 'Hindutva'.

It is also worth noting that at this time across India, there was wide unrest against British rule. The atmosphere throughout the land was summed up by one word, *swaraj* (self-rule). Keshav, who read the *Kesari* newspaper, was deeply influenced by the writings of Tilak and other nationalists such as Shivram Paranjape, who was the editor of *Kal* newspaper and also called for complete independence. This was in marked contrast to other nationalists who would insist on their loyalty to the crown but wanted a greater role in governing their own country, people such as Dadabhai Naoroji. According to Palkar, Keshav was immersed in an atmosphere where everyone was talking about *desh bhakti* and *swaraj*. Phrases like desh bhakti are difficult to render in English. A lazy translation would be patriotism; lazy and not wholly wrong because it does communicate something, but without any of the worthwhile flavouring and use of the term, while still keeping all the contrite baggage it has in the pan-European psyche. A slightly more evolved rendering would be 'serving one's land', in the sense of upliftment of the poor or downtrodden. Again, not wholly wrong but just very tame. The term *desh* to Keshav might have meant something more aligned to the word 'soil'. It is often lazily translated to mean country or state. Both would be to misconstrue. The term *bhakti* from Sanskrit literally means to attach, to love for any endeavour, fondness for, pay homage to, devotion or purity. The term desh bhakti has a deep sense of reverence and sacredness attached to the land itself. The people, their institutions, the minerals, trees and rivers come much later down the track. The soil itself is sacred. It is worthy of worship. Desh bhakti for Keshav would have meant something akin to complete devotion to the land. For Keshav, his 'patriotism' was not steeped in some political ideology or religious dogma but rather to the idea that those who view the land itself as sacred and divine are insiders no matter their race, class or creed. And by the same token, those that do not see the land as sacred but as something to be dominated, to be exploited and to be subjugated are the outsiders no matter their race, class or creed.

The European fear that Voltaire so aptly rendered in his work *Dictionnaire Philosophique*:

> 'Il est triste que souvent, pour être bon patriote, on soit l'ennemi du reste des hommes. L'ancien Caton, ce bon citoyen, disait toujours en opinant au sénat: Tel est mon avis, et qu'on ruine Carthage. Delanda est Carthago. Être bon patriote, c'est souhaiter que sa ville s'enrichisse par le commerce, et soit puissante par les armes. Il est clair qu'un pays ne peut gagner sans qu'un autre perde, et qu'il ne peut vaincre sans faire des malheureux. Telle est donc la condition humaine que souhaiter la grandeur de son pays, c'est souhaiter du mal à ses voisins. Celui qui voudrait que sa patrie ne fût jamais ni plus grande, ni plus petite, ni plus riche, ni plus pauvre, serait le citoyen de l'univers.'[19]

An English translation would read:

> It is lamentable that to be a good patriot we must make of ourselves the enemy of the balance of humanity. That good citizen the Cato the Elder

> always concluded his senatorial orations with the formula: This is my opinion, and Carthage must be destroyed. "Delanda est Carthago." To be a good patriot is to wish our own state be enriched by commerce, and powerful by arms; but such is the condition of humankind, that to wish the greatness for our own country is often to wish evil to our neighbours. He who would bring himself to wish that our country shall always remain as it is neither larger nor smaller, neither richer nor poorer, would be a citizen of the universe.

Voltaire rightly warns us, and on the whole European commentators have continuously highlighted the dangers of patriotism, in that it pits one part of humanity against another. Understanding the term desh bhakti in its rightful use and expression nullifies, to a large extent, Voltaire's fear. Desh bhakti is not centred around any one type of people; the people can be multifarious and distinctive with only one binding clause: *reverence for the soil.* It is an inward-looking expression, not an outward-looking one. Desh bhakti need not necessarily need an 'other' to fear, so long as all those who live on the land put its interest first and centre. This is a fundamental realization that most analysts, and writers alike, fail to unearth. To understand Hedgewar and Hindutva as projected by the RSS, this notion of desh bhakti must be fully understood.

Desh bhakti leads to what John Hutchinson calls cultural nationalism and this is where the RSS is rooted.[20] Whereas, patriotism often leads to political nationalism and is where the BJP sits. Researchers, commentators, and academics alike have often conflated the two, and misunderstood not just Hedgewar, but also his creation—the RSS. The difference between the two are significant, and not to be taken lightly. Hutchison writes that for patriots and political nationalists like the BJP,

> their ideal is a civic polity of educated citizens united by common laws and mores like the polis of classical antiquity. They reject existing political and traditionalist allegiances that block the realisation of this ideal, and theirs is a cosmopolitan rationalist conception of the nation that looks forward ultimately to a common humanity transcending cultural differences. But, because the world is divided into a multiplicity of political communities, they are forced to work within a specific territorial homeland in order to secure a state that will embody their aspirations.[21]

Whereas for cultural nationalists such as Hedgewar and the RSS, Hutchinson write,

> by contrast, the cultural nationalists perceives the state as an accidental, for the essence of a nation is its distinctive civilisation, which is the product of its unique history, culture, and geographical profile. Unlike political nationalists, who is fundamentally a rationalist, a cultural nationalist … affirms a cosmology according to which humanity, like nature is infused with a creative force which endows all things with an individuality. Nations are primordial expressions of this sprit; like families, they are natural solidarities. Nations are not just political units but organic beings, living personalities, whose individuality must be cherished by their members in all their manifestations. Unlike the political nationalists, the cultural nationalist found a nation not on mere consent or law but on the passions implanted by nature and history.[22]

The Sangh, that is RSS, and its affiliate organizations are a composition of political and cultural nationalism, but the RSS, and in particular Hedgewarian thought, is firmly rooted in the latter.

The line drawn, as it was, on desh bhakti meant that Hedgewar, and then the RSS, would always run into problems with the two Abrahamic faiths, namely Christianity and Islam. Both creeds originated from outside India. Both saw their holy of holies outside of India, one at the Vatican or Jerusalem, and the other in Mecca. Both faiths at the time saw the ancient Indian civilization as essentially barbarous. For both, their religious dogma, especially their fixation surrounding idolatry, would directly juxtapose with desh bhakts. How do you reconcile two directly contrasting red lines? The religious dogma of the 'isms' states that to worship anything but God is idolatry, especially something as crude as the land. For the desh bhakts it was the land that was the cornerstone of their identity, their ancestry and ultimately their traditions. The two, even today, struggle to coexist. The only way they can coexist is by having to perform some fantastic mental and legal gymnastics to render both terms in their most diluted forms, whilst hoping that nobody notices.

These red lines posed problems in Keshav's society too. Just as there was the soft murmuring of *swaraj* on the lips of many, so too there was the call from the minarets of Istanbul, the capital of the Ottoman empire; seat of the *khalifat* (caliphate), that Muslims in India should call for pan-Islamism.[23] Whereas, most Hindus thought that *swaraj* meant self-rule; some Muslims began to speak of a Dar al-Islam, a land connected from West Asia to the Indian sub-continent ruled and governed by Islam. Where the Hindus began to draw inspiration from ideas such as desh bhakti, Muslims drew inspiration from those calling for a theocratic rule in India based on the *shari'a*. These ideas were akin to tectonic plates pushing against each other and were occurring across the Indian landmass. The shifts were slow, almost invisible, but when the plates jolted, the earthquake came suddenly and often violently. Between 1900 and 1930, so-called Hindu–Muslim riots increased in frequency throughout the country. What Keshav would have witnessed, which he later recollected, was the meekness and servile nature of the Hindu masses in the face of Muslim aggression during (Hindu) festivities and the increasingly draconian British state apparatus.[24]

Throughout his teens, Keshav visited the *akhada* several times a week. Coupled with the early influence from his brother, and then seeing the plight of those who were meek, it's easy to appreciate why any self-respecting young man would want to strengthen himself. It was a time of revolution, and young men everywhere were busy becoming tough guys. It was here in 1904, at Shivram's Guru's *akhada* that Keshav really begins to meet a like-minded peer group, and where he met the handsome, charismatic, populist and the man behind the gym, Dr Balkrishna Shivram Moonjay.[25 26]

Dr Moonjay had been a commissioned medical officer in the Imperial Indian Army and had fought in the Boer wars. He was a wealthy man. He had at least two clinics in Nagpur run in partnership with his three friends—Dr Pardhi, Dr Jatkar and Dr Gadgil.[27] He had the best of a British Indian education, and by all outward appearances one could quite easily have mistaken him for an Anglophile. A polished Englishman by all accounts. He was a smooth talker and, in his younger days, enjoyed the company of women (especially British women, many of whom reciprocated his attentions). But looks are often deceiving. Dr Moonjay was raised in a tradition where he was taught Sanskrit as a young boy, grounded in Hindu traditions. He was born in 1872, a mere fifteen years after the first war of Indian Independence of 1857, and the memories of that brutality would have been fresh in the minds of his parents who would have ensured that their son was grounded in Hindu traditions equally as much as modern western ones.

Dr Moonjay was thirty-two years old when he and Keshav first met. Keshav was a bright-eyed, quick witted, ambitious fourteen-year-old. Dr Moonjay was an eye surgeon, had experienced warfare first hand in South

Africa and had travelled much of North India to appreciate the state of the country. He had formed views about the world and his place in it. Dr Moonjay could have excelled at pretty much anything. He had an inner urge to be a writer. He wanted to be the writer that would bring Indian culture, that is Hindu culture, back to the fore.[28] But alas, he had decided that his time would be better spent for the freedom struggle. He let his friends operate the clinics on a day-to-day basis, while he focused on political matters. He had become a 'Tilakite', one who followed and supported Bal Gangadhar Tilak's vision of a free India.[29] Whereas Tilak operated out of Pune and Mumbai, Moonjay was given the task of organizing the youth in Nagpur and throughout the district of Vidarbha more generally. It was to that end that Moonjay both funded and visited *akhadas*.

Tilak was travelling all over the country to win support for swaraj, and he became acutely aware that if freedom was to be won from the British, then India would need to re-industrialize. He was aware that after a century and a half of British rule, his fellow countrymen had fallen well behind the rest of the world in manufacturing technology. He had identified bright young men from middle-class Indian families that were educated in Japan, USA and Britain in all types of technology and was encouraging them to set up their own enterprises instead of working for the British. The slight snag to his plan was start-up capital; ironically something which modern India is still facing with its twenty-first century tech entrepreneurs. Where could young men with the right skills find the capital required to start-up businesses and thereby disseminate the skills they had acquired to their countrymen? Tilak's answer was the 'paisa fund'. A paisa was the lowest denomination of coinage in India at the time. He had first written about the idea of raising a fund from the public at large in *Kesari* in 1900.[30]

His call was taken up by a villager who moved to Pune to work on collecting one coin from each citizen in 1902. Ananta Damodar Kalay and his team across Maharashtra had raised over 53,000 rupees by 1904.[31] That was a significant amount of money in those days, well in excess of 100 million rupees in today's currency. Kalay had visited over 200 villages all over Maharashtra, giving lectures. He traced India's decline to its de-industrialization caused by British policy and asserted that if India was ever to be free again then it must learn to generate wealth.[32] In 1904, Moonjay recruited young Keshav into the fund-raising team at Nagpur. Soon, Keshav led a small team of friends who would organize themselves by neighbourhoods. Boys were teamed into pairs, and each pair was arranged to visit a set number of streets in every neighbourhood. They were equipped with nothing more than a coupon to give to the householder in exchange for their contribution, a pencil and paper to capture the details of the residents, and a small letter from Dr Moonjay explaining what the boys were officially tasked with. At the end of each day, the boys would come to the *akhada* and tally up. Keshav would tally up the day's raise and give it to Moonjay, who would top it up with a generous contribution and send it to Pune.

Palkar tells us that Keshav was 'thoroughly enthused' by the responsibility assigned to him.[33] It would not have gone amiss by Moonjay that in front of him was a young man, recently orphaned, full of idealism and displaying all the hallmarks of a desh bhakt. His familiarity with Tilak's *Kesari* newspaper also would not have gone unnoticed. Moonjay described him as an earnest young man who was clearly eager and equally talented at organizing his friends and keeping them motivated, to carry out the beat; street by street, house by house, for months on end. Moonjay had Keshav marked from then on.

The 'paisa fund' went on to give capital to many entrepreneurial young men who had manufacturing skills and know-how. One such success story was that of Ishwar Das Varshnei, born in Aligarh, south-east of Delhi. He was born to successful cloth merchants and was sent to study at Tokyo's Technical Institute between 1902 and 1904, and then to the famous Massachusetts Institute of Technology (MIT) between 1904 and 1905. He specialized in various different glass manufacturing techniques. With the help of the paisa fund and Tilak, he was able to acquire land near Pune and build the first glass manufacturing factory in India. He went on to create a second factory in 1916.[34] He became the founding chair of the All-India Glass Manufacturers' Federation (AIGMF) and created the Ishwar Das Technical Institute. He dedicated himself to re-skilling the Indian population as well as creating employment and wealth. Initially, he employed four glassblowers from Japan to start the factory and then trained Indians in subsequent years.[35] Hundreds of young entrepreneurs were assisted by Tilak's paisa fund, which in turn was raised by hundreds of volunteers, one of whom was the young Keshav. He, with the support of Moonjay, would go on to administer large amounts of the fund in subsequent years.

By the time Keshav was sixteen years old, his relationship with Mahadev had gone from bad to worse. Mahadev would argue that they were 'too poor' to be getting involved with the likes of Dr Moonjay and his political activities. Furthermore, Mahadev wanted his little brother to remain at home, study and earn money. The ship of mediocrity had sailed by, and Keshav was not getting on it. The two brothers who were once close were soon poles apart. The atmosphere at home became unbearable for Keshav, and with the support of Moonjay, he spent less and less time there. He would often stay with Moonjay and his family. And Moonjay, by all accounts, had taken the place of Keshav's father and his older brother. Above anyone else, Moonjay planted the seed in Keshav's mind to become a medical doctor and to train in Calcutta, the centre of power, rebellion and political intrigue. With Moonjay's patronage, all sorts of opportunities emerged. Opportunities to study at the best institutes; opportunities to earn money; opportunities to build an international network of desh bhakts; opportunities to further one's knowledge of European society and the Christian faith and opportunities to deep dive to the seabed of the struggle for freedom. Keshav grabbed all these opportunities with both hands and dove deeper than even Moonjay could have imagined.

While at school, with his mentor's guidance, Keshav and his three friends set up a discussion group. The theme of this group was the natural rights of Indians to self-govern. Themed talks around 'make in India' were organized where expert speakers could come into school and talk to the students as well as the teaching faculty. That age-old adage that 'history repeats itself' comes to mind with a wry smile when the Indian prime minister, Narendra Modi, launched a campaign across India as recently as 2015 called 'Make in India'. Under the guise of discussions, several objectives were met. First, young men of intellect were attracted. Second, the most dedicated were allowed through to an inner working society which Keshav led. Third, teaching staff could be influenced. And fourth, parents of the children, many of whom were shopkeepers, were influenced to only stock 'made in India' products.

According to Keshav's childhood friend Balwant Mandelkar, Keshav, with Moonjay's support, selected the most committed members of the discussion group to join a secret bomb-making workshop.[36] At this workshop, the attendees were informed about the political situation of the country, especially Bengal and Maharashtra. This is just one workshop that we know about, but many took place where political expediency coupled with martial skill and a readiness to deploy what was taught was encouraged. These meetings are the stuff of legends. If Mandelkar is to be believed, and there is no reason not to, these locations were basements that were lit by flickering candlelight. Rooms were dusty, voices kept low and those not quite in the inner circle were asked to keep watch outside for snoops. Keshav, now becoming the Hedgewar we will come to know, was the boy in charge. Apart from Moonjay and the bomb-making experts, all of whom were ex-military, Keshav was the most senior boy.[37]

In European renderings of these incidents, Moonjay is described as 'another Hindu supremacist', along with Savarkar, and Hedgewar as his protégé.[38] Christophe Jaffrelot, the French academic who, through no fault of his own, is branded by Indian academics as the 'Godfather of Hindu Nationalism', describes these activities as 'terrorist' in nature.[39] The image of Jaffrelot as being the 'Godfather', a shadowy figure who is the master and overlord of all intellectual ideas of modern India is not without irony, and use of unintended clever wit. But humour aside, contemporary readings of these events are tinged at best, and downright prejudiced at worst, with Eurocentrism.

An idea coined by the Unitarian minister and prominent American Transcendentalist Theodore Parker is apt when revisiting these murky spectres of history,

> 'I do not pretend to understand the moral universe; the arc is a long one, my eye reaches but little ways; I cannot calculate the curve and complete the figure by the experience of sight; I can divine it by conscience. And from what I see I am sure it bends toward justice.'[40]

As we travel down the arc, slowly but surely, Moonjay will be re-interpreted. History may call him a reformer, a reactionary and a man with essentially a Kautiliyan nature, but not a supremacist.[41] In the same way as is rightly argued by modern-day feminist writers that it is no longer appropriate to call the suffragettes terrorists even though they took part in what can only be labelled as 'terrorist' activities. The reason they give is that these women were essentially using force and bomb-making as a last resort in a society that was so patriarchal in nature that there was no other way to shake them from their prejudice. In a bigoted society, reason has to be jolted into action. A few bombs detonated often does the trick. The suffragettes were essentially fighting for rights, something which we now accept as natural and quite right. Modern renderings of the suffragettes state that they fought a 'struggle'.[42]

In the same way, one has to look at the activities of Moonjay and the young Keshav not with imperialistic eyes but rather from a perspective of a suppressed people struggling for their right to govern in the face of a leviathan. Moonjay, as did the suffragettes, was struggling for rights and liberty. Something that today we see as natural. Like the suffragettes, Moonjay did not target civilians or innocent people but rather the military complex and the British officers governing the country. Moonjay, if he were alive today, would most certainly be horrified by the terrorists we see now —those who, in the name of Islam, blow themselves up, killing innocent people indiscriminately. The similarities between the struggle of the suffragettes and those that were struggling for India's independence draws on other similarities. Both struggles faced a leviathan that would not give them any room for political recourse or demonstration. All forms of protests were outlawed. In the face of such suffocation, people who are travelling down the arc had no choice but to shake the global conscience from its deep slumber. A sense of desperation had crept into the Indian people of that time, especially after the measures taken in Bengal.

The trajectory of the freedom struggle had taken a sudden change. The tectonic plates between the *passive* Hindu majority and the *assertive* Muslim minority had just shifted, and it caused an awful great quake in the form of the Partition of Bengal in 1905.[43] At the time, the Viceroy of India, Lord Curzon's official line of reasoning was that the divide between East and West Bengal was for administrative reasons. Bengal, Curzon had said, was simply too large to administer with a population of 78 million.[44] Even at a superficial glance, those in favour of a united India could see that the dividing lines were based on communal grounds. West Bengal was predominately Hindu and East Bengal was predominately Muslim. According to Hermann Kulke, Lord Curzon only after partition realized East Bengal was predominately Muslim and West Bengal Hindu.[45] If this was indeed the case, then it was a blunder of enormous scale and one that sparked the beginning of the end. The partition took place with little or no consultation from the wider population. And those that were consulted were all part of a group that would, a year later, become the All-India Muslim League.[46]

The British were clear that the entire country was going through a political awakening with the call for swaraj. Consequently, the sheer use of force whilst pacifying the old guard composed of Nawabs and local rulers would not be enough to keep the masses at bay. The working man was becoming aware that they were essentially being exploited. With advances in mass communication, print and global travel, anti-colonial sentiment was on the rise throughout the British Empire. It is no surprise at all that Indians, too, began to question the status quo. There could be a plethora of reasons for why the British partitioned Bengal, but the fact that the vast majority of Bengalis felt that their land had been usurped from them and unfairly divided sparked what western historians would go on to dub as 'radical nationalism'.[47]

In East Bengal, where Hindus had suddenly become a minority, they began to agitate. Soon agitation became militancy. A range of shootings, bombings and violent attacks on the state machinery took place. 'Vande Mataram' became the battle cry. It was a potent war cry. It evoked in the mind of every Hindu, the imagery of children rising against those who wish to harm their mother. This fused with the imagery of Kali, the Goddess which destroys those that are practising *himsa*, or harm, and you got an otherwise passive meek Hindu population suddenly rising with deep emotional energy, which, if uncontained, can unleash a great deal of violence. Agitation and protest spread across Northern India from Punjab to Maharashtra. The leviathan was being challenged from all sides.

One ally that the leviathan could always count on to be 'reasonable' was the Indian National Congress. After all, it was founded by a sensible Brit with foresight, a senior civil servant by the name of Allan Octavian Hume. He had a look that matched the grandeur of his name. He was ostensibly regal looking. The Congress was founded in December 1885 and was presided over by another remarkable man, Umesh Chandra Banerjee, born in 1844. Banerjee was the Englishman's Indian. Made in the image of his master, he was erudite, a wealthy barrister who would go on to live in Croydon, England, where he would even run for a parliamentary seat for the Liberal Party. Although he would not win the local election, he did go on to form the first Indian Parliamentary Committee in England. He was Lord Macaulay's 'word made flesh'. An Indian with an English outlook, English appetites, English sense of decorum and most importantly, he had developed an Englishman's love for liberty and a sense of fair play. It was this latter trait that ultimately led Banerjee to take on the first presidency of the Indian National Congress.

The first congress was attended by seventy-two delegates. It was a gathering in Mumbai of a select group of British civil servants and an elite group of Indians, who were unrepresentative of the Indian masses.[48] The aim of the Congress was to meet annually and begin to intermediate between the needs of the Indian educated elite and their political masters. Hume had felt that unless the Indian elite were empowered to represent their aspirations, they would eventually transfer their frustrations to the masses who would rise again, and this time, it would be a greater economic disaster than the first war of Independence (1857). William Wedderburn in his biography of Hume (1913) writes,

> Mr Hume became convinced that some definite action was called for to counteract the growing unrest. From well-wishers in different parts of the country he received warnings of the danger to the Government, and to the future welfare of India, from the economic sufferings of the masses, and the alienation of the intellectuals.[49]

The first ten years or so of the Congress went by in impotency. Banerjee had already emigrated to England with his family. He would continue the struggle for the right for his class of men to rule India (on behalf of the Crown) for decades to come. He would, in his own way, prove very useful in providing the rhetoric and reasoning for swaraj in the years to come. By 1906, twenty-one years had passed by since the days of Hume and Banerjee. The Congress had changed. It had a new momentum. A new purpose. And yet, it still had the mandate as Hume had set it: to be a steady hand for the British. To represent the aspirations of the Indian educated elite.

The momentum of the people was at odds with the mandate as set by their political masters. The Congress was fracturing under the pressure. On one side, there were those that wanted complete independence and liberty. History, as one comes to discover, is not without its own sense of humour. Those who wanted complete liberty and independence for the Indian people, as was their natural right, were dubbed as 'extremists'. Alas, the smirk that must be on the face of history as she taunts those that walked against the 'arc of the moral universe'. These 'extremists' were none other than the likes of Tilak, Lala Rajpat Rai, Aurobindo Ghosh, Ajit Singh (uncle of Bhagat Singh) and Moonjay amongst others. On the other side were those that wanted to play to a safer, less antagonistic tune, and indeed were, on the whole, advocating for colony status to be awarded to India, in the same light as Canada and Australia. In other words, self-rule but under the Crown. These were dubbed as 'moderates'.

The 'grand old man' of the Congress, none other than Dadabhai Naoroji, presided over the meeting.[50] For the first time in twenty-one years, the Congress was arm-twisted into adopting the resolutions which would seed its own internal divisions a year later. These resolutions were to clearly state the commitment to swaraj: the embargo of British goods, make in India initiative and promotion of national education. He addressed the Congress, 'We do not ask for favours we want only justice. Instead of going into any further divisions or details of our rights as British citizens the whole matter can be comprised in one word – self-government or swaraj like that of the United Kingdom or colonies.'[51] Naoroji, even though cajoled, was wily enough to balance both sides of the divide, he toed a line between the 'advocates', namely those that wanted to remain under the crown, and the 'republicans', who were those that wanted complete liberty. This would be the last time he would preside over the Congress. As the session ended, the 'republicans'—Tilak and his allies—were gleeful, ignorant of the deep seeds of division that were sown.

In 1906, Keshav got the chance to meet Tilak as he passed through Nagpur. Keshav was instructed to organize public talks for Tilak amongst the student fraternity. Keshav would later recall Tilak's fiery speeches that hypnotised the audience and stirred them into action through the war cry 'Vande Mataram'. Aurobindo, after his political stint, would recall that the mantra 'Vande Mataram', in those heady days of revolt, became a kind of religious calling for the masses.[52]

The annual Congress came around again. It was December 1907, and this time the location was Surat in the west of the country. This session would go down in history as the 'Surat split'. Initially, Nagpur was to be the location of the Congress but internal fears of Tilak becoming the president and the city being a hotbed for agitating youth meant that another more suitable location had to be found. Surat being in Tilak's home state automatically meant that he could not be president that year. He was by default made to give way to an 'advocate'—Ras Behari Ghosh. Under Pandit Madan Mohan Malaviya's chairing, Tilak was not allowed to even speak at the Congress, much to the annoyance of his supporters. Tempers swelled. Exasperated voices became irate. Soon, Tilak's supporters began throwing eggs at Malaviya and a few even threw their shoes at him. The Congress became a shambles. 'Advocates' wanted to work in conjunction with the British authorities to reform India and constitutionally build a model for swaraj (for themselves). On the other hand, the 'republicans' wanted to force the hand of the authorities through agitations, boycotts and non-cooperation.

At the Congress, the 'republicans' decided to have a separate private meeting and agreed to create their own political party, one that would have a mandate to act. These were the political churnings that would create the Hindu Mahasabha in the years to come. By 1906, the All-India Muslim League had already been formed by Syed Amir Ali after the partition of Bengal. Ali unequivocally felt that Muslims could not share power with Hindus.[53] At the Congress, they were aligned to the 'advocates'. A natural place for them as both were essentially representing the aspirations of an upwardly mobile class who felt they had a natural right to govern. Albeit govern separately! Within the 'advocate' circles the Muslim faction was causing divisions. Under the influence of Syed Amir Ali, an Islamist reformer and a loyalist of the Crown, a promoter of Urdu as the national language for all Muslims and essentially a separatist, who loathed the Congress and its aims of a united Hindu-Muslim India.[54] Amidst all of this was Moonjay, a natural 'republican' and a Tilakite. His experiences would go on to shape Hedgewar's perspective.

As the tectonic plates were shifting and the Indian political landmass was radically changing, young Keshav was becoming Hedgewar. With Moonjay occupied, Keshav went to stay with his father's cousin, affectionately called 'Aaba ji,' whose real name was Moreshwar Shridhar Hedgewar, in a village called Rampayali.[55] Today, by Indian road standards, this is a three-hour drive. In Keshav's time, this would have taken the best part of twenty-four hours in what was effectively the rural backwaters of British India. Moreshwar was a tax collector. He had built himself a small house, bought a small piece of farmland, just enough to grow the food he and his family required and lived a placid life. In these parts, people would have only recently come to know that their country was ruled by a foreign power but would have, on the whole, passively got on with the task of living. Life was slow and uneventful. Over the years, Keshav visited Rampayali during school holidays. He had built himself a small group of friends. It comes as no surprise then to find out that even here in the peaceful utopian backwaters of Maharashtra, on the banks of the swift meandering Chandan River, Keshav started soliciting his own brand of the freedom struggle.[56] He encouraged his growing band of village boys to adopt Tilak's four-point plan and bring the swaraj movement to Rampayali. Decades later, Narharish Thakur recounted the story to Palkar how boys from around the village would gather to listen to Keshav.[57]

'Keshav', he tells us, 'spoke with a fire in his belly. He would talk to us for hours on end. He would have copies of Marathi and English newspapers to quote from as ammunition in case anyone had doubts.' [58] He told stories of Tilak, Moonjay, Aurobindo and cities like Bombay, Calcutta and Delhi. These would have been the names and places that would have been inconceivable to village boys like Thakur. For kids at Rampayali, Nagpur would have seemed like a different world, and so to talk about other states would have been simply beyond their imagination. As with such things, if you can mesmerize people with stories of far-flung places and with names that are larger than life, superheroes in effect, one is sure to pull in the punters. Thakur tells us that 'Keshav was a powerful speaker, well-read, did not hold back; physically intimidating; and enigmatic to us. We all dearly admired him'.[59] It was this admiration and Keshav's sheer doggedness that ended up bringing this quiet backwater into scandal, around which regional folklore would be crafted for years to come. People would wear it as a badge of honour to share with their children.

Keshav had arrived just before the Hindu festival of Dussehra. This festival marks the defeat of Ravana, the tyrant king of Lanka, defeated by Rama in the epic, the *Ramayana*. To this day, all across India, and in every diaspora community in the world, Hindus mark the occasion of Dussehra. It is the build-up to Diwali. On Dussehra, all the pujas (devotional ritual) and celebrations culminate into the burning of Ravana's effigy in a great bonfire. That night, on 27 September 1906, the procession progressed through the colourful streets with an unusually large number of young people taking part, as noted by one dignitary, along with the village elders and some junior civil servants like Moreshwar. Just as the procession reached the effigy of Ravana, Keshav broke rank, ran to the front, stood on a pre-arranged box and shouted 'Vande Mataram'. Not one for half-heartedness, he and his friends sang the entire poem; a poem that was outlawed by the British. It was effectively a battle-cry. No sooner had he scandalised his audience, in front of local civil servants who were obliged to act, including his own uncle, he started to deliver one of his fiery sermons. Bhagode remembered it as a night he would never forget. His sleepy village had suddenly become the hotbed of national fervour. Keshav compared the British administration with Ravana's tyranny. He challenged his dumbfounded audience to take up the example of Rama and fight this tyranny. He spelt out in rapid-fire Tilak's four-point plan to bring down the tyrant, and on and on he went.[60] As he stepped down from the box, people didn't quite know where to look. Should they tell him off? Should they arrest him? Should they congratulate him? People were torn between falling foul of their tyrannical overlords and following their own inner convictions for swaraj.

No sooner had the sun risen the next morning than the police arrived at Moreshwar's home looking for the young upstart. Keshav was arrested. This would not be the last time. The charge against him was treason. He had made a 'seditious' speech. A serious charge indeed, and one to make an example of more than anything else. His two comrades were not spared. Bhagode and another boy called Dabir were picked up from school and expelled immediately by the headteacher for disgracing the school.[61] Thankfully for Keshav, Moreshwar informed a sympathizer. He was a lawyer by the name of Purushottam Deo. Through his appeal to a Mr Armstrong, who was the prosecuting solicitor, charges against Keshav and his friends were dropped. The boys were reinstated at their school. Keshav was barred from public speaking in Rampayali.[62] He was ushered out of the village and returned to Nagpur to tell the tale to his friends and mentor. He had returned home with his first 'battle tale'.

Even though Keshav got off lightly, his uncle faced the brunt of his nephew's political yearnings. He was effectively removed from office and asked to transfer to another district. It was impossible for Moreshwar to simply leave his family and move. He was forced to resign. To what extent did Keshav know about the severity of his actions and the problems it would cause those who supported him? We simply do not know. One can take this in one of two ways. Either Keshav knew full well the severity of his actions and felt that it was worth it, or that he was a teenager fired by the ideology of swaraj, fuelled by testosterone, who blindly and regrettably, caused serious setbacks to his own family. We can never answer these questions. Hedgewar never spoke of this incident.

Further trouble was just ahead for Keshav. The swaraj movement had caught traction and British imports were down. Swadeshi goods, that are made in India, even though often handmade and poorer in quality, were preferred. Demand for British goods began to fall. In response to this, the authorities began to create draconian tax measures for landlords who were letting out shops selling swadeshi goods. Many *akhadas* were closed down too for good measure. It became increasingly difficult to get permission for public gatherings. Then came along the infamous 'Risley Circulars' named after a famous British ethnographer, Herbert Hope Risley, who though being intelligent and earnest, got so much wrong and misled so many. He was the man that falsely merged caste and race as one.[63] He is the man that sowed the seed of casteism in the political body of India; something which India is still trying to untangle. The Risley Circulars were draconian in nature. They reeked of imperialism. The circular made it impossible for schools across the country to teach politics to students, and simultaneously prohibited students from engaging in any political activity whatsoever. Phrases like 'Vande Mataram' were strictly forbidden, as Keshav had just found out, and the cost borne by Moreshwar.

The circular arrived at Keshav's school. Teachers had been asked to report any student activities that were political in nature to the authorities. At Keshav's school, teachers were, on the whole, passively supportive of the 'republican' agenda and Tilak's four-point plan. They had even allowed discussion forums to take place propagating the idea. Now they were, in effect, asked to put an end to all talk of swaraj, liberty and fairness. An internal dissonance occurred within the teachers' union. On the one hand, they must teach the English value-system, emphasizing reason above passion; science and mathematics; the importance of economic development and an emphasis on liberty and fairness, while restricting those values from being practised. With the advantage of hindsight, it seems like an obvious blunder by the authorities—one of many they seemed to be making around this time. In what sense did they hope that such a proclamation would quell the idea of swaraj? Many schools, including Keshav's Neil City High School, turned a blind eye to many such activities. Teachers and administrators themselves were part of the agitation programme. Things remained as they were until inspectors arrived. The school and students had to toe the line for one day before returning to normal. Keshav, however, had tasted rebellion and discovered the thrill of being a thorn in the backside of tyranny.

On the day of an inspection, as the inspector entered the hall where the students were in assembly, what appeared to be a spontaneous cry of 'Vande Mataram' rang around the hall. Groups of students, scattered across the lines, were shouting at the tops of their voices, the war cry in defiance of the new regime. The inspector is said to have become red-faced and stormed out of the hall with the principal, Janardan Vinayak

Oak, in quick succession. 'Without a word', recalled Mr Vazalwar, a teacher at the school, 'he left the school barking instructions at Principal Oak to dismiss the hooligans behind this stunt'.[64] Oak, by all accounts, seemed a reasonable man. But to his distress, he was about to find out that reason had abandoned those students he admired so much. They were fully in the grip of a national fervour.

In RSS literature, one gets the impression that Hedgewar was a rabble-rouser, a dynamic die-hard hero who was going to stick his two fingers up at the authorities no matter what. It also leaves you with the impression that it was spontaneous in nature; it was based on the emotion of students and the charisma of Hedgewar. Yet, reality is always filled with more intrigue than simple droll narratives. We know that Keshav was held in high regard, and there is ample evidence that he was a student leader; yet was he capable of acting as a lone ranger in this way? Was he that reckless and emotionally charged? It seems to go against his grain. Hedgewar, through Moonjay, had learnt that organization was key. He would have known the limitations of rage, anger and spontaneity from the writings of Ramdas and the deeds of Shivaji. It seems far more likely that this was orchestrated by a small group of youth leaders at the Neil City High School and Morris College (the girl's school). Keshav led the charge at Neil City and another youth, who has regrettably been forgotten, was in charge at Morris College. It seems likely that Moonjay would have known about what was going to happen. He was ready with a defence for the students, as were statements from Tilak in Pune, and other 'republicans' in Maharashtra. News can travel fast, but when organized, it travels that much faster, and Keshav knew this.

Oak hauled himself back into the hall and addressed the students. He was sympathetic to the student cause but advised that a school was not the place to express these sentiments and so the culprits ought to step forward and apologize to the inspector. No sooner had he finished his sentence than 'Vande Mataram' started to echo around the room. This time even students who had no inkling to get involved began to chime in. Oak was furious. By now, a letter had been written and sent to Sir Bipin Krishna Bose, the chairman of the School Managing Committee, by the inspector. Both schools run by the Shikshan Mandal, Morris College and Neil City had responded in the same way. Now students at other schools were getting in on the act. The authorities would need to set an example. A heavy hand would have to be applied on the culprits. That heavy hand fell on Keshav.

The ring leaders were rounded up and expelled.[65] This only further stirred the hive. All two thousand students began to boycott the school in the following days and weeks. The strikes continued for two months.[66] Each day that went by was a public-relations disaster for the authorities. Newspapers were writing editorials on the student protests in Nagpur. The public came to know what was happening in schools across Maharashtra. Students across Nagpur would chant 'Vande Mataram', in defiance, showing solidarity with Keshav and his class. These mass shows of protest took place after school every day. People began to agitate, debate and support the students. Through an equal measure of pleading with and coaxing the students and parents, one by one students were promised to be reinstated back into class and all would be forgiven if they simply apologized and gave the name of the student(s) in charge. The latter request was met with silence. Parents of many students panicked and further pressured their children to give the names of the ring leaders. Police were escorting school children to and from school to ensure order. Over time, pressure wielded its inevitable results. Eventually, with the intervention of another republican, and peer of Moonjay, Achyut Kolhatkar stepped in to help. He pleaded with the students, and to everyone's surprise, they listened. The demonstrations came to a sudden halt. Students went back to school.[67]

According to eyewitness accounts, suspected students who might have known the ring leaders were hauled into Oak's office under the oversight of Bose. Each student was asked simply to nod with an affirmation if the right name was presented to them as to who the ringleader was. Keshav was highlighted by several peers. Keshav himself refused to cooperate.[68] He was duly expelled.

THREE: 1907–1909

Expulsion and Revolution

The one thing that had given Keshav some sense of order, learning and friendship was suddenly gone. Without a job, income and Mahadev's support, his life had become seriously precarious. RSS literature describes this period in its usual long-winded hyperboles. In older narratives from the 1970s and 80s, Keshav is portrayed as a 'stubborn', 'resilient', 'daring', 'patriot' who would never be willing to retract his 'love for the motherland'.[1] In later renderings, Keshav moves swiftly and somewhat seamlessly from Neil City High School to another school over 160 kilometres away. Sinha writes, 'Leading nationalists arranged for his education at Yavatmal's National School'.[2] Who were these 'nationalists'? How had this been arranged so quickly? Who paid his fees? None of these questions are considered by any RSS literature. One can only suspect that they felt this kind of detail is of little use in instilling 'patriotic fever' in the minds of young men. It is an unnecessary distraction from the business of 'nation-building'. It goes without saying, but nevertheless it needs to be said, and John Wooden says it best, 'It's the little details that are vital. Little things make big things happen'.

Keshav had moved in with one of these nationalists. Dr Moonjay and his family housed the young rabble-rouser. We know practically nothing at all as to the living arrangements, or Keshav's relationship with Moonjay's wife, Krishna, or their two children. Keshav was almost eighteen years old when he moved in with one of the most affluent families in Nagpur. Keshav was gregarious. He was a self-assured young man, but one who was always contained in front of Moonjay and Krishna. There was a demureness to him, while equally being playful with the younger two children. Keshav split his stay between Moonjay in Nagpur and his uncle

Moreshwar in Rampayali for the best part of a year.[3] On one occasion, while Keshav was in Rampayali, a homemade explosive was detonated near the police station. No one was injured, nor was any property damaged. Those who knew Keshav was in town were quietly confident as to who was behind the disturbance. Police interviewed a few people and likely knew that the explosion and the arrival of the young militant were linked. But alas, with no proof, the matter had to be dropped.[4] During these times, all we know is that Keshav was heavily involved in organizing and training the youth of Nagpur and its surrounding districts. It's well within the realm of possibility that Keshav was spreading revolution to sleepy Rampayali by teaching its young men everything from how to organize public protests to bomb-making techniques. It is hard to decipher, however, much else as to his whereabouts and activities while he was staying with Moonjay.

Even Moonjay's diaries, all written in immaculate English, fail to mention, even in passing, any reference to his wife and children, let alone Keshav. By all accounts, this negation of one's wife and children seems deliberate. It seems puzzling to any modern reader as to why this might be the case. One obvious point is that Indian writers, on the whole, have simply not been interested in the details. Understanding the 'why' of any situation has simply not appealed to them; partly because they have already decided upon the 'why'. Indian writers are nearly always partisan. This is the case across the landscape of Indian historical narratives, especially biographies of its national heroes and villains. For many decades, Hedgewar had been the supreme villain. On the other side, many RSS books are often protracted rambles of heroic deeds of Herculean magnitudes where details are bulldozed aside as if they played little or no part in making the protagonist.

It seems quite likely that it was Moonjay who, at the very least, had inspired and supported Keshav in launching a student protest. It was a real coup for those popularising swaraj. The news of student protests spread far and wide across Maharashtra. Newspapers ran front-page stories, especially Tilak's *Kesari* and *Kal*. It was paramount for young people to join the swaraj movement, and this was a sure way to get everyone talking, including the authorities. Keshav, on the one hand, was now under observation from the police. The state apparatus had picked him up and labelled him as 'treasonous' as it did with all those who opposed Imperial rule.[5] Simultaneously, he had become a student leader, recognisable by name and reputation. Parents were polarized. Some felt admiration for the young man, while others felt that he had effectively ruined his education, and certainly wouldn't want their children to follow suit. Moonjay knew the sentiments of the people. He also knew the leviathan had eyes on Keshav.

Keshav had been very close to graduating high school. Moonjay, along with his uncle, the ever-reliable Moreshwar, now arranged for Keshav to move to a small school in Yavatmal. The Yavatmal National School, called *Vidya Gruha* (House of Knowledge) was small and privately-run, with a nationalist curriculum, the type that the Crown loathed.[6] A young man, freshly graduated from Calcutta University, with a degree in Law and a new barrister in town, was appointed to administer the school as a trustee. His name was Madhav Shrihari Aney.[7] He was short but sturdy in build. Although twenty-seven years old, he still chose to wear the customary circular top-hat, worn by families of high learning dating back to the heady days of Maratha rule. He was a keen advocate for Indian society to take control of its own educational curriculum and teach young people all that was to learn of its own land and customs. Like Keshav and Moreshwar, he too was a Deshastha Brahmin from the same region as the Hedgewars. His family name 'Aney' was a 'Maharashtralisation' of Annamraju, from the Telugu-speaking areas. It was Aney, through a fusion of familial solidarity with Moreshwar and deep respect for Moonjay, who accommodated Keshav not only in school but also provided accommodation in his own house. Keshav kick-started his education in 1908.[8]

Aney was an intelligent man. Well educated. A desh bhakt. He joined thousands of others in the struggle for India's independence. He was a significant actor in the post-independence years, initially becoming the Governor of Bihar, before going on to become a member of parliament between 1962 and 1967.[9] A man who became well-known for his decency and spent decades building India's rule of law and educational establishments. He died in 1968. Keshav had the good fortune to live with Aney for almost fourteen months, a man who was only nine years his senior.

His brother Mahadev was replaced by another.

Keshav, if nothing else in his life, had the incessant blessings of Sarasvati, the goddess of knowledge. Through plague, death, upheaval and family breakdown, his education was always somehow catered for. Moonjay provided the funds while Moreshwar worked the family connections. Well-wishers who saw some latent talent in the young man imparted education to him. Sarasvati may have blessed him, but he was firmly a devotee of *Bharat Mata*, the personification of culture of India and her land. Even in Yavatmal, Keshav couldn't help himself in setting up 'extra-curricular' discussion classes where Tilak's four-point solution for Self-rule could be presented and argued.[10] Keshav's 'cell', as dramatized by many modern historians, kept links with 'discussion' groups throughout Vidarbha district. The school was funded by a small but committed army of well-wishers who generously donated money, food, books and furniture. Behind this army was a man who had given everything he had in terms of time, money and mind for the struggle. His name was Narhari Shivram Paranjape, popularly known as Babasaheb. He had made it his personal mission to fund any teacher that wanted to set up an independent national school in the region. His character preceded him, and so people were always more likely to donate to any school Babasaheb supported.

Classes were held near the Vitthal mandir, where a deity of Vishnu presides. Keshav's school days were between 11 a.m. and 5 p.m.[11] He was an early riser, usually awake between five-thirty and six just as the first rays of the morning sun hit the dew-covered grounds. He would pick up a large circular clay pot, walk over to the water well and pull out a few buckets of water to fill up his pot. Walking across the yard, he would go over to the bathing area. Using a combination of soapberries (from the Sapindus tree) as a cleansing agent and pouring cold water over his lean body, he would bathe. The soapberries, which are known to be anti-bacterial, would release a pungent smell and clean the skin much the same way as modern soaps do today. In South India, soapberries are still used in villages. Having bathed, he would complete his morning prayers, a routine he had carried forward from his father. In between his daily prayers and grabbing a morsel of food consisting of a *bhakri* (a type of flatbread made out of millet flour) and a glass of buffalo milk, he would experiment with facial hair.[12] It was around this time that he began to grow his Nietzschean style of moustache. He had adopted the German expression of masculinity, knowingly or unknowingly, through his moustache, a feature that in later years would contribute to his image as the 'tough guy', 'the authoritarian', 'the man's man' and 'the bigot'. The rest of the morning would have been spent either studying or engaging with his wide foray of 'extra-curricular' activities. Just before heading to class, Keshav would join Aney for lunch. Keshav's diet consisted of legumes, vegetables and rice. Even though a large number of Maharashtrians ate meat and fish (near the coast), Brahmin families were on the whole vegetarian. The two of them would talk with the older steering the younger.

Just across the square opposite Aney's house was the mandir where classes were held. After class, at five, just as the sun began to cool, he would devotedly attend the *akhara* to exercise. Either in the morning or as the cooling sun set, Keshav would regularly find the time to read. He would read the dailies and weeklies to stay on top of political news.[13] But he also read books. Moonjay, who was fascinated with European enlightenment thinkers, especially the Italian political theorist Mazzini, certainly encouraged Keshav to read his treatise on Nationality and his book titled *The Duties of Man*. Others like Aney and Aptey would have signposted him to a wide array of Indian and European authors. He then read the essays of, and about, Vivekananda, the Hindu monk who had extensively travelled the USA and Europe to refocus the thrust of modern Hindu thought, and who had died a few years earlier in 1902.

Keshav never met Vivekananda, but through his writings and speeches, it is safe to assume that he was sufficiently inspired by the trailblazing monk. Vivekananda called for wholesale change in the outward manifestation of Hindu society by rejecting the bigotry that accompanied any caste-based society. His was a voice for reason and modernity, while unabashedly signalling a move away from superstition and ritualism. In his time, Vivekananda was a polarizing figure.[14] He resurrected the Hindu emphasis on *seva* (service of humanity). He founded and ran an order of monks who would live amongst the people and seek to reform society rather than seek *ananda* (bliss) in some forest hermitage. The Ramakrishna Order of monks, to this day, has deep links with the RSS. Years later, Hedgewar would encourage one such monk to not join Vivekananda's order but instead take on the responsibility of the RSS as its *Sarsanghchalak*.

Keshav had found himself as a frontiersman discovering new thoughts every day, helping him reimagine his world, how it had come to pass and importantly, his place in it. If he wasn't to be found reading on the balcony of the mandir, he would be seen sitting under a beautiful kachnar tree, which, when in bloom, ripens into a radiant ball of pink flowers. Often perched on the lower branches would be the long-tailed shrike—a small black-headed bird with a small beak and a long narrowing graduated tail. In shade and with birdsong as company, Keshav devoured many books. These few years were deeply formative for Keshav, surrounded as he was by such learned men, in an atmosphere of study and reflection. He carried with him the resonance of temple bells and the murmurings of ancient Hindu incantations, grounding him in a deep, primordial past, while his mental journey was unfolding at lightning speed into modernity through science, reason and an exposure to global thought. During these two years, between 1908 and 1910, Keshav seems to have blended his ancient Hindu world with a global sense of modernity.

There would have been little doubt left in him that the European societies had far out developed anything the Indian civilization had to offer in terms of scientific discovery, material development and invention, political institutions and generating economic prosperity. He would have become irrepressibly aware of the social backwardness of the Indian society, from the state of its women to the grotesque rootedness of caste in Indian custom. And yet, he would have seen the inherent racism and bigotry of the European mind, its obsession with consumption and materialism. Its distinct inability to deal with genuine liberty and plurality both in religious and political terms. The unconscious seeds of the RSS and its attitudes towards modernity are rooted here in these years where Keshav was coming of age. Unbeknown to him at the time, Keshav was trying on the clothes of a man of destiny and he would soon discover that they fitted him handsomely.

The school at this time had fifty students. Each student was funded by a patron and other donors were found to pay for the teacher's salaries. Every student was encouraged to attend public gatherings and festivities to raise funds for the school.[15] Keshav, unlike many of his peers, was always keen to fundraise and he would often mobilize the students for such tasks.[16] Many schools like Vidya Gruha were manned by teachers who, in their own right, were educated men and more than capable of getting jobs within the civil service. The civil service was a straight one-way ticket to life-long security, with a stable job and good pay. Yet, thousands of middle-class Indians during these times decided to not join the leviathan and instead set up schools, many of which were for disabled children and the downtrodden.[17] The British did nothing to support these initiatives. Teachers from the Vidya Gruha, some of whom were prominent historians and mathematicians, went on to write their own accounts of India's contribution to their respective fields. One teacher at the school by the name of Ketkar went on to establish a large institution for orphans in later years. These are the stories that are untold and will always remain so. The thousands of Indians who quietly gave up the possibility of a comfortable career, risking jail sentences, while settling for a meagre existence when they could have had so much more materially is what constituted the backbone of the revolution across the country.

Vidya Gruha was designated by the British authorities as an 'unrecognized' institution of learning. In other words, this was a school that could not issue formal certifications, and its students were not subjected to any central curriculum. By 1911, there were some 39,000 unrecognized schools across the country.[18] State provision of education was non-existent at the time so most of these schools were supported by the local community and wealthy patrons. These unrecognized schools could teach subjects that recognized schools could not. Subjects such as Indian history, native languages, martial arts and whatever else trustees saw fit to be part of their curriculum. Every 'unrecognized' school was different in size and quality.[19]

In a population of 252 million, there were only 193 colleges and universities; 6,400 secondary schools; 1,20,000 primary schools; the provision of education was sparse; places few; people many. Literacy rates amongst women were as low as 1 per cent, and for men, they were around 10 per cent.[20] Many of these schools were funded by Christian missions, especially Jesuits. Many were madrasas funded by Istanbul, the capital of the Ottoman empire. In Keshav's time, education was a big deal. It was a sure way out of poverty. So, for Keshav to be literate in English, Marathi and to some extent in Sanskrit placed him comfortably within the top 10 per cent of the population. He was, whether people like it or not, from a simple background but incredibly lucky and well networked. The *parivar's* interpretations of these times are fanciful at best. Sinha writes that he was simply a 'brilliant student' and 'family problems, poverty, or state repression – nothing could defeat Keshav's irrepressible resolve'.[21] This type of superfluous showboating does nothing to really bring about the truth of the matter. Keshav was, first and foremost, a beneficiary of lady luck, in the form of a father who had decided to enrol him into an English school and then by the likes of Aney and his uncle to have supported and funded his education, followed by opportunities to live with India's elite, people like Moonjay. There is little doubt that Keshav himself was bright, studious and tenacious, but it becomes hard to imagine where his tenacity would have taken him had it not been for the blessings of Sarasvati.

Indian society had found itself at an all-time low. Her people had not always been so decrepit. Keshav, and many like him, knew through oral tradition that their people had flourished a few centuries earlier. The British, and to a lesser degree, the Mughals before them had undermined the traditional methods of *guru-shishya parampara*, 'in which students would live with their teachers and imbibed an entire way of thinking'.[22] During the Pala period, between 750 CE and 1200 CE, India saw a number of monasteries emerge in modern-day Bihar and Bengal. The five most famous centres of higher learning were Vikramashila, Nalanda, Somapura Mahavihara, Odantapuri and Jaggadala—these were elite institutions of learning and attracted students from Turkey in the West to Japan in the East.[23] Nalanda had a campus housing two thousand scholars and over ten thousand students from all over the world. It had a library nine floors high. Subjects students could enrol into included fine arts, dance, music, chemistry, medicine, mathematics, astronomy, politics and war.[24] It is worth noting that at this time European centres of learning, such as Oxford and Bologna, were, in comparison, fledgeling in scale and knowledge. Will Durant, in his *Case for India*, writes, 'When the British came, there was, throughout India, a system of communal schools, managed by village communities. The agents of the East India Company destroyed these village communities and took no steps to replace the schools; even today [1930] they stand at only 66 per cent of their number 100 years ago'.[25]

Keshav was enrolled into an intermediate studies programme that every student had to complete before being able to enrol into a university degree. Colleges at the time encouraged rote learning, the regurgitation of which was required to pass exams. Failing these exams was very common. It was so common that many Indian students who got this far would proudly flaunt BA (F) as credentials to signal that they had reached a degree level but had failed.[26] Getting a bachelor's degree in these days was widely considered to be a rare and considerable achievement.[27] Keshav had to pass the year to be considered for further studies. He had missed the best part of a year and had much to catch up on. Living with Aney was one key factor as to why, despite it being an uphill task, Keshav was able to catch up on all his material in under six months.[28] One would have thought, however, that a sensible young man would have got his head down and focused on the matter at hand. Not Keshav.

He and his comrades, of which he had many in Yavatmal, especially after achieving 'semi-rockstar' fame amongst nationalists, decided to keep up the momentum of spreading anti-British sentiments throughout the town. Keshav was the 'go-to man' for all budding nationalists. At this time he lived with a very educated man who was an upcoming barrister in town. He was the one who had played a key role in organizing public events when the great man himself—Lokmanya Tilak—came to town, after all he was the 'adopted son' of Moonjay; and had an incredibly popular uncle in Moreshwar. He was also the young rabble-rouser who had caused two months of student strikes in Nagpur and held the badge of honour of being expelled. Now his fame continued to grow for being the local 'tough guy'. As a direct consequence of his rising fame, the leviathan was watching. Waiting. It only needed the slightest excuse to shut the entire school down.

On 5 April 1909, four days after Keshav's twentieth birthday, the entire town was celebrating Hanuman Jayanti (the birth of Hanuman). One must also keep in mind that Hanuman is the patron deity for young tough guys. He is the deity at every *akhada*. During these celebrations, Aney gave strong emotive speeches articulating exactly why colonialism had to be resisted. Then, youth leaders like Keshav were given a platform, rallying the young men of the town into a kind of frenzy.[29] Cries of 'Vande Mataram' filled the air. In this kind of agitation, there was a real danger from the throng of angry men gathered towards anyone who represented their oppressors—police officers, tax collectors and anglophiles of any sort. Public buildings were often targeted. Law courts, police stations and the homes of senior bureaucrats were often set ablaze, typically followed by a series of 'lathi charges' by the police who, in turn, brutalized anyone caught in their wake. Hundreds would be arrested, beaten and then discharged. The ring leaders would be rounded up and charged.

On this occasion, the leviathan had its hundred Indian eyes fixed on the Vidya Gruha. Babasaheb was quickly rounded up and taken in for questioning. He was well treated due to his seniority and the respect he commanded from everyone concerned. The local police officers who were doing their master's bidding would have been aware of the sentiments of the locals. Any harm to Babasaheb could have resulted in a full-scale riot. He was nevertheless quickly suspended from speaking in public. He signed his bail documents and was released without further charge. Then came the menace.

Parents were approached by senior police officers, warning them about what could happen the next time their children visited the school. 'Unfortunate incidents are becoming common these days', was often their parting message to already frightened parents.[30] After having visited parents, they went to known donors and well-wishers. Officially, these visits were merely to inform the local townsfolk about the 'extremism' in their neighbourhood, but eyewitness accounts suggest a far more intimidating presence from the authorities. A permanent police check was put in place directly outside the mandir. Police officers would randomly, and without explanation, conduct 'stop and search' on students. Books would be confiscated. Little clips around the ear were often administered to the boys on their way home from the school. Eventually, the pressure paid off. Parents began to withdraw students from school. Then the final nail was struck through the courts. Officials declared that the school was illegal and posed a 'seditious' threat to the wellbeing of the public. Just like that, Vidya Gruha was shut down by the autumn of 1909. Even Aney, being a barrister and a trustee of the school, was not spared. He had been seen to give seditious speeches and his license to practice law was revoked for one year.[31]

Well-wishers and patrons of the school who were not frightened off began to transfer their students to different schools, which were sympathetic to their predicament. Aptey and Aney, who by now had grown very fond of Keshav, planned for him and two other boys to complete their final exams in Poona (Pune)—the home of Tilak. Through a deep web of guardians and well-wishers, Keshav was quickly enrolled into Samarth School and accommodated at the Maharashtra Boarding House for boys near the Narayana Peth vicinity. Located in the old city, it was a crowded hive of commerce with crisscrossing narrow lanes and alleys. Fees were naturally paid for by patrons, Moonjay being the foremost. Keshav spent two months in Pune studying for his finals. Then in July 1909, Keshav sat his intermediate examinations. According to Sinha, Keshav achieved an upper second and passed out of high school.[32] He then swiftly went onto take the entry examinations at Amaravati for Calcutta's (now Kolkata) National Medical College and Hospital to enrol onto its four-year programme.

Why did Keshav choose to pursue medicine? Was he aware of the prestigious nature of his application? Was he aware of the rarity for Indian boys of his background to even consider applying for such a course? Did he understand that only 630 students were selected out of thousands that applied? How was he to fund his studies? We simply do not know if these considerations passed through his mind. RSS literature is unhelpful, and all we are told from these sources is that 'Keshav's patriotic heart was thirsting for the sight of that beehive of revolutionaries'.[33] There is little doubt that one of the considerations for studying in Bengal was to be at the epicentre of the struggle. Furthermore, we know that Moonjay, a medical doctor himself, and incredibly well connected through his time in the Imperial Indian Army, not only funded Keshav but also systematically guided him to apply. To be a medical practitioner in India in those days was exceedingly well respected. Doctors were few and far in between. Demand from illness was high. The British knew that modern medical provision was woeful across India, and 'natives' would have to be educated if India was to remain their 'jewel in the crown'.

Having submitted his application to study medicine at one of India's premier nationalist institutions, Keshav returned home to Nagpur in July 1909.

FOUR: 1909–1914

Into the Beehive

In December 1909, five months after returning to Nagpur, Keshav received his formal certification, having achieved an upper second class pass in his examinations.[1] He was now, in terms of education, in the top 5 per cent of Indian society. Around this time, he also received his acceptance letter from Calcutta National Medical College & Hospital. He was about to enter the top 1 per cent.

He left Nagpur in July 1910 and travelled some 1,100 kilometres by train to the throbbing heart of revolution. Hedgewar, as always, was a bundle of layered complications. Unlike most privileged students who lounged around during the summer, waiting for their schooling to begin, Hedgewar was suffused in revolution. Another layer to Hedgewar's onion-like life was that he became, in some sense, an 'adopted' son to Moonjay. This meant that he not only lived with the great doctor during these times, but he was constantly involved in activity of a seditious nature.

Hedgewar, in many ways, was knowingly entering a dangerous world. A world where revolutionary activity could involve murder, being murdered in turn, capital punishment or a lifetime of hard labour in one of the leviathan's many gulags. He went from being a radical youth leader into becoming a dangerous revolutionary in the many eyes of the leviathan—a fighter for freedom in its most pointed form. Knowing he was about to depart for Calcutta Moonjay assigned him a role that would earn him much-needed trust points with the secret societies in the hive of Bengal. His reputation would precede him, as it had done amongst students of Vidarbha.

A Bengali man by the name of Madhavdas Sanyasi, of whom we know little, was sent to Nagpur in the autumn of 1909. This, as far as we can tell, was not his real name. He was a man on the run. The imperial police wanted him alive so that they could be the ones to make him dead. Moonjay assigned Hedgewar to keep Sanyasi safe and out of sight. Sanyasi was a member of Aurobindo Ghose's Anushilan Samiti, a secret society, whose members were clear about their ends—complete freedom for India from the British through any means available. Their chosen technique was to terrorize the British. Bombs and assassinations were their preferred options. Interestingly, Anushilan, pronounced 'Ōnū-shī-lōn', meant bodybuilding. Started in 1902, it was at its height during these times. Frustrated young men with a growing political consciousness, who were eager to win their freedom, began creating branches all over Bengal. It had over 500 branches where hand-to-hand combat and training with daggers and lathis (bamboo sticks) was taught by ex-army officers. Today, in the West, Aurobindo is mostly known as a yogi, a poet and a mystic, who brought ancient wisdom from the east, and was one of the leading intellectual voices championing what later became the global environmental movement. Today, thousands of Europeans and Americans flock to his ashram in Pondicherry to find solace and peace and to live in environmental harmony. Few would connect the yogi with the nationalist. But a nationalist and a republican he was.

Aurobindo was a close friend of Tilak and Moonjay. All three led the republican side of the National Indian Congress. In fact, almost a decade earlier, it had been Tilak that inspired Ghosh, a Cambridge educated classics scholar, to join the struggle.[2] As the leaders of the Samiti were being arrested, Sanyasi made his escape to Maharashtra. While he managed to escape, many of his comrades were not so lucky. Sanyasi, being on the run since May 1908, was planning to make his final escape to Japan where a growing number of 'wanted criminals' fled. The Japanese, who clearly had imperialistic ambitions of their own that had not come to pass just yet, housed the enemies of their imperial rivals. Sanyasi was wanted by the authorities for his involvement in the Alipore bomb plot.

In May 1908, the leviathan, through infiltrating the secret societies, discovered a bomb factory at 33 MurariPukar Road in Calcutta. The authorities carried out stealthy raids under the cover of darkness and found bombs, detonators, revolutionary literature and details of names, addresses and correspondences between societies. The British had stumbled unknowingly into the nerve centre of its nemesis. A major coup for the British. A disaster for the struggle. It would lose many members through exile, imprisonment, execution and trauma.

A series of assassination attempts on senior British administrators, some successful, had led the leviathan to crack down on the Bengali secret societies. A massive intelligence gathering task force was commissioned by the Crown between 1906 and 1908, which resulted in the senior leaders of the Samiti being rounded up, arrested to be put on a public trial. Over a thousand artefacts and 222 witnesses were produced by the prosecution as the trial dragged on for months. A key witness for the prosecution, Narendranath Goswami, who had been a member of the Samiti, decided to turn King's witness. Weeks before he was to be summoned to give his account in the dock, he was murdered in jail by two of his former friends and fellow Samiti members, Kanai Lal Datta and Satyendranath Bose, both of whom were executed in November 1908. The stakes were high indeed. The judge at the trial, Charles Porten Beechcroft, found Aurobindo innocent due to the 'flimsy nature' of the evidence produced by the prosecution. Aurobindo may have been released after twelve months of largely solitary confinement, but he was no longer the same man.

> Friday, May 1, 1908. . . I did not know that that day would mean the end of a chapter of my life, and that there stretched before me a year's imprisonment during which period all my human relations would cease, that for a whole year I would have to live, beyond the pale of society, like an animal in a cage. And when I would re-enter the world of activity it would not be the old familiar Aurobindo Ghose. Rather it would be a new being, a new character, intellect, life, mind, embarking upon a new course of action that would come out of the ashram at Alipore.[3]

Aurobindo would abandon the struggle. He had paid too high a price. Under his leadership, young men had been executed, arrested and imprisoned for life in the leviathan's gulag, or had to flee to foreign lands abandoning their loved ones. One tragedy above all others may have tipped him over the edge.

Khudiram Bose was hanged on 11 August 1908 in Alipore Jail. He was just eighteen years old. Born in the same year as Keshav, just a few months younger, he too came from a humble family. He was arrested several times for handing out seditious literature and was involved in the struggle from a tender age. Aurobindo's younger brother, Barindra Kumar Ghose, had taken the young Khudiram under his wing and trained him in bomb-making techniques. For all we know, it was Barindra Ghose who had instructed Khudiram and another nineteen-year-old by the name of Prafulla Chaki to assassinate the Chief Magistrate at Alipore, a man by the name of Douglas Kingsford. On the night of the assassination attempt, the two young men had been tipped off as to which was to be Kingsford's carriage. Unknown to them, Kingsford had sent his daughter and wife ahead and took a later carriage. Prafulla threw the bomb in the carriage and inadvertently killed the two Englishwomen. Both men thought their mission was complete and made a run for it in separate directions. Khudiram was picked up the morning after having travelled twenty-five kilometres to a village outside the city by two police officers. He instantly panicked and gave away his identity. Having heard of Khudiram's arrest, Prafulla committed suicide rather than be caught by the authorities. News of the failed assassination attempt reached the Samiti and the Ghose brothers the next day to their complete dismay.

On the day Khudiram was executed, thousands lined the streets of Calcutta, garlands in hand. All the appeals for leniency fell on deaf ears. The authorities were bent on making an example of the young man. As in all Indian renderings, Khudiram was brave and even smiled just before he was hooded and noosed. In reality, one cannot help but feel that a young eighteen-year-old boy would have known what lay in store. The final walk from his tiny rat ridden cell to the gallows. He would have no doubt hoped that his neck would break quickly, shortening his final journey through the valley of death.

When Khudiram was executed, Aurobindo was in the same prison, a few metres away. What would he have felt as he sat in darkness, completely alone? Was it his vision of revolution that had taken a young man to the gallows? Just months later, two more young men would be executed, and this time, simply to ensure that Aurobindo would be saved. How does a sensitive, self-aware man such as Aurobindo live with that? His own younger brother would spend the best part of eleven years in a labour camp on the Andaman Islands, off the coast of India. It was Aurobindo that had enrolled his kid brother into the secret societies and was present during the oath of allegiance, where each recruit promised to offer everything, including life itself, on the altar of freedom. Now the time had come where freedom was demanding sacrifice and Aurobindo was the high priest committing those life sacrifices.

Hedgewar, through his growing influence across Maharashtra, managed to successfully house Sanyasi in a small village one hour away (by modern road standards) from Nagpur. It was a sleepy place where birdsong would have been the loudest thing one could hear by day, and by night, it would have been men and women singing around the campfire, retelling ancient stories of Rama and Sita and their eventual victory over the tyrant king Ravana. Here, in these settings, in Mohpa, where fewer than a thousand people worked and toiled the land, someone by the name of Appa Halday,[4] a local landowner, agreed to save Sanyasi's life by risking his own. Hedgewar, back in Nagpur, raised money from sympathizers to purchase Sanyasi's one-way ticket from Mumbai to the harbour in Osaka, Japan.

Hedgewar followed the Alipore bomb case closely. It was the first public trial of its kind. The case provided daily headlines for India's burgeoning press. *Kesari* covered the case extensively and ensured that the public across Maharashtra knew what was happening hundreds of miles away. Hedgewar was instructed to raise funds on behalf of the defendants to help cover the legal costs associated with the trial. Seshadri, in his usual magnifications, tells us something about the state of mind Hedgewar was in during these turbulent times.

> His one consuming passion was how to cleanse the motherland of the stigma of foreign slavery. It was hardly surprising that Keshavrao and other like-minded fiery youth saw armed rebellion as the only solution.[5]

These were heady days. A strong concoction of excitement and anger coupled with forethought and ideas of duties as a desh bhakt provided continuous highs for the young man, overpowering all other 'normal' thoughts. He was just twenty years old. Most young men are high on thoughts about status, sex and money. This is certainly the case today, as it was back then. Hedgewar, however, does not ever consider marriage or settling down in the traditional sense. He never seems to have entertained the ideas of drinking and womanizing, both of which were on the increase in urban Indian society. He never picked up any bad habits such as chewing tobacco, something that plagues Indian society even today. There is little doubt that he was raised on solid foundations, and he had the legacy of dead generations upon his shoulders. His older brother, Mahadev, had the same upbringing but he took to drinking and fell prey to the ills of the society. Hedgewar, we know, was lucky in some significant sense. He was, by all accounts, taken under the care of his uncle, Abba, and more significantly Moonjay, who not only financed his education but also gave him a home, as well as a network of dedicated and self-driven personalities. Role models are paramount. Hedgewar had plenty. Moreover, when it comes to women in Hedgewar's young life, we know little. He never said much in later years, nor have any of the RSS commissioned biographies said anything, and yet we know that women would have constituted fifty per cent of his relationships. Or would they have? In Hedgewar's time, at the turn of the twentieth century, women could only be seen in the home or toiling the fields or as maids. Very few girls attended formal schooling. It seems unlikely that Hedgewar would have had very many women in his life. Krishna bai, Moonjay's wife, would have been a carer for him; Moonjay's daughter would have been a younger sister; his aunts and sisters (if they were still in touch) would have given him some perspective, but how deep and meaningful would these relationships have been?

One thing we do know is that Hedgewar was exposed to radical ideas about womanhood. From his letters, diaries and later attempts to empower girls, Moonjay made it clear that for a strong Indian society to rise, women had to be educated, at the very least, and then made physically competitive with their male counterparts. Moonjay, in years to come, would be an open advocate for women's equality and argue that women were as capable as men, and in certain respects, more so. He had also been exposed to plenty of European women and was keen to Indianize European concepts of women in science and literature. There is little doubt that Hedgewar would have been exposed to all these emerging ideas. Twenty-five years henceforth, unbeknown to him, he would put into practice these ideas that were percolating in his intellectual universe.

10 July 1910, Hedgewar was twenty-one when he set off for Calcutta. He was at the height of his physical and intellectual powers. For the first time in his life, he would cross the borders of Maharashtra and venture to the other side of his beloved nation. He did not know it at the time, but greater India would teach him more, so much more, about his people, about the leviathan and most importantly about himself. He was about to

start his education at one of the most prestigious institutions in Imperial India—Kolkata's National Medical College and Hospital. He was armed with a letter from Moonjay, financial support from a collection of well-wishers from Nagpur and most importantly, he had a mission.

Upon arriving in Calcutta's bustling Howrah train station, where crowds thronged, he would have been greeted by scores of faceless strangers. Just by taking a short walk across the station at the time, he would have come to know much about the mastery of the British and the new world they were creating. He would have seen more white faces in the first hour of his arrival than he would have seen in years. Howrah station was the epitome of Imperial India. It was grand and majestic. It had been rebuilt in 1905, just five years before, and Hedgewar, like so many at the time who saw it for the first time, would have been in awe of the monument. Red bricked, with great arches lined across the front and a great central clock at its massive entrance. With fifteen platforms, it was by far the largest station in India and probably Asia. A melee of *chaiwalas*, makeshift food kiosks and coolies would have been hustling for Hedgewar's attention as he walked by, wide-eyed and dazed by what lay before him. The station is located on the banks of the Hooghly River, which was once known as Kati-Ganga. Hedgewar would have known it by this name. A sacred river, some 160 kilometres long, sweeping thousands of tonnes of silt into the Bay of Bengal. At points, the river is almost a kilometre wide.

Today, the famous Howrah Bridge, some 705 metres long, dominates the landscape connecting Howrah to Calcutta. In Hedgewar's time, as he came out of the station already in a state of astonishment, he would have gazed to his left, to find another breathtaking piece of engineering. The predecessor to the current Howrah Bridge was Pontoon Bridge, built in 1874. It was 465 metres-long and 19 metres wide with 3-metre-wide pavements on either side. At dusk, Hedgewar would have seen the bridge be mechanically raised to allow great ships safe passage. It was illuminated by electric lampposts, powered by the dynamo at the Mullick Ghat pumping station.[6] Hedgewar would have found himself staring at the cutting edge of what Industrial Britain, a world superpower, could produce. These experiences would further punctuate his feelings towards the British. To see such an engineering marvel in his own country would have further conceptualized his lifelong respect for European ingenuity, creativity and sheer audacity to get things done.

He would cross the 465-metre-long bridge, wide-eyed, staring at the city in front of him. He was in one of the greatest commercial cities in the world. If it wasn't for the scores of his fellow countrymen transporting heavy goods on bullock carts and ferrying around their white masters in the scorching sun, the architecture all around him would have made him think he had been transported to another world. As he turned right from the bridge and walked down the Strand, he would have seen what is today called Raj Bhavan. But in Hedgewar's day, this was the Government House where the Treasury was located. A majestic building, built in the Hellenistic style, draped in white stone and surrounded by green lawns and leafy, quiet roads where the riff-raff was not allowed to walk. As he gawked at the Treasury, he would have already passed statues of Queen Victoria, the Royal Exchange, countless churches, Canning's statue and then he would have seen the Ochterlony Monument—a tall, erect column made from white stone, visible for miles around, named after David Ochterlony who defended Delhi from the Marathas in 1804. Here he would have stopped to look up at the forty-eight-metre-tall column reminding him of how his own beloved Marathas were undone by the British.

As he walked through the lush green gardens, marked by wide roads, he would cross Lord Mayo's statue at the centre of the cross junction. Once the Viceroy of India, the statue, which is no longer there, would have shown a proud man riding elegantly on his steed in complete control. It would not have been lost on Hedgewar that Mayo was the master of all, in complete control, dispassionate in his approach, guiding the way forward. Mixed and muddled feelings would have been churning in him as he explored his new world. All around him, he would have seen statues of all those who had succeeded in colonizing his own people. Statues, marking the collapse of the Indian civilization, paid for, and built by the subjugated, with sharpened bayonets pricking them on the lower back, not enough to pierce them through, but enough to draw blood to let the victim know what lay in store if commands were not followed.

On his left, he would have passed Robert Clive's statue just as he saw the entrance to Fort William. He would not have been allowed in, but had he ever joined the leviathan as a senior bureaucrat, he would have entered the true power centre of Imperial India. Fort William is sprawled across 70 hectares. As he passed the entrance to the fort, he would have come to one of the grandest buildings ever built. The Victoria Memorial in white stone with a great dome in the centre and a gigantic archway for an entrance was the show of pomp of the leviathan. In Hedgewar's time, this was where the leviathan ruled 300 million subjects.

And then, just like that, after crossing the 30-metre-wide road, Hedgewar would have been back in the India he knew. He would see no more white Mughals, no more green lawns, no more wide roads, but instead, the small streets packed with his own people, albeit speaking a language he would hardly understand. He made his way to 70 Bowbazar Road, to Maharashtra Lodge. At the end of what would have been a mammoth journey in those days, at the height of summer, Hedgewar arrived looking dishevelled with the few possessions he had, only to find that the lodge was already full. There was no space for him. Hedgewar, as he was, carried Moonjay's letter of introduction, with clear instructions for the house manager to take care of him. The great man's letter could not be ignored. Temporary arrangements were made, and Hedgewar spent a few weeks sleeping on the floor of the manager's office.

By day, Hedgewar explored his new surroundings and met people at the helm of the struggle. He was specifically instructed to meet and work closely with Pulin Bihari Das, who had just completed a two-year prison sentence for committing an armed robbery in June 1908, with which arms and ammunition were purchased. Das was completely taken in by the idea of defeating imperialism through an armed revolution. He would go to any lengths to accomplish this end. He saw himself as a Robin Hood—stealing from the rich to feed the revolutionaries with arms. He was an expert fighter with the *danda* (the bamboo stick). He used to fence and was a fierce fighter with knives and daggers. Das was involved in several assassinations of British administrators before his arrest in 1908. The leviathan had no intention of letting someone like him wander freely around Calcutta. No sooner was he released, he was arrested again in July 1910, and this time, was sentenced to life imprisonment. He was duly transported to the cellular prison on the Andaman Islands, off the coast of East India. Hedgewar never met Pulin Das.

The manager at Maharashtra Lodge had requested students living nearby at 18 Premchand Boral Street to accommodate Hedgewar at their place. Moonjay's letter was a bane for the poor manager of the lodge. He was stuck and so did what he could—pass the buck. Anna Khaparde had enrolled at the medical college a year before Hedgewar and lived with a group of friends on the second floor of the building. Space was tight. Initially, Khaparde turned the manager down, but then was handed

Moonjay's letter. Khaparde could not turn Hedgewar away so easily and so agreed to accommodate him. Khaparde was the son of a wealthy lawyer who supported the struggle. His name was Ganesh Srikrishna Khaparde, who, it just so happened, was a close friend of both Tilak and the omnipresent Moonjay. Khaparde junior had no choice and, against the wishes of his roommate Shankar Naik, agreed to house Hedgewar in their room. Hedgewar slept on the floor, in between Khaparde junior and Naik's beds. The room was small with balconies on both sides. This was simple living with minimal comforts.

Khaparde, Naik and Hedgewar were at odds from the beginning. All three were of different temperaments. Naik called Hedgewar 'Head gawar', which loosely goes something like 'ignoramus' or 'chief of the ignorant'. Naik was rancorous. In turn, Hedgewar was the tough guy who would often annoy Naik by hiding his books, especially just before exams. Hedgewar took joy in seeing Naik get riled. Years later, Hedgewar would confess that what kept the three quarrelsome roommates together over the years was that each was a 'foot soldier' for the struggle.[7] Anna Khaparde would dedicate the best part of his life to the struggle and become an ardent follower of Gandhi's revolutionary movement in years to come.[8] With all three roommates at odds with each other, it is somewhat ironic that Anna named his flat Shantiniketan meaning 'the house of peace'.

The 'Head gawar' was never one to be taken lightly, at least by those he didn't like. For all his fierceness, he was equally gentle and playful with his friends. A case in point is his relationship with a group of young medics from Punjab. He spent quite a lot of time at the Punjab youth hostel with Niranjan Singh and Shivdatta Parashar. The three became close and would often study together, cook for one another and generally 'hang out'. Even though both boys were sympathetic to the plight of the country, they never, as far as we can tell, joined the Samiti. They remained well-wishers and nothing more. For Hedgewar to spend time with these two would have given him respite from his otherwise intense life.

Hedgewar, years later, recalled an incident which summed up his character in those days. The story goes something like this, as retold by Palkar in Marathi; Niranjan's early morning ritual of singing excerpts from the Guru Granth Sahib at the top of his voice, with windows wide open to allow for the fresh morning air, naturally disturbed the residents of an otherwise quiet cul-de-sac.[9] After a few complaints from the neighbours and Niranjan's complete dismissal of them, tensions began to rise. The locals, at the best of times, weren't thrilled to have students living nearby but now with a daily 'call to prayer', which no one understood, the polite 'can you stop singing, please' turned into stone pelting through the open window. On one such occasion, Keshav happened to enter their room in the morning just as Niranjan was completing his morning dose of shrill singing to the pain of everyone when stones began flying through the window and into the apartment. Both men took cover and waited for the bombardment to stop before deciding to take matters further. As soon the pelting stopped, both men ran downstairs to catch the perpetrators. There was no one there. They knocked on the neighbours' doors, but no one answered. That same day, as dusk fell, stones began crashing through the windows again. This time, they were bigger and more menacing. Both men ran downstairs and entered the cul-de-sac. Looking around in the shadows, they saw a group of men standing around. Without a second thought, both ran up to the group of five or six men and began landing blows. In a matter of minutes, fists and kicks were flying around; men grappling with each other and flinging some poor soul into the cement walls. A few minutes on, five men were beaten, bloodied and defeated.

Hedgewar and his Punjabi buddy had made their point. The cul-de-sac returned to an eerie silence.

The National Medical College was less than a ten-minutes' walk from their 'abode of peace' if they took a straight route down Premchand Boral Street. On his daily route, he would pass the Lady Dufferin Zenana Hospital, an institution that exists even today. This would have been a daily reminder to him of the internal weakness of Indian society. In the late nineteenth century, Indian women, by and large, had no access to medical care. What care there was, was delivered at home, and often by other women of the house. Thousands died needlessly. The society at the time did not permit male doctors administering care to women not related to them. Women themselves would rather risk infection, or worse death, than to allow a man to even touch them. Consequently, after seeing the death toll of women rise unremittingly, it was Queen Victoria herself who ordered the Viceroy of India at the time, Frederick Hamilton-Temple-Blackwood, the first Marquess of Dufferin and Ava, in 1884 to do something to resolve the situation. He gave the task to his wife, Lady Dufferin. She was regal in mind and look. She came from an established family and had connections to philanthropists with deep pockets. She created the Lady Dufferin Fund and raised money to build hospitals for women and children only. With the women's-only hospitals came the need for all-female medical staff. And so, she also encouraged Indian women to become medical practitioners and join the nursing colleges. She ended up building hospitals across India; seven in total, and one each in Calcutta and in Nagpur.

These soft impressions on Hedgewar's mind would shape the attitude of the RSS and, consequently, modern India in the decades that followed. He would have been all too painfully aware that as much as independence was the birth right of every Indian and worth fighting for, he also knew that Indian society was in need of serious reformation on every front, especially when it came to the empowerment of his mothers and sisters. He was all too aware that for India to become a respected nation amongst the family of nations, its women would need to bask in the light of education and social liberty.

Teaching hours at the college were between 11 a.m. and 5 p.m. everyday Monday to Friday. As he walked across the oval, a small but well-maintained patch of green, he would enter the administrative building, which housed the iconic clock tower and the principal's office. According to Palkar, the principal of the medical college was an alumnus of Edinburgh, a Dr S.K. Mallik, who, having been educated at the elite institutions of his times and raised as an avid admirer of all things British, was now vividly aware of the despotism that subjugated his people.[10] Hedgewar was particularly struck by Mallik's insistence on speaking Bangla and Hindi to students when outside of formal lectures. He was chiefly harsh on anglophiles who would use their fluency in English to distance themselves from the common folk who worked at the college as clerks, cleaners and porters. In the early part of the twentieth century, medical education was not what we might come to expect today. Medical schools were too few and far in between. Formally trained doctors were scarce, and most hospitals were philanthropic institutions. Training doctors was not very formalized either; theoretical lectures in chemistry, biology and physics were taught in educational institutions, while surgery and medication dispensing were done wherever possible, usually—but not always—at a hospital. The fact that the medical college and the hospital were purpose-built and on the same campus, a unique set-up in those days, meant that Hedgewar was one of the few students of his day to receive a 'university and a hospital education'.

Hedgewar was, by all accounts, fairly studious and kept up with his studies and assignments. Having said this, it was quite apparent to all those around him at the time that his real focus lay elsewhere. According to Palkar and a stream of other authors who have cited the only source we have, Ramlal Bajpayee, who was in Bengal during these years and was a member of the Samiti along with Keshav, wrote years later in his autobiography, 'Keshav's principal purpose to go to Calcutta was not to study medicine but to learn and connect with the secret revolutionary societies, and bridge the movements in Maharashtra and Bengal.'[11] Ramlal, a lawyer, eventually left India and settled in the United States and married an American woman who had convinced herself that she was a 're-incarnated Hindu' and her mission in life was to spread classical forms of Indian dance around the world. He went onto become the president of the India Welfare League, a lobby group in Washington.

Hedgewar was joined by other talented young men, many of whom would go on to make a name for themselves, either as political figures in independent India or in their respective disciplines. Narayan Savarkar, the younger brother of the famous Vinayak (Veer) Damodar Savarkar, studied with Hedgewar. Through Narayan, Hedgewar would eventually meet and become close to Ganesh, eldest brother of the three Savakars, who in literary circles was named Babarao. It would be Babarao and Hedgewar's friendship that would become the fertile soil in which the seeds of the RSS would be sown in the decades to come. Narayan would become a doctor, practising in Maharashtra and supporting the freedom struggle throughout his life. Narayan would suffer a most unfitting death when contrasted against the backdrop of a life lived with utmost integrity. In 1948, soon after Mahatma Gandhi's assassination, mobs were organized and sent out to seek vigilante justice. The 'evil-doers' had to be punished. But who were these begetters of evil? The angry mob had its gaze firmly fixed on Brahmins—any would do. Brahmin houses were torched, looted and men were killed on the spot.[12] Thousands would face serious injury, and hundreds would die. In these desperate and tragic days, Narayan, a respected doctor in Mumbai, was helping neighbours, friends and innocent bystanders escape the fury of the reckless mob. A large stone hit Narayan on the back of his head. He fell and never recovered. A year later, in October 1949, he died.

Along with Narayan and Hedgewar, there was a young medic with an unpronounceable name, Trailokyanath Chakraborty. He was a radical, a fact completely unknown to his middle-class Anglophilic family. Chakraborty was knee-high in revolutionary work by the time Hedgewar met him as a classmate in 1910. Both were of the same age. Chakraborty was the one who educated Hedgewar on the who's who and 'who's-in-prison' stories. Chakraborty, many decades hence, would go onto become a member of parliament, and a heavyweight at that, in what would become East Pakistan, after the partition of India. Chakraborty, even as a politician, was a radical democrat. He was arrested and subjected himself to an exile away from all political work from 1958 after martial law was introduced by the Pakistani establishment. Chakraborty, in 1910, along with Pratul Ganguli, became the de facto leaders of the Samiti after the arrest of Pulin Das. Chakraborty was caught up in a murder trial in 1912 but, through a lack of evidence, the charges were dropped. Then in 1913, eighteen months before graduation, he and Ganguli were arrested for what became known as the 'Barisal Conspiracy case'. Forty-four were arrested. Twelve were charged, of which five were given lengthy sentences and transported to the Andamans. Both Chakraborty and Ganguli would spend decades in prison for trying to incite British Indian troops to mutiny. These stories, which were unfolding around Hedgewar, could have so easily led him to extraordinarily long prison sentences of his own but, somehow, a combination of luck, his working style and his focus on Maharashtra instead of Bengal probably just about managed to keep the leviathan at bay.

The Samiti was a secret society. It was involved at the sharp end of the struggle. Due to its very nature and its opacity, it is difficult to know what role Hedgewar played in the Samiti. Contemporaries who went onto write biographies either in prison or many decades later give tantalizing snippets, but alas, ultimately leave us gasping for more. Nalin Kishore Guha, who became a quasi-famous author, wrote in his testimony, 'Hedgewar was a true revolutionary in every sense. He was known in the Samiti for his constructive thinking and work.'[13] Jogesh Chandra Chatterjee, a contemporary, described in his book, *In Search of Freedom*, how the Samiti was organized, and one can deduce from his words the environment in which Hedgewar was submerged. He tells us that each district had a District Organizer (DO) who was in overall command of a region. Each DO was in touch with other DOs from neighbouring districts. This was a tightly regulated and centralized system. There would be cooperation between the DOs, but each was independently run. The DOs reported to the heads of the Samiti, to which there were several branches—the Dacca and Calcutta branches being the biggest. Hedgewar had joined the Calcutta district and was under the de facto leadership of Trailokyanath, who was a DO. It was the role of DOs to execute and prioritize activities as commanded by the central leadership. These activities were not for the faint-hearted or for those living in the realms of non-violence. Indeed, to drive the point home, the Samiti had, according to Jogesh, a Department of Violence, who in turn would have experts in the fields of murder and dacoity (armed robbery).[14]

> The leaders of the Violence Department could not move in a district without the permission of the DO of the district. He generally knew the experts personally. Before a dacoity was committed for money, the person in charge of the Violence Department went to two or three districts, heard of the possible places from the DOs and then selected one target in one district. If it was a boat dacoity, expert boatmen were requisitioned. If an iron safe had to be broken open, the in-charge of the Violence Department requisitioned persons accordingly. If, say, 12 men were required in a dacoity, the leader of the Violence Department, would, in collaboration with the Centre and the DO of the district assemble these men from different places at a pre-arranged place after nightfall so that they were unable to recognize one another in the dark. They would then reach the place under the leader's direction and different persons would perform their assigned work. As soon as a whistle is blown, they would stop their work, stand around the leader, who counted them and ordered them to march on. After reaching a specified place the booty and stolen arms would be handed over to new men, who in their turn would carry them to safer custody. Every individual was searched to ensure that nothing was left with any one of the group which committed the dacoity. The perpetrators went back empty-handed to their own places. If they somehow were caught, they could not be prosecuted for a lack of evidence. The same was the procedure for murder.[15]

To what extent was Hedgewar involved in murder and dacoity? We can be fairly certain that he was not involved in any murderous activity. He may well have known about them, being, as he was, in the inner circle. What we do know is that Hedgewar, during this time, was systematically connecting revolutionaries from Maharashtra with the Samiti. There was a belief amongst a section of Maharashtrian society that secret societies such as the Samiti and their model of working were the only way to fight the struggle against despotism. To that end, between 1911 and 1913, Keshav made regular journeys back to Nagpur carrying a special cargo with him, namely guns. It was through a series of armed robberies committed by the Samiti, which allowed them to; first bribe British soldiers to hand over guns and ammunition for the struggle; which then eventually came to Hedgewar who would personally transport these items to Nagpur. If he had ever been caught, the punishment would have been severe —a one-way trip to the cellular jail on the Andamans, where so many of those who struggled were rotting away.

On 13 and 14 December 1910, armed police were drafted across the city. Keshav was a bystander. This was the Islamic festival of Eid al-Adha, honouring that arcane memory passed from generation to generation, cross-pollinating between ethnic groups and regions over thousands of years—that moment when a despotic, some would argue insecure God commands Abraham to sacrifice his son to prove his loyalty, to which Abraham readily agrees, and just before he is about to cut his own son's throat, the merciful God replaces his son with a ram. It is the re-enactment of this myth that takes place every year across Dar al-Islam, where an animal is sacrificed to show one's allegiance to God. Thousands of cows were slaughtered on the roads in broad daylight. The cow, as we have already come to know, is especially dear to Hindus. From the Hindu perspective, this was open provocation. 'Why', Hindu elders asked, 'was it that Muslims across the world sacrificed a lamb or goat, but in India, and especially in Bengal, they were adamant on culling a calf or a cow, if not for openly defying Hindu sentiments?' According to several newspaper reports in Britain, nothing much happened, and the police were soon withdrawn. They mention some localized scuffles breaking out in the suburbs of the city followed by a closure of shops in the Hindu quarters, which caused great losses to those businesses.[16] In reality, Muslims did indeed sacrifice animals, as they do today, but most Bengali Muslims quietly got on with it, in their own quarters, and usually sacrificed goats, not cows. Slaughtering cows was an expensive business and most certainly was not going to win you friends from the Hindu community. However, there was a group of Muslims who were openly walking cows onto the street corners near Hindu quarters and cutting their throats to the sheer horror of passers-by. Seeing cows in torment before their eventual demise is not something anyone wants to see in a civilized society. And yet, a small group of (Muslim) Pathans from the border regions of Afghanistan, who had moved to Calcutta, did exactly that to intimidate Hindus.[17] Hedgewar noted that, on the whole, everyone was sufficiently outraged, but no one dared to stand up to these provocateurs. To make matters worse, some of these Pathans began looting businesses in the Marwadi quarters. Marwadis are known to be merchants, often wealthy, and tight-knit. No one came to help. Hedgewar became further distraught to hear fellow Samiti members make off-hand remarks about the Marwadi traders, '... They deserve it. Where were they when we said to boycott British goods during the partition of Bengal?' This was true. The Marwadi community was single-mindedly commercial. They do not generally let something like nationalism get in the way of trade. Yet, clandestinely, many Marwadi families supported the struggle all over India.

On the second day, 14 December, Hedgewar mobilized some of his friends from college and decided to set up a medical relief camp in the suburb where rioting was most acute. At the same time, the Samiti was not going to take this lightly. Small bands were quickly arranged and went out hunting Pathans. While Hedgewar was providing first-aid to an unconscious man caught up in the riots, he saw a security guard leap on top of a Pathan who was busy looting. After a few sharp thrusts with his straight-edged dagger and some loud grunts from his victim, the guard made a run for it and the Pathan dropped to his knees, continuing to scream, convulsing and trembling like a rabid animal, with blood flowing profusely from the gaping hole in his side. Immediately, Hedgewar and his friends split up. Two carried on nursing the unconscious man, while Hedgewar and one other went over to attend the Pathan. No sooner had they reached him did they realize that the police were on the prowl and any Hindu near a half-dead Pathan would most certainly be incriminated. All it would take is for the Pathan to accuse them of the stabbing and they would be done for. After quickly cleaning and applying dressing on the open wounds, they too made a run for it. That day, Hedgewar made a lot of new friends from both the Marwadi community and Bengalis at large.

Between June and August 1913, fifty-five inches of rain fell on the Chota Nagpur Plateau, which is almost four hundred kilometres away from Calcutta. The plateau feeds the 'river of sorrows', which itself is hundreds of kilometres long, snaking its way through Bengal to join the Hooghly River. The Damodar today is one of the most polluted rivers in India and somewhat tamed through a series of dams built in the 1950s. But in the early part of the twentieth century, the river was wild, feared by farmers and loathed by the British. The river had burst its banks and had completely engulfed the town of Bardhaman, a district capital, with a population of almost 2,00,000. The authorities were overwhelmed by the sheer scale of flood damage. Tens of thousands had been left homeless, thousands were missing and huge amounts of irreparable damage had been done. Water levels had reached a staggering two metres, and most of the population were marooned on rooftops, exposed to the elements.[18] Dehydration was the biggest killer of young children and cholera was rampant. News of the unfolding catastrophe reached the medical college in early August. Hedgewar and five other medics who, according to Seshadri, joined the Ramakrishna Mission, which was one of the leading organizations in the region carrying out relief work.[19] Over a period of a week, Hedgewar and his small band of friends travelled by boat, going house-to-house transporting grains and lean water, and providing medical support.

Cholera was sweeping across large parts of rural Bengal. Hundreds of people had volunteered to help, but there was a chronic shortage of medically trained staff. Hedgewar saw for himself how a poisonous cocktail of poverty, illiteracy, cultural backwardness and casteism exacerbated the problem. Working fourteen hours a day, attending to sick and desperate people, was not only heart-wrenching for him but also life-changing. These were formative experiences. He witnessed how the rich, land-owning classes were always able to secure their position, often with no regard for the peasants who worked the fields. Women often bore the brunt of the disaster and faced a higher mortality rate than men. Orphaned children would often beg to survive whilst girls were taken in as domestic servants.[20] Being a male medical student almost certainly ruled him out from attending to lots of women who needed treatment. He would have seen women suffer needlessly because of arcane rules that dominated Indian society at the time and prohibited women from engaging with men who were not their kin. Years later, these experiences would culminate in developing a weltanschauung that would shape not just his life but that of the RSS and subsequently of millions of women in modern India.

Back in Calcutta, Hedgewar continued with his studies. Initially, unbeknown to him, the local police department had decided to keep a permanent watch on the students at the medical college. As time passed, the police grew increasingly aware of who's who and naturally identified Hedgewar as a potential ringleader. At some point during the winter months of 1913, the police went to great lengths to enrol a student by the name of Gopal Vasudev Ketkar, a Maharashtrian, into their service. The police in the Central Provinces had twice searched the houses of Moonjay and Hedgewar. They found nothing incriminating but were onto a strong scent. Ketkar was also interested in Narayan Savarkar, who had already spent a short stint in prison before starting his medical degree. Hedgewar and Savarkar were close. Both were in the same classes, and although Savarkar had taken a step back from seditious activities, his name preceded him wherever he went. Ketkar, always wanting to be close to them both, had made Hedgewar particularly suspicious. Hedgewar was trained. He would have known from his training in Nagpur, and then with the Samiti, of how to 'smoke out a rat'. Hedgewar was cautious from the beginning. According to Palkar, Hedgewar found a note incriminating Ketkar as a spy working for the police, but instead of humiliating the poor fool, he made sure that everyone fed Ketkar an endless stream of misinformation. Ketkar was none the wiser and indeed began to believe that he was slowly breaking into the inner circle.

About the same time, Hedgewar, along with his friend Prashar, would visit one of their chemistry professors in the evening. There was already some suspicion that the professor's office was watched day and night. Visitors would be noted and then, in turn, watched. Professor Chowdhary was under surveillance because there was some anecdotal evidence that emerged from the Alipore conspiracy case that he was teaching members of the Samiti bomb-making techniques. On one occasion, so the story goes, Hedgewar visited the professor on his first-floor office in the red-bricked administrative building. As he crossed the oval, he saw several shadows lurking around the front foyer of the building just through the front archway. Having noted the shadowy figure with a book in his hand that he clearly had no interest in, he went up the flight of stairs to reach the first floor. Through a pair of double doors and down the corridor, he came to the professor's office. Just as he entered and greeted his teacher, Hedgewar once again noted the shadow at the top of the staircase. Hours passed. What was discussed we will never know. What we do know is that for Hedgewar one-on-one meetings were important. He spent most of his day, when not in lectures and in theatre, with people. He was not a recluse. He didn't really have the luxury of being one. There was no space in the city that he could call his own. He was forming a wide network of friends and colleagues, people, that in some way, no matter how small, could play a role in the struggle.

That night, the conversations dragged out well past midnight. As the professor and the two students left his office and began to walk down the staircase in the dark, Prashar, always keen to show off his night vision skills, rushed on ahead. A few moments later, the shadow that was Prashar stumbled and fell, and simultaneously another shadowy figure let out a groan, with a clear sense of panic and shock. Hedgewar, only a few steps behind, held the professor back for his safety and continued down. He heard an annoyed Prashar ask the shadowy figure, 'Who the hell are you?' The shadow had no intention of answering and decided to run off into the dark. He shoved Prashar, who was still getting to his feet and ran. Hedgewar pursed him. The shadow ran onto the oval and Hedgewar, within a few minutes, was on him. With a quick but powerful jerk of the shadowy arm, Hedgewar had caught him and immediately slapped him across the face. By now, Prashar and the professor were watching from the entrance of the building and could see the tall figure of Hedgewar smack a kneeling man, who was feebly trying to protect his face. After a few firm smacks across the face, the man was going nowhere. He curled up on the cool, damp lawn, awaiting whatever fate had in store for him. Hedgewar signalled to Prashar and the professor to come over. Hedgewar threatened to take the man straight to the station for loitering on private college grounds. The man muttered forgiveness and asked to be pardoned. Instantly, Hedgewar realized that the man was no threat. Just a police stooge out to make a quick buck. He had inadvertently dozed off out of sheer boredom after waiting for hours in a dimly lit stairwell. Hedgewar picked him up by the collars and commanded him to his feet. He forcefully put his arm around the man's shoulders in a gesture of friendship, but with a menacing overtone and suggested that since they were all friends now, he should walk with the three of them and treat them to freshly made jalebi from a street vendor. The professor never saw the man again.

Stories, as retold by Palkar, tell us something about the Hedgewar of 1913—a twenty-four-year-old tough guy, charismatic, forceful but also sensitive to the world around him. He, like his father and older brother, could be a hothead, while at other times, he was soft and warm to those he respected. He had an affinity for his teachers, who often warmed to him. Hedgewar is often lauded in RSS circles as a man who chose to live in poverty and always smiled his way through life and its challenges. We know that the first is certainly true. Throughout his life, Hedgewar had numerous opportunities to lead a normal life, earning a lucrative salary as a doctor. However, he always turned them down, dedicating himself instead to the unpaid work of struggle and upliftment of his people. The latter could also be true, especially considering the people he encountered in Calcutta. Just as he had political role models in Moonjay and Tilak, he also found intellectual inspiration in his professors; he even had role models of the hardened militant type in the form of Pulin Das and the countless other hard line members of the Samiti; but he also drew, in later years, from an altogether different set of role models. One was a simple man, meek and short in stature, named Shyam Sunder Chakravarty, twenty years his senior. And another was a Maulvi, a Muslim scholar.

Chakravarty was, first and foremost, a journalist. The type that despotic regimes abhor because they write with a penetrating wit and flair that can unshackle the reader from their mental slavery. He was a learned man. He had that rare thing called a degree in English, coupled with a mastery of Sanskrit and Bangla. As a trilingual investigative journalist who feared no one and paid no heed to British interests, he quickly became a public enemy. His writings were too inflammatory for the authorities to handle, and he was swiftly exiled to Burma, today's Myanmar, in 1908. Being barred from writing and having whatever he owned usurped by the authorities, he was made destitute. After years of scraping out a living in Burma, he was allowed to return to India. When he returned, the world had changed. So many revolutionaries had been arrested, imprisoned, exiled or executed, and equally as many newspapers and journals were shut down—he found himself in a type of literary exile. He was monitored twenty- four hours a day and had become a pariah for any self-respecting newspaper. Of course, by self-respecting, they meant censored. He owned nothing. He lived in a single rented room. To his list of prized possessions, he had one set of clothes, a traditional dhoti and a khadi top, and a small collection of books that he treasured.

He would often visit Shanti Niketan and engage the young men in conversation and debate and brief them on the news of the struggle from across the country. Some students did not take too kindly to this poverty stricken, timid man. While others, like Hedgewar, found immense inspiration from him. Hedgewar recognized the literary brilliance of the man, and his deep-rooted connection with the struggle. He knew that that his sorry economic state was inversely correlated with his menacing intellect. Hedgewar would often invite Chakravarty to eat with them, knowing full well that he was living day-to-day and often went without a meal. What's more is that having recognized the man's brilliance, Hedgewar wanted to ensure that as many students as possible heard Chakravarty speak. Sure enough, he became an inspiration to many young men who consequently joined the struggle. What was particularly remarkable about Chakravarty was his pleasant demeanour. He was never seen in despair. He never became bitter about the hand life had dealt him. He never complained. But above all, Hedgewar could see a fierce fire behind the older man's otherwise submissive nature. That fire in the face of the most acute adversity was what inspired Hedgewar, and the example of Chakravarty would stay with him throughout his own life, especially after 1925.

Today, those that have spent any meaningful time with prachaaraks or prachaarikas will immediately feel a similar demeanour about many of them. Prachaaraks draw great inspiration from the deeds and actions of Hedgewar, just as Hedgewar himself emulated those who inspired him. Prachaaraks own almost nothing. The rule of thumb by which they live is that life should be as simple as possible. They will own only that which is necessary—often two or three pairs of clothes, a laptop, a mobile phone and some basic toiletries. They have no home, nor family. They will not even spend money on a bottle of water unless absolutely necessary. Their complete dependence rests on the broad landscape of the Hindu community worldwide. These are devoted actors with incredibly sharp intellects who live on less than $7,000 (Rs 5,97,744) per year in the developed nations and on even less in India, and other developing countries. The Hindu landscape is vast, both geography and culturally, leading to the deification of prachaaraks in some areas, while in other places, such as the United Kingdom, they are seen as real men and women of flesh and blood. Men and women such as these provide the faceless leadership for the worldwide parivaar.

Liaquat Hussain was a Shia Muslim scholar and had studied at an Islamic seminary. He was a man in his sixties by the time Hedgewar met him in Calcutta. Like many others, he too had learnt to be thrifty. A simple man who had spent many years in prison, constantly in and out for misdemeanours against the Crown. He was relentless in his commitment to the struggle. He took life as it came and often quipped to young audiences at his morning rallies that he had begun to enjoy 'government hospitality'[21]. British officials saw him as a charlatan posing as a pious Muslim, while in reality he was merely a stooge for Tilak and his 'Make in India' campaign. He was one of those few Muslims at that time who strayed from the common path as defined by Muhammad Ali Jinnah and Sayed Ahmed Khan who proposed a two-state solution, claiming that Hindus and Muslims could not share a country. Liaquat Hussain went as far as to stop wearing his Turkish styled black top hat and started wearing the Indian white cap in what is now known as the Nehru-style cap. As time went by, his Muslim followers decreased and by the 1930s, he was a pariah amongst them. By the end of his life, he had a handful of students around him to help him through his illness. It is unclear what he died of, but we do know that he died poor and in relative isolation.

Hedgewar, during his time, saw a man at the height of his influence. Although he was often unwell, and for many months, Hedgewar and his friends nursed him through his illness, he nevertheless was incredibly active. He was a tireless worker, organizing morning peaceful protests outside colleges and government buildings. He would sometimes get Hedgewar to step up onto the podium and say a few words to the audience about buying only 'Made in India' goods. Interestingly, Hussain also ran his own goods store called Kuber General Stores where, not surprisingly he sold only goods that were made in India. At some of these morning marches, crowds would gather, often drawn in by no more than curiosity. Some, however, would stand on the by lines and jeer and taunt the speakers. On one such occasion, some poor fool stood adjacent to the podium and was heckling the old Maulvi as he spoke. Hedgewar, listening intently to the fool, one amongst the congregation, suddenly burst out from amongst them, grabbed the heckler and beat him indiscriminately. Eventually, some of his friends ran over to stop him from causing any more serious damage. When he was asked what provoked him, he said 'no one should be allowed to speak of the Lokmanya with such disregard'.[22] These were polarizing times, and Hedgewar wasn't one to be trifled with.

Conversations with the Maulvi would have given Hedgewar a deeper understanding into the underlying currents that were afoot in the Islamic world. The Ottoman Empire, the seat of the Caliph, the leader of the Muslim Umma and the protectorate of all the faithful, was no longer the power it used to be. Endless corruption, a declining economic power and blatant show of poor leadership as far as the mullahs and the pious were concerned, all created an increasing feeling of unease amongst Indian Muslims. Muslim leaders were generally anti-British with the overarching dream of returning India back to Dar-ul-Islam. There was a small, and ever decreasing number of learned Muslims who felt otherwise. These few, amongst whom Maulvi Hussain was one, believed that India must be composed of a Hindu–Muslim unity underpinned by being children of the soil first—that is 'desh bhakts'. Of course, for most Sunni Muslims, this would be tantamount to idolatry, and so was a non-starter. Maulvi Hussain knew that his was an unpopular position amongst his fellow clerics and preachers. By 1919, events in Europe would spell the end, once and for all, of a Hindu–Muslim unity pact in the Indian struggle for Independence. The only problem would be that no one would tell the Congress leadership, especially Gandhi. When people did try to tell him that his dream of a unified Hindu–Muslim country was a pipe dream, he would dismiss such claims as simply undue pessimism or throw charges of bigotry on those trying to reason with him.[23]

On 28 July 1914, Britain entered the first World War. It was a war that clearly no one had quite expected, but once triggered through a series of complicated alliances between nation states, 70,000,000 combat personnel would be mobilized throughout its duration.[24] Of these, 1,500,000 Indian soldiers would be drafted into a European theatre of war, of which at least 74,000 would end up killed and a further 64,000 wounded. Many were illiterate and used scribes to send letters back to India. They were subject to racism and maltreatment and were woefully under equipped to deal with the cold European climate[25]. None of this was known to Hedgewar and his bolshie friends when the British called up medics to join the army to support the war efforts in Europe. Completely unaware of the tragedy unfolding in Europe, his friend, N.S. Moharir, went to the recruitment office to sign up. Hedgewar accompanied him. Both thought that experience of real fighting would somehow prove useful for the struggle. It's safe to say that these were young medics who were naïve at best, drawn into the propaganda of the times—'that real men joined the army to fight'.[26] Both were rejected immediately for being blacklisted and identified as 'working against the interest of the Crown'[27]. It turns out that Hedgewar had been blacklisted and was on the police watchlist ever since his Neil City School days. The police were given a book titled *Political Criminals* of India in 1914, which verified Hedgewar as a danger to the interests of the Crown, it even described him as being 'well over six feet in height and was of stocky build'[28].

It is difficult to say with any certainty whether Hedgewar was serious about joining the Indian Army to fight in World War I or was it a stunt pulled by two young men to get a quick laugh and jeer with their comrades. Certainly, his personality and wit were such that British officers would have certainly appreciated it. A humorous cocktail of bravado and sarcasm mixed in with a dash of daredevilry. He was most certainly officer material, but sadly, as far as the British were concerned, he was on the wrong side.

For all his extracurricular activities, he managed to score fairly decent grades in all his examinations throughout his time at the Medical College. In September 1914, he passed his finals. He scored 70 per cent as an average across all his modules. He scored particularly well in physiology. In 1915, he went on to intern at Calcutta's state-of-the-art Albert Victor Hospital, which, just three years earlier, had been given a donation of Rs 5000 by King George V to complete the hospital.

Hedgewar, during his five years' stay in Calcutta, had transformed from being a high-energy, emotively driven young man eager to fight the British into a 'tough guy' who had proven himself against the best of them and was a respected member of all the hard-line secret societies of Bengal. He had learnt the 'tricks of the trade' and had experimented with new ones. He had seen his fellow revolutionaries charged ready for the fight, when suddenly they would bow out with a whimper. He saw strong men arrested and imprisoned, facing life sentences. He witnessed murder. He witnessed first-hand the dastardly intentions from certain sectors of the Muslim community, especially around their vision of returning India to a perceived golden age under Dar-ul-Islam. He saw the trauma of poverty, illiteracy and cultural backwardness of his own people. He had witnessed how misplaced women were in his society and how caste played havoc across it.

He had become increasingly cultured, and with it, nuanced mentally. He had been exposed to British engineering, the height of their bureaucracy, the discipline with which they operated, their music, art and above else their thirst for knowledge through science. He had become increasingly respectful of the British and their achievement as much as he maintained his resistance against their tyranny. He had become aware that the British in every quarter had advanced well beyond the Indian. British superiority seems to have only further motivated him to bring his own people on par; to create a fair playing field. Knowing what we now know, it is clear that it was during his days in Calcutta where he recognized that the root of the Indian problem lay within a culture that had mutated from what it once was into a highly fragmented, superstitious, illiberal and grossly hierarchical. These were learnings. He had diagnosed the problem but the cure remained elusive. It would be another decade before he would realize it. The cure would be a hard pill to swallow, and the recovery arduous.

Doctor Hedgewar returned to Nagpur in late 1915.

FIVE: 1915–1919

Guns and Inner Storms

Twenty-six years old, the boy Keshav had become a respectable man.

Anyone familiar with Hindu society knows that being a doctor is one of the most respected professions a person can purse. Even today, the Hindu diaspora in the United Kingdom, which represents less than 2 per cent of the population, produces something close to 12 per cent of all doctors in the National Health Service (NHS).[1] Quite literally, Hedgewar had the world at his fingertips. He could have had financial security, and prestige and entered a class of elite Indians if he so chose. At the time, there were only seventy-five registered doctors in the entire Vidarbha district, which, in 1915, had a population of well over 11,000,000.[2] He was clearly aware of what lay ahead. After all, he was the protégé of Dr Moonjay, a man with two eye clinics and one of the wealthiest men in Nagpur.

When he arrived in Nagpur, Hedgewar decided to go and stay in his family home with Mahadev and Sitaram. We know that during Hedgewar's time in Calcutta, he seldom kept in touch with Mahadev. The two brothers had irrecoverably parted in mind and spirit. There was no reconciling with Hedgewar's drive to remain dedicated to the struggle, no matter the personal cost, whereas Mahadev's yearning to find security with a little dignity in life was all there was in his mind. Mahadev would have certainly hoped that now, with his younger brother's earning power, easier days had surely arrived. Mahadev eagerly waited for Hedgewar to announce his new job and, more importantly, his pay packet. He would see his younger brother leave the house in the early hours of the morning after bathing and completing his ritual puja. He would return late evening, say a few uninteresting words and then head to bed. Days became weeks. Still no news. Mahadev increasingly became aggressive. As his aggression increased, Hedgewar proportionately spent less time at home. To add fuel to the raging fire in Mahadev's mind, Hedgewar turned his upstairs room into an office and began inviting people to his home for private consultations. We have little insight as to whom he was consulting or on what matter. But we can be sure it was not medical in nature. The nectar of rupees that Mahadev had so looked forward to was nowhere in sight. And there was no sign of it ever appearing. Mahadev remained in a financial desert, much to his growing frustration.

While Mahadev was conjuring up mirages, struggling to make ends meet and edging towards destitution, Sitaram had been in Indore, a city some eight hundred kilometres away, learning to become a *karma-kānd* Brahmin. He went to train as a priest. Having memorized thousands of aphorisms and verses from medieval texts, and endlessly complicated rituals for every occasion of civic life, he had returned home at almost the same time as Hedgewar. Sitaram and Hedgewar remained close. It's uncanny that both brothers had finished their respective training at a similar time. Even though there is no evidence, there is an ever-present scent that fills the spaces in between their letters, which suggests that the two brothers had planned their return. Both were going home to confront Mahadev's tyranny.

Even though Sitaram and Hedgewar made some attempt to get along with their oppressive older brother, it soon dawned on them that things were not going their way. Hedgewar spent most of his time with Dr Moonjay and Tatya Fadnavis, while Sitaram was now making his livelihood through performing rituals every day and administering to the neighbourhood. Both ate out. Sitaram, as was the custom of the day, was fed well by his customers—the devoted, and somewhat superstitious Hindu families. While Hedgewar had no shortage of houses he could call upon. No one cooked at home. The home had become just a house.

It transpired that while Sitaram and Hedgewar were away studying, the house had been rented by Mahadev, which became his only source of regular income. We do not know where Mahadev lived. What we do know is that the house was rented by a Mr Wamanrao Dharmadhikari. His family lived there for around four years. The house had fallen into disrepair, and Wamanrao had been the one to renovate it. By all accounts, Wamanrao and his family had a happy home, and naturally felt it was time to move when the two brothers were due to return from their respective studies. Wamanrao was another 'troublemaker' as far as the authorities were concerned, albeit a minor actor, and one they didn't really bother or keep an eye on. He and minor actors like him would go on to play a significant role in the years to come, but that was yet to manifest itself.

Between 1914 and 1916, Nagpur suffered from several small outbursts of the plague. According to the historian Ira Klein, at the American University in Washington DC, outbursts of plague continued to occur throughout Asia, the Middle East and Africa between the late 1800s and the first half of the twentieth century. Klein believed that the regular occurrence of the plague in India was largely due to 'British economic policies, where village sanitation remained almost non-existent, modern transport and modern irrigation made it that much harder to contain the disease, and the overall density of people living in squalor' all helped in spreading the disease.[3] Having said this, it is also clear that the British did indeed learn lessons from the disaster of 1902 when almost three-hundred people died daily, including young Hedgewar's parents. The British developed quick response units that would isolate the sick, evacuate families to the suburbs in makeshift huts and provide vaccinations, which were available, to the poor.

Like hundreds of other families, Sitaram and Keshav left their home to seek shelter in the outskirts of the city. Mahadev did not come with them. Instead, he took it upon himself to stay back and guard the local neighbourhood from small-minded bandits, scavenging from people's derelict homes. We cannot be sure why Mahadev did not listen to people's advice to leave his home. He was stubborn; we know this. Maybe he was trying to replicate the heroic deeds of his parents during the 1902 outbreak. Maybe he was trying to redeem himself and show his younger brothers that he was still capable. Maybe he was just overcompensating for his sorry state by showing courage in the face of the disease, which had killed so many. Or maybe, just maybe, he was at some unconscious level seeking to end it all. This was his route through the fire exit. Mahadev died in the same way as his parents had. Except he died in pain, and alone, in his home. It would be several days before his rotting corpse would be taken away and cremated. His was a life of such potential that had been derailed so early.

As best as we can tell, Mahadev died in early 1916. Palkar, however, writes in a footnote that during his efforts to collate Hedgewar's life, there were people who felt that Mahadev had died in 1914, one year before Hedgewar graduated. We know that Hedgewar travelled by train in 1914 to visit Nagpur, but we cannot be sure if this was to smuggle arms or because a calamity had befallen his family. Hedgewar never spoke about Mahadev; he never wrote anything and as far as we can tell, it was as if Mahadev was there one minute and gone the next. There are no death certificates, or records to be found, which can corroborate these memories. Mahadev just fell out of history, as do the vast majority, but his death would have certainly left its mark on Hedgewar.

Hedgewar was twenty-six years old, a doctor and, infinitely more interesting, one of the most eligible bachelors around. Visitors came from far and wide to see his uncle Abba to ask if he would permit an introduction to the dashing young man named Keshav. Abba was keen, all too keen, to see his troublesome nephew get married, settle down and take up some real responsibility. Horoscopes came in thick and fast from fathers with daughters, a custom, albeit a dying one, that still pervades the Hindu world. Horoscopes must match. Hindus of Hedgewar's time saw to it that the moon and stars were all going to play a helping hand in the life of their son or daughter before giving or accepting a suitable dowry. Even in superstition, one ought to manage risk.

Hindus still practice arranged marriages. But what this actually means is something most people cannot pin down. There are draconian child marriages, which thankfully have all stopped. But in Hedgewar's time, it would have been quite common. His parents and grandparents would have been wedded as children, although they would have commenced their life as a couple only after the girl had reached the wise old age of sixteen, often to husbands who were ten or more years older. Then there was the practice of what Hedgewar was experiencing. Elders, mostly men, in the community, met in semi-secret parleys, sipping on small shots of sugary chai, arranging the marriages of nieces and nephews. Boys would often, but not always, get a say in who they meet and marry, but girls seldom did. They accepted whatever life dished out to them. It was a gamble. Finally, and broadly speaking, there are arranged marriages which effectively legitimizes dating first, and both boys and girls have a say in how they feel about getting married. This is what today's Hindu world calls arranged marriages.

Then there is that issue of the dowry—an arcane hand-me-down from a bygone tribal age. Dowry in India was outlawed in the late '1960s, but the practice carries on to this day, although now it is confined to the marginal elements of society, and mostly in rural India. Hedgewar's uncle was offered a princely sum of Rs 5000 as a dowry by one family. In modern money, that is worth almost Rs 4,00,000, nearly £4,500 (Rs 4,81,050). As much as Abba wanted his nephew married, he knew very well that it was his older brother, Sitaram, who had to be settled first. Hedgewar throughout this period dodged and ducked his way through matrimonial offers, often hiding behind customs that were convenient. Then, to Hedgewar's delight and dismay, probably in equal measure, Sitaram got engaged that year, and by the middle of 1917, he was married.

There was nowhere to hide now. There was a line of suitable maidens for the dashing young doctor. Hedgewar would signpost every prospective elder towards his uncle in Rampayali. His uncle Abba was then left to deal with enthused families seeking his nephew's hand. He was constantly encouraging Hedgewar to take some time out and meet a few girls. But to Abba's growing frustration, Hedgewar never came clean and he remained elusive and non-committal. In the winter of 1917, Abba had enough. He called time on the young bachelor. In a letter to Hedgewar, he wrote, 'It is high time you made your stand clear in regard to your marriage'.[4] Palkar tells us that Hedgewar was eventually collared by his uncle and given a good dressing down for 'misleading anxious parents, and he should make clear his intentions once and for all!'[5] Hedgewar, after some reflection, wrote to his uncle. The letter today sits in Nagpur at the headquarters of the RSS. With somewhat of a heavy tone, he explains to his uncle that he had decided to remain unmarried all his life. He felt that his life had already been committed to the 'Motherland, and her welfare'.[6] In these dangerous times, living under a tyrannical state and in a society that could hardly feed itself, he felt that it would have been grossly unfair on any young girl to marry him. He was intent on spending the best part of his life dedicated to the struggle, which he knew meant living in relative poverty in an existence on the edge. Hedgewar was in the midst of organizing an armed struggle. In fact, it seems odd that Moonjay and Abba, who knew exactly how deep in it he was, were encouraging him to get married. They too would have seen countless young men behind bars, leaving behind young children and a wife to fend for themselves in such an uncertain time.

In RSS literature, this decision is held up in quite a prosaic manner. The myth of Hedgewar goes something like this: he was so dedicated to uplifting his people and upholding Dharma that he decided to lead a celibate life and dedicate his heart and mind towards the struggle. Indeed, all this may be true, but if left there, we fail to recognize the nuances of Hedgewar's life. He was well aware of, and somewhat discontented with, the lot of women in his society. He knew that Hindu society did not, on the whole, treat women well. Furthermore, and much to his dislike, he knew that the prevailing customs and traditions were unconducive to empowering half of the Hindu world. As Vivekananda, fifteen years earlier, had stated, 'Without liberty for women, a society could never progress and would remain backward.' [7] Hedgewar had witnessed and seen what the fate of women who were widowed was—especially for the class of women he was to marry. According to Lucy Carroll,

> The problem of widows-and especially of child widows-was largely a prerogative of the higher Hindu classes among whom child marriage was practiced and remarriage prohibited. Irrevocably, eternally married as a mere child, the death of the husband she had perhaps never known, left the wife a widow, an inauspicious being whose sins in a previous life had deprived her of her husband, and her parents-in-law of their son, in this one. Doomed to a life of prayer, fasting, and drudgery, unwelcome at the celebrations and auspicious occasions that are so much a part of Hindu family and community life, her lot was scarcely to be envied. On the other hand, the lower, particularly Sudra, and the so-called Untouchables who represented approximately eight percent of the Hindu population – neither practised child marriage nor prohibited the remarriage of widows.[8]

Was the welfare of some future potential wife troubling him when he decided that marriage was not for him? Was it that he was embarking on a truly dangerous journey in organizing an armed revolt against the thousand-eyed leviathan that had him worried? Did he think that he was bound to end up in prison, or worse dead, sooner rather than later? Speculations can go further, and somewhat more nuanced: had Indian society already reformed and given equal rights and protection to women to marry and remarry, would this have meant he chose differently? Or was this, as the RSS literature suggests, a spiritual quest with nationalist coverings, and as such a celibate life was the only real option for a reforming social leader. It is true now, as it was then, that to be celibate meant instantaneous respect from lesser mortals in Hindu society. The 'nub of the matter' we may never know.

Soon, the message got out that Dr Hedgewar was a man on a mission. 'No wife, please' was communicated loud and clear. Soon, the horoscopes and letters stopped arriving, and Hedgewar moved on. As far as anyone can tell, he never entered an intimate relationship with any person, nor did he forge close relationships with any woman thereon in. As was the custom in those days, Sitaram's wife moved into the Hedgewar house, a house that she seems to have quickly turned around. Hedgewar told many friends that his house finally felt like a home again. His sister-in-law was caring, sensitive and gregarious. She brought laughter and play back into the house. Food was cooked there again, and the house well maintained. Friends could be invited over for dinner. A warmth that had left their lives since the passing of their parents had returned, and Hedgewar cherished it. Soon, Mahadev's beloved gym was transformed into a living area, and all his gym equipment was donated to surrounding akhadas. As with all things Indian, details surrounding the lives of women are scanty, we have no record of her name or where she had come from. Like Hedgewar's sisters—his sister-in-law, who gave him such warmth and care—passes out of history.

The World War I was well underway. Britain was in a crisis at home and abroad. It had become a protracted war. Indian soldiers under the Crown were asked to fight in the Persian Gulf to secure oil fields from the Ottoman armies, all the way through to Flanders in France and across the Western front. Indian troops fought in what was to become Israel, and across parts of Africa and even took part in the human carnage that was the Gallipoli campaign. What perplexed Hedgewar during these times was the attitude of all the national leaders—from Gandhi to Tilak, all supported the British war effort. On the one hand, they ceased all activity to undermine the government, while, and infinitely worse, they were leading the effort to recruit young men to go and fight in the war. Hedgewar, it seems, was dumbfounded by the actions of his leaders; men he had modelled himself on—namely Tilak and Moonjay. In fact, Moonjay wrote a letter of confidence to Mr Slocock, a fairly senior bureaucrat, of how bullish he was about the recruitment prospects of signing up young men for the war efforts.

> I wonder why our province alone should not be able to supply us a standing reserve of well trained, able-bodied young intelligent, partially educated men, fifty or one hundred thousand in number.[9]

All the Republicans, those men who only five years earlier were vehement that the British must be pushed out of India, were today recruiting on their behalf and had ceased almost all subversive activities. The Associates were rather more naturally capable of aligning themselves with the British, but the Republicans? He couldn't wrap his head around it. For Hedgewar, the equation was somewhat simplistic. The war meant that British resources were stretched. They were too thinly spread. The demands of war, coupled with a complete lack of, and cooperation from, Indian troops and money, would mean a greater chance of the tyranny ending. Surely this could only be a good thing! According to Sinha, Hedgewar coined the phrase 'Britain's crisis is India's opportunity'.[10] Sadly, for Hedgewar, almost none of the senior leaders of the struggle agreed with him. Hedgewar, while training to become a respectable and educated man, had completely been out of the loop when it came to the work of the Indian National Congress (INC).

The war changed the dynamics between all the main players. The Crown needed unity and stability in India. More than that, it needed money and men. The moderates within the INC, who now led the party, were, on the whole, men who saw it as their destined right to rule India once the British left. These men were often from elite families—either royal or from commercial families that had benefited greatly from British patronage. These were men built in the image of their masters. Then there were the Republicans, those that history called extremists, but only because they felt that India had its own destiny and not one which played second fiddle to British interests. These men wanted full independence right away in one united India. Then there was the Muslim question. The Muslim League under Jinnah had already parted ways from INC and was lobbying for Muslim rights, and more significantly for a Muslim India to be carved out. In reality, of course, many of these men too were made in the image of their masters, but their allegiance was not to the Crown, but to the Caliph in Istanbul, the seat of the Ottoman Empire. Then there were the thorns—those good for nothings—who were willing to kill, maim and steal to overcome the struggle. These were the secret societies, the ones that Hedgewar had spent so much time with and learnt so much from. The lines between these groups were never finely drawn but came in shades across a wide spectrum of beliefs and motivations.

Two things seem to have perturbed Hedgewar. First, that none of the leaders saw the war as an opportunity to further the cause of independence through direct action. And second, that suddenly, all those forces who had very differing 'ideas of India' were seeming to come together to support the British through these difficult times. 'How and why?', asked Hedgewar of Moonjay. The answer Hedgewar received was simple. If we help the Crown now, we will get concessions and a timetable for India's dominion status after the war. Hedgewar asked quite pertinent questions—how could they be sure the British will honour their side of the agreement? What would happen if Britain lost the war? What about the Muslim League? We cannot be sure what answers Hedgewar received from Moonjay, but clearly, they were not enough to quell the fire of rebellion inside him. Moonjay then invited him to go and see the great man himself—Bal Gangadhar Tilak in Pune. In his meeting with the great man, Hedgewar found out that all the factions, including the Republicans, had agreed with the Crown to install what were called the 'Defence of India Rules'. These rules effectively gave the government absolute power to take drastic measures against any subject of the Crown, whose actions hampered the war efforts. There is something rather Orwellian about the 'Defence of India Rules'. Now Hedgewar was truly flabbergasted. All the work he had done in Bengal, and all the illegitimate work he was knee-high in, risking his life and the lives of other earnest revolutionaries, were all traded for some uncertain benefit in some unknown future.

By the end of 1916, the Lucknow Pact was signed. The British had got what they wanted. Everyone else jockeyed for influence. The new unity pact called the Home Rule League was somewhat of a mongrel movement as far as ideas were concerned. It was eventually agreed that it would be an ancillary body to the INC. Reading the personal letters of Gandhi, Nehru, Tilak, Moonjay and Jinnah, one gets a sense that this was as much about personal power as it was about Indian independence. Jinnah was particularly under pressure from many sections of the Muslim community for signing up to the pact, which was blatantly to help Britain defeat the Ottomans.[11] As far as most Muslims were concerned, Istanbul was the seat of power and the ultimate protectorate for all Muslims, not the Crown. Muslims had increasingly begun to distrust British motives after an incident in 1913 in Kanpur, where some thirty Muslim rioters were killed or wounded.[12] The rioters were demonstrating against the plans of the authorities to expand a road, which would mean that part of the mosque would need to be demolished and rebuilt at the rear end. This was clearly unacceptable to the crowd, and once stones began being pelted at the police, things quickly escalated. Jinnah, however, stood firm. He made it clear that unless the All-India Muslim League joined the Home Rule League, he would be forced to resign his post.

For Hedgewar, and somewhat less for Moonjay, all these moves only served narrow individual interests. Hedgewar, for the first time, began to doubt Tilak and his motives and capability to lead his people to total independence. Tilak was the hero of the hour in late 1916 when for the first time newspaper headlines throughout the country proclaimed that Hindu–Muslim unity was possible. Hedgewar watched sceptically from the sidelines. He made his points silently, and much later, Moonjay would concede that the price paid for this so-called unity was high indeed. Moonjay may well have been sceptical from the outset, but he was wedded to Tilak. Under the pact, Muslims would be entitled to a separate electorate, as well as extra weightage in proportional representation as compared to Hindus, and they were granted special concessions and rights to guard their social, political and religious interests. These were the seeds signed in 1916 that would eventually result in a non-uniform civil code for Independent India. Muslims would have their own law courts and privileges that Hindus and other minorities would not.[13] Indeed, the recent announcement by the Supreme Court of India that triple-talaq is unconstitutional was a reversal of privileges which find their seeds in this Lucknow Pact of 1916. It was clear for Hedgewar that Tilak had made a diabolical blunder, and what, in the short term, seemed like a victory for unity and reasonableness would soon transpire into partition and an independent India would, forevermore, struggle to identify itself as a nation for Hindus. History would prove Hedgewar right and Tilak wrong.

Even though Moonjay gave Hedgewar the nod and implicit support to carry on with his agenda for revolt against the British, he publicly distanced himself from all revolutionary groups. Hedgewar and Moonjay were men under constant surveillance. They seldom met in public. Hedgewar would often visit his mentor and father figure at his home, which was almost like a second home for him. He would come after dark and stay long into the night talking with Moonjay and other revolutionaries. His childhood friend Bhau Kawre would often join him.[14] Kawre had been widowed after his wife passed away due to complications during childbirth. He had a stout heart and a lean firm physique. Their meetings were conducted in code. Words which appeared banal at first glance would mean something altogether different to the initiated. They would laugh and cheer loudly in the night, as men who had nothing better to do than to make merry. Observers in the shadows reported back to the authorities that there was nothing much happening at the Moonjay house except merrymaking. In fact, what they were planning was nothing short of treason as far as the law was concerned. That was nothing new for Hedgewar, but now he was a known man.

Hedgewar and Kawre formed the Narendra Mandal, which was registered as a humanitarian organization that raised money for the poor and downtrodden. In reality, the Mandal used the money to buy and supply arms to every revolutionary group across Northern India—from Punjab to Bengal. The money would be raised at weddings and public festivals. Wealthy donors were also found who helped transport purchased arms and ammunitions along with their regular business merchandise. Kawre was not highlighted by the secret service as a threat and so was mostly ignored. He looked after the operations on the ground, whereas Hedgewar, who was under the ever-watchful eyes of the leviathan, tried his best to come across as a man without a purpose. He visited different people across the central provinces to engage them in 'humanitarian work' and coordinated from afar. Recruits, much like in Bengali secret societies, were tested first. Their loyalty and commitment to the cause were of paramount importance. Reading was obligatory. Books on the list included the political theory of Mazzini, the biography of Joan of Arc, the complete works of Shivaji and Savarkar's writings.[15] Hedgewar was transposing what he had learnt in Bengal into Maharashtra and Punjab.

Kawre and Hedgewar were close. Having grown up together, they had an implicit understanding of one another's temperament and style of working. Both were tall and stout. Hedgewar was a relentless networker, whereas Kawre managed the operations. Hedgewar spent his time travelling from neighbourhood to neighbourhood across Nagpur, and then to neighbouring villages and towns looking for disgruntled young men who had the sense to take on an armed struggle against the British. Hedgewar established libraries by harnessing local support. Libraries that would have the kind of literature, European and Indian, that would remind an otherwise downtrodden people of the 'magnificent past' and express the reasons for their desperate state now and what a free and independent India might be like. Local volunteers would be responsible for collecting books, finding a vacant building and raising whatever funds were required to set up these modest libraries. Classes were held by local teachers to teach adults basic literacy and numeracy, and Hedgewar insisted on making it available for men and women.

Hedgewar always ensured that publicly he was seen as the good doctor trying to kick-start his career as a local travelling medical professional. Some of their main donors were zamindars.[16] These were men who owned ancestral land, which had been taken over by the British, who, in effect, were tax collectors on their behalf. Zamindars were entitled to keep 40 per cent of all tax collected while the vast majority went to the Crown. These men were, on the whole, rather wealthy and of elite stock. Many held hidden dreams of ousting the British off their lands for no other reason than self-aggrandizement. These men were not desh bhakts but opportunists who were willing to risk their necks to have other men overthrow their masters for them. Hedgewar was a pragmatist. He was well aware of their motives and the potential for them to turn at any time. The risk of allowing a Trojan horse into the inner circle was always on his mind. He had read Greek history well enough to know as much. Hedgewar often gathered a handful of these zamindars together under the patronage of a senior who would host a feast to mark a successful harvest and the upcoming tax revenues. These were parties—nothing more. Hedgewar was constantly under surveillance. He ensured that the spies, whomsoever they were, also got a good glimpse of the zamindars. If even one turned on the Narendra Mandal, then all the zamindars could potentially go down with them. Having secured as best as he could his downside risk, he and Kawre managed to collect tens of thousands of rupees from these parties to purchase guns and ammunition.

The arms were purchased and sent by trusted couriers across India—from Calcutta to Hyderabad to Goa; arms were flowing far and wide. Hedgewar sent trusted lieutenants to most of the princely states in Rajasthan and Punjab. Of particular importance were two brothers, both of whom had spent time in the military and were designated to train young recruits in hand-to-hand combat, shooting and general fitness. The Talatule brothers, particularly Nanasaheb, the younger of the two, would remain with Hedgewar for decades to come, playing a defining role in the early years of the RSS. Along with the Talatule brothers, there were some 150 young men of varying talents and motives working tirelessly, and somewhat dangerously, with the Narendra Mandal. Hedgewar didn't even leave his tenant alone. Dharmadhikari, who had lived in the Hedgewar home with his family, had also been convinced to join the struggle. He was often sent to Goa to deliver arms, as well as to organize the young men to keep an eye on the ports reporting on the comings and goings of the military.

Then in 1918, a group ambushed a train leaving Nagpur to steal trunks of ammunition designated for the war effort in Europe. Eyewitness accounts described how soldiers boarded the train at Nagpur station and were the ones who forced the robbery in broad daylight. A later police investigation revealed that around ten men dressed in military uniform boarded the train with false identification papers, entered the secured carriage, forced the train to halt, unloaded the cargo and made off into the forests. No one was ever caught. Hedgewar was behind these missions.[17] According to Seshadri, Hedgewar had befriended military personnel, who had become members of the Mandal and supplied the group with uniforms and papers. Moments after the robbery, the men made their way deep inside the woods where they had planted a change of dress, and some other volunteers dressed as day labourers came to empty the trunks. The uniforms were quickly burnt and the ashes scattered into drains and woodland. The goods were sent across India by volunteers often dressed as women using trains and buses. Hedgewar was, in no uncertain terms, planning and shaping a full-blown revolt by a popular armed uprising.

It is worth mentioning that these men were not just disgruntled, unemployed youth, frustrated at their lot. Quite the contrary, many of these men were of good pedigree and well educated. Many were employed by the State or were aspiring businessmen. They had much to lose. Furthermore, the Talatule brothers created audacious, verging on the downright ludicrous, entry examinations for aspiring members. Examinations included jumping down a dark well, holding hot coal in your palms, wrestling each other and even showing one's ability to kill by catching and then decapitating a chicken. The latter, to the modern mind, just seems melodramatic. But when we consider that most of these young men were Hindu Brahmins from very middle-class backgrounds, for whom to even eat meat was an abomination, to actually catch and kill another living thing in cold blood was truly a ghastly thing to do. Many failed the tests. For those that were crazy enough who managed to join the Mandal, they were made to take an oath of secrecy in front of a picture of the great king Shivaji and his teacher Ramdas, with one hand stretched out over a lit candle which was close enough to leave a burn on the right palm of every recruit. You were literally scarred for life.

Then on the eleventh hour, of the eleventh day, of the eleventh month, in the year 1918, the Great War ended with the defeat of Germany and her allies, including the Ottoman Empire. The allies had won after a drawn-out crippling war; a victory that would be the beginning of a slow drawn out end to European hegemony worldwide. To Hedgewar's mind, Germany's defeat had come a little too soon. He wanted more time to organize his army of revolutionaries. With the end of the war, he knew that the British Indian Army would soon return home, and the chance would be gone once more for a free and independent Indian nation. As the allies celebrated, as did many throughout India, including many on the Republican side, Hedgewar brooded over how to undo what he had begun. He sat long into the night thinking, mulling over what his next steps would have to be. He would sit on a swing on the front porch, swaying ever so slightly, lost in thought. He knew that even the slightest mishap would mean that many of his comrades would be arrested and imprisoned on charges of treason. The mood was such that no one would publicly support such men who had plotted during the war.

Something deep inside shifted in him that November in 1918. An epiphany of sorts struck him. No doubt with much regret, a heavy heart and somewhat damaged pride, Hedgewar, still under the age of thirty, decided that revolution was not the way. He would never return to the idea of forceful revolt. Never again would he rest his hope on the spontaneity of Hindus to revolt against their Imperial masters in a bout of bloody revolution. In effect, he had rejected Marx, in particular, his idea that popular revolution is necessary to overthrow the system. This seed would germinate over the next seven years and lead to the founding of the grassroots organization that would go on to change modern India, and consequently the world. In the twenty-first century, it would directly influence one-sixth of humanity, and indirectly more than half of the world's inhabitants. The basis of this seed would be evolution through reformation, not revolution.

Over the coming months, the Mandal was disbanded. Arms and ammunition were thrown into the sea or buried in the dead of night in wooded areas around Vidarbha. Coded letters were personally delivered to every part of India where the Mandal had been supplying arms and training. The instruction was to disband and to do so quietly. Not everything went to plan. In the North, Arjun Sethi, a young member of the Mandal, had been arrested for treason. He had been beaten, faced long bouts of isolation in a dark cell, waterboarded and then beaten some more. He was finally released in 1918. In RSS literature, this incident is often shown as an example of a man who was so brave, so robust and trustworthy that no amount of torture could get him to 'spill the beans'. In reality, Arjun knew nothing. The Mandal operated surreptitiously. Everyone was on a need-to-know basis and identities were never shared with local operatives. The British time and again found that the chain ended abruptly every time they arrested a Mandal member. Had men like Arjun known the links of the Mandal network, it may well have been a different story for Hedgewar and his men-at-arms. Having been released from prison, Arjun was in a bad state. He was mentally unstable, suffering from sudden bouts of panic attacks, amnesia and incoherence. Hedgewar arranged for him to be moved to Wardha district, near Nagpur, where he could be taken care of. Never directly going to see him, Hedgewar, through Appa Joshi, ensured that Arjun was taken care of and nurtured back to full health. It took four to five years before Arjun Sethi returned home.

Hedgewar also learnt the unscrupulousness of men. Not all pistols were returned; large sums of money disappeared, and entire units of the Mandal vanished. 'Naming and shaming' was not an option as it would compromise everyone. No public scrutiny could be applied. Hedgewar, we know from his conversations with Kawre, his number two, became resigned to the fact that with Indians, particularly the Hindu character, was the problem at the core. India could never return to her former glory so long as her people lacked the basic character traits required to build a decent society, honesty, stout hearts, noble thoughts and a spirit of nationhood. Furthermore, he realized through many such bitter experiences that young men often took to revolutionary work out of some short-term emotional reaction. But as soon as they came across a pinprick of a challenge, all their hot air and bravado left them, leaving behind a mess of human self-doubt.

Discipline and honour, Hedgewar felt, were traits that Indians severely lacked. He noted how Indians in the British Army were so well drilled, largely loyal to the Crown and cooperative, putting behind narrow individual interests. They were also tremendously brave in battle, often showcasing the ultimate act of altruism. The revolutionaries, on the other hand, were also brave and daring but lacked any real coherence. They were emotional, difficult to command and control, ran on narrow self-interest and consequently lacked the kind of cooperation required to mount a serious sustainable threat to the thousand-eyed leviathan. Indians also could not bring themselves to trust each other. There was no honour code between them and nothing to bind them. Indians, on the whole, were self-divided by caste, creed, religion, language and geography. There was familial honour, and honour between members of the same *jāti*, but nothing beyond, to the detriment of the entire civilization.[18]

Hedgewar began to realize, slowly, organically and over time, that for India to flourish, it would first need to rediscover its past before all the various forms of colonialism it had undergone over the last millennium, first from Islam, then from the European powers. Hedgewar could see that Europe was ebbing away and would fall under its natural contradictions. Between 1918 and 1925, he publicly carried on making speeches on Indian liberty. Privately, however, he was building a substantial critique of Hindu society with a view of reforming the basic individual from the ground up, with an abiding mission of instilling nobility and character, wrapped around patriotism rooted in that age-old idea—Dharma.

SIX: 1919–1920

Seeds of Division

Winston Churchill once said, 'History is written by the victors'. Victors also have an uncanny tendency to simply ignore and suppress the inconvenient truth.

In early 1921, two Muslim organizations in Kerala, called the *Anjuman-i Khuddām-i Ka'ba*, meaning the 'Servants of the Ka'ba' and the Central Khilāfat Committee, began to plot a conspiracy. The repercussions of which would reverberate into the present day, something which the Hindu world, as hard as the Indian authorities tried, could never forget. A conspiracy which would manifest into the indiscriminate murder of tens of thousands of Hindus, forcefully converting scores more to Islam and causing a human exodus of biblical proportions. A conspiracy which would take the British Imperial Army over three months to quell, by exerting even more brutality, all culminating into the execution of thousands of mostly poor Muslim Mappila men. A conspiracy which would ignite other atrocities across India throughout the 1920s, albeit on a much smaller scale. Hedgewar would follow this human tragedy while serving a one-year prison sentence for seditious speeches and even come to experience it first-hand during the Nagpur violence, which inadvertently would lead him to create the RSS.

Mappilas are an ethnic group found mostly in Kerala. They account for something like 26 percent of the population of the state and are mostly Sunni Muslim by faith. They claim to be descendants of the first Arab merchants[1], who also later settled in India before the Islamic conquests arrived on the scene. In reality, the Mappilas are descendants of any native convert to Islam, or a mixed descendant of any Middle Eastern Arab or non-Arab individual.[2] The Mappilas were spice merchants from as far back as the seventh century. Over centuries, they have become a fusion of Islamic custom and beliefs with native Indian culture—art, dance, diet and language. They became prosperous during Mughal rule, and often joined the invading Muslim armies in fighting local Hindu Kings. Over time, the Marathas took over much of Kerala, and the Mappilas were stripped of their patronage.[3] In the following centuries, they became poor and descended to the lowest rungs of the Indian social hierarchy. First the Portuguese and then the British distrusted the Mappila community, stuck as they were in stories of bygone centuries when they were landowners and wealthy merchants paying homage to the Muslim rulers of the time.[4] The halcyon days were long gone, but the memories persisted. With each passing century, their memories kept on fuelling a bitterness towards the Hindus and the British.

With the fall of the Ottoman Empire after 1918, the seat of the Caliphate was no more. The power of Islam was humiliated. With humiliation came a crisis of faith.[5] With fragmentation and no political power on the world stage, the Islamic community reacted in exactly the way one would expect from such a diverse and disparate community held together by prestige, trade and empire.[6] Many in the Arab world thought that Islam was the problem and must be abandoned to create a new form of Arab nationalism where modernity could be compatible with culture. Mustafa Ataturk best exemplified this reaction. He founded the modern state of Turkey in 1923 and envisaged it to be run on modern western secular lines while celebrating and building on the rich culture of the Turkish people.[7] Then there were those that felt that Islam must stay but had to be modernized and brought in line with modern values. Mainly artists, writers, journalists and students fell into this camp.[8] Finally, there were those that laid the blame squarely on the hypocrisy and corruption of the political elite and their modernizing allies, who had strayed from the will of God.[9] The defeat of Islam was a punishment from God. These thoughts seeded the revivalist Salafi movement in the twentieth century.[10] The word salafiyya means a call to return to the Salaf, or pious predecessors.[11]

For these people, the answer lay in the 'original' Islam, the Islam of the Rashidun—the rightly guided ones. Movements such as the Salafi, called for a reorientation of Islamic jurisprudence away from case law, and directly back towards the examples set by the prophet and his early followers.[12] They called for an inner and an outer Jihad, a holy struggle against the forces of God. These enemies included the West—the great

Satan—and to reassert Islam's claim over all the lands of the infidels—including Hindus in India.[13]

Out of these volcanic memes sprang forth a new topography of ideas and movements. The infamous Muslim Brotherhood was founded in 1928. The founder of Jamat-e-Islami, an organization that would dominate the minds of South Asian Muslims into the modern-day, began to formulate his views after the Great War. Sayyid Abul A'la al-Maududi's cry for orthodoxy amongst Muslims still holds huge sway in mosques across India and Pakistan today. Deobandi Islam caught traction after the War, another form of conservative Islam, which is prevalent across Western Europe, especially the United Kingdom amongst Muslims from the Indian sub-continent.

Between 1919 and late 1921, an All-India Khilafat movement was launched to initially pressure the British to not disband the seat of the Caliph, and then when that failed, to actively work to free India from British rule. The Associates of the Congress, led by Gandhi, immediately supported the Muslim League and insisted on joining the Khilafat movement with a gusto that even surprised the Muslims. Gandhi and his associates wanted to show solidarity with their fellow Indians. Hedgewar, in close touch with Moonjay, watched. He was perturbed by what was happening in India and how its leadership were blinded by utopian ideals of universal brotherhood, internationalism and a growing socialism.

In 1921, the toxicity of radical Islam began to show itself in Kerala amongst the Mappila community. Sermons across mosques proclaimed loud and clear that India under the British was *dār al-harb* (the land of War). Every pious Muslim was to fight the British, and if this could not be done, then Muslims should think about moving to Islamic lands.[14] The power of the clerics was such that around 18,000 Muslims vacated their homes from the North-West and emigrated to other countries to live in *dār al-Islām*, while many others took on the call for jihad.[15] Knives, swords and spears were being secretly manufactured in Mappila dominated villages and townships.[16] According to Ambedkar, in August of that year, the police were attacked first in an area called Eranadu, near Kozhikode. Power lines and telegraph wires were cut first. Railway lines were put out of use. Blockades were erected on every major road coming into the area, and simultaneously, red flags of the new Caliphate were raised on every Muslim household and mosque. Eranadu was declared as the first Islamic kingdom, and Ali Musliyar was announced as its King.[17] Ali Musliyar was a Sufi Muslim, a scholar and an imam of a large mosque in Tirunrangadi district. He came from a family of scholars and was given the highest Islamic education that one could receive. He studied at some of the best Islamic seminaries in India, and then was sent to Mecca to complete his education. Musliyar had masterminded the entire uprising. What is often missed out from the current rendering is that Musliyar was a leading member and scholar of the All-India Khilafat movement, which Gandhi had so enthusiastically joined.[18] The Khilafat movement had officially announced him as Amir-in-waiting for when the day came for the British to leave, and India to be brought back into *dār al-Islām*. All revenues and taxes would go to the King's treasury.[19] Musliyar had recruited a peasant army of nearly 30,000 men, all of whom had uniforms, carried swords and were made to swear allegiance to the Caliphate on the Quran.[20]

Having killed several police officers and burnt the station, they moved on to attack the small army barracks nearby. Taken by surprise, the dozen or so men on duty had no chance to resist the violent onslaught that was meted out to them. They were simply overwhelmed. None survived. Having tasted blood and a sudden surge of power, they turned their attention towards their neighbours—the Hindus of the district. Groups of Muslim Mappila men, with the certainty that they were doing Allah's work, and with vengeance flowing through their veins, attacked, pillaged and burnt everything in their wake.[21] Every day, Muslim men went house to house dragging out Hindus—often killing the rich landlords and all male heirs and raping their wives and daughters before forcefully converting many of them to Islam.[22] Many who were raped became the second, third or fourth wife of the man who raped her. As the days went by, and there was no sign of the law, gruesome acts continued and ramped up another notch. Once the rich landowning Hindus had been dealt with, they turned their attention to thousands of poor Hindus. These were people as poor as the Mappilas, yet these people were marched out of their houses, the men beaten, many women raped and then forcefully converted. They would sometimes be force-fed beef, knowing that for a Hindu this was the final disgrace, and they would never again be accepted into the Hindu community.[23] Stories of extreme brutality spread far and wide across India, where Mappila men cut open pregnant Hindu women butchering them if they resisted conversion or rape. Not only humans but all things sacred to Hindus were targeted. Cows were butchered, and their entrails were cast all over deities in temples.[24] Skulls of men and cows were hanged outside temples as a warning to any who might be thinking about seeking refuge with their heathen gods. According to Ambedkar, this was not a Hindu–Muslim riot; this was unprecedented barbarity by Muslims on Hindus.[25]

By September 1921, Lord Reading, the British Viceroy of India, received an urgent telegram from one of his officers, '…the situation is now clearly actual war and famine; widespread devastation and prolonged rebellion can only be avoided by prompt measures.'[26] It took the Royal Dorset Regiment six months to crush the rebellion and restore order. In the end, over 2000 Mappila men had to be killed in the process, over 6000 sent to prison all over the country and over 30,000 men forced to surrender. This was a rebellion ignited by the sorry condition of the Mappila community, coupled with a genuine attempt to overthrow the British, but all tragically fuelled by radical militant Islam yearning to create a *dār al-Islām* in Kerala.

The Army was brutal in turn. They went house to house pulling out anyone who had any tentative links to the rebellion, and they were either beaten till they revealed more information or sent to prison. Those that were considered to be ring leaders were arrested and charged with the death penalty. There was also an incident where over two hundred Mappila men had surrendered to the Dorset Regiment and were summarily executed and buried in mass graves, which lay forgotten for decades.[27] So many Mappila men had been either killed or arrested that there were only women left to dig the graves for their dead.[28] Hundreds were executed including their leader, the scholar Sufi King of the Mappila, Ali Musliyar on 17 February 1922.

Gandhi and his colleagues in the Indian National Congress could only distance themselves from the rebellion carried out in the name of the Khilafat movement, and quipped that the rebellion was 'just an outburst of fanatics'. To Ambedkar, and Hedgewar's utter horror, Gandhi went onto question the victims,

> It is they (Hindus) who should find out the causes of the Mappila fanaticism. Hindus will find that they are not without blame; they have hitherto not cared for the Mappila community. They (Hindus) have either treated him (Mappilas) as serfs or dreaded him. They have not treated him as a friend or neighbour, to be reformed and respected. It is no use now becoming angry with the Mappilas or the Muslims in general.[29]

Gandhi wasn't finished. He went after the Government and took a paternal tone towards the Mappilas.

> The Government has thoroughly exploited the Mappilas' madness. They have punished the entire Mappila community for the madness of a few individuals and have incited the Hindus by exaggerating the facts. Malabar Hindus, like the Mappilas, are an excitable people and the Government has incited them against the latter. The outbreak would not have taken place if the Collector had consulted the religious sentiment of the Mappilas.[30]

In contrast, Moonjay received a heart-wrenching letter from a friend who lived in Malabar, which described in detail the horror that was unfolding. He describes to Moonjay, '…the wells and (water) tanks in Malabar were full to the brim with the dead bodies of Hindu women who had committed suicide by jumping into them in order to save their honour'.[31] Moonjay left Nagpur and travelled to Malabar to see for himself what was happening. To his utter horror, the letter had failed to describe the full devastation, which was unfolding. Moonjay writes in his diaries that he was brought to tears on several occasions while travelling from village to village witnessing the barbarity of the rebellion. He was surprised to find that the Congress Enquiry Committee was busying itself whitewashing the entire episode and organizing relief camps for the Mappilas who were injured by the Dorset Regiment's attempt to regain control.[32] Moonjay could smell the stench of Gandhi's politics all over the published report, which claimed that there were only three cases of forced conversions, whereas, the official government report written by William Vincent told the central legislature that 'the number of forced conversions probably runs into the thousands'.[33] Moonjay, dissatisfied with the findings of the Congress, commissioned the Servants of India Society, a grassroots organization dedicated to the welfare of the poorest and most downtrodden in society, to investigate the atrocities. Led by a well-educated, unassuming man called Gopal Gokhale, the Servants of India Society reported that conservative estimates indicated over 1500 Hindus were killed in little over a month, more than 20,000 were forcibly converted and something like 30,000,000 dollars' worth of property looted and damaged.[34] The report was accepted by the Crown but rejected as out of hand by the Indian National Congress.

Moonjay recognized that the mostly poor Hindus who had been forcibly converted had a right to return to the fold. But Hindu society, steeped in superstition and arcane practices, often resisted anyone who had converted once, to return. Moonjay promoted the Shuddhi movement, a nationwide campaign involving many religious and social leaders of Hindu society to accept all converts who wanted to return to the tradition of their ancestors. The response was haphazard. Many like the Arya Samaj responded to the call, but overall, the response left Moonjay exasperated. Hindu society, according to Moonjay, was simply not aware and lacked the political consciousness to mobilize. In time, history would forget Moonjay, the Mappila atrocities, the British crackdown and most significantly, the Congress cover-up.

Hedgewar, while in a psychological state of flux, and experiencing an intellectual reformation, continued, as was his way, to toe the line with the greater cause. He resisted his inner doubts and sided with the Indian National Congress, and against every grain in his body, he too supported the Khilafat and Non-Cooperation Movement.[35] He may have simply sucked it up because he saw no other way of resisting the leviathan especially in the light of the Rowlatt Act, which was passed on 21 March 1919 by the Imperial Legislative Council. The Act, by a quirk of fate, had ushered in Gandhi's era of politics. The Rowlatt Act effectively gave the state an indefinite extension of all the powers given to them in the Orwellian themed Defence of India Act of 1915. The Defence of India Act was meant to be a temporary war measure granted to the government to imprison any person suspected of seditious activity in British India for up to two years without trial. The unpopular legislation provided for stricter control of the press, arrests without warrant, indefinite detention without trial and juryless trials for proscribed political acts. The accused were denied the right to know the accusers and the evidence used in the trial.[36] The Rowlatt Act, named after the unfortunate Sir Sydney Rowlatt, gave an indefinite extension to these powers.

The act allowed the British Imperial Army to squash the Mappila rebellion a few years later. The unprecedented brutality that was unleashed on the Mappilas would be later criticized by posterity, especially when unmarked graves were found all over northern and central Kerala. The act clearly seemed to have given the Army immense confidence to be judge, jury, jailer and when deemed necessary, executioner. As soon as the act was passed, Gandhi began his *haṛtal* (non-cooperation). He knew the way to hurt the British was through commerce. The people's *haṛtal* meant that the entire country ground to a halt. Mass mobilization of emotionally charged desperate people, faced by a police force which had recently been empowered to take decisive action against any anti-national threat was the ideal concoction for trouble.

The first riots occurred in Punjab in April 1919. People were shot, shops were burnt by rioters and the police was generally unable to cope with the mass protests, which were meant to be peaceful under Gandhi's strict orders. On 10 April, the police arrested two prominent Congress leaders and secretly transported them to Dharmshala in the mountains. On the same day, the authorities made it illegal for any groups to gather in a public space. Yet, three days later, in an act of defiance, on 13 April, people congregated peacefully with their families at Jallianwala Bagh. Several thousand had gathered to mark Vaisakhi, the solar new year based on the Vikram Samvat calendar, and the day when the Sikh Khalsa was formed. Without doubt, fiery speeches were delivered, and non-cooperation and pro-Caliphate movement leaflets were distributed. The Army, under the infamous General Dyer, was drafted in. Troops entered the garden through the only entrance and took position on a mound, effectively blocking anyone from escaping. Without warning, the troops were ordered to fire. Dyer had manifested, in a ten-minute bloodbath, what everyone in Congress had feared—what the state would unleash upon innocent people if it misread the situation. Dyer and his loyal Indian troops killed over 400 people, including women, children and the frail, while seriously injuring another thousand citizens.[37] Dyer's massacre will always go down as an infamy for British rule.

From the very beginning, the Rowlatt Act was a disaster for the British. It was a bane of their rule. First, it brought Gandhi into the fore. Next, it led to the massacre of hundreds of innocent citizens at Jallianwala Bagh, and finally, it led to the ruthless assault on the Mappila rebellion. In March 1922, one month after sending Ali Musilyar to the gallows, the Rowlatt Act and twenty-one other repressive laws were retracted.

Even though Hedgewar re-engaged with the Congress, he was increasingly at odds with the leadership—both Associates and increasingly the Republicans. The Congress of the central provinces, which included Nagpur and the wider Vidarbha area, was effectively organized and run by an outfit called the Rashtriya Mandal, which somewhat loosely translates as the National or Nationalist Group. Tilak, Moonjay and fourteen other populist leaders were part of this group. They were a powerful lobby within the Congress. Hedgewar, through the influence of Moonjay, was working with this group from mid-1919, although he was never formally made a member. We cannot be sure as to the reasons why he was never allowed to join this populist group of nationalists, but Palkar tells us that Hedgewar was a little too outspoken for their liking.[38] Hedgewar openly and forthrightly made the case for India's immediate and complete independence, whereas this powerful Republican lobby led by Tilak and Moonjay was discussing a compromise with the Crown, to become an autonomous region within the realms of the British Empire. Hedgewar could never quite stomach this. For him, this was simply too obsequious.

By the end of 1919, he had reached his breaking point He swiftly formed another group called the Nagpur National Union (NNU), which would openly voice the call for complete and immediate independence of India. It is somewhat unclear if Hedgewar had the blessings of Moonjay to set the NNU up. Hedgewar certainly did not tend to break ranks or to act spontaneously and whimsically against those that were working for the struggle. Moonjay may well have given him the silent nod of approval. We know that Moonjay was disgruntled with the direction of the Congress but was trapped by his loyalty to Tilak. Many associate members of the Rashtriya Mandal joined Hedgewar's NNU. One could read this as yet another clue that even though official documents suggest a mild rebellion from Hedgewar, in reality, it may have been a ploy to allow those nationalists who wanted to take on the British in the here and now, could continue to so, without being smothered by the day-to-day politics of the Congress.

The NNU launched a local Hindi journal to push forward their agenda called *Sankalp* (sacred oath). Hedgewar travelled all over Vidarbha to get people to subscribe to the new initiative. He was effectively acting as a revolutionary entrepreneur crowdsourcing his seed capital by going to one house at a time, through villages, often not knowing anyone, and constantly being refused. Raising money for anything is a humbling experience. By travelling on dusty roads, on crowded buses and hitching rides on the back of bullock carts, Hedgewar was developing a trait that would serve him well after 1925—humility. Moonjay, it so appears, had set him the task of collecting three-year advance subscriptions from well-wishers. It didn't work. 'People do not like to give advance subscriptions, and that too for three years. The reason for this is that in the past funds collected for public purposes could not be utilized properly', he wrote in a letter to Moonjay.[39] But perseverance is everything, well almost. Perseverance he had an abundance of, but he had also perfected the art of storytelling, which made Hedgewar extremely successful at convincing people to support anything he was a part of. A few months later, cheques began to arrive at Moonjay's house. Moonjay, in his diary, logged the amounts. 'He (Hedgewar) sent five hundred rupees and then on the 25th of the month, he sent another six hundred rupees.'[40] Hedgewar travelled for three continuous months. He visited the breadth and depth of rural India. He met the landed gentry, the artisans, the teachers, the farmers and the indebted labourers. He was, unknowingly, refining the skills which would one day be part and parcel of what was required to join the prachaarak order of the RSS.

While growing up, Keshav displayed a rascality that was first innocent and later turned militant. Hedgewar, now in his early thirties, was a full-blown reformer, and a radical in the minds of those that blindly followed the arcane customs of the day. Somewhere around late 1919 and early 1920, according to RSS folklore, a story which Palkar also mentions in his book, tells us how Hedgewar helped a friend who had unwittingly agreed, under peer pressure, to have his young teenage daughter marry a man old enough to be her grandfather. During the cooler months, Indians, now as then, prefer to get married between December and February. Gangadhar, Hedgewar's friend, regretted his decision but was too meek to now reverse the wedding plans. As soon as the news reached Hedgewar, he immediately sent a letter to the bride and another to her mother who lived in the neighbouring village that should their daughter not want to get married to the decrepit old man, she should make plans to leave the village on the wedding day with her father. Hedgewar reassured Gangadhar that he would see to the arrangements personally. Hedgewar stayed in Arvi, a small farming village on the main road between Nagpur and Akola. The odd couple were to be married in Arvi. A tiny backwater where custom ruled over common law; where the birth of a little girl was seen as a burden the father would have to carry for years to come and where a father would have to toil for years to save enough money to pay the dowry on the day of his daughter's wedding. Hedgewar detested these customs.

The wedding was only two days away. The entire village congregated to witness the ceremony. Leading up to the wedding, Hedgewar made himself known to the village chieftains. These were always men; often the landed gentry, loyal to the British and who ruled their fiefdom with an iron fist. He spoke to everyone cordially but made it apparent how odd it was that such an old man would want to marry a girl so young. Hedgewar was a respected man.

He was a doctor, and therefore especially useful. As soon as people knew that a doctor was in the village every man, woman and cow wanted to see him. He did what he was obliged to do. The grandees of the village were all thrilled that such a national leader was staying with them and in the two evenings that remained before the wedding, he had dinner with the people that mattered.

On the day of the wedding, he had it confirmed by Gangadhar that his daughter had no desire to marry. While the bride's family spent the morning erecting the mandap where the sacred vows would be taken, Gangadhar and his daughter fled the village. They were picked up by a local farmer who was a friend of the Hedgewars and taken to a safe house. Indian weddings are colourful and noisy affairs. They always have been. Custom dictates that the bride's family must welcome the groom with colourful and noisy fanfare. Musical instruments accompany such entrances, often played out of tune, and loud hubbub welcomed the old man, of whom we know nothing. Hedgewar watched the procession as a dignified guest of the whole village. Then, when it was time for the bride to arrive at the mandap with her father, the fiasco began. The groom was obviously outraged, his anger rooted in complete and utter humiliation. His family lashed out at the bride's relatives, who looked here and there, dumbfounded and somewhat embarrassed at the whole affair. Then according to Palkar, Hedgewar stepped up to the withered pitiful groom, in the *mandap*, completely dwarfing all those around him who were shouting accusations to the other side. Hedgewar had always been a rabble-rouser; it was in his nature. Furthermore, he was supremely confident in his ability to look after himself if it ever came to fisticuffs. With this combination of nature and nurture, Hedgewar made a short but fiery speech, condemning the whole occasion as sacrilegious, and stating that such a perverted wedding ought to never have been allowed in the first instance. To the surprise of the bride's family, the village elders agreed with Hedgewar, isolating the groom and his relatives.[41] Having shouted down the guests with his superior rhetoric, physical presence and the unambiguous support of the elders, there was nothing for the groom and his guests to do but leave with a whimper and a grumble. All we know from Palkar, who interviewed some of those present, is that the village soon avidly outlawed such marriages and created an atmosphere of shame for any hoary man that did try. The young girl did eventually get married, and although Hedgewar was affectionately invited, he was a trifle too busy getting himself arrested.

While fundraising for the nationalist journal, Hedgewar, wherever he was known, was often invited to speak publicly to the young and old alike. He was constantly giving speeches about the glory of India's far, near-forgotten past, as well as the days of Shivaji and his band of Marathas. He was inspiring the old to allow their young men to rekindle and celebrate the height of India's once glorious past, all with the aim of igniting a political consciousness in his people and generating recognition of the exploitation and degradation of their own folk. Hedgewar, while taking on the fundraising responsibility, was also appointed as the general secretary for another local organization whose single aim was to celebrate Indian culture and its heroes through festivals and public gatherings. He spoke in village greens and outside village temples.

During these days, Hedgewar was accustomed to travelling with only a satchel consisting of two pairs of clothes, a reading book, notebook and pen, a basic first aid kit consisting of a stethoscope to hold clinics wherever he was called upon to do so, and finally his trusty walking stick. The walking stick was more of a sign of respectability than a tool to aid him to walk. He wore a white dhoti, with a white shirt and a khadi waistcoat underneath a blazer and his customary black cap to signify his standing in society. By now, he had grown and was confidently wearing his Nietzschean style German moustache with its customary bushy brow partially covering the top lip. He oozed the masculinity of his times. He projected strength and power through his physique. His education was indicated by his walking stick, blazer and black cap. His contemporaries would have also immediately known that he was a Brahmin from the black cap and his haircut. His political views were clearly demonstrated by his fusion of east and west—his dhoti with his blazer—indicating that he was a Congressman and a Republican.

Being a Congressman himself, he was constantly writing his displeasure addressed primarily to Moonjay about the state of his peers. 'Congressmen are good orators', he wrote to Moonjay, 'who impress people in the first meeting but their impact on people's minds vanishes in two or three days. They are busy in their pursuit for money and don't have time for public work'.[42] In another letter to Moonjay, he writes, '…They wish to get service done through others but are not prepared to do it themselves'.[43] These private exchanges reveal Hedgewar's growing discontent with the Congress and its leadership. He felt that cadres, that is those who had newly joined the Congress having received some basic organizational training, were simply poorly equipped in character, motive and ability. He realized that the Congress had already been corrupted by nepotism—an illness that Indian society still suffers from. Meritocracy was a distant dream. In fact, to be meritorious actually worked against you in front of the leadership. If there was even the slightest sign that one would get ahead of one's own designated station without the tacit approval of the hierarchy, their days were numbered. India's mongrel social hierarchy had crept its way into the heart of the Congress.

He realized that those Congressmen who were not in the limelight were often the hardest working, competent and earnest. Yet, these people were nowhere in leadership roles. They were, on the whole, not even noticed by the leadership. Hedgewar constantly highlighted such individuals to Moonjay. To Moonjay's credit, he met many of them and often spoke to Tilak and the leadership about the observations Hedgewar was making at the grassroots. But in the hubbub of daily politics, as is still the case, reason is all too often snuffed out.

Moonjay was surprised to learn that Hedgewar was introducing him to men who held views that were completely poles apart from his own. Hedgewar held the company of men who often vehemently disagreed with him about the fundamentals of Indian society and its ills. They shared a different 'idea of India'; many were communists, from across the spectrum; yet Hedgewar respected these people, and even supported them wherever he could. Hedgewar's only criteria of support were earnestness, character and talent. The views held by another were of little consequence. He could argue for hours with his friends, and then continue to share a sugary shot of milky chai the moment after, sharing personal joys and sorrows with each other.

The end of the monsoon season, around the end of October, on the night of the full moon called Kojagiri Purnima, marked the beginning of the harvest season. On this day, people from all strata of society gathered to talk, sing, dance and make merry long into the night, basking in the light of the full moon. Hedgewar thoroughly enjoyed Kojagiri. Between sixty and seventy of his closest friends and associates would meet over an endless supply of thick frothy saffron enriched milk, topped with almonds, nutmeg and spices. The drink of the Gods. The night would be full of laughter, interspersed with rancorous discussions on the state of the society, what to do about the leviathan, the Hindu problem, the Muslim problem, the Communist problem, the mercantile problem, the destitution of their countrymen, the state of women, on history, on war, on philosophy and on statecraft. No subject of contention was barred. Hedgewar thrived. He would mostly speak in a style of Hindi spoken by the learned, use traditional Sanskrit aphorisms to make oral jabs to his opponents' weak spots when they were rabbiting off about the worthlessness of ancient India, interspersed with dollops of only the very best of the Queen's English for knockdowns. These were nothing short of lyrical sparring matches between the best of orators and learned men. After everything was said and done, Hedgewar would stand and thank everyone, pay due respect to those whom he fervently disagreed with and then round the night up with some put-down humour, often with a little dose of self-deprecation.

Even as Hedgewar continued to work tirelessly for the Congress, *Kala*, the personification of time in Indian culture, was about to play his game of dice, altering the fate of some two-hundred and fifty million people, and the outcome of India. Gandhi had recently entered the fray of Indian politics and joined the Congress. His rise had been meteoric. His vision coupled with his character and ability to mobilize millions of people, was game-changing. He had the pulse of the Indian masses—mostly the Hindus. He displayed immense coherence and integrity. He could simultaneously speak to the most downtrodden of society and the elite in a single breath. He led a shrewd campaign. He was a cocktail of sheer power of will verging on despotism to ram through his worldview, while simultaneously running a public relations campaign the likes of which no one had ever seen. He would be a continuous thorn in the proverbial backside of Winston Churchill. This new *deva* of the Indian National Congress was going to collide with a pre-existing Lord of an earlier age. *Kala* would choose to snag his coat on the new nail.

As 1919 came to a close, Hedgewar made his way with Moonjay and the rest of the powerful Nationalist lobby to Amritsar, Punjab, where the massacre of Jallianwala Bagh had taken place, to attend a session of the Congress. The who's who of the Congress visited the site, where bullet cases and bloodstains would have been visible throughout the ground. Even today, visitors can see the bullet holes on the walls surrounding the Bagh. Hedgewar never spoke about his visit, but we do know he made a second visit by himself on the first night. The narrow lanes would have been clogged with people, with the air thick with the smell of spices, open latrines and human sweat. The Bagh would have been under guard by a lone sepoy. I doubt he would have put up too much resistance against

Hedgewar's visit. Hedgewar spent several hours sitting on the dehydrated earth contemplating.

The Amritsar Congress came and passed. But something changed. Gandhi and Tilak were engaged in one-on-one verbal combat. Tilak represented a completely different approach to what Gandhi was advocating. Their exchanges were public and were creating visible tears in the fabric of the Congress. Tilak was not used to be taken on in this way by a much younger adversary who had moves that Tilak had never encountered, for that matter even the British and Churchill would not know how to adequately nullify this upstart dressed in a single piece of cloth. 'Lokmanya Tilak', wrote Gandhi in a publication called *Young India* in early 1920, 'represents a definite school of thought of which he makes no secret. He considers that everything is fair in politics. We think that the political life of the country will become thoroughly corrupt if we import western tactics and methods'.[44] Gandhi made the opening shot and made his intent clear. Tilak, the grand old man of the Congress, a stalwart and a national celebrity, a man respected by millions for his cause and character was being challenged so openly and with words such as 'corruption' and 'western tactics'. This would have given a mighty prick to Tilak's ego.

On 28 January 1920, Tilak responded through his publications.

> Politics is a game of worldly people and not of sadhus, and instead of the maxim "we should conquer anger by opposing it with tranquillity" as preached by the Buddha. I prefer to rely on the maxim by Shri Krishna: My response to the devotees is in perfect harmony with the manner of their approach. Both methods are equally honest and righteous, but one is more suited to this world than the other.[45]

Then, in a very un-Tilak-like manner, he concluded his response with a slight tetchiness unbecoming of a seasoned national politician. Tilak wrote, 'Any further explanation about the difference will be found in my Geeta Rahasya!'[46] Gandhi must have revelled in the pettiness of the response by Tilak.

Seeing the old man out of his depth, Gandhi moved in for a knock-out blow,

> ...with deference to Lokmanya Tilak I venture to say that it betrays mental laziness to think that the world is not for Sādhus. The epitome

> of all religions is to promote "purushārtha". Purushārtha is nothing but a desperate attempt to become a sādhu, that is to become a gentleman in every sense of the term. Finally, when I wrote the sentence about everything being fair in politics according to Lokmanya's creed, I had in mind his oft-repeated quotation "tit for tat". To me, it enunciates a bad law.[47]

Gandhi's own recollection of events is somewhat more subdued. 'The idea of having to differ from such seasoned, well-tried and universally revered leaders', wrote Gandhi, 'was unbearable to me'.[48] Yet, his public rhetoric was nothing short of confrontational towards these 'revered leaders'. Gandhi was radical in his approach and had set his stall out nice and early in the struggle. For the Associates within the Congress, they had found their messiah. The Republicans who had been in the ascendancy for a number of years now found themselves an adversary who oozed moral authority and played by a set of rules unknown before in pre-independent India. Things were about to get worse for the Republicans, much worse.

The Congress of 1920 was held in Nagpur—the home turf of the Republicans led by Tilak. Naturally, it was felt that the Republicans would sweep the floor by holding a majority in all crucial voting. Gandhi was now effectively all but leading the Associates, whom he deemed as having a closer vision for a united Hindu–Muslim India. He was suspicious of the Republicans and their links with violent revolutionaries. He was also at odds with the Muslim League, whose raison d'être was to create a Muslim India. Whereas the Republicans were a necessary pain, which had to be managed, he had to actively 'woo' the Muslim League to move away from their reason for existence—a steep climb indeed.

Tilak was generally quite keen on Gandhi's involvement in the Congress. Gandhi had proved himself to be a very competent draftsman, drafting up bills and reports, as well as being an excellent fundraiser. Gandhi had been given the task, with the approval of Tilak, of raising funds for a Jallianwala Bagh memorial. Gandhi had proved effective with his sharp intellect and unassuming appearance. Tilak's concern lay in Gandhi's approach and worldview. Tilak was not convinced by Gandhi's push for *swadeshi*—something that Tilak himself had promoted over two decades earlier when Gandhi was still making his career as a lawyer. Tilak understood that India had been de-industrialized, and so it was a problem of supply, not demand. Gandhi's push to buy only Indian made cloth would mean that the demand for such goods would increase without resolving the supply side of things, which would create an inflationary pressure on home-made goods. More expensive Indian goods would harm the poorest and not help quality. Tilak encouraged Gandhi to visit several mill owners before the Nagpur Congress due to be held in December 1920. Gandhi recollects one of these conversations in his autobiography. Gandhi went to see Umar Sobani, a man who had been generously supplying Gandhi's new ashram near the Sabarmati River, in Ahmedabad, Gujarat, with much-needed funds to buy yarn, and set up his rural initiative to spin cotton. Gandhi's vision was to supply every woman in rural India with a spinning wheel and yarn. The cotton spun by these women could supply the manufacturers, providing a dignified source of income for India's rural women. Noble in thought, but impractical, decided Tilak. Sobani was one of the wealthiest mill merchants in India; he warned Gandhi not to be naïve and to understand mercantile economics. Gandhi tells him,

> My idea is to get these women to spin yarn, and to clothe people of India with Khadi woven out of it. …on the contrary to the extent that it can add to the cloth production of the country, be it ever so small, it will represent so much solid gain.[49]

Sobani gave a well-mannered but succinct response, 'Whether the spinning wheel can make headway in this age of power machinery is another question. But I for one, wish you every success'.[50]

Gandhi remained convinced of his drive for swadeshi. He felt that the symbolism of the spinning wheel would act as a tremendous vision and touch the sentiments of the poor. He was right, and shrewd enough to know it. Gandhi seemed to completely ignore Tilak and Sobani's warning that swadeshi, as a tool for anti-British propaganda, would only cause Indian cloth to become more expensive. For Gandhi, the economic turmoil, and not addressing the supply side of the equation, was not important. First, and foremost, he was a politician, and as such, he knew that such a campaign would be popular with the masses. It was a public relations drive par excellence. Tilak, on the other hand, was too busy fretting about real-world problems. For him, India's salvation lay in industry, skills development and capital accumulation. None of which would appeal to the masses. Gandhi was winning popular support, whereas Tilak was being outmanoeuvred, partly by not reading the changing times, further exacerbated by his poor health.

Tilak had spent a lot of time in prison throughout his life. These episodes of incarceration did eventually catch up with his health. Throughout 1919 and 1920, Tilak had been suffering from incessant bouts of chest infections. In early July 1920, he began to exhibit a whooping cough and soon developed breathing problems. He found himself coughing incessantly and severely out of breath after walking only a few steps. He managed to write throughout July, communicating with Moonjay in Nagpur who was busy planning the Congress. By the end of July, Tilak was bed-bound, tired and severely ill. Doctors were sent for, but it was a little too late. On 1 August 1920, he died of pneumonia.

Tilak, for all his flaws, and there were certainly many, had devoted his life to the struggle. He had inspired countless numbers of his countrymen, men like Moonjay, to join the struggle. His untimely death had caused a tremendous vacuum in the Congress and at the helm of the Republicans. With the Nagpur Congress now only months away, Hedgewar encouraged Moonjay to arrange a meeting with Aurobindo Ghosh—the Bengali revolutionary and Congress leader, who had narrowly escaped life imprisonment in the Alipore bomb plot a decade earlier. But his conscience had paid too high of a price. He had seen too many killed, hurt or left destitute. He had spent ten years with a small, but growing band of followers in French-occupied Pondicherry in South-East India. He had abandoned politics and civic life, to explore what he considered to be higher matters—to contemplate on the spiritual evolution of humanity. Hedgewar knew that only Aurobindo—a British trained classicist with a spiritual backbone, discipline and charisma—could unify the Congress and lead the Republicans to victory. Hedgewar also knew that if anyone could halt Gandhi in his tracks, it would be Aurobindo. The NNU, the powerful Republican lobby within the Congress led by Moonjay, readily agreed.

A letter was dispatched immediately to Aurobindo inviting him to take the presidency of the Indian National Congress with the full support of the Republicans. On 30 August, the response came. It would disappoint everyone, Hedgewar more than any other. Ghosh's letter was succinct, with a tone that exemplified a 'matter of fact-ness'.

> I find myself unable to accept your offer of the Presidentship of the Nagpur Congress… The central reason, however, is this that I am no longer first and foremost a politician, but have definitely commenced another kind of work with a spiritual basis, a work of spiritual, social, cultural and economic reconstruction of an almost revolutionary kind, and am even making or at least supervising a sort of practical or laboratory experiment in that sense which needs all the attention and energy that I can have to spare. It is impossible for me to combine political work of the current kind and this at the beginning. I should practically have to leave it aside, and this I cannot do, as I have taken it up as my mission for the rest of my life. This is the true reason of my inability to respond to your call.[51]

But Hedgewar was not one to give up. The letter, although disappointing, made it also clear why Aurobindo Ghosh was the right man. Ghosh was the closest person in Hedgewar's mind to Plato's Philosopher King—the one who does not seek power must have it. Hedgewar and Moonjay left for Pondicherry within weeks of Tilak's death. The meeting was arranged for early September 1920. The train journey took two days. Moonjay, as was his taste, travelled via first-class carriage, whereas Hedgewar travelled in the third-class compartment, what Shashi Tharoor so aptly called 'cattle class'.[52] Tightly squeezed together, Hedgewar had passed his time reading and talking to the folks around him. He would enquire about their lives, their family, what they thought about their country and so on. He would have shared his space with men, women, children and even animals. The air would have carried a thick stench of sweat and spices. People shared stories with each other, looked after one another's children or animals, and Hedgewar would have freely consulted people about their health, as well as the health of the country. Moonjay, on the other hand, spent his time in relative isolation reading, writing and sleeping in comfort.

RSS folklore is full of incidental stories about Hedgewar. One such incident occurred a few stops away from Madras, now Chennai. The story captures how the mood of the country was changing. How Hindus were beginning to express some sort of political consciousness and a sense of history. The story goes something like this: at long stops, Hedgewar would leave his carriage to stretch his legs. He would often walk over to the front of the train and check up on Moonjay, who was, after all, his mentor and father figure. On one occasion, Hedgewar was checking on their bags in the first-class carriage when suddenly, the train began to leave the station.

No sooner had Hedgewar realized, a ticket conductor tapped him on his shoulder and asked for his ticket. Hedgewar began to explain that he was just checking up on his friend, and he was promptly on his way back to his compartment. The conductor was having none of it. 'If you don't show me a valid ticket right now, you'll have to pay for a new one,' he snapped, while never quite making eye contact, instead looking past Hedgewar.

Moonjay, who heard this, got up to stand next to his friend and tried to make a plea. 'Look', said the short stubby conductor glaring up through his spectacles at the two tall, imposing figures in front, 'show me a ticket or buy a new one' pointing menacingly at them. Moonjay, so the story goes, lost his cool. 'How dare you speak to me with such a tone. I am the customer, and you are here to service my needs. I am the master, and you are the servant, or have you forgotten?' seethed Moonjay. The conductor, instead of being cowed by the much taller man, clearly from wealthier stock, flared up, not intimidated in the slightest. 'You are no longer the masters of this country. This is a Hindu country, and you have no right to treat me as your servant anymore', he blustered, red in the face. With one look at each other, Hedgewar and Moonjay burst out laughing. Moonjay pulled out his wallet, bought a new ticket and even tipped the conductor. Bemused, and somewhat thrown off balance, the conductor smiled awkwardly, not sure what to make of what had just happened.

The conductor had taken one look at Moonjay and immediately assumed that he was an aristocratic Muslim. Moonjay, with his greying beard, tall slim stature, short hair and black cap, could have fit right into the committee of the Muslim League. What had impressed the two men was that this poor conductor, an ordinary man by all accounts, was confident enough to stand up to people that were not only clearly above his station, but that he could do so with a clear sense of purpose and political awareness. Hindus, on the whole, were a cowed bunch. They were meek and passive. Having been ruled over for seven centuries by one invader after another, they had developed a subservient mindset—all too ready to please. But not this man. The conductor, to Moonjay and Hedgewar, showed all the signs of the ordinary Indian realizing that India was their country first and foremost, and they would no longer tolerate being called a servant, nor treated like one.

Eventually, the train rolled into French Pondicherry. Divided into 'white town' and 'black town', one need not stretch their imagination too far to understand what the names represented. The white town, which is now romanticized as the Indian Côte d'Azur, with its straight roads cooled by the shade of trees lined in front of French colonial buildings housed the French merchants and political elites. As romantic and picturesque as this might sound, by the time Hedgewar and Moonjay had arrived, the French were a spent power. They had deforested the surrounding area to such a large extent that outside of white town, one would have been lucky to see a single tree. Much of the tree line outside of the white town was planted in Independent India, decades after the two doctors made their only visit. Ghosh, at this time, had been living like a recluse. They found him living on the edge of the white town across the canal in a dilapidated French building, with high ceilings and large windows with white wooden shutters.

Ghosh was a shadow of the man that he had been a decade earlier. He spent his time in meditation, reading and writing, completely at the mercy of well-wishers, especially a French lady who had moved to Pondicherry earlier that year in April, called Mirra Alfassa. Moonjay and Hedgewar would have known him as Aurobindo, a man who had not lost any of his penetrating intelligence, wit or humour. All three men met in private over four days, often spending three to four hours every morning discussing matters of politics, culture, philosophy and society. Mirra Alfassa would drop in every now and then, at which point Moonjay would divert the conversation to more mundane matters. It remains unclear as to what exactly was discussed in these meetings, but we know that Ghosh was completely at odds with the journey of the Congress, especially Gandhi's obsession with the Caliphate movement.

> On the other hand, a gigantic movement of non-cooperation merely to get some Punjab officials punished or to set up again the Turkish Empire, which is dead and gone, shocks my ideas both of proportion and of common sense.[53]

Even though Aurobindo Ghosh did not change his mind, Hedgewar, the junior of the three listened intently on the thoughts and ideas expressed. Ghosh considered himself to be a revolutionary.

> I am an idealist to the marrow and could only be useful when there is something drastic to be done, a radical or revolutionary line to be taken,

> (I do not mean revolutionary by violence) a movement with an ideal aim and direct method to be inspired and organized.[54]

Ghosh, although uninspired by the status quo, was undoubtedly committed to India's struggle for freedom. Like Hedgewar, he was a critic of Hindu society. He had boiled down his complete critique to the simple statement that Indians, and Hindus in particular, had lost their strength, or as he phrased it 'their shakti'. Indian civilization had become old and decrepit in will.[55] The civilization had to be reborn. The culture was producing individuals that were weak, both in character and skill. 'Without ability, how could an individual respond to challenges and threats?' he quipped. A society impotent to confront its challenges was doomed to be subjugated. What Ghosh revealed to Hedgewar was nothing short of revolutionary. Hedgewar mostly sat engrossed, absorbing what was being revealed. Unbeknown to Ghosh, his dream of creating tens of thousands of men and women strong in will to serve society and reform it from the grassroots up would not be achieved by his own endeavours, but by the younger man, the junior, relatively unknown figure sitting opposite him. Ghosh further dreamt of devoted actors with a missionary spirit, completely dedicated to the resurgence of India's great civilization. Men and women, well trained, noble in character, culminating in tremendous ability, who could live in synchronicity with Dharma to reawaken the spirit of India. These devoted actors would not come from his endeavours, but from the RSS and its pracharak order. It was Ghosh, above all others, in these private meetings that seeded the idea in Hedgewar's mind of the pracharak—one who willingly forsakes everything for the upliftment of a culture.

Ghosh further elaborated his vision that Hindu culture was not only worth preserving for its own sake but because it had something tremendous to offer the world. It guarded Dharma itself and ideas of Ahimsa (non-harming); Karuna (compassion) and Moksha (the ultimate expression of liberty) were its greatest gifts. Ghosh accepted that the West had mastered nature; she had harnessed her energy but lacked a teleology. The Hindu had a clear teleology but had fallen into the dark recess of life—impotent and weak. Ghosh also expressed as coherently as any before, that the Abrahamic faiths were dangerous and imperial in nature. Hindu culture could offer an alternative for humanity. 'But alas for its people!'[56]

Over four days, Hedgewar, in the midst of a mental churn, found Ghosh to be nothing short of inspiring. Ghosh had unknowingly crystallized in Hedgewar's mind the same stream of thought that he was churning. The truth of Ghosh's words would take a further five years before they germinated, but the seeds were planted in Pondicherry in 1920. Where Aurobindo's ashram would burn bright for a few decades before itself falling into relative insignificance, ultimately straying far from Ghosh's dream of producing men and women of vigour and wisdom, the RSS still to this very day in its daily *prarthana* (oath) talks about building people with the highest skill and character, those that have the greatest ability and those that seek nothing in turn. The daily oath of the RSS encapsulates, in some very significant sense, Aurobindo Ghosh's vision.

On 10 October 1920, the new president of the Congress was elected. With Moonjay's reluctant support and Hedgewar's abstinence, Chakravarti Vijayaraghavacharya (CV) came to the fore. CV was of the old guard. Already sixty-eight years old at the time of his election, he was seen by both the Republicans and the Associates as a safe pair of hands who could act as a unifier. He was one of the founding members of the Congress thirty-five years earlier and an alumnus of Presidency College, Calcutta, where he graduated as a lawyer. He was bright, articulate and much like Hedgewar, his influences were a mixture of Hindu orthodoxy and elite western education. He entered the public life somewhat accidentally when he had been falsely accused by the Crown for having started a riot between Hindus and Muslim in Salem, Tamil Nadu in 1882. He fought his corner, and the nationalist papers of the time, including Tilak's *Kesari,* labelled him somewhat prematurely as the 'Lion of South India' when he was acquitted and compensated one hundred rupees.[57] In 1895, he was elected to the Madras Legislative Council where he served for six years. During this time, he became close to Hume, the founder of the Congress, and even helped him write the constitution. He was a respected figure who sat on the 'top table' of the Congress alongside Motilal Nehru, the late Tilak, Naoroji and Lala Rajpat Rai. Moonjay, now with no real influence on the top table, decided to back CV, hoping that his powerful lobby from the Central Provinces would tip the balance to favour the Republicans. Nothing of the sort happened. CV was his own man. He never allied himself with either half of the party, and firmly walked the middle way. A paper reporting on the president's speech wrote, 'we are unable to fathom whether the Congress president has spoken in favour of the Non-Cooperation Movement or has opposed it'.[58]

In December 1920, Gandhi's agenda of swadeshi, non-cooperation and supporting the Caliphate movement were all unanimously passed by the Congress. Over 20,000 delegates attended from all over British India. Even though everything was going contrary to what Hedgewar had wanted, he nevertheless led 1200 volunteers and took charge of organizing the Congress. Hedgewar was the youngest member of the organizing committee that included close friends, among them Dr Paranjape and Harkare. Hedgewar, still only thirty-one years old, had gained a reputation as an organizer. Everyone, including Gandhi, noticed how the young man organized his teams, how he commanded from the back and his complete absorption in the task at hand. A gargantuan marquee was erected where over 14,000 people could be seated. All around the main marquee were smaller sub-tents for break out meetings, food and drink, toilets and a first aid tent. The land where this mammoth event took place is still called Congress Nagar in Nagpur.

Even though Hedgewar left the Congress with an enhanced reputation, the two doctors had struggled to manage and coordinate a relatively disorganized bunch of volunteers. Motivation amongst the main teams ebbed and flowed, as well as their general ability to follow instruction. His countrymen were lacklustre, poor in spirit and quite incapable of solving day-to-day problems. Often infighting and prejudices held back progress. Individual egos would clash too frequently. Hedgewar began to muse, and brood, as he often did. He would sit on his porch late into the night. What did the Indian character lack? Why were Indians so disorganized, haphazard and unable to cooperate with one another? He recollected after the Congress how even though he had been praised for his leadership, on the whole, no one would have wanted his role. To be a *swayamsevak*, that is a volunteer, was subservient, and something about the word connoted being low in the social hierarchy. Today, the word itself is the hallmark of the RSS. To be a *swayamsevak* is to be a well-trained, disciplined and a highly capable volunteer.

Having passed the non-cooperation bill, the country went into lockdown. Hedgewar was responsible for Nagpur and surrounding districts. Under his watch in early 1921, schools, law courts and other administrative functions were boycotted. The Central Provinces report noted, 'the dangerous and anarchist principle of non-cooperation has grown rapidly and has struck a far more serious blow on the cordial relations between the government and the people than any other propaganda hitherto'.[59] Hedgewar was leading the charge through an endless series of powerful, evocative, as well as provocative speeches. He would have known that the leviathan was watching, and sooner or later, its eyes would capture enough for him to be prosecuted. Yet, he carried on. In May 1921, he was arrested by the police who presented a warrant outside his house. Hedgewar quietly gave himself up, without a fuss, and with relative calmness. His brother Sitaram and his wife watched Hedgewar being marched out handcuffed.

By 1922, Hedgewar, while serving his prison sentence, watched with equal curiosity and dread as Indian Muslims began to agitate against British rule. He saw all too clearly that the loyalty and the heart of the Muslim lay not in India, but in Istanbul or Tehran or Mecca. Religion came before country. Belonging was drawn from a global *umma*, and not from one's ancestry or rootedness with the land. Nationalism was an anathema for most Muslims as it was a form of idolatry. Hedgewar mused how could this be reconciled? How could a militant Islam seeking a *dār al-Islām* and re-establishment of the power of the Caliphate be part of a progressive secular nation? Islam, he discovered was universalist, it recognized no borders, whereas, he was a nationalist, with a clear rootedness in his ancestry and land. He further mused as to how was it that other communities such as Parsis, who are Zoroastrians from Persia who fled their homelands and found refuge in India could assimilate, but Muslims could not. For Hedgewar, Islam was a system of belief, in the same way as all the other religions of India were, yet all others, on the whole, had assimilated into the wider culture of the land. But Muslims, who were mostly Hindu converts, were breaking all bonds with their kin and ancestry. Nehru, in his biography, writes 'many westernized educated Muslims who were not religious minded began to grow beards and observe religious rights'.[60] Why was this? These questions percolate in Indian discourse even today. Increasingly, the West has had to start asking these types of questions—how is a Muslim to reconcile their Muslimness along with their Americanness or Britishness?

SEVEN: 1921–1922

Shackled Freedom

Sedition.

A charge we seldom hear in today's liberal democracies. But if we were to venture a little beyond the shores of our liberty, we would find that in totalitarian states such as China or Saudi Arabia, many people are not only arrested for sedition but convicted and executed. This was the charge levelled against Hedgewar. In May 1921, this could have easily led to a lifetime of hard labour on the Andaman Islands, or worse. As Hedgewar sat in the police station, listening to the charges being read out to him, his heart would have had palpitations about what the immediate future may have in store for him. He would have been more than familiar with the gruesome stories about what happens to a man when he is hanged from the gallows. The long drop, as it was known, if miscalculated by the executioner, could result in bloody decapitation. If done exactly right, then the victim would die in seven seconds after suffering a sharp, excruciating pain in the neck just before it breaks. Hedgewar sat silently, perfectly still, as dark thoughts flooded his mind. But according to the police records, he showed no outward expression of any kind.

Hedgewar had been openly and somewhat brazenly giving public speeches that incited revolution and resistance against the Crown. His speeches were confrontational. Hundreds had heard him speak. His speeches were at times so fierce that Congressmen would privately speak to Moonjay and question the doctor as to why Hedgewar was chosen to give speeches.[1] His speeches in Bombay were particularly noted.[2] He was part of a double act with his old medical colleague Narayan Savarkar, the younger brother of the famous 'Veer' Savarkar. Moonjay was raising funds off the back of these fiery speeches and had no appetite to hold Hedgewar back. People were roused, only momentarily, but just long enough for many to financially support the struggle. According to Palkar, a contemporary who heard Hedgewar speak during these times, 'whenever the topic of foreign rule, or foreigners came up, Keshav could not rein himself in and would let out a torrent of blue language'.[3] Many nationalist newspapers at the time were reporting on these speeches. This was not some covert underground operation, far from it, it was a cry for independence in one year. Many newspapers openly reported on the content of the speeches describing them as 'patriotic rallying calls', 'spirited' and other such euphemisms, but never quite writing enough to vindicate Hedgewar for sedition.

On 14 June 2021, Judge Smiley presided over the court hearing. All RSS literature humorously, and somewhat mischievously, calls the Judge, Judge Smelly or Smeley.[4] Smiley's courtroom was a large rectangular room with large windows on two of the sides overlooking the courtyard of the law courts. It was hot. The air was dry. Several wooden benches making up the public gallery were packed mostly with well-wishers on the day of the hearing. Several members of the local press were present reporting on the case. Smiley, dressed in his black robes and typical grey wig, with a small set of spectacles decorating the top of his nose, entered the room. He was known to be a stern man, who would follow the letter of the law, no matter how unjust. Hedgewar had no money, but he had plenty of social capital. Two men stepped up to represent Hedgewar named Bobday and Mandlekar.[5] Bobday was the barrister and the other man, the junior of the two, the solicitor. As was the custom, Hedgewar and Bobday sat in the front row to the judge's right and the Crown's prosecutors to the left. The wooden dock was in the front to the left, on a slightly raised platform.

Two speeches were read out as being seditious, both delivered on 2 October 1920, in a town called Katol, sixty kilometres away from Nagpur. The sub-inspector of Katol was the first witness called upon by the prosecution. After the sub-inspector had identified Hedgewar as the man who had chaired and given the speeches at the meeting, Bobday came up to question the witness, who, by all accounts, was quite a simple man from a backwater town doing what he believed was his job—following the instructions of his superiors. Bobday interrogated the witness. He wanted it out in the open as to who had commanded the lowly inspector to raise these charges? Once it had been verified that it had come from high above, the judge appealed to Bobday to get on with his line of questioning. It is worth noting that at this time, in a period of non-cooperation, a certain anarchical belligerence had taken over the minds of those who were fighting the leviathan. Every courtroom struggle was an act of defiance. It was a show to be communicated to the outside world, with a hungry audience eager to see their own defy that which was once impossible to defy. As such, the struggle embraced the actor, even rewarding many with fame. It was also an opportunity to use the British instrument of 'justice' against itself. The British prided themselves on fairness and being a civilizing force in the world. The law had to prevail regardless of how unjust it was, and this was exactly what Hedgewar and Bobday wanted to show the Indian public.

In the spirit of the act, Bobday continued with his line of questioning, which was designed to bring to the fore the desh bhakti of Hedgewar, and the natural rights of every Indian to self-govern. They were effectively showing the world that to be an Indian who yearned freedom was a crime in Imperial India. Judge Smiley was no fool and was experienced enough to spot such micro acts of anarchism. Questions from Bobday infuriated the judge and the prosecution. The experienced, but hot-headed, Smiley lost his cool when Bobday asked the fuddled police inspector, 'Is it not true that Dr Hedgewar propounded the principle of India for Indians in his said speech?'[6] The judge, having had enough and on the verge of losing a power struggle with the defence, asked for the question to be expunged from the records. He then went onto warn Bobday that this line of questioning was not in the spirit of the court. Bobday, to Smiley's horror, was not done yet. Upon being admonished for his questioning, Bobday turned towards the public gallery exclaiming, 'This judge is prejudiced and obstructing the process of impartial cross-examination.'[7] An accusation of the most heinous type as far as any would-be judge was concerned. Bobday, in an act of melodrama, announced to the court that he could no longer do his job in such a repressive environment and resigned his post as defence counsel. There was a flurry of activity and some hushed murmurs arising from the public and press gallery. Bobday marched over to his side of the court, packed his papers, shook Hedgewar's hand and exchanged some solemn glances before storming out of the courtroom. No sooner had Bobday left the room, Hedgewar stood up pleading that his case be heard by another judge, as this one was not fit for purpose. Complete havoc broke out in the back of the room where the public sat. Smiley had effectively lost control of the proceedings. With great embarrassment, Smiley was compelled to adjourn the proceeding for the day.

Hedgewar wrote a plea to the District Magistrate, Irwin:

> Mr Smiley does not possess even an elementary working knowledge of Marathi, whereas all my speeches and statements are in Marathi. Therefore, he is not worthy to adjudicate this case. Evidence of this can be gauged from the blank sheets of paper for disposition. Despite a lengthy hearing on the 14th June, he was unable to pen down even a single word. In addition to this, his political awareness is also questionable. That is why he raises objections to every question raised by the counsel. He has to make an effort to understand the purpose of every question put, before the proceedings can even move ahead. Owing to a lack of understanding of the proceedings, he dismisses questions being asked as "irrelevant", "unrelated" or "out of context". Had those questions not been dismissed and the public prosecutor forced to answer them, it would have been proven that there was no sedition in my speeches.[8]

The letter was swiftly rejected on the 27 June, with Irwin stating that, in his opinion, Judge Smiley was more than capable.

The next date for the hearing was set on 28 June 1921. Smiley was seething when he arrived in court. The front pages of all the newspapers in Nagpur had made a mockery of the judge and his court. The late Tilak's *Mahratta* newspaper was covering every word uttered in the courtroom, much to the Crown's annoyance. Hedgewar, who had never been in court before, understood that Smiley would try and put him in a difficult situation. To that end, Smiley ordered Hedgewar to submit a written statement as a defence plea to the court. Hedgewar refused, stating that it was his right to first hear all the witnesses and the arguments as presented by the prosecution before he would submit a statement. Smiley tried to assert his authority but to no avail. As the *Mahratta* reported the next day, Hedgewar made it clear, 'I have stated whatever it was that I wanted to say. I am firm on that. I shall give my statement only at the end.' [9] Once again, Smiley was forced to concede and set a new date for the hearings to proceed.

On 8 July, a hot sticky Friday, the court resumed. The public gallery was full. People were sitting shoulder to shoulder, sweating and almost breathless. They wiped their faces with their napkins every few minutes. Hedgewar was brought into court by the guards. He was going to represent himself. The air, as he entered, would have been pungent like the 'dirty sock smell' of a locker room produced by the overheating of flesh and little ventilation. The doors through which the public arrived were kept open for everyone's sake. Hedgewar's aims were threefold: first, to demonstrate through the media the injustice of British rule, and that he was being asked to prove himself in a criminal court for openly expressing his patriotism and candour for a free and open society; second, to minimize his prison term and finally, having accepted that a prison sentence was assured, to cause mischief in the court and show that Indians will not be cowed. Of course, Hedgewar's fancy legal footwork around Smiley was being helped by the daily advice and guidance received from Bobday. He was aware of the buttons he could push, and how the judiciary could be used to further the cause of 'India for Indians'.

Hedgewar was particularly fired up on this day. He had access, as was his right, to the testimony provided by eyewitnesses. He spent most of his days studying the evidence, line by line, in a pensive mood. He appeared in his typical white dhoti, white shirt, a waistcoat and a well-worn grey khaki blazer with elbow patches, which he had stitched himself. His upper lip was covered by his bristling black moustache, and the white of his eyes contrasted with his darkened skin at the top of a large frame. He was intimidating for any man at the best of times. But in a courtroom, where Hedgewar could cross-examine the witness himself, it would prove to be a daunting day for the inspector from Katol, a diminutive character by the name of Gangadhar.

Hedgewar's line of attack centred around Gangadhar's competency, initially calling into question his ability to write in the dark, and then on his ability to transcribe speeches accurately. Inaccuracies were hurled throughout the cross-examination, where Gangadhar claimed that Hedgewar spoke at a tortoise rate of twenty-five words per minute, whereas Hedgewar challenged the court that he spoke at 200 words per minute, which would have made him excruciatingly difficult to understand.[10] With exaggerations on both sides, the truth is often in the middle somewhere. Gangadhar did concede that his understanding of Marathi was not quite up to scratch and that his grammar lacked any precision. Hedgewar clearly enjoyed bringing to everyone's attention that according to Gangadhar's transcript on the night in question, 'I had spoken about wives and children' [11] said Hedgewar holding up the transcript in the air, much to the amusement of the public gallery. His central argument was that this evidence, as presented by the simple police inspector from Katol, could not be taken seriously. As the day's session was ending, Hedgewar asked for other witnesses to be brought forward for cross-examining. Smiley refused. Incensed by this, Hedgewar launched into a monologue. Smiley promptly asked the clerk to expunge whatever it was that he said in court from the official records. But *Mahratta* published some of what was said.

> I know that my defence would have no impact on a government that has unleashed a cycle of repression against the devoted children of the motherland. I reiterate the fact that Hindustan belongs to its devoted children and 'Swarajya' is our mission. If the declared promise of self-determination for Hindustan by the British Prime Minister and Government were a sham, then you can pronounce my speech treasonous. I have full faith in God's Justice.[12]

The speech, although only partially recorded, does nevertheless reveal the subtleties of Hedgewar's inner world. Phrases such as 'repression against the *devoted* children of the motherland'; and 'Hindustan belongs to its *devoted* children' reveal some of his ideas. These ideas would be the underpinning of one of the largest and most successful movements in the world—the Rashtriya swayamsevak Sangh. These phrases reveal that the leviathan, as far as Hedgewar was concerned, was targeting only those who stood up against its rule, suggesting that those that simply kept their head down were left alone. His notion of 'devoted children of the motherland' is also interesting. Who were these children? Were they of a specific religion, ethnicity or language, or was it built on some other common factors of fraternity? As far as we know, he never defined these terms in court, or if he had, we certainly have no record of it. The common academic literature tells us that the RSS, from its very beginning, was a Hindu fascist movement, calling India the land of Hindus.[13] This rhetoric has been prevailing for so long now that it has become a verisimilitude, something that is simply taken at face value. But Hedgewar, of whom modern literature has extraordinarily little to say, was not so simple. We know that he was equally inspired by patriotic Muslim scholars from his time at university, as much as Moonjay, his role model and guide. We know that he was stirred by people from all strata of Indian society—rich and poor—and seemed to completely see through caste and creed. He was equally a radical for his time when it came to women's rights and clearly perceived the backwardness of Hindu society at large. Hedgewar, above all else, was critical of Hindu society. The point of fraternity for him lay only in two things—the individual's character and patriotism for the 'motherland'.

The next time the court convened was on 5 August 1921. He stood on the dock that day and read out his written final statement. The statement further reveals the mind behind the man. It is worth presenting in full.

> I have been called upon to answer whether I have been delivering speeches which were calculated to rouse discontent, hatred and treason against the British government established in law and create enmity between Indians and Europeans. I believe that for Bharatiyas (Indians) to be tried and judged for their deeds by a foreign power is an affront to the dignity of this great nation.
>
> I am surprised to hear that a government established in law exists in Bharat (India). What exists here is a reign of terror foisted upon us by brute force, where the law is only its handmaiden and the courts but its instruments. The only government that has any right to exist in any part of the world is a government by the people, for the people, and of the people. All other forms of government are a subterfuge run by rogues with the aim of looting the people.
>
> I have tried to rouse the affection in my countrymen for our downtrodden motherland. I have tried to instil in their hearts that Bharat belongs to her children. If a Bharatiya cannot expound this principle without committing treason and cannot talk plain facts without creating enmity between Europeans and us, then I fear that those who call themselves the government of India should recognize that their time for a dignified retreat has passed.
>
> I have seen before my very eyes that evidence has been produced in this court against me which is inaccurate, broken, and misrepresenting of what I have said in my speeches. But I am not worried in the slightest. The principles governing my behaviour towards the British and other Europeans are reciprocal, nothing more. Whatever I have said, is with the view to establish the rights and freedoms of my countrymen. Furthermore, I am willing to take complete responsibility for, and defend every word from my speech and I affirm that all of it is fair and just.[14]

Hedgewar passed his statement onto the clerk and stood facing the judge. According to the *Mahratta* reporter, Hedgewar pressed on.

> The prosecution has only produced police officers as its witnesses. It is far more fitting to call them prosecutors rather than witnesses. Bharat belongs to Bharatiyas. This is why I demand 'Swarajya' (Self-rule), which was the theme of my speech at the night in question. It is not enough to just speak about freedom, I also must explain how to achieve it and how to maintain it once begotten. I fear that otherwise my countrymen will begin to emulate the British. The British, who are unsatisfied with their own country, always seem ready to plunder other countries. The British have enslaved and exploited so many nations. If their own independence was under threat, they would least hesitate to draw the sword and be the cause of rivers of blood. A case in point was the European war that has just passed in which so many of my countrymen died. I have encouraged people to not emulate the British, and that it is unjust for one people to rule over another.
>
> This brings me onto our current political situation. It is clear and visible that today Bharat is being ruled unjustly by foreigners. Maybe the public prosecutor can tell me if there is any such law that enables one country to rule over another? Is this not unnatural? If indeed there is no such law, and wholly unnatural for one people to rule over another, then who gave the right to the British to rule over us? Are the British of this land? Then on what basis do they rule? Is this not a murder of all that is just and moral?
>
> We do not wish to snatch away the freedoms of the British people and to rule them. Just as the British rule over Britain, and the Germans rule over Germany, we too, people of this land, wish to be our own masters. We have no wish to be ruled by the British. We want complete freedom from foreign rule, and we will not rest until we have achieved this. What law is broken if one wants to live in freedom and dignity in one's own country? I passionately believe that the law exists to uphold the principles of justice and morality and should be applied in its defence.[15]

At 12.30 p.m., on 19 August 1921, Hedgewar was to be sentenced. A few hundred people gathered outside the courthouse. Going to prison for the sake of the struggle was a rite of passage. It was a celebration. People gathered to cheer Hedgewar on; in some sense he was expected to metamorphose into a new man, a man worthy of leadership on the national stage. As Hedgewar arrived in the courtroom, Judge Smiley wasted no time. He declared that Hedgewar's statement to the court was more treasonous than the charges. Smiley, to no one's surprise, charged Hedgewar as guilty. However, to everyone's surprise, Smiley ordered a bail of Rs 1000 and for Hedgewar to refrain from any more speeches for twelve months. A light sentence indeed.

A game of cat and mouse was being played between the Crown and the revolutionaries. The Crown understood that, for many, spending time in prison was a rite of passage to higher positions and, often, fame. Therefore, judges often gave light sentences to simply demean and mock the defendant. The judge would have had no desire to see the likes of Hedgewar in high office, leading bigger struggles in the future, and so better to put him in his place now. But Hedgewar had been expecting prison all along. One could even speculate that Moonjay had suggested to Hedgewar that the time was ripe for him to spend some time in prison, to earn his badge and come out ready to take some senior leadership roles in the Congress. The public loved nothing more than a leader who had spent some hard time in prison. To that end, Judge Smiley may have wanted to thwart such a plan.

A fine of Rs 1000 was somewhat of an insult to a revolutionary of the stature of Hedgewar. Even though Hedgewar had little money of his own, he had enough social capital from those around him to easily raise the bail amount and be released. Instead, Hedgewar refused to pay any fine and claimed his innocence, leaving the judge with no choice but to send him to prison for twelve months instead. We cannot be sure if the judge would have been happy to send Hedgewar to prison because it was a well-known fact that some revolutionaries were more dangerous in prison, where they became recruiters for otherwise would-be petty criminals.

As Hedgewar left the court, hands shackled, Palkar tells us that Gokhale, on behalf of Nagpur Congress, garlanded him. All the city and district leaders were present outside the courtroom. Petals were thrown to greet Hedgewar. People cheered and shouts of 'Vande Mataram', the new-age battle-cry, filled the courthouse. Hedgewar was finally greeted by Moonjay, his father figure and mentor. Hedgewar bowed to the older man, a few secret words were exchanged between them and Hedgewar turned to face the crowd.

> I defended myself on the charges of treason. Many think that it is wrong to defend oneself. The fact that so many of you have assembled here implies that you do not think this. When charges are laid against us, we must defend ourselves to prove the meekness of our opponents. This is

> a service to the motherland. Not defending oneself, I think, is suicidal. If it does not suit you do not defend yourself, but do not feel that one who defends oneself is less worthy. We should be prepared for any sacrifice including transportation and death. But do not spread the delusion that going to jail is heaven and that by itself will lead to freedom. Keep in mind that there are several things one can do to serve the motherland outside of jail. I will be back in one year. I would not know the affairs of the country until then. I believe that the movement for complete independence of the country from the British would have started. Hindustan cannot stay under foreign rule anymore. It cannot be enslaved anymore. My heartfelt thanks to each one of you. I take your leave for the year. Namaskar.[16]

With that said, and a final glance at Moonjay, Hedgewar stepped inside his prisoner carriage and was drawn away. He was sent away to prison with the continuous chanting of 'Vande Mataram' and 'Doctor Hedgewar ki Jai' from his friends and colleagues.

His final speech is revealing. It was clearly bothering Hedgewar that some people among his circles felt that he ought not to have defended himself. Some of his colleagues preferred that he take the honour of prison gladly. It speaks to the culture of his time among Indian revolutionaries that firstly, going to prison was an honour, and secondly, that to defend oneself was a show of cowardice. Hedgewar was clearly troubled by both norms. For him, it was paramount to stand up against the Crown and use its own sense of justice against it. Furthermore, it seems very much the case that liberty was a universal self-evident truth for Hedgewar, one which Indians ought to appeal to at every given opportunity.

That evening, the Congress had organized a gathering to celebrate Hedgewar, a custom that had emerged from the first war of independence when the British imprisoned hundreds of Indian soldiers who had taken part in the mutiny. As each soldier was imprisoned, he was celebrated as a hero by his local community. Each soldier, therefore, became a role model. It became an act of courage and righteousness to stand up against the leviathan. This custom had now spread into the revolutionary movement. Families attended the gathering. Sweets were given out to the young children, and speeches were made trumpeting Hedgewar's character and life. A week later, on 24 August, the *Maharatta* newspaper published an editorial on the life and 'self-sacrifice' of Hedgewar.[17] The article, as was the way, embellished him, especially his complete insistence on independence.

Hedgewar had become comfortable with the police. He had spent countless days in custody, and was accustomed to police attention, harassment and the occasional roughing up. He was not too anxious as he entered the archway of Nagpur's Ajani Jail. Yet, twelve months in a district prison would not be easy.

The Indian response to jails was not what one may have expected given that imprisonment as a form of punishment was something very colonial, and not native. Indian society, from the ancient to the classical periods, did not put any emphasis on incarcerating citizens as a form of punishment. In classical texts such as the *Arthasastra* (4th century BCE), a treatize on political economy, fines are the most common forms of punishment in classical India. Short-term imprisonment was only a mild punishment. For severe crimes or violations, punishments could range from bodily mutilation, to amputations, exile or even death.[18] Ancient India, as a rule, was free of thought when it came to prisons, even though they did exist as mild punishments. Prisoners had basic rights. Kautilya, the author of the *Arthasastra* mentions that no prisoner should be deprived of his or her right to 'daily avocations as sleeping, sitting, eating or excreting'.[19] He goes so far as to mention that keepers of prisoners should face severe punishments if they needlessly torture prisoners or deprive them of their basic rights.[20]

During Muslim rule in India, the role of the prison changed. For Muslim rulers, supported by clerics, prisons became places where the sins of men could be washed away, and where a place could be found in heaven even for the lowliest sinner. As such, prisons were dark places, meant to cause suffering and pain to the incarcerated. Even though prison sentences were not encouraged in Mughal India, prisons were forgotten institutions—decrepit and hellish.[21] This is how the British would have found them when they arrived in the late eighteenth century—diabolical and for the most unfortunate.

For the English, prisons were the by-product of the industrial revolution and the abolition of transportation of prisoners to the penal colonies. For the English, prisons in the sixteenth century were for beggars and young hoodlums.[22] The Land Enclosure Act in England led smallholders and landowners to go bankrupt. They were forced off their ancestral lands and forced to move to cities looking for work in factories. In 1830 in England, 85 per cent of all arrests by the new police force resulted in imprisoning vagrants, that is beggars and the homeless, rather than people who were criminals.[23] According to Karl Polayi, 'enclosures have appropriately been called a revolution of the rich against the poor.... The lords and nobles were upsetting the social order, breaking down ancient law and custom, sometimes by means of violence, often by pressure and intimidation.' [24]

Britain's industrial revolution came at a great social price, one that the elite and beneficiaries felt was worth paying, given that Britain, an island with near zero resources, no great history and few people, within a century had become a global superpower par excellence. In India, a similar strategy was being played out, although, the Europeans in their hubris felt that Indians were never quite up to the mark as being civilised, as they had interbred with low-ranking dark-skinned Dravidians—a race theory that was prominent amongst Indologists of the day.[25] One can argue that the British were sincerely carrying out an enlightenment project, even a civilizing project, bringing humanity and prosperity to savage peoples all over the world, including India. It was a pain worth enduring for these races because it would pay off over the long term. Of course, even with all these good intentions, the path to hell is still the same. The leviathan was speeding down the path by 1921.

Indian prisons were full of political prisoners during this time. The British had introduced the prison system into India as early as 1810, and by this time it was an evolved system of incarceration. In the early part of the nineteenth century, the British had such a severe penal code that judges simply could not apply the law by the book as it would have resulted in the execution of thousands. Instead, in 1829, a penal code was introduced where the application of capital punishment was replaced by longer prison sentences.[26] This was the main reason why, between 1829 and 1920, there was a mushrooming of prison infrastructure across India. The East India Company, and then the Crown, in their quest for efficiency and profit, appointed select inmates, deemed as 'appropriate' with extra authority. These were 'convict officers', in effect petty criminals who would get their rations increased, receive extra bedding or maybe a cell to themselves if they were deemed 'very appropriate'. Convict officers would act as supervisors on behalf of the Crown. Throughout the nineteenth century this system had caused wide scale corruption and convict officers often misused their powers.[27] By the time Hedgewar had arrived in prison, this system had been recognized by the authorities as flawed, but the economic benefits were too great to really change it. Hedgewar, along with hundreds of revolutionaries, would take full advantage of this flawed and corrupt system to work against the leviathan.

Hedgewar, as with so many other aspects of his life, never really spoke openly about his experiences in prison. What we do know is that he came out of prison a year later 25 pounds (11 kilograms) heavier.[28] RSS biographies, as expected, extol the hardship Hedgewar faced in jail, and how he ungrudgingly faced up to his lot. The reality, as always, is more nuanced and far more interesting. Prison schedules reveal what a 'day in prison' may have been like for Hedgewar.

Upon arrival, Hedgewar was stripped of whatever few possessions he may have had, including his watch, pen, notebook, clothes and any spare change he may have carried. Stripped naked in a small room, he was asked to take off his *Upanayana janeu*, to which he flatly refused.[29] Knowing the sensitivities of such actions, the Indian wardens often turned a blind eye to such sensitivities, something which white officers would often enforce through physical violence if required. Hedgewar wore his *janeu* under his prisoner uniform. Had Hedgewar not been who he was, the usual custom was for convict officers to give a mandatory beating to the new incumbent as a way of instilling discipline. His hair and precious moustache were shaved. With no footwear, and given only one set of underwear, a thin mattress to sleep on, an even thinner blanket and a metal plate and a tumbler, he was led to his cell. Sanitary conditions were dire. Lice were rampant amongst the prison population, and rats found their way in and out through open latrines.

Wake up calls began at six in the morning. Hedgewar would step out of his cell and squat with his hands behind his head along with all the other prisoners. After a quick search of the cell by the wardens, prisoners would have an hour to wash and queue for breakfast. Bathing consisted of ten prisoners at a time walking over to an open tank of cold water. Nothing could be done without an explicit order from a guard. They would be commanded to strip off, and at every whistle thereafter they would first pour water with their tumbler over their bodies, followed by a quick use of berries and cheap soap to scrub, followed by another whistle where they could wash off. The final whistle was a command to dry off. Within three minutes, the bathing ritual was complete. Hedgewar, with nine others, twice a week, would wash in this manner for another twelve months. Marched back to their cells with their clothes still in their hands, they were made to walk almost naked, with just a loin cloth loosely wrapped around them. Once in the cell they could get dress in their prisoners' uniform. This was routine prison life, something which Hedgewar acclimatized to astonishingly quickly. Breakfast consisted of a tumbler of tea, some spiced poha and a morsel of roasted chickpeas or upma. Lunch and dinner consisted of rice and dal, and if the guards felt generous, prisoners were given a single banana before lights out.

After breakfast, prisoners worked for small amounts of money, or for some traditional poor man's cigarettes called beedis. Hedgewar was assigned to paper polishing duties in the prison's carpentry unit. An unpleasant job at the best of times, it often left his palms rough, sore, and blistered. His wrists would swell.[30] The air was often laden with microfibers from the wood polishing, and without protective wear, Hedgewar would suffer tremendously with poor respiratory health in years to come. According to the sub-inspector Nilkanth Rao Jathar, Hedgewar never complained. Guards could see that he was often in pain, and his work slowed, but he never asked for time off or for redeployment[31].

Then, come noon, it was lunch. Rice and dal would be dished out, every lunch and dinner. A completely unbalanced diet, full of carbohydrates and sugars, with little protein and vegetables, coupled with little to no outdoor exercise all resulted in long term health problems in later years. Having said that, for many inmates, Hedgewar included, the diet would have been familiar. Rice and dal were staple foods for most of the working poor. The main difference was that they were locked in a cell most of the day with little ability to exercise. After lunch, Hedgewar began a routine of going to the 'prison library', a grand description for what was, in essence, a stack of tattered books damaged by woodlice, which very few bothered to read. Most prisoners, at this time, would go back to their cells and take an afternoon nap or consume the time away in idle gossip.

Hedgewar began reading the great Indian epic, the Mahabharata. With 1,20,000 verses, it is the longest piece of literature known to man, dwarfing the combined remnants of Homer's Iliad and Odyssey. The Mahabharata is a mammoth body of literature from classical India, with the earliest known version dating from the second century BCE. But orally it is much older. Originally known as *Jaya*, meaning victory, the text is an amalgamation of the work done by hundreds of writers over hundreds of years who have each added something extra to the text. A story upon a story, upon a story. Each layer adds a metaphorical and literary richness to the text. It is a timeless text in Indian culture, and almost every Indian child across the diverse strata of society will know something about the main plot and characters therein. The Mahabharata describes the spectrum of human character from sublime virtue right the way through to belligerent egoism. Each afternoon, Hedgewar would read for an hour in his cell. Eventually, his four cellmates joined him, and they started a book club of sorts.

The prison was full of political agitators and Hedgewar's cell was no different. In a small three by three metre cell, he shared close quarters with four other oddities. The first was a lawyer by the name of Raghunath Pathak. He was a self-respecting man, who spoke little, his confidence in his own people was a little jaded, but a sharpness remained. The next was a radical by the name of Radhamohan Gokul, an ardent follower of the Arya Samaj—a neo-Hindu religious movement that was responding to the Abrahamic charge that Hindu customs are baseless. The Arya Samajis were people who responded to the challenge by advocating that the Vedas should be regarded as the 'holy book' of the Hindus. They were also ardent, to the point of militant, believers in removing all idolatry from Hindu society. A reformist organization which wanted to do away with 'caste' in all its manifestations. They had imagined a purer past where a 'Vedic' society existed, a time when such societal mutations such as prejudice, idolatry and subjugation from foreign powers was not possible.

Then next in was a skull cap wearing, energetic twenty-year-old conservative Muslim called Inamullah Khan. He had been incarcerated for agitating against the Crown too, but not for a free India, but rather to re-establish the Caliphate in Istanbul or anywhere for that matter. He was young and intense, the brooding sort, one that Hedgewar could all too readily understand. The prison authorities no doubt took great delight in putting the likes of Gokul and Khan next to each other. The prison was no different to the outside, where the British made sure that individuals never got beyond group identities. They made sure that Khan would collide with his cellmates and continuously create a sense of discomfort and division among them, making it easier for the guards to control inmates. As if this was not enough, a few days later, Hedgewar's old friend and co-worker was not only sent to the same prison but given the same cell to share.

Hedgewar must have been delighted that his long months in a rat-infested, foul-smelling cell would be made that little bit easier now that his friend and confidant was with him. Putting Harkare and Hedgewar in the same cell was either a gross oversight by the prison authorities or it was their way of getting another prisoner to overhear their conversations and leak out vital information. Nevertheless, they found themselves in the same cell. Harkare, unlike Hedgewar, was a hothead, quick to anger, and ready for a fight at any given quarter. It was only a matter of time before Khan and Harkare would clash.

Hedgewar, once joined by Harkare, began to read his books out aloud in his cell, and Gokul could not help himself from getting involved in the discussions. With always something to say, passionately, and with no restraint, he would infuriate Khan, who was trying to nap in the cell. Eventually, Pathak joined in and added a much-needed critical element to their discussions about the Mahabharata. Then, to their surprise, sub-inspector Jathar showed up outside the cell one afternoon. He took a chair and sat outside, listening to the rendition of the epic, and even joined in with the ensuing discussion. Eventually, the news reached the prison Superintendent, an Irishman by the name of Ford, who was somewhat sympathetic towards the struggle Indians faced. He suggested to Jathar that if Hedgewar's so-called book club would be a positive influence on the overall well-being of prisoners, then he should be given space in the communal areas for all prisoners to benefit. After a cursory meeting with Ford, Hedgewar was given more time every afternoon and had the lunch area to conduct his rendition of the Mahabharata. Soon, several more convict officers sat and listened. Most of them would have been illiterate. Accompanying them from time to time were other political prisoners who would eavesdrop on the discussion around Dharma, and good conduct, the inalienable rights of people and virtue ethics. Hedgewar was coy, he never went into the politics of the day, but often spoke about pre-British India, and the 'golden' age of Hindu kings around the eighth and ninth centuries.

It was clear to the wardens, especially to Ford and Jathar, that Hedgewar was no ordinary prisoner. He was learned, nuanced and above all else, earnest. According to Deshpande and Ramaswamy, Jathar once remarked to them sometime in the 1950s, when they were researching Hedgewar's life, 'the Doctor had no ulterior motive. He wanted no extra favours or some underhand arrangement.' [32] Jathar went on to admit that 'even though we were servants of the Crown, we were nevertheless so drawn to him by his amiable conduct and character. After his release, whenever the chance came, many of us would go and visit him at his home.'[33] Hedgewar's congruence had won the hearts and minds of his prison wardens. Hedgewar was an open book—a man on a mission, and that mission was transparent—a free India, for Indians, governed by Indians. His convictions were rooted in deep metaphysics and epistemology. They were nourished by his exposure to the best education of the day, and his understanding of political thought, especially European thought. He was not a blind reactionary, or a desperado out to make his name. He was clearly a composed individual, still only thirty-two years old, who oozed a maturity beyond his years. Of course, it probably helped that he was protected high-on up, by the good and the great of the Indian National Congress and the Hindu Mahasabha.

Days went by. They became weeks, and soon months. Hedgewar had become a personality in the prison, and even the convict officers treated him respectfully. He was no longer made to squat at five in the afternoon when cells were checked. He could get dressed in the bathing area, rather than making the walk back to his cell with just a loin cloth on. Given the state of the blisters on his hands and wrists, he was given lighter tasks. But Hedgewar never accepted any of these leniencies. He did as was expected by all the inmates, further winning the hearts and minds of the prison population.

Often, when political leaders were incarcerated, they were treated with more dignity and respect. They were separated from petty criminals and riff raff. Nehru, who spent something like ten years in total behind bars, wrote his best books there. He was even allowed, in Dehradun prison, the luxury to keep a cat who kept him company. He was allowed visitors and could even occasionally convince the wardens to rustle up one of his favourite dishes—a good old tandoori chicken. The British were sensitive to political prisoners with high office being ill-treated, due to the outrage it would cause on the streets. Most prisoners of Nehru's ilk were considered to be on writing sabbaticals when in prison. The best of them wrote poetry, novels and even autobiographies. Nehru did all three. He even educated his daughter through distance learning by writing long letters, educating her about Indian history. It is hard to imagine Nehru or Gandhi, for that matter, many of the Indian elites being told to strip off, bathe to the sound of whistles and march back naked to their cells.

Hedgewar wrote nothing in prison. He did read, however, a great deal it must be said. Only a few months into his sentence, Hedgewar heard about the Mappila carnage in Kerala. It devastated him. A cocktail of anger, hopelessness about the state of his country and general frustration swept through him. Limited correspondence between Moonjay and Hedgewar had continued throughout his incarceration. To the untrained eye, their letters were a fusion of banality and the mundane, completely unworthy of political prisoners. But to Moonjay and Hedgewar, every word they wrote meant something. To this day, it seems unclear exactly how they communicated through these letters but communicate they did. Moonjay had visited Kerala and seen first-hand the butchery that had taken place there, and how the Congress leadership had tried to cover it up. Hedgewar came to know of Gandhi's neglect of Hindus in Kerala. While life for Hedgewar was a routine, the outside world was in tremendous flux. Removed from the action, he was able to see, somewhat, what ailed his countrymen, the political leadership and the hopelessness of it all.

At some point in his incarceration, Hedgewar seems to have come to a realization that Indians, and its political elite in particular, were not fit to govern. He saw all too clearly that when the British left, and he had no doubt that the British were on borrowed time in India, the elite, divided as they were between Hindus, Muslims and pseudo-secularists with socialist hearts, were simply going to tear India apart. The foremost blame, he argued, lay on the general meekness and lack of political consciousness of the Hindu majority who were steeped in poverty, casteism, superstition and division. He saw that the Congress leadership, led by Gandhi, in their misplaced hope to pacify the Muslim League to not seek an independent Muslim nation, were drowning the interests of the majority. He considered many of these men at the top of the pile as privileged, power hungry and entitled. He saw them as essentially British in aspiration, taste and mind, with an Indian topsoil, and a socialist core. Many were well intentioned, but that would not be enough. A democracy handed to an illiterate majority, meek and subservient, was ripe for exploitation.

The most significant revelation for Hedgewar during these unremarkable, anxiety-ridden months was that everyone concerned—from the British at the top of the pecking order, through to small religious and political leaders in villages—saw Indians not in terms of individual flesh and blood human beings, with their own individual tastes and aspirations, hopes and fears, but rather in terms of group identities. There was no individual in India—everyone had to be either a Hindu, a Muslim, a Marathi, a Bengali, a Brahmin or Sudra, and so on. It was always about groups. All rhetoric and policy making revolved around groupthink. Everyone saw the Indian nation as a hotchpotch of distinct groups trying to live together, primarily split by religion, then by language and finally by caste. Democracy, for Gandhi and his elites, was about accommodating each group so that they could live according to their own customs and norms with minimal conflict. He recognized that the likes of Nehru were after building a socialist utopia where India, and he (Nehru) in particular, would be the darling of the world- non-aligned, peaceful and a beacon for other new democracies emerging out of colonialism. Nehru wanted to show the world how a modern, industrial India could accommodate disparate groups and live peacefully.

But alas, during his time in prison, in the quiet of long, sleepless nights, Hedgewar came to realize that, in many ways, he and the Congress leadership—with Gandhi and Nehru at the helm—shared a striking similarity in their diagnosis and prognosis of India's ailments. And yet, for all their collective endeavour, they were irreconcilably different in what each believed to be the right course of treatment and way forward for their people.

Hedgewar would have agreed with much of what Nehru believed about India and her rich history and contribution to humanity throughout the centuries. Nehru's rendering of Indian civilization in his *Discovery of India* and Hedgewar's would have almost been in perfect harmony. Both agreed on its rise, its plurality, its ability to absorb all outsiders and 'Indianize them', its contribution to humanity and even how the social stratification of people had given great stability to the society over millennia.[34] They agreed on almost all aspects of India's slow, steady decline. For Radhakrishnan, the second president of India and an Oxford scholar at All Souls College, Indian society lost its rigour with the loss of political freedom. But Nehru rightly asked, as did Hedgewar, 'But why should political freedom be lost unless some kind of decay has preceded it?'[35] Hedgewar would have broadly agreed with Nehru's explanation for the cause of India's decay, 'probably this was the inevitable result of the growing rigidity and exclusiveness of the Indian social structure as represented chiefly by the caste system.'[36]

Yet, for all their intellectual agreement and complete commitment to the struggle, their outlook for what India ought to be was polarizing. The result of which, one can see all too readily in modern India. Fundamental differences arose in their differing childhoods and upbringing. Nehru had the best education money could buy and was effectively a prince of the realm. He was educated at home by English tutors in palatial settings and deeply influenced by Anne Besant's *Theosophy* where he was introduced to Hindu philosophy and culture for the first time. He went on to study at

Harrow School, one of the premier institutions in 1905. His nationalism, by his own accounts, was aroused by the Japanese–Russian war, and the writings and deeds of Garibaldi. He had visions of acting out similar deeds in India—he had always wanted to play the liberating and unifying hero.[37] He then went on to study at Trinity College, Cambridge, which even today is considered a premier institution amongst the elite colleges of Cambridge. He graduated in 1910, and went on to study law at the Inner Temple in London, where he was deeply influenced by writings of socialist philosophers who were all Fabians.

One must contrast this with Hedgewar. Both were peers. One from a lower stratum of society, the other from an elite. One lost his parents to the plague, the other had all the advantages of wealth and patronage. While one was adopted and influenced by local, on-the-ground happenings, the other was influenced by global events in distant lands. Both read European political philosophy—one read under a tree in a temple courtyard, and then at medical college in sticky hot Calcutta, sleeping on the floor between two beds, while the other read at Harrow School and Cambridge. One was living nationalism working in the grassroots, while the other was intellectually excited by it. These differences, although leading both to nationalism, could not be reconciled, and their understanding about what India fundamentally was, was different, resulting in different means to achieve different ends.

For Hedgewar, India—or Bharat, as he would have called it—was something altogether different. To him, Hindu culture was Indian culture; it was the *atma*, or essence, of Indian society. Earlier, invaders had eventually been absorbed, or as Nehru would have expressed it 'become Indianized' and had essentially become Hindu. India's plurality lay in Hindu Dharma. When the Mughals arrived, they considered themselves not only different but also superior.[38] 'Indianization' of the Mughals was partial, whereas the Islamisation of Hindu India was thorough and changed the fundamental character of society.[39] On the other hand, for Nehru, it mattered not what religion you believed, it was all ultimately faith-based and superstitious. Rather, it was the shared ancestry that made one Indian. Indeed, Nehru went so far as to say that if every Hindu converted to Islam, this would still not deprive them of their heritage, just as the Greeks after their conversion to Christianity did not lose their pride in the mighty achievements of their ancestors.[40]

Hedgewar would have sneered at such lofty naivety. He had witnessed first-hand what it meant to be a Muslim in India during the early twentieth century. He knew that Islam was anti-culture in that it was fundamentally rooted in Arabism, where all things Indian were to be seen as backward and untouchable, which ultimately led Muslims to suffer a collective amnesia about their heritage.

Hedgewar cared principally about Dharma, something which Nehru seemed to appreciate intellectually, but was equally ambivalent as to its application. Hedgewar's nationalism was not rooted in dreams of heroism. The hard knocks of life he endured would never allow such delusions of grandeur to be entertained. Hedgewar was a product of his father. He had seen his father risk his life during the plague when many others had decided to put themselves or their families first. Hedgewar had role models in the form of Moonjay, who had dedicated the best part of his later years and much of his wealth towards the struggle; Tilak, who had inspired the Republicans of the Congress and had genuinely attempted the re-industrialization of India; Dr Malik, an Edinburgh trained physician who returned to India to support the struggle and the charismatic writer, Shamsunder Chakravarti who had lost all his worldly possessions and faced years in exile for the cause. These were some of the men who had shaped the inner life of Hedgewar.

Possibly, one can advance the thought, somewhat safely, as to these experiences being central in Hedgewar's emphasis on individuals first and foremost. He prioritized the individual over all group identity. Most commentators and historians alike in modern renderings of Hedgewar completely fail to recognize this point.[41] Hedgewar was a man of the people—a people composed of individuals. He saw the well-being of India not through industrialization as Nehru did, for that would inevitably come later. Rather he saw that the primary goal was to build the social character of every citizen, so that Bharat became worthy of a democracy—for the people, by the people and most importantly, from the people. This is patently clear from what he devoted most of his life to after leaving prison.

Months went by, and prison life had become somewhat normalized. Hedgewar tried to resist normalizing such a routine, but prison is meant to be mundane and brain rotting. Hedgewar, in the final months, had become close friends with the sub-inspector, and as such, was given extra time to read and converse with interested prisoners. 13 April 1922 marked the third anniversary of the Jallianwala Bagh massacre. Hedgewar marked the day with his fellow cell mates by refusing to work all day. Even the hot-tempered Khan had agreed to join in. Jathar turned a blind eye to the day, as did Ford, and allowed Hedgewar to openly speak to the prison population about nationalism and why it was important that they contribute something to the struggle. A few weeks before the monsoon rains began, at the hottest time of the year, Harkare was released early for good behaviour. A few days later, at the daily morning cell check, as Hedgewar positioned himself in the usual squat position, Jathar placed a letter at his feet. Hedgewar had received his release date—11 July 1922, at noon.

A few weeks before Hedgewar's impending release date, local nationalist newspapers had begun informing their readers that their man was soon coming out. The usual fanfare was made by the local Congress. A few days before his release, the monsoon had started. The heat had cooled considerably, and a freshness had returned to dry earth. Anyone that has been in India at the time of the first monsoon rains knows the fresh earthy smell that scents the air. For Indians, the arrival of the monsoon is sacred. On the day of his release, Ford and Jathar had come to see him off. Hedgewar had made many friends on the inside, many of whom would go on to join the RSS in years to come. It was pouring. The skies thundered and the heavens opened. Hedgewar, after almost a year, got dressed in his familiar freshly ironed white dhoti and shirt, khaki blazer and black top hat. He walked out of prison to be met by hundreds of well-wishers, mostly activists and the Congress leadership. Everyone, including Hedgewar, was soaked through. For Indians, to be soaked in the first rains is considered a blessing. The afternoon was full of hugs, polite bows, prostrations from younger activists and handshakes from his colleagues. His brother, Sitaram, and his wife came to the front of the crowd, garlanded him and took him home.

EIGHT: 1922–1925

Crossroads

The rains fell all evening. Hedgewar sat on the porch, on his brooding swing. Swaying to and fro, ever so slightly, he stared into the darkening sky, listening to the heavy drops of rain. Something in Hedgewar had changed. One year in prison, away from all the hustle and bustle, the politicking and dealing with the skulduggery that came with the struggle, had given Hedgewar new insights into himself and the social character of his countrymen.

It had taken an hour for Hedgewar to reach home from the prison gates. In that hour, he had been bombarded by Congressmen about upcoming rallies, meetings and a complete lowdown on the state of the struggle. His brother had left him a series of newspaper cuttings with headlines about his impending release from jail. One article read, 'his patriotism is above all controversies. Hedgewar has proven his sincerity in jail. His extraordinary sacrifice has made his inborn patriotism shine with ever greater lustre. His stay in jail, too, has been spotless.' [1]

Hedgewar did not care for such claptrap. This is what many of his colleagues in the Congress craved and even went to prison for—for praise and fleeting fame. He came to recognize that those who wanted power in the new world would need to pander to fame and therefore it was the nature of democracy. Public image would come before integrity for many of his colleagues. The nature of the ruling classes, connected as they were to popular opinion, would be bent on manipulating the masses to form deeper group identities instead of transcending them. Of course, they knew very well that their rhetoric should always be an opaque veneer, one that would hide their divisive intent. Democracy in India required politicians who would pander to and harness group identities. Could he be part of such a democracy? The effectiveness and moral value of a democracy was solely dependent on the social character of individuals who formed composite parts of a society from which politicians came and served.

Hedgewar had bought into his own rhetoric and that of others. He believed people at face value when they said we must alleviate poverty, caste, superstition, and so on. But it dawned on him that even though there were many earnest people in the Congress, many with good intentions, the nature of democracy, as it was germinating in India, meant that group identities would only be further entrenched, and the Hindu society further exploited through lines of caste. He had become acutely aware that only European political thought challenged the ills of Hindu society. There were isolated and disjointed attempts by religious and spiritual gurus to combat ills such as poverty, illiteracy and general backwardness, but with few resources and disconnected from the wider social milieu, how effective could these be? There was no adequate indigenous response to what a post-colonial Indian democracy ought to look like.

He knew that Moonjay and the Hindu Mahasabha, the Hindu wing of the Congress, had groomed him effectively to step up to a national leadership role. He had earned his final badges in prison and was now ready for seniority, having achieved credible popular support from the central regions. Hedgewar was a known man—respected by all the major factions vying for power in a post-British India. That night, he knew he was at a fork in the road. In front of him lay the straight road into politics. A future where he would play some significant role in firstly resisting the leviathan and then shaping the country through politics. A path that, for years, had looked brightest and most likely to uplift his people from the squalor that history had punished them with. Now, suddenly, this path looked only partial. Did he want to pander to the masses? Did he want to climb the greasy pole? Did he want to harness the illiterate masses through identity politics? Was he prepared to sacrifice the means for an end? Did he want to be a political leader within a Gandhi-led Congress? Could he accept Gandhi's negationism, especially when it came to the 'Muslim challenge'? Could he reconcile his concerns about Muslim aggression with Gandhi's insistence on Hindu–Muslim unity? Could he accept the gross injustice meted out to his fellow Hindus by some of their own leaders, especially in the light of the grotesque violence they suffered in Kerala? Could he accept Congress's concealment of the record of Islam in India? If he could accept these things, then the path to power lay straight ahead. All he had to do was step onto it.

Yet, there was another path, one less trodden. A darker path with no certainty. A path most likely to lead him to obscurity. A thankless path, one in the grassroots. A path that, in all likelihood, may have been inspired, in part, by his exposure to Aurobindo Ghosh, who had spoken extensively to both Moonjay and Hedgewar about the need for a transformation in the consciousness of Hindus. This transformation could not come through any political initiative or tropes of freedom and equality, but rather through hundreds and thousands of men and women being prepared to venture forth to build virtuous character. Ghosh had argued that if it took a thousand years for the Hindu civilization to become so decrepit, then it would take at least a few centuries for the civilization to re-establish itself. This had resonated at some deep level with Hedgewar. Ghosh's ideas, much like the man, were lofty, nebulous and unformed. There was no blueprint one could follow.

To what extent this alternative path had been formed in Hedgewar's mind is unknown. His tendency to stay on the porch late into the night was customary. Whereas usually he would be surrounded by colleagues and workers planning for campaigns or some rally or another, this time he was alone and silent, with just the cooling rain to keep him company. His actions the following day would reveal much about this thought process.

The next day, Hedgewar, with his brother and sister-in-law, along with a string of friends, neighbours and well-wishers, walked ten minutes up to Chitnis Park, where the Congress had organized a welcome rally. Today, Chitnis Park is surrounded by densely packed low rises. It is a poorly maintained cricket ground where concerts and other public events are held. In Hedgewar's day, the park would have been greener and surrounded by trees with a maintained lawn. The floodlights and the ugly tiered seating around the ground would not have existed.

The rains began once more. At the entrance to the grounds, he was met by none other than Motilal Nehru, who had been the elected president of the Congress two years earlier. He was the father of Jawaharlal. Next to him stood Hakim Mohammad Ajmal Khan—a doctor and an educator. Both men, smiling, were at the top of the Indian political and social hierarchies. Motilal with his palms clasped together in the usual way that Hindus greet each other using a namaste, whereas Ajmal Khan bowed courteously, as refined Muslims did, with an *adab*. Hedgewar would have been briefed that both men were attending the rally and so the gravitas of the occasion would have been clear to him. Hedgewar greeted the older man first with a reciprocal namaste, and just slightly lowering his gaze from Ajmal Khan with the words *tasleem*. After an exchange of smiles and handshakes, both men, with Hedgewar in the middle and Moonjay trailing just behind, walked into the park to meet the throngs of people who had gathered.

Motilal Nehru was a lawyer turned politician who, although having had a difficult career, had become stupendously wealthy.[2] His father, Gangadhar Nehru, had ensured that Motilal was given the best education money could buy in India—one in Urdu and Persian. Motilal learned English before he had really mastered Hindi, as was the way in the mid-nineteenth century amongst wealthy families looking for patronage from the political elite. The Nehru family had benefited tremendously from the patronage of the Muslim court and later the British, where he had become a member of the privy council, which advised the head of state. Only a few years earlier, he had begun his own national publication called The *Independent*. Gandhi had been a huge influence on him, and he had given up wearing the attire of an Englishman and took to wearing traditional Indian clothes. Gandhi, the first truly masterful public relations expert in India, knew that the leaders of the Congress in an emerging democracy had to look like their subjects, at least somewhat. Gandhi himself had obviously taken his own advice to its utmost limit. Although inspired by Gandhi, Motilal was his own man. He had recently fallen out with his mentor and openly criticized Gandhi for abandoning the non-cooperation movement. Motilal was forming his own party to rival the Congress. He along with his fellow rebels, including some other heavyweights of that time—Subhas Chandra Bose and Vitthal Patel, the elder brother of the famous Sardar Patel—had just formed the Congress-Khilafat Swarajya Party.

In 1922, National Legislative Councils were to be elected, and since 1909, a limited number of Indians could stand for election. Gandhi wanted nothing to do with them and insisted that Congress boycott the election. Nehru had other ideas. He wanted to participate and felt that only through legislative council elections could the Congress enjoy any real political power. Ever the pragmatist, he was out on the campaign trail searching for candidates that he could back. Motilal was hunting for talent, and it is quite likely that he had his eyes on Hedgewar.

Ajmal Khan came from a long lineage of physicians. They specialized in Persian medicine and served the Mughal courts over generations. Ajmal

Khan, with the patronage of wealthy Arabs from the Middle East and Nawabs of India, had co-founded the Jamia Millia Islamia, an educational institution, a few years earlier in 1920. Today, the university is a fully-fledged institution and is ranked amongst the best higher education institutes in modern India. The other co-founder was a man called Mahmud Hasan Deobandi, who was a Sunni (Hanafi) Muslim scholar and a disciple of the man who founded the conservative Deobandi movement. Most Muslims in the West of South Asian descent practise a Deobandi form of Islam—highly conservative and orthodox, which has often intricately been linked with, and sometimes openly supports, extremist Wahhabi forces within Islam.[3]

Deobandi Islam was founded in 1866 in a small seminary in Deoband, a village in Uttar Pradesh, India, with a revivalist spirit. It was vehemently anti-British and propagated the idea that Muslims had to cleanse themselves from corruptions of Western influence to regain the grace of God and re-establish a Dar al-Islam on Earth.[4] For Khan, India had to be liberated to fuse it with a wider Dar al-Islam, something which would have been unthinkable for Hedgewar, Moonjay and the Hindu Mahasabha.

As Indra cut loose his monsoon clouds, the rain lashed down. According to Palkar, the rally was quickly moved to the nearby Vyankatesh theatre.[5] As the dignitaries all arrived at the large hall, they would have been somewhat surprised by the crowds that had already found themselves some room to stand in. Not everyone could be housed, and scores of people were lined around the edges of the theatre and seated in the gangways. Nehru and Khan addressed the crowd in turn. Both men, polished and articulate as they were, had their voices drowned out by the sound of rain lashing the corrugated roof. The *Mahratta* newspaper made quite a song and dance about the crowds and their enthusiasm to hear Hedgewar speak. As he rose to address the crowd, he knew the crossroads that lay before him; on one side, if he played to the tune of the political elite, Hedgewar was destined for a life in politics at a national level. However, if he chose to say what he really felt, he would have to leave politics, rethink everything and 'watch the things he gave his life to, broken, and stoop and build 'em up with worn-out tools'.[6]

The only source of what he said on that day comes from newspaper clippings.

> The fact that I was a guest of the government for a year has not in the least added to my merit; and if it at all has increased, the credit for it should go to the government. ... We have today to place before the

> country the highest and noblest of ideals. Any ideal short of complete freedom will take us nowhere. To expound to you the method whereby that goal can be achieved would be an insult to your intelligence, as all of you doubtlessly are aware of the lessons of history. Even if death were to stare us in the face, we are not to shirk from our path; we have to keep the ultimate goal constantly burning in our minds and calmly carry on the fight.[7]

Even though he went on to speak throughout the central regions at the behest of regional Congress leaders throughout 1922, with every speech Hedgewar gave, he was becoming increasingly sceptical about the future of his society. Outwardly, he delivered powerful, uncompromising speeches, but inwardly, a melancholy had set in. Neither Nehru nor Khan approached Hedgewar to run for election on behalf of their breakaway party, nor did Hedgewar show any appetite for such a venture. He had knowingly picked the path less trodden, thereby avoiding a poisoned chalice.

Hedgewar became the general secretary of the provincial Congress. He witnessed, in an exacerbated form, the indiscipline and poverty of character across the organization. Those at the higher echelons of leadership, Hedgewar's peers, saw volunteers as simply bodies to order and command.[8] Those further down in the pecking order were treated badly, without any respect or care towards their well-being. Decisions would be made impulsively without any discussion or consensus, and volunteers were expected to follow these decisions as soon as the order was given.[9] Morale was low. The attrition level amongst volunteers was high. Furthermore, Hedgewar saw how caste lines further exacerbated the problem of unfairness, where leaders would only favour and promote those that they knew, were related to or were from the same caste. Hedgewar, in these moments, saw the future of an independent Indian society—a society incapable of working together, developing itself in unison, with fairness and equality across the strata. He witnessed how very few women joined the grassroots movement, not out of want, for he knew there were many women who would, and could, contribute to the struggle if the prevailing culture would allow them to do so.

By December 1922, the Congress machinery had been split in two. On one side was Gandhi with his *padawan* (Jawaharlal) Nehru,[10] both in prison at this time, who was advocating a complete boycott of the National legislative elections; and on the other side was the (Motilal) Nehru–Das faction supported by Moonjay and members of the Hindu Mahasabha, to participate in the elections and win significant seats. Hedgewar had refused to take sides and consistently called for consensus and unity. His stance made him the perfect candidate to chair meetings and facilitate public discussions. At a two-day Congress session on 16 December 1922, Hedgewar chaired the acrimonious occasion. Hedgewar pleaded with all those who spoke 'to be loyal to our principles and not to individuals'.[11] His call had partially worked, and key resolutions around cow protection, gram panchayats (village/parish councils) and swadeshi (indigenous) goods were passed. However, when it came to the elephant in the room—the issue of the legislative council elections, he knew that the resolution for participation would win, further alienating Gandhi's followers. Seeing that he, as chair, had little choice but to allow a split vote, he saw 'the pro-entry faction sail through'.[12] Hedgewar's personal reputation soared amongst both factions of the Congress, and he remained the only unaligned senior political figure.

While the Congress was tearing itself apart into many different factions, the Muslim League, while vying for power amongst themselves, was also busying itself championing the Khilafat movement, galvanizing Muslims to work against British interests while raising the political consciousness of its members. 'Muslims in India', argued clerics, 'must help re-establish the Caliph in Istanbul.' [13] But by late December, at the same time as the Congress was taking place, Turkey, the old seat of the Ottoman Empire, was in civil strife. Within the Muslim world, Muslims were seeking an alternative narrative to what the orthodox clerics were spouting in India. Within Turkey, a progressive, secular nationalist movement arose known as the Turkish National Movement led by Ataturk, who would eventually, in 1924, turn Turkey into a secular modern constitutional state and remove the power of the Caliph altogether.

Hedgewar, who would have been following the news closely, was dumbfounded at how global affairs in a post-war Muslim world were playing out in his backyard. While many Muslims the world over were seeking to abandon orthodox Islam and embrace a western style liberal secular democracy, Muslims in India were ghettoising themselves, and an ultra-conservative Islam was forming through the Deobandi school.[14] Muslims outside of India were moving towards modernity, while inside India, even British-educated Muslims who had no genuine religious feelings began to grow beards and observe religious rituals as an outward show of their piety and support for the Khilafat movement.[15] Muslims across the Middle East, Egypt, Northern Africa and Iran were seeking to reform their societies and fuse modernity with their Islamic heritage to become progressive, scientific and secular. The exact opposite was happening in India. To make matters worse, the Congress leadership under Gandhi was prepared to go to any length to maintain the Hindu–Muslim unity pact, including turning a blind eye to Muslim aggression in India, a case in point being the Mappila uprising in Kerala. Indeed, Gandhi is accused by many commentators of being responsible for 'jettisoning sane, secular, modernist leadership among the Muslims of India and foisting upon Muslims, a theocratic orthodoxy of Maulvis'.[16]

Gandhi was adamant and unwilling to negotiate on the matter of a Hindu–Muslim pact. The majority (Hindus) should do whatever it takes to pacify the minority (Muslims), where 'the test of friendship is assistance in adversity, and that too, unconditional assistance'.[17] With such a belligerent stance, Gandhi managed to single-handedly fragment all the political forces in a single strike. The Hindu camp was now split into three. The first camp was the Hindu Mahasabha—the Republican side of the Congress wanted nothing to do with the Khilafat Movement. They saw it as a complete waste and distraction from the cause of complete Indian independence. Furthermore, they wondered why the Muslim organizations were whipping up support for a cause that the Turks themselves did not ask for, nor desire for themselves. The second camp was those Hindus who were willing to support Gandhi's Non-Cooperation Khilafat Movement but with conditions. This camp was also suspicious that Muslim sentiment was straying towards the establishment of Muslim rule in India, and so, as a litmus test, they proposed that in return for Hindu support, that Muslims should give up cow slaughter. The third camp was Gandhian. This camp consisted of the likes of Nehru, Rajagopalachari and Rajendra Prasad. These were people who felt that if Hindus were willing to go to any length to appease Muslim demands and concerns, then eventually, the Muslim sentiment would turn, and a unified India would emerge. Gandhi was dismissive and uninterested in speaking to the Hindu Mahasabha. According to Gandhi's own *Young India* journal, the second group was simply told to get in line. In effect, there could be no litmus test.[18] Gandhi asked Hindus to effectively take a leap of faith that the Muslim leadership would take a conciliatory tone in time.

For Muslims too, Gandhi's strategy caused division. There was the Muslim League, which, since 1906, had been trying to mobilize the Muslim voice to ensure that an independent India recognized its significant minority population. The League was not run by orthodox conservative Muslims, but rather opportunists, whereas Gandhi's backing of the second group, the Khalifatites were most certainly conservative orthodox Muslims in nature and intent. The third Muslim group felt that India was a land of the *kufr* and that unless India could be brought under Dar al-Islam,[19] it was better for Muslims to migrate to Afghanistan.[20] Around 18,000, mostly Muslim peasants, answered this heinous call and left their homeland in search of some Islamic paradise. The Muslim leadership too was divided, at least for a while. Hedgewar witnessed Gandhi's stratagem fail with tremendous consequences. For Hedgewar, the nightmare scenario of a Partition looked increasingly more likely under Gandhi's leadership. The evidence for this pessimism came thick and fast.

An incident in November 1923 in Nagpur crystallized the challenge for India. Muslims began targeting Hindu families who were participating in a religious procession that happened to go by a *mazar*.[21] This small mark on the road had grown into a small *dargah*, and by 1923, it had become a small place of worship, no more than a single room where five to ten men could participate in Friday prayers. In every Indian city, even to this day, one can find small, tiny mosques, poorly constructed and illegally built on the side of roads in predominantly Hindu areas. On the whole, this is an aspect of plural society in Hindu India today; however, in the 1920s, with the rise of the Khilafat Movement fuelled by the conservative Deobandi strand of Islam, intolerance grew and ruptured the plural fabric of Indian society. As such, Muslim leaders passed an edict that no kufr-led musical procession could pass by the mosque, especially one carrying *murtis* (statues), which Muslims and Christians wrongly identify as idols.[22]

The problem was that, right next to the shack-like structure, was an older Hindu shrine dedicated to Ganesh where every year Hindus started their procession. In November 1923, local Muslims managed to get an injunction from the District Collector against playing instruments near the mosque during the Ganesh festival. The festival was essentially postponed until the following month when a 30-day-long Hindu ritual called *Kakad arti* was to take place. Every day, between the early hours, a procession would go past the same mosque, which would have been empty at the time. After much discussion, the Muslim leadership agreed to allow five Hindus to walk by the mosque. This was quite naturally unacceptable and preposterous to the Hindu community. Tensions rose. Soon, police constables were deployed to guard the illegal mosque in a predominantly Hindu neighbourhood, which only further exacerbated the tensions, as now the leviathan was seen to be taking sides. A few days later, the procession was pelted with stones by a small group of Muslims to stoke Hindu anger. As tensions continued to rise, temples began to be desecrated at night, and carcasses of dead cows were left at the entrances. Soon, Hindus equipped themselves with bamboo sticks to protect themselves and organized night vigils near temples.[23]

During these riotous times, Hedgewar led from the front. He would see how frightened and anxious Hindus became as they passed by mosques or how singers would stop singing kirtans on the off chance that they might draw an unwanted challenge from Muslims who were passing by. Hedgewar, during these occasions, would himself pick up an instrument and begin playing it. He would sing, too, rather boisterously.[24] Every evening, he would go door to door to remind sturdy youth from local gyms to attend the morning procession. Irked by this, Muslim groups began sending anonymous letters with threatening undertones to Hedgewar and Moonjay.[25] Both continued with their daily life without any outward display of fear. Moonjay would always have some form of security with him, whereas Hedgewar, who always considered himself a tough guy, would insist on walking alone.

Hedgewar was acutely aware that the Khilafat movement, in the hope of mobilizing Muslims against the British, was also infusing a dangerous sectarian consciousness against Hindus. The chances of total Muslim rule in India were small, but certainly, if enough momentum were created, then India would be partitioned into Hindu India and Muslim India. He further saw that Hindu society was ill-equipped to deal with what was emerging all over the country. Hedgewar saw the violence that lurked in unsaid words and scarce glances between Muslims and Hindus. He witnessed increased intimidation from Muslims who, only a few years before, worked and lived side-by-side with their Hindu neighbours. Suddenly, lifelong Hindu friends had become the *kuffar*; and India, the home of their ancestors, became a land that suddenly belonged exclusively to Islam. These incidents had a profound effect on Hedgewar.[26]

In 1923, Veer Savarkar was in prison in the notorious Andaman Islands. Ganesh, the elder of the three brothers, was very close to Hedgewar.

Named Babarao by friends and family, he too had spent thirteen years between 1909 and 1922 in prison.[27] He worked tirelessly with Narayan, the youngest of the three, who also studied with Hedgewar, to have his brother released from prison. Hedgewar also played his role in the campaign. The Republican side of the Congress was organizing rallies across Maharashtra to create awareness amongst the public to have Veer Savarkar released. According to Seshadri, Hedgewar never minced his words:

> In convicting Savarkar the government has murdered justice; and if the government is interested in washing off this blot, let it forthwith release him. The government will not be bestowing any special favour if it was to release him now, after fourteen* years of cruel incarceration. If even now the government does not care to release him, it will only be one more evidence of its evil intentions towards our country.[28]

For most of his adolescent and adult life, Hedgewar had fought outwardly with the British. Inwardly, he fought with increasing intensity to make sense of the decrepitude of his own people—his own society. Outwardly, he pulled on themes similar to that of Calcagus, the Caledonian chieftain, a pagan warrior, in Tacitus's *Agricola*. The Hedgewarian mindset can be easily understood by using Calcagus's speech as mental scaffolding to help us understand his deeper narratives that ultimately shaped his mission. Tacitus, who is otherwise full of Roman praise in his chronicles, noted the following speech as apparently given by Calcagus on the day of battle to his 30,000 strong pagan army in the highlands of Scotland. It is worth quoting in full:

> Whenever I consider the origin of this war and the necessities of our position, I have a sure confidence that this day, and this union of yours, will be the beginning of freedom to the whole of Britain. To all of us slavery is a thing unknown; there are no lands beyond us, and even the sea is not safe, menaced as we are by a Roman fleet. And thus in war and battle, in which the brave find glory, even the coward will find safety. Former contests, in which, with varying fortune, the Romans were resisted, still left in us a last hope of succour, in as much as being the most renowned nation of Britain, dwelling in the very heart of the country, and out of sight of the shores of the conquered, we could keep even our eyes unpolluted by the contagion of slavery. To us who dwell on the uttermost

confines of the earth and of freedom, this remote sanctuary of Britain's glory has up to this time been a defence. Now, however, the furthest limits of Britain are thrown open, and the unknown always passes for the marvellous. But there are no tribes beyond us, nothing indeed but waves and rocks, and the yet more terrible Romans, from whose oppression escape is vainly sought by obedience and submission. Robbers of the world, having by their universal plunder exhausted the land, they rifle the deep. If the enemy be rich, they are rapacious; if he be poor, they lust for dominion; neither the east nor the west has been able to satisfy them. Alone among men they covet with equal eagerness poverty and riches. To robbery, slaughter, plunder, they give the lying name of empire; they make a dessert and call it peace.

Nature has willed that all man's children and kindred should be his dearest objects. Yet these are torn from us by conscriptions to be slaves elsewhere. Our wives and our sisters, even though they may escape violation from the enemy, are dishonoured under the names of friendship and hospitality. Our goods and fortunes they collect for their tribute, our harvests for their granaries. Our very hands and bodies, under the lash and in the midst of insult, are worn down by the toil of clearing forests and morasses. Creatures born to slavery are sold once and for all, and are, moreover, fed by their masters; but Britain is daily purchasing, is daily feeding, her own enslaved people. And as in a household the last comer among the slaves is always the butt of his companions, so we in a world long used to slavery, as the newest and most contemptible, are marked out for destruction. We have neither fruitful plains, nor mines, nor harbours, for the working of which we may be spared. Valour, too, and high spirit in subjects, are offensive to rulers; besides, remoteness and seclusion, while they give safety, provoke suspicion. Since then, you cannot hope for quarter, take courage, I beseech you, whether it be safety or renown that you hold most precious. Under a woman's leadership the Brigantes were able to burn a colony, to storm a camp, and had not success ended in supineness, might have thrown off the yoke. Let us, then, a fresh and unconquered people, never likely to abuse our freedom, show forthwith at the very first onset what heroes Caledonia has in reserve.

Do you suppose that the Romans will be as brave in war as they are licentious in peace? To our strife's and discords they owe their fame, and they turn the errors of an enemy to the renown of their own army, an

> army which, composed as it is of every variety of nations, is held together by success and will be broken up by disaster. These Gauls and Germans, and, I blush to say, these Britons, who, though they lend their lives to support a stranger's rule, have been its enemies longer than its subjects, you cannot imagine to be bound by fidelity and affection. Fear and terror there certainly are, feeble bonds of attachment; remove them, and those who have ceased to fear will begin to hate. All the incentives to victory are on our side. The Romans have no wives to kindle their courage; no parents to taunt them with flight, many have either no country or one far away. Few in number, dismayed by their ignorance, looking around upon a sky, a sea, and forests which are all unfamiliar to them; hemmed in, as it were, and enmeshed, the Gods have delivered them into our hands. Be not frightened by the idle display, by the glitter of gold and of silver, which can neither protect nor wound. In the very ranks of the enemy, we shall find our own forces. Britons will acknowledge their own cause; Gauls will remember past freedom; the other Germans will abandon them, as but lately did the Usipii. Behind them there is nothing to dread. The forts are ungarrisoned; the colonies in the hands of aged men; what with disloyal subjects and oppressive rulers, the towns are ill-affected and rife with discord. On the one side you have a general and an army: on the other, tribute, the mines, and all the other penalties of an enslaved people. Whether you endure these forever, or instantly avenge them, this field is to decide. Think, therefore, as you advance to battle, at once of your ancestors and of your posterity.[29]

We know that Stuart's translation of Tacitus's work was being circulated as early as 1915 amongst scholars, intellectuals and revolutionaries throughout the colonies to highlight the leviathan's obvious and flagrant hypocrisy.[30] Did Hedgewar read Stuart's translation? We cannot be sure. Certainly, it would have been in his ideosphere. Calcagus' charge that Romans were 'robbers of the world', 'rapacious' and had a 'lust for dominion' were charges that Hedgewar would have quite readily applied to the British. Even Calcagus's words, 'in the very ranks of the enemy, we shall find our own forces', would have deeply resonated with Hedgewar, for it was not lost on him that some of the heinous crimes against humanity that the British were guilty of were, in fact, carried out by loyal (to the British) Indian soldiers. The war cry of Calcagus and his draw to the land, to his kin and ancestors were all resonant to desh bhakts. They often wondered how could a country (Britain) that valued freedom so much be so committed to taking the freedom of other nations away. The world Calcagus found himself in 85 CE in the northernmost reaches of the Scottish Highlands, helps us understand the Hedgewarian perspective.

While brooding over such themes, he toured the central provinces, speaking on a range of issues, often drawing on the same visceral language as Calcagus to stoke the passions of freedom in his audiences. He was also fundraising for what would turn out to be one of his worst ideas. As it happens so often with outliers, their best idea is often preceded by their worst.

In mid-1923, Hedgewar decided to raise money from investors through a cooperative model to launch a daily newspaper. They named it *Swatantraya*. Swatantraya is a homonym, which can mean self-sufficient, freedom, sovereign or self-determining. The daily was meant to give a narrative in support of radical revolutionaries and drip feed gusto and political fervour to a sleepy, lethargic and divided Hindu society. The aim of the paper was to reshape the narrative that was being consumed by the literate masses and challenge what was coming out of the mainstay press, most of which was in a weekly, monthly or quarterly format. Media, which was in general favour of complete independence, was far and few in-between. The papers that were present, with sizeable circulation and readership, often divided themselves between advocating Gandhian 'Muslim appeasement' and angry communist revolution, which was not only anti-British but anti-everything that was Indian too. For Hedgewar, this situation was not tenable, and someone had to challenge the established news houses.

The newspaper was quite naturally based out of Nagpur, a regional centre, but by no means at the heart of anything significant. Furthermore, Nagpur would have had a smaller readership and even smaller number of people actually willing to pay for their news through subscriptions. Anyone who has run a publication knows that for a daily to be sustainable, it has to occupy a space in the market, which is not only uncatered for by existing media but also have a readership that is sizeable with disposable income to spend on the written word. Nagpur had very little of both.

Somehow, and it's not too difficult to imagine how, six friends, with Hedgewar and Khare in the centre, convinced themselves that it was a splendid idea to launch a media house on a sixpence. Exactly how they thought it would have been possible to run around the central regions, raise the cash from sympathizers, produce daily news pieces and build a distribution channel across Nagpur and surrounding districts all in a matter of months is a mystery. It was the surest sign of intelligent, earnest and very capable men, who, although well-intentioned, were blind-sided with overconfidence, who sadly failed to realize between them that they did not have the foggiest on how to run a commercial enterprise.

Six friends launched *Swatantrya* in mid-January 1924. It declared with great enthusiasm:

> The Indian National Congress has been working for the last three years towards the attainment of India's political goal, but that issue has not yet been properly solved. This daily has been started with the avowed object of defining in clear and unmistakable terms, the national goal of India... This daily will try its best to place before the public an ideal, quite in keeping with the dignity and tradition of Mother India.[31]

The language is unmistakably Hedgewar's. In the same tone, he went on to write that 'the independence we aim at is not the goal of any particular party but of the nation as a whole, and it is hoped that all the political parties in India would sink their differences and work in a united manner for the common cause.'[32] The underlying message of overcoming parochial identities and recognizing the fundamental unity of all Indians was, and still is, the central message of Hedgewar's creation—the RSS.

The intention may well have been constructive, but the new *Swatantraya* only proved to be divisive amongst the nationalist and the Republican side of the Congress. Hedgewar and his editorial team were uncompromising, and in their attempt to win the popular narrative, they lost the unity amongst nationalist papers. Their heavy-hitting editorials certainly made a mark and boasted a subscription base of 1200 in the first six months. This is rather remarkable considering that the well-established and influential *Mahratta* weekly had a base of 6000. The problem, as always unseen beforehand, was that the pro-independence media outlets were cannibalising their own support base. As *Swatantraya* launched and quickly gained traction through fire and spice in their editorials, subscriptions at the *Mahratta* fell from 6000 to under 5000. Coincidence?

Well, maybe, but quite unlikely. The Tilakites were not too pleased with this new upstart from Nagpur.

Even though the subscriptions rocketed temporarily, financially, the newspaper was in a tailspin, which further exacerbated the internal differences between the editors. By the end of 1924, the newspaper had a debt of approximately 11,000 rupees, which is equivalent to almost 1,500,000 today. Another way of looking at it is that an annual subscription cost around Rs 12, which gave the paper an annual income of less than Rs 15,000. The costs were spiralling out of control. Like all start-ups, recruiting and keeping talent is always difficult, especially when the business is under-capitalized. Writers came, made a quick splash and left as soon as they realized the newspaper was in financial difficulty. Hedgewar's pleas of doing the 'right thing' and 'for the nation' simply did not stand to reason in the face of market forces. Hedgewar himself never took a salary, and increasingly, as 1924 progressed, he ended up working harder and longer hours than any other. After all, the burden of debt was on his shoulders. No matter how hard he worked, ultimately, it was a sinking ship. And in early 1925, the newspaper was closed. People were made redundant, and investors were told that their money was lost.

Success, they say, has many fathers, but failure is an orphan. Hedgewar was that orphan. He wrote the last editorial. Hedgewar's little creation had a big bark, little bite and inadvertently had alienated many on the same side. The newspaper was uncompromising. It attacked anyone who showed even the slightest amount of hypocrisy, and none in politics can survive without a little hypocrisy. Even Moonjay was attacked for his remark that the Hindu Mahasabha should welcome the British Prime Minister's trip to India. In September 1924, a man called Moropant Joshi, a leading barrister who often defended the Hindu Mahasabha, had been offered a knighthood by the leviathan, which he readily accepted. This caused immense displeasure to the editors of *Swatantraya*, and they openly attacked the character of such lawyers. The paper had no support from any party, nor would the government ever advertise with it, and with little to no advertising revenue, the paper was untenable and losing friends fast.[33]

Finally, to rub further salt into a gaping wound, Hedgewar, out of principle, faced a legal lawsuit on behalf of the paper on a defamation charge. When asked to provide a list of authors and editors, he refused, out of solidarity with his colleagues who, on the whole, had abandoned him to face the music alone. The court case dragged on well into 1925, and in the end, it was dropped by the prosecution, largely because Hedgewar had little to no wealth, and the paper was bust.

Valuable lessons were learnt. First, that newspapers do not shape behaviour, especially in a population that was mostly illiterate. Second, money and resources matter. Third, idealism has its place, but it alone will not suffice in a commercial or political enterprise. Fourth, by being earnest and forthright, friends and allies can be lost, an outcome Hedgewar did not want. Fifth, and probably the most important, the social character of his fellow countrymen was such that petty interest and loyalties superseded the interests of the larger body politic.

RSS literature, in its usual overstated manner, makes a song and dance about what a remarkable endeavour the *Swatantraya* was. The reality seems to point in the opposite direction. Khare, a year later, wrote in another newspaper called *Tarun Bharat* that 'a lack of financial muscle and people not having a habit of reading dailies was the major cause for the experiment to fail'.[34] *Swatantraya* was a painful experience for Hedgewar. It was yet another setback. Since his release from prison, Hedgewar's life had been in a state of flux. He had no desire to pursue politics. A clarity had formed in his mind that politics was not the panacea to cure the real ailments of his country. He had reluctantly given up on armed revolution, realizing it was doomed to fail—his countrymen lacked the mettle to endure such a bloody escapade. He realized that the Congress, especially under Gandhi's leadership, was taking the country on a disastrous course to partition. Why was Indian society, and particularly Hindu society, in such dire straits? What was really at the root of this malaise? The answers, as difficult as they may have been to accept, were slowly being revealed in his mind's eye, and the solution, too, began to appear through the spectres of history and were seeded in his own setbacks.

In late 1924, when Ganesh 'Babarao' Savarkar came to Nagpur, his ideas further crystallized. Ganesh was an intense character. He was ferocious, even for the hardiest revolutionary. He was staying with Hedgewar's close friend Vishwanath Kelkar. The three of them would meet in the afternoon and be lost in discussion, exchanging viewpoints and even arguing late into the night. The three lamented the state of the Hindu society, its utter fall in word and deed.[35] All three were hardcore revolutionaries at heart and had completely dedicated their lives to the struggle. Ganesh was a youth magnet. Young people, often frustrated and angry at the dire state of their society, would gather around him and listen to his discussion forums. Ganesh was a poor public speaker but had tremendous presence and charm one-on-one. Even though he had the ability to motivate, he lacked the ability to implement anything significant from an organizational perspective. It was all too apparent to Hedgewar that the fire that raged inside Ganesh could not be wielded consistently and coherently. Ganesh himself was incapable of controlling his passions, which was the root cause of his inability to build anything substantial and long-lasting. Ganesh also knew his own limitations and was deeply aware that his own constitution had become frail after years of punishment endured through hard labour on the prison island—the Andamans. 'Sometimes', wrote Elizabeth Berg, 'serendipity is just intention unmasked.'[36] Perfectly apt. In Hedgewar's mind, he knew perfectly well what he had to do. These conversations, stretching late into the night, crystallized his mission and seemed to have just tipped him over the edge to start putting into motion the foundations of what would quickly become an organizational force to be reckoned with.

Even as his newspaper venture was coming to its unavoidable end, and he was going through the trauma of making people redundant and informing angry investors that their money was lost, he was increasingly spending his spare time with young people—coaching and mentoring.

On one such occasion, a group of boys from Ganesh Sarvarkar's Hindu Tarun Sabha—a group formed to instil the revolutionary spirit in youth—were being trained by Hedgewar. They were learning to swim in a nearby tank of water no more than five to ten metres in each direction. A thirteen-year-old boy was walking by, gazing at the group of boys splashing about in the cooling water. Hedgewar caught his eye and, as was his way, asked the boy if he too wanted to join the rest of the boys in the water. The boy meekly said he could not swim. Hedgewar, in his usual cheery manner, said, 'So what? Jump in if you dare.' The boy quickly stripped down to his shorts and took a running leap to bomb the pool. Hedgewar was impressed with the audacity of this strange boy and his sheer gusto to take on a challenge.[37] This was how Gopal Rao Yerkuntwar, as a teenager, came to know Hedgewar. The two would form a deep connection in the form of an inspirer and inspired. Gopal Rao would go on to become a lifelong prachaarak of the RSS and one of its early pioneers. Another boy in that same group many years later recounted how Hedgewar in those days would walk around the city and meet as many youths as possible, generally asking about their welfare, studies and families.[38] This boy also became a lifelong swayamsevak of the RSS and a distinguished professor in later life —Professor P. K. Savlapurkar.

Why did Hedgewar, at age thirty-five, begin to re-orientate himself in this direction? This is not the act of a man who desired power. Indeed, it's even more odd when we consider that Hedgewar was on the cusp of what so many men crave for—political office. Yet, Hedgewar was already aware of how such an opportunity could also be a poisoned chalice. Rather, this was a man who consciously rejected power and fame while already having drawn conclusions that the nature of democracy would only lead to further disintegration of his society, until, the social character of the individual could be transformed. There were two things driving Hedgewar in those days—first, he probably found a little solace when he was in the company of youth with their raw energy coupled with ingenuity, wit and creativity. Second, he was now beginning to observe how that which was percolating in his mind might manifest.

On 12 and 13 July 1924, Muslim communalism reared its ugly head again. Hindu festivals and noisy processions were an anathema for Muslim clerics. They quickly made plans to disrupt proceedings. This time, Hedgewar and Moonjay were better prepared. Their year of planning and training youth in self-defence, fitness and strength, and a martial art that involved the wielding of a bamboo stick rather ferociously, was their main hope of protecting pilgrims. They knew that most Hindus were meek and frightened by intimidating Muslim gangs.

On 12 July 1924, a Muslim gang attacked a small Hindu procession at a place called Rajwada in Nagpur. It was twenty minutes away by foot from where Hedgewar stayed. Only a year before, at the very same place, the Maharaja had supported the Hindu community in its rights to observe religious ceremonies in the city. Now this particular Muslim gang, incited by clerics, had chosen this very spot to start the intimidation. On another occasion, the Maharaja and his family may have been intimidated and backed off, but this time, Hedgewar and Moonjay had organized youths in small squads to patrol key junctions and locations. They had also evacuated

Hindu families in Muslim majority areas a few days earlier. According to some eyewitness accounts, around thirty Muslim rioters were injured, and what was reported as a Hindu stand was actually the stand made by a minority of Hindu youth who had been well-drilled and organized.[39] The Hindu community of Nagpur and Hedgewar, in particular, took much heart at what was possible if only a few Hindus could be organized, trained and spirited to protect land and kin.

NINE: 1925–1927

It Begins

Hindutva, a term that for the faithful represents resurgence, modernity, decoloniality and progress.[1] This is a term, for many, that sheds the colonial tropes and prejudices that have plagued the Hindu identity for centuries. For those who are the intellectual descendants of the British, 'the brown sahibs', the term means anything from fascism to ethnic absolutism.[2] In late 1924, Hedgewar came across Vinayak 'Veer' Sarvarkar's book, *Hindutva*, which crystallized everything that had been percolating in his mind—spirited ideas that had no form, now finally had a lexicon. Hindutva gave Hedgewar the scaffolding he required to articulate what he felt was the problem with Hindu society and its potential indigenous remedy.

In March 1925, Hedgewar, along with his friend Vishwanath Kelkar, went to see Vinayak Savarkar. Hedgewar's university classmate and friend Narayan Savarkar, Vinayak's younger brother, also joined them eight miles outside of Pune at a place called Shirgaon. Vinayak was a household name, and his legacy remains as important and pronounced as Gandhi's and Ambedkar's in shaping modern India. Vinayak had spent eleven hard years in the leviathan's prison island of Andaman. He was a resident of the notorious Cellular Jail. After eleven hard years of labour, he was released and, in turn, vowed never to participate in any revolutionary activity. Vinayak's body had become frail and somewhat diminutive, but his mind was as sharp as ever. Even after his release, he was confined to travelling and living only in Ratnagiri, a small port city in south-west Maharashtra. Ratnagiri was somewhat of a sleepy backwater town, a place that the British could easily watch over. The three friends stayed together with Vinayak for three days.[3] We have no records of what was discussed, nor did anyone present ever speak about this meeting. It is, however, uncanny that Hedgewar met all three brothers in quick succession between 1924 and early 1925 before taking the most significant step of his life.

Hindutva, which means Hinduness, was originally a pamphlet that was turned into a short book in 1928. It is written in a prose more akin to a fiery speech than an academic essay, where statements are often unsubstantiated, and assumptions presented as arguments. Having said that, the ideas contained therein are nothing short of revolutionary for any desh bhakt. The prose is direct, descriptive and penetrating. The ideas in the book attempt to explain the identity of the Hindu—who are the Hindus, from where have they come, and makes the argument for India being the natural home of the Hindu people. Vinayak was not a religious man; indeed, quite the opposite, he was a well-known atheist.[4] His atheism made no difference to him or his Hindutva. He effectively carved out Hindu culture and civilization from religion. He also goes on to make claims about how it was that Hindu civilization fell from grace and into the depths of a long servitude—first with the Islamic conquests and then under the European colonial project.

His argument revolves around the fact that the Hindu culture, first with the rise of Buddhism and then under the weight of its own corruption, had forgotten its own martial spirit and had deviated too much towards renunciation and asceticism. The height and aspiration for the Hindus became otherworldly, all the while neglecting worldly matters of economy, war and human welfare. Its best progeny was vacuumed up to become monks and nuns rather than warriors and administrators. The Hindu worship of 'shakti', that is, energy or potency, was replaced by a worship of milder deities, which were only interested in a release of suffering and an existence in other higher realms. Consequently, the Hindu became increasingly confused, careless about worldly matters and even callous, especially towards one's own.

He also argues that Buddhism's universalism and somewhat cultural relativism led the Hindu to be accepting of anyone and anything, which effectively made the culture wide open for exclusivist ideologies, such as Islam and Christianity, in later years. He writes 'The foe that has nothing in common with us is the foe likely to be most bitterly resisted by us just as a friend that has almost everything in him that we admire and prize in ourselves is likely to be a friend we love most.'[5] Buddhism in its search for universal appeal inadvertently made every culture 'the same' as a means to find common grounds with foreign peoples. For Savarkar, this meant 'everything that is common in us with our enemies, weakens our power of opposing them.'[6] Furthermore, the national spirit, according to Savarkar, was corroded when the Buddhist fraternity began to favour 'outsiders' so long as they were sympathetic towards Buddhism. Often, these outsiders were foreign warlords fighting fellow Hindu kings of their own soil. He compares this to how 'Catholic Spain could always find some important section in England to sympathize with their efforts to restore a Catholic dynasty in England.'[7] While critiquing Buddhism, Savarkar continuously reminds the reader that this is no reflection on the Buddha and his Sangha (community), for they are Hindu and have contributed immensely to the national character.

For Savarkar, the Hindu was, in essence, anyone who was a desh bhakt. While Dharma was indeed universal, one had to understand that the Hindu civilization was a unique cultural unit designated by not only geography and a collective history but also through custom, tradition, language(s) and culture. What Hedgewar most liked about Savarkar's argument was his call that the Hindu identity was not negationist as the British, and their colonial intellectual prodigy would believe—that a Hindu is anyone who is not a Christian, Muslim, Jain, Buddhist, Sikh and so on.[8] For the British, there was no real substantive thing called a Hindu. Hindu meant clumping together a multitude of tribes and clans with a diversity of beliefs and traditions that could be broadly called Hindu. For Hedgewar, being a Hindu was a positive identity. Savarkar made his point in 1924 in the following manner:

> If some Indian, as gifted as that Englishman who first the coined the word Hinduism, coins a parallel word "Englishism" and proceeds to find out the underlying unity of beliefs amongst the English people, gets disgusted with thousands of sects and societies from Jews to the Jacobins, from Trinitarians to Utilitarians, and comes out to announce that "there are no such people as the English at all", he would not make himself more ridiculous than those who declare in cold print "there is nothing as a Hindu people".[9]

These arguments still prevail in modern scholarship and the battlelines remain stark as ever. There are those who claim that there is no objective identity that is Hindu. Rather, the term itself denotes just a basket of different cultures and traditions. Most Western academics still build their understanding of modern India through this assumption. It is one of the reasons why the West still cannot see India for what she really is and fails to understand her in any meaningful way. The foundational constructs of the West are rooted in the colonial project. Until and unless the West is prepared to re-root its assumptions about India and her civilization, Hedgewar's India will stride ahead, remaining at best 'exotic' and, at worst, a 'false ghost'—one that is contrary to Western universal values and therefore resisted. To understand the RSS, one must understand how Savarkar's word was made flesh by Hedgewar in 1925.

Interestingly, had the Indian author and politician Shashi Tharoor and Hedgewar ever met, there would have been much they would have agreed on. Much like Hedgewar, Tharoor buys into the idea of India as a 'land of his ancestors' and 'a sacred geography knit together by countless tracks of pilgrimage'.[10] His ancestors were Hindu, and the pilgrimages he refers to are also Hindu, dating back thousands of years. The land Tharoor claims as his own is, therefore, Hindu. Hedgewar, much like Tharoor, is rooted in the same philosophical substratum as many respected intellectuals such as Radhakrishnan, Aurobindo Ghosh and Tagore. The differences between them are not all that divergent regarding the Hindu society. Almost every historian accepts that Hindu society is rooted in a primordial past. They also agree that it has lasted a very long time, having reached great heights of civilization and knowledge, which then declined in thought and deed. They would also concede the point that serious reformation was necessary. Some differences emerged in their solutions. However, the major differences came in how to make sense of the non-Hindu, or those that had the same ancestry but now had adopted a completely different religion—namely Islam, and a mongrel culture of Hindu, Arab, African, Persian and European.

Savarkar's Hindutva gave language and clarity to Hedgewar. Savarkar gave him the language to focus on mobilizing the Hindus to reform their own society. In other words, Hedgewar was able to reconcile the heights of the Hindu past with the need for rapid and total reformation of Hindu society without rejecting its central tenets and traditions. Hedgewar, much like today's social justice movement, was against all forms of caste—period! Social justice movements in India presuppose a social order that is non-discriminatory and people-orientated, one in which disparity, inequality, and inequity do not characterize social, economic and other aspects of life.[11] Hedgewar would have signed up to this without too much hesitation. The challenge for Hedgewar, and today's RSS is that liberal-minded social justice warriors supported by the likes of Tharoor, have diluted what it means to be a Hindu to such a degree in order to accommodate illiberal, exclusivist and intolerant elements, which ultimately could not have a place in modern Hindu society. Karl Popper says it best, and Hedgewar would have agreed:

> Less well known is the paradox of tolerance: Unlimited tolerance must lead to the disappearance of tolerance. If we extend unlimited tolerance even to those who are intolerant, if we are not prepared to defend a tolerant society against the onslaught of the intolerant, then the tolerant will be destroyed, and tolerance with them.—In this formulation, I do not imply, for instance, that we should always suppress the utterance of intolerant philosophies; as long as we can counter them by rational argument and keep them in check by public opinion, suppression would certainly be most unwise. But we should claim the right to suppress them if necessary, even by force; for it may easily turn out that they are not prepared to meet us on the level of rational argument, but begin by denouncing all argument; they may forbid their followers to listen to rational argument, because it is deceptive, and teach them to answer arguments by the use of their fists or pistols. We should therefore claim, in the name of tolerance, the right not to tolerate the intolerant. We should claim that any movement preaching intolerance places itself outside the law and we should consider incitement to intolerance and persecution as criminal, in the same way as we should consider incitement to murder, or to kidnapping, or to the revival of the slave trade, as criminal.[12]

Popper was a Hedgewarian; he just didn't know it.

After his brief but impactful meetings with Vinayak, he returned to Nagpur. Between March and September of that year, he resigned from all his political posts. Moonjay, who was a father figure, mentor and confidante for Hedgewar, would have known but not understood why his political protégé was undoing everything he had achieved over the last few decades. Even though it is quite likely that Moonjay did not understand Hedgewar's drive and direction, he would have had a father's instinct—he would have known his protégé had outgrown any vision he could have had for him. Moonjay was the bow from which Hedgewar's life's arrow was released and now travelling swift and far.[13] He would have sensed the depth of his boy, a depth that he could not fathom. Yet it was there. Stirring deep within. Hedgewar was thirty-six years old.

On 27 September 1925, Hedgewar invited a handful of friends to his house. He ushered those who arrived through a side entrance that led them to an upstairs room. His sister-in-law played the host and offered guests chai and a customary water pitcher. It was a Sunday. Everyone arrived by three in the afternoon. It was an auspicious day in the Hindu calendar—Vijaya Dashami. For nine continuous nights leading up to this day, Hindus all over India mark the occasion of the hero King Rama having won a war against the tyrannical King Ravana. Hindu culture is full of festivals based on the great Hindu epics—the Ramayana and the Mahabharata. Vijaya Dashami commemorates the eventual victory of *satya* (truth) over *avidya* (ignorance). It is generally misconstrued in modern renderings of Hindu epics as good versus evil—but of course Hindu culture has never thought in such frameworks.

Hedgewar stood steady as the invited friends took their seats on the floor, sitting cross-legged. Vishwanath Kelkar, a childhood friend, lawyer and local member of the Hindu Mahasabha; Bhaauji Kaavare, another childhood friend who had been at the helm of the local struggle from their days in school; Prabhakar Daani, a seventeen-year-old boy who would dedicate his entire life to the RSS, and would go onto become the powerhouse of the movement, and become its General Secretary (Sar-kar-ya-vaha) in 1946; Dada (meaning brother in Marathi) Parmarth, who would also go on to become a life-long prachaarak, developing the work of the RSS in India's North-East; Bala Huddar, another inspired and capable young man who would lead an extraordinary life by becoming one of the leaders of the RSS in the years to come, before joining the Spanish Civil War as a committed Communist and who would later join the Communist Party of India. All these young men, with their destinies still unrevealed, sat looking at Hedgewar. There were ten other young men in the room that day.[14]

'Today', declared Hedgewar in somewhat of a poised tone, 'the Sangh begins'.[15] He could have said I, or we, will start the Sangh today, but he chose to speak in the third person. This is telling of Hedgewar's inner world. The young tearaway who thought he could liberate his country by sheer brawn had grown far deeper roots than any had suspected. To say that the 'Sangh begins' is to suggest that *we* are not the doer of deeds but rather the vessels through which the Sangh manifests. The Sangh, according to Hedgewar, has an independent life of its own, and it has now found swayamsevaks, that is, loyal volunteers, who will embody it. The Sangh, therefore, is a collection of timeless values, traditions, the dignity of a people, the belonging of a people to its land and a collective memory of a civilization, all driven towards a particular destination—that of *Vishwa Shanti* (world peace), something which has been codified in the daily prayer of the RSS.

He went on to spell out what he believed were the root causes behind the fall of Hindu society and, ultimately, Indian society. First, Hindus lacked any coherent sense of nationhood, without which there was nothing to bind them into anything meaningful. After centuries of persecution and political obscurity, the Hindu mind had lost all sight of what it meant to belong to one's own nation and be in control of one's own destiny. Second, there was a serious dearth of desh bhakti in the common person. Without a sense of love and affection for one's own land, a people would not be willing to come together to make that land and her people prosperous and progressive. A people who only have disdain for what is theirs will, at best, neglect their heritage and, at worst, look to destroy all traces of it in an attempt to liberate themselves from their own self-delusions. Third, without a sense of desh bhakt*i*, the common Indian lacked any substantial sense of self-respect. When a society en masse feels that all things that are other, foreign and exotic are always better than anything indigenous, then that society will lose its capacity to create and will become completely dependent on external forces. Fourth, he spelt out the inherent selfishness of the common Hindu, who had become so parochial and trapped in his own creation of caste, tribe and religion. In the Hindu's parochiality, one had lost all sense of what it meant to be a responsible citizen—someone who cared for his fellow neighbour, who saw their neighbours as their own and ultimately understood the interconnectedness of their own well-being with that of the community's. Fifth, stuck as they were in their own ghettoized hierarchy of caste and creed, the Hindu society was incapable of solving any of its own problems. It had become a stale society over hundreds of years, where innovation had largely dried up, and knowledge fossilized in the hands of a few. Finally, the Hindu, who could personify Bharat Mata (the Earth as a mother) and worship her, had nevertheless lost all sight of what Bharat was: her geography, her landmass, her customs and traditions and so on. The common Hindu could no longer psychologically connect with any other person who was outside one's own caste, creed or language belt.[16]

'The Sangh begins today to rehabilitate Bharat (Indian society) from these ailments.'

With these lofty aims, one could be forgiven for thinking that there may have been some deep discussions on the name, charter, finances and promotion of the new organization. Nothing of the sort happened. The only thing that was decided was that it was paramount that men between the ages of twelve and thirty be contacted and encouraged to attend the local *akhadas*. Here, they would train and go through some form of diluted military training. The hope was to build a community of young men that was disciplined, fit and martial. Furthermore, his hope was that through the training, these young men would become fraternal and thereby transcend their prejudices linked to their group identities. He hoped that they would learn to judge individuals on merit—not caste or creed. Hedgewar's vision, with respect to human development, was individualistic and egalitarian from its very inception. The focus lay on each individual regardless of his background. What mattered was his reliability. Was he an organizer? Was he courageous? Was he intelligent? Was he articulate? Was he able to learn and then teach others?

It is, therefore, somewhat perplexing that modern renderings from respected academics such as Christophe Jaffrelot still hark on colonial tropes; namely that the Sangh was started to maintain caste hierarchies.[17] This trope is particularly potent in the minds of journalists and commentators, and it has been reported so many times that it has become common sense amongst historians of modern India. However, nothing from Hedgewar or the early swayamsevaks suggests anything of the sort. Indeed, while academics and journalists buoyed by each other have been misrepresenting the Sangh, the organization itself just keeps on working tirelessly—a behavioural trait that should be expected. One only has to understand Hedgewar's childhood influences such as Ramdas's *Manobodh* to get a sight of his real motives.

As much as the Sangh was about consolidating Hindu society and training its young men to be physically stronger, better disciplined and politically conscious, there was another side to the movement. This was its martial spirit. Hedgewar knew that the state no longer monopolised violence. The massacre of Hindus in Malabar was the most significant case in point, but even recent incidents in Nagpur and countless other towns and cities had shown Hedgewar that the state, without a monopoly on violence, was incapable of protecting the Hindu community. The

Hindu community was headlong committed to Gandhi's non-violence movement. It had completely opened itself to abuses of all sorts—from minor miscreants harassing Hindu women to full-blown genocidal attacks. If the state was incapable of monopolizing violence and thereby treating each subject equally under the law, then the Hindu society would have to become capable of wielding just enough force to repel any would-be aggressor. To that end, Hedgewar was clear that Hindus had to rely on their own martial spirit to protect life and property. Robert Rotberg, in his book, *When States Fail*, describes the Hedgerwarian perspective well:

> States fail because they are convulsed by internal violence and can no longer deliver positive political goods to their inhabitants. Their governments lose legitimacy, and the very nature of the particular nation-state itself becomes illegitimate in the eyes and in the hearts of a growing plurality of its citizens.[18]

The British state, having lost its legitimacy with an increasing number of its subjects, was becoming impotent against the increasing anarchy that was becoming prevalent in Indian society. Assertive communities, which were ambitious enough to take advantage of a growing power vacuum, were increasingly using force to get what they wanted. In reprisal or fear, other communities mobilized and asserted themselves, which further fed the cycle of threat and violence. The first to assert themselves after the Great War were Islamic groups with their yearning for the re-establishment of a Caliphate and for India to become part of the wider Dar al-Islam.[19] The Communists were not far behind. At this time, there were many small, uncoordinated groups working throughout India against the leviathan. However, they were also deeply influenced by foreign powers, who were hostile towards Hindu culture.[20]

Because of these reasons, Hedgewar asked Anna Sohoni, a well-built martial artist, to introduce hand-to-hand combat skills, martial skills with the *danda* and even deadly dagger training. Sohoni was charismatic, and his martial skills attracted plenty of young boys to the Sunday training sessions held once a week. In the early days of Hedgewar's creation, boys were expected to join a gym and exercise daily. Additionally, extra sessions were held every week—one for Sohoni's martial arts training and the other at local houses, twice a week, to run what became called *Bauddhik* sessions. In Hindi, the term means intellectual. In the Sangh, bauddhiks were designed to build the political awareness of swayamsevaks. They would often take the shape of storytelling to inspire the young men and instil a particular sense of pride towards oneself and one's cultural heritage. These sessions were taken by Hedgewar himself or his friend Kelkar. At these sessions, swayamsevaks were instructed to read copiously, especially in English. Then there was Martand Jog, a former soldier of the Imperial army of the leviathan, who taught them militarized marching techniques and drilled them in formations and organizational training. He initially split his time between the Sangh and the Congress Seva Dal, which was the youth wing of the National Congress. In time, he would completely dedicate his time to developing the Sangh.

Hedgewar's Sangh was organizing and militarizing Hindu boys in Nagpur. Young men flocked to the training offered. Numbers swelled without much effort. Every man across Nagpur felt the need to organize, mobilize and train to protect one's own. In these days of increasing anarchy, brute force was becoming right. With a lack of law and order, Hindus were compelled to protect themselves. Hedgewar was creating the means through which the society could do so. Throughout this period the Republican side of the Congress, now renamed as the Hindu Mahasabha, supported Hedgewar's experiment from afar. Moonjay was always kept informed, and he often attended and spoke at many of the gatherings. Additionally, Ganesh Savarkar remained close to the Sangh during these early days, often encouraging those in his sphere of influence to attend its almost daily sessions. Ganesh was effectively encouraging existing youth groups, which were created two years earlier by the Hindu Mahasabha as a reaction to the Islamic militancy in the town, to merge into the Sangh. There was an active consolidation happening amongst Hindu youth groups. The Sangh, in a matter of months, became the youth movement of Nagpur with clear support from its political class.

Soon, Hedgewar and his band of merry men needed more space. They found a disused patch of land that had been overrun by shrubs at a place called Mohite Wada in the Mahal area near Hedgewar's home. The word 'wada' refers to a large set of wooden doors, which were often entrances to the private courtyards of the rich. This patch of red dusty land backed onto some old walls and a pair of gates at least three hundred and fifty years old. Volunteers cleared the land and claimed it as their own. This is where the first daily shakha, meaning branch, was started. Today, this patch of soil is almost sacred for the millions of men and women across India who have been inspired or touched by Hedgewar's creation. Every day since 28 May 1926, daily shakha has taken place on these grounds. Adjacent to the dusty ground are trees, which provide a much-needed cooling effect to the ground in the hot summer months. Behind these trees are now the Nagpur central offices of the RSS, a place which is surprisingly sleepy, and which is a residence for retired lifelong prachaaraks who are taken care of by local volunteers. It is also home to the archives that have been pivotal in researching this book. There is an entire room dedicated to all the letters and correspondence relating to Hedgewar's life. It's austere in its décor, clean and cool. It is surprisingly welcoming with a jovial atmosphere among the volunteers and residents. The general ethos of the place was nicely summed up by one of the prachaaraks resident there. 'Take the work seriously, but not yourself', he exclaimed, while grinning ear to ear, showing his teeth underneath the longer bristles of his whitened moustache.

The grounds at Mohite Wada in 1926 had become overgrown with shrubs, and the grand house had fallen into disrepair. It was once owned by a wealthy widow who was a sympathizer to the independence struggle. She had often allowed meetings to be held in her home fifteen years earlier when Hedgewar was a young rabble-rouser and led the youth movements in Nagpur. He remembered the house well. The lady of the house had died with no heirs, and her property had become derelict. With the leaders of the city on his side, he had got permission to use the property as he saw fit. He and his fellow volunteers of the Sangh began to clear the grounds. Hedgewar, as was his manner, led from the front with shovel and spade in hand. In the scorching thirty-five-degree sun, they removed the rubble from the grounds. The basement of the house was still intact, but the rest of the house had caved in. After weeks of work, the ground was fit for physical activities, and the basement usable for meetings and small private gatherings.

It wasn't until 17 April 1926 that those organizing the daily activities decided that the movement should be named. Twenty-six organizers met at Hedgewar's home. It was a sweltering Saturday. The discussion of what the name ought to be had been going on for several months, and many names were suggested. Eventually, three were shortlisted of which, finally, the Rashtriya Swayamsevak Sangh was selected.[21] The word Sangh simply means community or group and was quite common in those days. Another common word was swayamsevak (Swa-yam-sevak), meaning self-volunteer. The word *Rāṣṭra* means nation. The suffix 'triya' after Rashtra broadens the term and adds a layer of ambiguity. The word itself is debated even today as to its exact meaning and application. The broad consensus suggests that it means nationhood. This is certainly how Hedgewar would have intended it. The Rashtriya swayamsevak Sangh (RSS) literally means the 'Community of Volunteers for the Nation'. A framing such as this will certainly disappoint those who have built an industry out of caricaturing the RSS as a dark menace, highly organized and militant, with a single-minded objective to harm anyone that gets in its way. The RSS, from its very inception, has been a movement to reform Hindu society first and foremost and then to promote the idea of Rāṣṭra amongst all citizens.

According to a young man present there that day, months previously, the name had been suggested and broadly agreed upon, but no final decision had been taken. Hedgewar was insistent that all formal decisions be taken in formalised meetings and appropriate minutes taken. Decisions should always be taken in meetings, and every person present at the meeting be given the opportunity to question, think and suggest alternative names.[22] Other names were considered, but ultimately all those present, after some deliberation, settled on the RSS. There is something to be said about this insistence on decisions being made in groups and through consensus building rather than through hierarchies or voting rights. Even teens, so long as they held a formal responsibility in the shakha, had to be consulted and their thoughts and opinions considered. This was quite revolutionary in the context of Indian society, which for millennia had been overly hierarchical and tribal—where groups had to simply concede to the whims of elders. The RSS today insists on an egalitarian structure among what it calls its 'karyakarini', a group of individuals who hold formal responsibility within the organization.

Hedgewar, with the help of senior volunteers, in May 1926, formalised the smallest organizational unit of the RSS—a shakha. According to the RSS, there are over 84,000 shakhas across every nook and cranny of India.[23] Back in May 1926, the first shakha was formalized. Each shakha would consist of roughly thirty to forty men. It was sixty minutes long, consisting of physical exercise, some martial training and organizational training. The shakha was run in a format one would have found on any military training ground, with clear instructions being barked out by the instructors in English. Early on, during the initial few months, the shakha would have appeared as any other outdoor gymnasium, but as the shakha became formalized and daily, it became apparent that Hedgewar's creation was something far more potent and with purpose. Martand Jog, at the behest of Hedgewar, created cavalry units, which caused a stir amongst the locals. To ride horses was the prestige of the few—the elite, the military, the police forces and the rich with titled lands. Hedgewar now had swayamsevaks from all strata of society learning how to ride horses, and not just for recreational use but something far more significant.

It is still said in the RSS that the shakha can take any form. Each shakha can be altered to suit the needs of its local people. The only two things which must remain consistent through every shakha are the saffron dhvaj *(flag)* and the recitation of the *prarthana* (prayer) at the end of each shakha. The original Sangh prarthana was a combination of Marathi and Hindi stanzas.[24] The Marathi words were taken verbatim from prayers sung in local schools, and the Hindi was taken from the Arya Samaj, which was another Hindu resurgence movement working against the leviathan.[25] The Sangh prarthana today has evolved and is quite a poetic work when sung in Sanskrit. It is an all-encompassing prayer asking whatever divinity there may be to instil virtue in everyone so that they may have what it takes to fulfil the Sangh's mission to build a harmonious, progressive and peaceful society. To date, commentators on the RSS seldom talk about the daily prayer sung after every shakha throughout India—this is puzzling considering the prayer itself clearly outlines the mission and purpose of the RSS and how it intends to fulfil it. The dhvaj is the symbol of Dharma. A timeless symbol of Hindu civilization, which everyone from the Buddha's Sangha to Hedgewar's Sangh has taken inspiration from. There are very few symbols that every Hindu can relate to—the saffron triangular flag is one of them.

That same year (1926), at a place called Ramtek in Nagpur, thousands of pilgrims descended upon the grounds to mark Ram Navami, a festival celebrating the birth of King Rama from the Hindu epic, the Ramayana. As usual, it was a bundle of chaos with few facilities, organization or security provided. The state could no longer deploy adequate resources. Anarchy once again reigned. This time Hedgewar, along with Raghunath Bande, who was the designated lead of the shakha, organized the swayamsevaks into units to provide a sense of order and some basic facilities such as drinking water stations, a place where first aid could be administered and a resting spot for elderly pilgrims to rest.[26] The swayamsevaks were, for the first time, in uniform. The uniform was wholly taken from the Bharat Sevak Samaj, an organization of the Indian National Congress, which was created to organize the Nagpur session a few years earlier and was overseen by Hedgewar and his friend Paranjape. The uniform consisted of khaki shorts, a khaki shirt and a matching double-buttoned cap. The intention was for the swayamsevaks to be noted not only by the pilgrims but also by the authorities. Those on security ensured a sense of gravitas and safety against pickpockets, con artists and those selling charms and other bits of hocus-pocus to often uneducated villagers. These were opportune moments for the Sangh to recruit new youth to its shakhas, which now numbered eight.

Hedgewar spent his days travelling the city and surrounding districts, meeting as many swayamsevaks as possible. He usually walked everywhere. He was courteous, caring and gentle with his own. He had seen from his days in the Congress how badly volunteers were treated. For Hedgewar, the RSS was to provide a deep sense of camaraderie and a feeling of well-being. He would enquire not only about the health and overall well-being of each swayamsevak, but also visit their families. He would use his deep and extensive networks to help people with finding the right job, pursuing further education or getting access to medical treatment. He would make himself useful for the Sangh. He ensured that swayamsevaks supported each other in all aspects and were never left to feel alone and isolated. He also broke customs prevalent in the Hindu community which he deemed as backward and prejudiced. He would eat at the houses of all Hindus, whosoever they were, and not allow the stigma of untouchability or backwardness to get in the way of building meaningful relationships. In these small acts lay Hedgewar's genius. To this day, the backbone of the RSS, with its millions of swayamsevaks, is relationship building. The original master of 'how to win friends and influence people' was Hedgewar.

Today, the RSS has tens of thousands of organizations that are in some way related to it. These organizations work independently in every stratum of Indian society, from health accessibility to poverty alleviation, providing quality education, elderly care services, workers unions, ex-military personnel support groups, women's bodies, organizations dedicated to removing caste consciousness, animal welfare groups, to even Muslim organizations dedicated to integrating young Muslims into mainstream society. Researchers and commentators who have never quite understood the organizational structure of the Sangh Parivar, that is the collective name given to these bodies related to the RSS, remain perplexed and confused at how they work in tandem.

When the shores of their knowledge are reached, they begin to imagine. And academics, especially those specializing in South Asia, have a mighty imagination. To read a well-cited book on the RSS, *Khaki Shorts and Saffron Flags: Critique of the Hindu Right*, one would think that the RSS is some deeply hierarchical patriarchal organization that has strict codes of command and control and millions upon millions of naïve Indians have been brainwashed to obey every command of their sinister supreme leader who sits on his throne in Nagpur.[27] Nothing could be more comical to the average Sangh worker today. To understand the RSS, one needs to understand the wheels that Hedgewar had put in motion as early as 1926.

The Sangh Parivar is not as it appears in the imaginings of academics sitting at Harvard or India's Jawaharlal Nehru University (JNU). In reality, there is no formal control whatsoever in the RSS. The entire Sangh edifice is built upon the relationships that have formed in daily or weekly shakhas between swayamsevaks over decades of working together. The RSS provides organizational training, skills and purpose to its swayamsevaks, nothing more. Countless swayamsevaks, having become aware and duty-bound to serve their fellow citizens, naturally see it as their responsibility to alleviate the ills they perceive. They venture off into the direction that compels them. They attract other like-minded people, those who have been trained in the RSS shakhas and those who may never have visited a shakha. These organizations work independently from the RSS, having been inspired by swayamsevaks, who founded the organization. These organizations are loosely held in tandem and lend support to each other through a network, a network even more subtle—the prachaarak order.

prachaaraks spend their lives meeting people and keeping a bond through a mild blend of friendship and purpose. Prachaaraks are men and women (prachaarikas) who devote large chunks of their lives to serve the Sangh. These are full-time volunteers who live incredibly simple lives and forgo family and personal ambition. Through the prachaarak order, the RSS maintains its subtle influence on thousands of organizations across the country. Yet, the prachaarak, although highly respected, has no formal authority or power anywhere in these organizations. They can only influence, advise and guide but have no formal jurisdiction to command. These are master organizers and highly capable individuals and through their talents they wield their influence, but nothing more. These were, and still are, the checks and balances to power that Hedgewar had put into place from the earliest years of the RSS. Hedgewar was the first prachaarak, and although that word was not in use in 1926, it was certainly in his mind.

In May 1927, almost two years into his experiment, Hedgewar and his inner circle felt that it was time to create an Officers Training Camp (OTC) where the most competent swayamsevaks would be selected to attend the camp for extensive training. The aim of the OTC was to train volunteers to a level where they could go anywhere in the country, set up shakhas and run them with minimal oversight. OTCs ensured that the decentralized nature of the RSS could be maintained and could continue to grow at speed with minimal control from any centralized authority. Once again, the ground reality of the RSS is very different to the perceived imaginings of the ivory tower. As a point in case, Tapan Basu writes, 'the shakha is an instrument where the individual is told to submit completely to the will of the supreme leader.'[28] Suppose one is to consider Hedgewar, his motives and inspirations. In that case, it becomes abundantly clear that the shakha was designed to do the exact opposite—that is, to enhance the individual to become a self-respecting, organized, conscious citizen and one who is critically minded. Indeed, the self-thinking swayamsevak has been one of the key reasons why the Sangh has spread so far and wide almost autonomously. H.V. Seshadri writes, 'The object of the programme was to equip the swayamsevaks to enable them to carry on Sangh activities on their own, wherever they might go.'[29]

The first OTC had seventeen participants. Days started at five in the morning, with two to three hours of physical and martial arts training consisting of hand-to-hand combat, dagger training and fighting techniques with the bamboo stick.[30] This kind of training certainly would not fit well into the sanitized minds of today's Europeans, or even Indians for that matter, but in a world of increasing anarchy and rising community tensions, with little law and order, one can appreciate the vanguard nature of the early Sangh. After a break at nine, the participants would gather again to participate in sessions concerning Indian history, colonialism and its effects on the Hindu mind, revolutionary theory, Mazzini's nationalism, Savarkar's writings on the First War of Independence and understanding Marxism.[31] From these humble beginnings, today's OTC is called Sangh Shiksha Varg (SSV), and tens of thousands of swayamsevaks gather each year to train and learn how to further develop the work of the Sangh. Needless to say, the dagger training has been dropped, as has most of the martial training, and the fighting with the bamboo stick has become more of an art form, and incredibly performative, rather than anything lethal.

In the meantime, Hedgewar's personal financial situation was becoming increasingly precarious. He was not earning any money and had not done so for many years. He was supported on a meagre stipend given to him by his older brother, Sitaram. Sitaram was always tight on funds, supporting the house and Keshav. It was also becoming visible to others. First, Hedgewar's clothes had begun to look worn and tired. His wardrobe was very limited, even for those days. Second, people noticed that Hedgewar was constantly working for the community and volunteering, first with the Congress and now with the Sangh. People observed that his entire life was being spent for the service of the community. Third, there was always an endless number of people visiting him at his home, and people who visited him noted the austere contents of the house. The local aristocratic family, headed by Lakshman Bhonsle, enquired through his private secretary as to the financial welfare of the Hedgewar household. Even though precarious, Hedgewar never responded to the financial support offered by the Bhonsle family. On another occasion, his uncle Appa Joshi broached this subject with his nephew, and once again, Hedgewar simply shrugged off the offer to receive financial support. Years later, Appa recalled Hedgewar's response to his offering help, 'I shall ask for it when there is need of it. Help should not feel like an obligation and should not strain one's mind. I have no objection in seeking help from people I am comfortable with, but right at present there is no need for it.' [32] Not accepting Hedgewar's answer and seeing it as his own pride getting in the way, they began to quietly hand over Rs 50 every month to his sister-in-law, who he had a very soft spot for. A few months went by, and soon Hedgewar picked up the scent of money coming into the house. Most likely, his loving sister-in-law purchased some much-needed new clothes for him, which no doubt aroused his suspicions. He soon picked up the trail and put a stop to his uncle's fifty-rupee contribution to the house. A few more months went by, and in late 1926, several swayamsevaks started an insurance company called 'Ideal'.[33] They employed Hedgewar on a pay-as-you-go arrangement and made him the Chief Medical Officer (CMO), who would be responsible for examining candidates who wanted insurance. Hedgewar accepted. He earned Rs 500 every year from carrying out ad-hoc medical examinations, something that is equivalent to around £400 sterling in today's money. This arrangement supported Hedgewar for another ten years. Although paltry, it provided great relief for Sitaram and the Hedgewar household.

Tensions around religious processions always remained high in Nagpur throughout the 1920s. After a series of incidents in 1923 surrounding Hindu religious processions going past a small mosque in a predominantly Hindu neighbourhood, a commission led by Motilal Nehru and Abdul Azad, another prominent Muslim leader, had decreed that Hindu processions were perfectly within their rights to go past any mosque so long as it was not during the time of Muslim prayers—the namaz. Even though the decree had been made and accepted by leaders of both sides, in reality, the Muslim clerics were unwilling to accept such a compromise. Clerics continued to encourage young Muslim boys to pester Hindus who took part in festivals or daily prayers. It was a constant nuisance in the city. But since 1926, tensions were on the rise once again, especially after several Hindu processions had been cancelled out of fear and intimidation by a small group of heavily armed Islamic extremists.

The local community elders complained to the local representative of the Congress. He, in turn, took it to Moonjay, who gave the nod to Hedgewar and the Sangh to mobilize and support the fear-stricken community. The incident would go down in history and, until recently, in infamy.

TEN: 1927–1929

The Godfather

Henry Kissinger, the charismatic Foreign Secretary of the United States, in the 1960s, once quipped 'that the point would come, inevitably, at which the relationship between the cause of conflict and political objectives would be lost' [1]. Misled by their clerics, the Muslim community of Wardha had already lost all sight of their intention for political unrest. Their intention had been to push the leviathan into recognizing and re-establishing the Caliphate of Islam. Instead, their frustration and anger now were directed at their neighbour, who was the 'other', the kafir.

In late 1926, in a small backwater town of Avri in the Wardha region of Maharashtra, one hundred kilometres away from Nagpur, misguided Muslim youth stopped a Hindu procession during Dussehra, the tenth day of Navratri. A relatively small scuffle broke out between some youths. The procession was quickly halted and prevented from going any further. The clerical objection to music being played near mosques was cited as the reason why Hindu festivals must be stopped. The British bureaucracy, which was tired, overstretched and without adequate law enforcement officers, decided to penalize the Hindu community and ordered them to postpone the festival by a month. By all accounts, given the circumstances, the authorities took the path of least resistance, or so they thought. Usually, the procedure went something like this: conservative Islamic clerics would rile up their youth during Friday prayers, who in turn would, drunk as they were on their own sense of piety, intimidate their neighbours—the Hindus. The Hindu community, disorganized as it was, was usually mild and would appeal to the authorities for protection. None would be forthcoming. The state was completely spent. The Hindus would continue to harbour a grudge against the authorities but passively move on.

This time, however, things would not go according to the playbook. Representatives of the Congress informed Moonjay in Nagpur about the rising tensions and postponement of Dussehra yet again. Moonjay immediately engaged the Muslim leadership, who had little clout on the Muslim community as a whole but could have access to the clerics who were the real agitators. Moonjay brought Hedgewar into the discussions. Sensing the impotence of the Muslim political class, who by all accounts did not want a clash, nevertheless had little to offer during the talks. The Hindu community of Avri was told simply to 'take it on the chin' for the sake of Hindu-Muslim unity, which had become the buzzword for the political classes. Hedgewar quietly sent word and activated Anna Sohoni to prepare the RSS units.

According to Dr Narayan Khare, a prominent member of the Congress who later became the leader of the Hindu Mahasabha in independent India, four men gave speeches in Avri to the community. He claims that both he and Hedgewar spoke firmly and asked the Hindus there to stand up for themselves.[2] The others that spoke were Moonjay and a barrister named Govind Deshmukh. No sooner had the four men left in Moonjay's automobile, a rarity indeed in these parts of India, they got news that another scuffle had broken out between some Hindu and Muslim youths. This time, the Hindu boys stood their ground. Four men died in the fighting. The authorities arrested and attempted to prosecute fourteen local Hindu leaders who had organized the gathering where Hedgewar had spoken. The authorities at Avri also tried to prosecute all four visitors who had spoken and allegedly had given inflammatory speeches. The Nagpur courts did not entertain the case. However, the local Hindu organizers at Avri were charged, and a court case arranged. Hedgewar and Moonjay led the drive to raise funds to hire lawyers. Hedgewar had a particular affinity for a man named Sudhir Mohrir, a fellow medical doctor who had trained with him at Calcutta.

Mohrir was, on the whole, a simple man who practiced his medicine with integrity and chose to do so in a backwater town. Very few practitioners wanted to work in towns like Avri, mainly because there was no money to be made. The people could not afford medical care, and so much of what Mohrir did was on a charitable basis. There was no way he could afford the court case and adequately defend himself. For Hedgewar, this was a great injustice. A man who was providing much-needed medical care in a town where there was no provision, who provided care to both Hindus and Muslims alike, was now accused of organizing a riot and faced potentially a sentence of life imprisonment. Hedgewar worked hard to raise funds. He, with Moonjay's support, managed to convince some heavy hitters from Nagpur and Mumbai to come and defend the fourteen men. But sadly, it was of no avail. The British authorities had made up their mind that these men had to be made an example of, and so they were found guilty, and Mohrir, on 13 December 1926, was given the harshest sentence of all—life imprisonment.[3]

Hedgewar could hardly believe it. He was dumbfounded at the injustice meted out. Mohrir's family was devastated. He was the sole earner in a family of six. His family faced destitution. Hedgewar spent over a month in Avri during and after the trial. He continuously visited Avri and would reassure the families of the fourteen men who had been imprisoned with financial and moral support. Many locals, instead of supporting these families who were victims of a great injustice, chose to shun them in the hope of not drawing the gaze of the leviathan. Hedgewar continued to travel the hundred kilometres from Nagpur at least twice a year to see Mohrir in prison until his eventual release in 1934. Mohrir, in years to come, would never forget the solidarity Hedgewar had shown and would become a pivotal actor in the rise of the RSS.

After this incident, Hedgewar requested Appa Joshi to start a Sangh shakha in Avri. He had been shown what a shakha was and how successful it had become in Nagpur. In February 1927, the first shakha outside of Nagpur was started in Avri.[4] Young men joined the shakha in scores. They too understood that the authorities could no longer protect the ordinary family, and justice had truly become blind. In the months to come, they would see, first-hand, what the RSS, and they as swayamsevaks, were capable of.

Ten days after Mohrir was sentenced to a lifelong prison sentence, another terrible piece of news reached Hedgewar. He had just reached Nagpur after a long journey, where people had stood at the entrance to his house, waiting for his arrival to tell him the news. A Swami by the name of Shraddhanand had been brutally murdered by a Muslim man, who had been arrested.[5] His name would go down in infamy. His actions would cause a ripple effect, which would go on to cause one of the largest Hindu–Muslim clashes of the twentieth century. Its tremors are still felt in modern Indian discourse. A man arrived at the home of the Swami early morning on 23 December 1926. He had asked the Swami's personal attendant if he could get an opportunity to have a personal audience with the Swami. The reason he gave is not one without painful irony, for he suggested to the attendant that he wished to alert the Swami regarding a growing Islamic threat. Abdul Rashid was led into the lounge. The Swami arrived, and both men cautiously greeted each other. The Swami was unwell and lay down on a bed propped up by pillows so he could see his visitor. The guest asked for a glass of water to which the attendant cordially obliged and left the room to fetch a glass. No sooner had the attendant left the room, Abdul Rashid got up from his chair, walked across the small room, pulled out a gun hidden in his jacket, and shot the Swami point blank. The Swami died instantly in his bed.[6] Rashid was later tried and hanged.

The murder caused a great ripple effect amongst India's movers and shakers. Gandhi, on 30 December, in his *Young India* journal wrote:

> The expected has happened. Swami Shraddhanandji passed a day or two at the Satyagraha Ashram at Sabarmati, now about six months ago, and told me, ...that he often received letters threatening his life. Where is the reformer who has not a price put upon his head? ...And there is nothing untoward in the assassination having taken place.[7]

He went onto praise the bravery and integrity of the Swami, and even called him a warrior, one who had achieved a martyr's death.[8] Gandhi, while acknowledging the militancy of Islam, called on the Hindu community to rise above this heinous act,

> 'Let us (Hindus) not ascribe the crime of an individual to a whole community. Let us not harbour the spirit of retaliation. Let us not think of the wrong done by a Mussalman (Muslim) against a Hindu, but of an erring brother against a hero.'[9]

It perplexed and vexed Hedgewar that in a single breath Gandhi could clearly acknowledge the aggressive tendencies of Islam but advise Hindus to see it as an individual act, while with the next breadth blame the entire Hindu community, and especially the newspapers, for inciting the violence against the Swami. Gandhi wrote, 'I wish to plead for Abdul Rashid. I do not know who he is. It does not matter to me what prompted the deed. The fault is ours (Hindus).'[10]

Gandhi's lack of compassion, indeed one can even say callousness towards the Hindu community, and his extremely lofty spiritual expectations not just for himself but for the common Hindu left Hedgewar feeling incredulous. Certain words echoed in his mind—'the expected has happened. The fault is ours.' In an increasingly lawless society, how was the Hindu community to react to one of its spiritual and social reformers being assassinated in broad daylight and so nonchalantly? Gandhi's call was to turn the other cheek. For Hedgewar, idealism aside, this was an untenable position to take, as one can only show forgiveness when one has the capacity to punish or react in some credible way. The Hindu community was completely incapable of protecting itself, and so it wasn't forgiveness that Gandhi was inciting, but rather cowardice, meekness and passivity in the face of mortal danger.

Hedgewar was aware of why Shraddhanand had been murdered. He was a Hindu monk ordained in the nationalist reformist movement called the Arya Samaj. He had been running campaigns to bring all those who had been forcibly converted to Islam back into the fold of Hindu traditions. This was quite a radical act in those times, as the perceived Hindu wisdom stated that once a person left the fold, there was no return for them. Shraddhananda, with the help of the Hindu Mahasabha and Moonjay in particular, was making it legitimate to return to the fold of one's ancestors without any shame. He had brought more than 1,60,000 people back into Hinduism from Islam. While this may seem like simply a battle for ideas and people having the right to choose their religion, in reality, when leaving Islam, it can be a very dangerous affair indeed. From the Islamic perspective, the Swami was inciting, and openly so, with celebration, apostasy—a crime so heinous in Islam that it is tantamount to treason and therefore, death.[11] Underpinning the act of murder was a deadly theology, an entire edifice that made common Muslims like Abdul Rashid into violent militants. Indeed, many Muslims celebrated the murder of the Swami as an act of justice being carried out. Hedgewar, along with the likes of Aurobindo Ghosh from far away Pondicherry, were the few people who could see that Islam's violence lay in its political ideology rooted in a particular theological framework and not just isolated in a few bad apples.

Early 1927 proved to be a hotbed for militancy and vigilantism in Nagpur[12]. Tensions were high. Hedgewar had been receiving threatening letters over several weeks. His usual response was one of amusement. He had always been supremely confident in looking after himself in fisticuffs. Others casually reminded him that he was no longer the fit, strong twenty-something that he had been a decade earlier. He would chuckle and swiftly move the conversation on. On one occasion, an editor from the *Mahratta* newspaper asked him about how serious he thought these threats were.

Hedgewar, with all sincerity, replied, 'Well, these days, I have to be guarded at all times.' Surprised by the answer and looking around the room, he asked, 'Where is your guard?' 'Right here', replied Hedgewar, pointing at a fifteen-year-old swayamsevak who had just appeared with some chai. Both men burst out in laughter, with the boy peevishly smiling, wrongly thinking that he was the butt of the joke. Hedgewar patted the boy on the back, reassuring him that the joke was not on him. The boy relaxed and smiled. This was a story as recounted by Gopal Ogale many years later to Palkar[13]. Jokes aside, Hedgewar knew that an impending fight was heading straight towards him, and it wouldn't be as straightforward as he often made out to everyone. Months went by, and Hedgewar, along with the growing number of RSS swayamsevaks, went onto a war footing. Increasingly, law-and-order issues came to Hedgewar, either directly from citizens or via the local Congress. Hedgewar would send Sohoni's units to different areas of the city to patrol in uniform with their bamboo sticks in hand. On one occasion, their presence alone was enough, for an adolescent Hindu girl to be released by a group of Muslim men who claimed that she had been married to one of them, which the girl firmly denied. She had been kept captive for over eight days.[14]

These kinds of incidents gave immense legitimacy to the RSS on the streets of Nagpur among the otherwise bewildered Hindu community. These unwelcome patrols were also duly noted by the clerics. They were determined to wage a struggle against the kuffar, especially any that strayed into their neighbourhoods. From the viewpoint of the clerics, the RSS patrols were intimidation tactics and an act of vigilantism. From the Hindu perspective, they were law and order enforcement officers, tightly controlled and disciplined, providing much-needed security in an otherwise chaotic world.

The fight soon came straight to Hedgewar's door. In the middle of the night, stones were pelted at the family home, scaring the life out of Sitaram and his wife. Hedgewar would immediately rush outside to confront the goons, but they would swiftly disappear into the night. These dastardly deeds continued for most of 1927.[15] The harassment of Hedgewar and his family was relentless. The more misled Muslim youth tried to intimidate Hedgewar, the more resolute he became; and in turn riled up the swayamsevaks, who were equally determined to join patrols around the city. This had become a cycle of intimidation between Hedgewar and his RSS swayamsevaks, and Muslim men who were directed by their clerics. One would feed the other's determination. Hedgewar was clear that sooner or later this heat would result in one incident which would trigger violence. Then, days before Eid Milad al-Nabi, the day of the Prophet of Islam's birthday, on 27 September 1927, a threatening letter arrived at Moonjay's house. The letter made clear that on the day of Eid, he would be sacrificed.[16]

Sohoni arranged his units to protect Moonjay day and night. On the night of Eid, according to Sheshadri, a small number of goons armed with knives and cleavers attacked Moonjay's home.[17] Swayamsevaks surrounded these masked teenagers and men in their twenties. swayamsevaks were under strict orders not to kill any of them but to give them a 'good thrashing'[18]. Surrounded and outnumbered, the young hotheads quickly realized they were well in over their heads. Many simply dropped their weapons and tried to make amends, while others went for a charge, brandishing their lethal weapons. The swayamsevaks on duty were well-trained, and quickly put down the aggressors, breaking a few of their limbs along the way. Those who surrendered were also beaten mildly, more to administer humiliation rather than physical harm. The night passed by without any further incident.

Throughout September, reports came to Hedgewar that gangs of Muslim men were walking around Hindu neighbourhoods, specifically marking out sites. It was unclear as to what was being planned. Suspicions on all sides were at an all-time high, and no measure of goodwill was given by any side. There was a third front faced by the early RSS and Hedgewar, namely the increasing tension between castes within the Hindu society. Hindu society was in turmoil. Its old prejudiced and hierarchical structure was being challenged from within. Reformers across the Hindu world were encouraging castes to share temples, live side-by-side, study together and even intermarry across caste lines, therefore breaking the endogamy of thousands of years. The ones opposing such movements were Brahmins stuck in tradition, which led to bigotry and dogma. Of course, the ones seeking social reform were Brahmins too. So, the simple caricature of Brahmins versus non-Brahmins is too simple and does not stand up to the reality on the ground.[19]

The Hedgewarian approach to mapping out the Hindu world went something like this: there are the castes, split into four fundamental buckets—the Brahmins, the Kshatriyas, the Vaishyas and the downtrodden Shudras. These buckets were broad indeed, with hundreds of professions in each. Over several centuries, these castes had become fossilised. In other words, a person born into one caste was almost doomed by their birth to stay in that profession till death did them part. It was a sorry situation, mostly caused by historical forces and dogma. Hedgewar had an established schema about how the Hindu world fell from its civilizational heights, but regardless of the causes, it was a fact that Hindu society was a shadow of itself. He felt that the caste structure had become stale and needed to be uprooted and gotten rid of lock, stock and barrel. Having said that, he was also aware that after thousands of years, the Hindu society could not simply remove its own shackles so easily. It would take a long time to reform the inner character of the average citizen, and free the individual from the tyranny of custom. The Hedgewarian approach is evolutionary, not revolutionary. In his mind, society had to be changed from within and not by external forces that had already done so much harm. The exploitation by the foreign powers was a case in point. He felt that the entire edifice of the Hindu society had to be reformed to free the individual from the shackles of caste while maintaining the continuity of wider culture, which had offered so much to the world and had much more to offer going forward.

Hedgewarian thought looks at the world not through the prism of caste but rather desh bhakti—that notion which has a deep sense of reverence and sacredness attached to the land itself.[20] The soil itself is sacred. It is worshipful. Desh bhakti need not be steeped in some political ideology or religious dogma but rather in the idea that those who view the land itself as sacred and divine are insiders no matter their race, class or creed. And by the same token, those that do not see the land as sacred but as something to be dominated, to be exploited and to be subjugated are outsiders, no matter their race, class or creed. In RSS adaptations, this desh bhakti is personified through the image of Bharat mata, which is Mother India.

Hedgewarian thought, having identified the 'ins' and 'outs', argues that the 'outsiders' must be kept at bay and never allowed into the centre of the society's body politic. One can trade with, learn from and, in turn, teach the 'outsiders'. Outsiders can be well-intentioned, but nevertheless if they do not hold the land as sacred, then a level of vigilance is called upon.

Outsiders can also be ill-intentioned; in which case they must be resisted, and a vanguard placed to oppose their efforts. Hedgewar's early RSS was a vanguard against all outsiders—Hindu and non-Hindu. The RSS was not, as far as one can tell, created to oppose Muslims and other minorities, as cited by so many academics and commentators.[21]

Then there were the 'insiders.' These were desh bhakts who revered the soil. No insider was to be resisted, for they were of the soil—not in some ethnic sense but in a philosophical or cultural sense. Having said that, Hedgewarian thought is clear that even insiders, although well-intentioned and part parcel of the body politic, can be harmful—those protecting caste-lines being one such example—those who supported child marriage being another. The general backwardness of Hindu women being the biggest blemish on the collective Hindu society was one more to reform. In this regard, Hedgewar saw Gandhi as immensely important for the struggle but ultimately misinformed and misled by his own self-created narratives. Gandhi's completely black-and-white response towards violence and the causes of violence was something that Hedgewar was repulsed by. Therefore, the RSS formally never supported any of Gandhi's initiatives except to provide first aid and medical support at events. Of course, individual swayamsevaks were free to join any campaign they saw as fit, but this would be in an individual capacity.

Hedgewarian thought, manifested in the early RSS, shows how challenges were categorized on a spectrum. The RSS was extremely hostile to anyone who wanted to create a society that was inherently different to the culture and historical legacy of the land—namely, Islamists who called for India to become part parcel of Dar al-Islam. It was also hostile to those who wanted partition, such as the Muslim League. It was hostile to Anglophilic Indians who felt that the Hindu culture itself had been the problem and needed to be removed and Western ideas, with her civilization, to be adopted. It was hostile to Christian evangelical churches, which used subterfuge to undermine Hindu integrity and inherently set its compass pointing West for its cultural direction. Communists were also categorized as outsiders as they espoused a form of political ideology, which was hostile to all culture and antiquity. In all these cases, the RSS could easily be hostile towards Hindus if they fell into the 'outside' category.

On the insiders' track, the RSS took a different approach. Here, it did not act as a vanguard looking to resist ill-intentioned programmes by those outside the land or those of the land who no longer had any reverence for it. Instead, the RSS looks to reform every stratum of society—grassroots, social customs and norms, religious dogma and institutions, political and intellectual. Hedgewarian thought for the insiders is infinitely patient, caring, cooperative and gentle. It will slowly but relentlessly make changes that will re-invigorate Hindu society so that it may harness its 'glorious' heritage to create a better, progressive and modern future. Removing caste sits within this framework, as does empowering women's welfare and the plethora of other problems faced by Hindu society. Anyone of any religion or persuasion can fit on the insider or outsider track from the Hedgewarian perspective. It just so happens that Islam as it is in India, and especially during Hedgewar's time, was inherently hostile towards Hindu culture and its categorization of Bharat mata as idolatrous was very unfortunate. In every aspect, the clerics, influenced as they were by a conservative, orthodox form of Islam, herded the Muslims of India on a collision course with the RSS. Something similar can be said of the evangelical Christian churches, which used charity as a guise to not only convert Hindus but then went one step further, imposing a Western universalist agenda in India—something which categorizes them as outsiders.

Hedgewar was born in a Brahmin family. Yet, he rejected all forms of caste in society. In 1927, however, there were increasing tensions between orthodox Brahmins who were trying to hold on to their way of life, no matter how erroneous, and other Brahmins, who were actively working to remove it. The tensions of 1927 were not between Brahmins and non-Brahmins but rather between reformers and traditionalists. Hedgewar was a reformer. The RSS was a reformist movement. Although the tension between reformists and traditionalists was at an all-time high, the bonds between them never broke, and the Hindu revival movements continued, on the whole, unabated. Muslim clerics certainly made attempts to create a political wedge between these groups but to no avail.

RSS patrols in July 1927 reported sightings of gangs training after dusk near the Nagpur railway station with daggers and swords[22]. By day, Hedgewar was moving through each area of Nagpur, alerting local community leaders of the impending threat of violence. Unlike in 1924, Hedgewar was heard this time. People were concerned but also intimidated. Muslim mobs, especially after Friday prayers, fuelled as they were by a militant piety, would stroll through Hindu neighbourhoods to irk anyone that they took a fancy to. On Friday afternoons, Hindus generally shut their stores early, and women remained indoors. Seeing this, Hedgewar realized that only a few men could be relied upon to really address the growing problem of intimidation. The police patrols were simply instructed to watch and report any disturbances. Hardly anyone was ever charged with vandalism, intimidation or assault, even though these things were a daily occurrence, and the victims were mostly Hindus[23]. Then, in late August, whatever doubts remained in Hedgewar's mind about the impending danger evaporated with a pamphlet— 'Al-Fatihah Rabbani'. It read:

> ..Muslim brothers are informed that Sayyad Mir Sahab expired two years ago. In his memory a procession has been organized on 4th September 1927 at 2 PM. The procession will proceed to Hansapuri cemetery passing through Nawabpura, Mahal, Walker Road, and Ganja Khet. All Muslim brothers are requested to gather at the Nawabpura Masjid at 12 PM to participate in the procession. This procession will bring fervour and heat and each one would richly share in the bounties.[24]

The title of the leaflet is a calling card— 'to the people (Rabbani) who believe and follow the creed of Al-Fatihah'. Al-Fatihah is the first surah (verse) from the Quran where Muslims pledge their allegiance to Allah and his will. In other words, the leaflet was addressing all Muslim men, regardless of what type of Islam they belonged to. It was a call for unification across sectarian lines. The man in whose honour the procession was being held was a Sufi cleric by the name of Tajuddin Muhammad Badruddin.[25] He was a holy man of the Naqshbandi Sunni-Sufi order who had died in 1925. The march was going to start at a mosque and then circle, meandering through major Hindu neighbourhoods, which would be celebrating the day of Maha Lakshmi, the day of thanksgiving to the goddess Lakshmi, on 4 September. They would decorate floats with gold and silver ornaments,placing murtis of the goddess clad in fine silks and jewellery, and take these out in an hour-long procession, which would be at its zenith around noon. Entire families would be out at this time, to view the floats and celebrate. For Hedgewar, the leaflet was the warning he needed. What peeved him the most was the final line of the leaflet—the reward for those who took part. Was it spiritual in nature, for the life hereafter or was it a dog-whistle to the mob that would also loot gold and silver, and the war booty would be shared out amongst the participants? Hedgewar was not going to wait to find out. Something had to be done.

He mobilized Sohoni to create a workshop in his house to make knives and daggers. Swayamsevaks came at nightfall and worked throughout the night by candlelight. In similar conditions, twenty years earlier, Hedgewar had been trained to make bombs in darkened basements. Hedgewar's training was being put to real deadly use. By day, bamboo sticks were left in innocuous bundles in alleyways at locations where both communities were likely to meet each other and clash. Meetings were held between the leadership of the RSS. Moonjay representing the Hindu Mahasabha, and maybe even the likes of Ganesh Savarkar attended, where it was decided for Hedgewar to leave Nagpur before 4 September. Exactly why Hedgewar, the man who always led from the front, who never feared a brawl, would be asked to leave Nagpur only a day or two before the dreaded day is unclear. Palkar suggests that it was a ploy to create the impression of unpreparedness on behalf of the Hindu community. The thinking went something like this: if the likes of Hedgewar are out of town, then the RSS must not have a clue as to what was being planned[26]. Another reason could also be that the leadership knew this could become a murderous affair, and bloodshed was very likely. Hence, it was better for Hedgewar to stay clear of such incidents to keep him out of any legal action undertaken by the state. Whatever the reason, Hedgewar left Nagpur somewhere between 1-3 September. He went on a speaking tour around Wardha district during the festive season.

On that ominous Sunday, 4 September 1927, the Hindu community was out as it had been the previous week. For the common Hindu family, this would have consisted of waking up early, bathing, participating in a morning puja and offering prayers. Many chose to visit temples, but many would have been in their own homes. Around nine in the morning, the processions began from each neighbourhood. At the front were the floats with the deity of Lakshmi riding high, laden with gold and silver and other valuable fineries. Slowly, these neighbourhood processions merged into one huge gathering of tens of thousands, all heading towards the Mahalakshmi temple in Nagpur. These processions were navigating themselves through predominantly Hindu neighbourhoods. Even though the atmosphere was tense for all the organizers and community leaders, the average family was out celebrating their faith without too much bother. However, when they passed a mosque, people felt reluctant to play musical instruments too loudly on the off chance that they would provoke the neighbouring Muslims. Little did they know that trouble was coming to them, whether they liked it or not!

Around noon that day, one hundred swayamsevaks gathered at Mohite Wada, the open ground that had become home to the first shakha two years earlier. They were formed into sixteen units of five and six people and sent across the route where the Muslim march would most likely collide with the Hindu procession[27]. A few of the younger boys were designated as runners who would pass messages between the units. Sohoni was mentally charged. His personality was hot-tempered at the best of times, and in situations like this, he was truly a force to be reckoned with. He placed himself at the front and centre of the procession where he could see what lay ahead. His associates were placed either side, and one to the rear, keeping an eye all around. They were armed and ready.

The heat that afternoon gradually built to a scorching 32 degrees; coupled with thousands of people congregating in tight roadways, the atmosphere was stifling. The smell of human sweat was pungent with tightly packed families as they walked shoulder to shoulder. Women broke the aroma with sweet-smelling jasmine in their hair. Children were carried on the shoulders of their fathers, enjoying the fanfare all around them. Then, just as expected, around two o'clock that afternoon, chants of the takbir 'Allahu Akbar' (God is great) began to be heard.[28] The sounds of defiance and aggression as far as the throngs of Hindu families were concerned. As the takbir became louder and closer, people began to panic. Families began to break away from the processions and started to swiftly make their way to safety. Others, the pious, kept the celebrations going. The few police present did what they were capable of—nothing!

As the band of fanatical Muslims crossed Walker Road, which separated the commercial area from the tightly packed streets and alleys of Mahal, Hindus realized what was going to happen. People began running in all directions. The oncoming mob marched onwards unabated. The police, which made a feeble attempt to draw the Muslim mob away from the Hindu procession, now just hundreds of yards away, were quickly brushed aside. Knives, cleavers, daggers and even spears were pulled out and waved in the air in sync with the war cry 'Allahu Akbar'. Hindus ran inside any building that would let them in, hoping it would be out of harm's way. Women and small children were especially at great risk. The sense of community and togetherness quickly regressed into 'every family for themselves'. The organizers of the procession, seeing the ensuing chaos, looked bemused and had absolutely no clue as to what they ought to do.[29] Eyewitnesses reported the hypnotic chanting of the takbir with ever-threatening potency. Something so sacred, could be turned into something so threatening—this has always been the power of the takbir.

The procession came to a stop on Killa road just metres away from the Kalyaneshwar mandir. Sohoni, with his five men lined up in front of the deity Lakshmi, armed with daggers and with a long bamboo stick in hand, waited in a fighting posture. Runners informed the other units to make their way to the front. Within a few minutes, thirty to forty swayamsevaks lined up in rows in formation with long bamboo sticks in hand, led by Martand Jog. Every one of them had a knife or a dagger under their shirts. The other units led by Bhau Kaware, Govid Cholkar and Krishna Joshi were watching the mob advance and were making their way in parallel through the backstreets. Two units, led by Ramachandra Kothari and Bala Sakhdeo, remained behind the mob to catch any of the miscreants that decided to make a run for it when the nastiness would begin.[30] swayamsevaks had encircled the mob clandestinely. The units following were instructed not to engage until the mob was fully committed to a frontal assault. Their job was to flank them and squeeze them into a tight space on what is today named Waiker Road.[31] The RSS units had been instructed to keep the violence restricted to a tightly held area to limit the danger to property and the public at large.

On Waiker Road, which led onto Killa Road, the mob began to unleash its violence.[32] Anybody who came in their wake was beaten, stabbed or simply trampled upon. Sohoni's unit engaged the mob at the junction of Waiker Road and Killa Road, a narrow pass where a handful of swayamsevaks could make a stand against much larger numbers. The mob was tightly squeezed by buildings on either side.[33] Ten young men, all under the age of thirty, led by Anna Sohoni, met the mob head-on and unleashed the lethal power of their long staffs. The mob was held in its tracks. Just yards from the fighting was the Hindu procession semi-abandoned on the road, with local organizers desperately trying to unmount the deity and take it to safety. The most precious valuables were gathered, while the silks and other ornamental fineries were abandoned.

The mob was met with such venom from Sohoni's unit that it backed away, trying to turn around back up Waiker Road. Except now, they were being met with serious force from all sides. Chaos ensued amongst the ranks of the mob. They ran helter-skelter. Those that managed to run past without taking lethal hits were met by the rear guard. Fighting broke out all around. The ten swayamsevaks were unable to keep the mob trapped on Waiker Road. The mob now let loose, setting fire to property as it retreated down Walker Road towards Chitnis Park.[34] Those Hindus who tried to run out of their houses or shops were quickly hunted down and beaten, and many were stabbed. RSS units pursued them, but the mob had broken loose, and the units were unable to contain the ensuing rampage. As the mob ran wild, people noted that an organized group of young men, clearly trained in the martial arts, were not only resisting the mob but quite clearly thrashing them in turn.

What happened next is best described by Edgar Albert Guest, who so memorably wrote, 'There are many to serve when the victory's near, and few are the hurts to be borne….'[35] Suddenly recognizing that the rascals were in for a good hiding, hundreds of Hindu men still in their dhotis came out of their hovels, sticks and rods in hand to help the swayamsevaks.[36] Very quickly, the mob was outnumbered, out armed, and with very few places to go. From the Muslim perspective, it looked as if Hindus suddenly had found the pluck to stand up for themselves. They noted that there were a few tough men amongst the Hindus who had stout hearts. In reality, the stout-hearted ones were all RSS swayamsevaks without their uniforms. As far as the Muslim mob was concerned, Hindus, out of nowhere and completely unexpected, had risen to fight. The RSS units maintained their discipline and never strayed too far from the Hindu procession on the off chance that the mob returned to loot the religious artefacts. Within a relatively short space of time, what looked like a battle forlorn now looked like a complete rout from the Hindu perspective. The afternoon became relatively calm.

But something darker had been unleashed. That evening, skirmishes broke out all over the city. Muslims attacked Hindu businesses and temples. Hindus kept vigil on their property and family. Others went out seeking bloody vengeance. Tit for tat became the rule. What had started as a clash had become a riot. Well over 150 people on both sides had been severely injured, mostly suffering stabbings or deep wounds caused by daggers and knives.[37] On the first night, temples had been ransacked, and a mosque had been torched. The police had lost all control of the situation. On the second day, RSS units led by Sohoni and Huddar tried to organize the Hindu mobs but to little avail. RSS units watched over temples and key junctions to stop Muslim mobs from attacking. But other Hindus went seeking revenge. Hindus had always vastly outnumbered the Muslims in Nagpur but, until this day, had never reacted with such force. Muslim homes were torched, and almost all that were killed were Muslims.[38]

In retaliation verging on utter madness, a small band of Muslim youths attacked a funeral procession of a by-stander that had been killed the day earlier.[39] In the ensuing fight, RSS units patrolling nearby were informed. In the response and fight that followed, a young man by the name of Dhundiraj Lehgavkar was killed.[40] It is unclear if he died of bullet wounds or a stabbing. He is widely known to be the first RSS swayamsevak to have died in such an incident. He would certainly not be the last. The RSS unit also killed three Muslims who were involved in the attack on the funeral procession.

In total, twenty-five men were killed over two days.[41]

By the third day, the leviathan had awoken. The Imperial Army had arrived with semi-automatic machine guns and armed to the hilt. They occupied every crossroad and junction. They patrolled the streets for over a month until calm had returned across what looked like a war-torn city. The Muslim community had felt the brunt of the Hindu reaction caused by a misadventure encouraged by Islamic clerics. Those clerics remained in their place and continued to preach hatred and violence. But the Muslim community had been shaken. It was visibly frightened and took refuge when the military arrived. Had the army not arrived, Nagpur may well have seen a greater exodus of Muslim families leaving their homes.[42]

Leaders from both sides were brought together and forced into a truce. Reports were commissioned. People were arrested and put on trial. Hedgewar, as expected, received word that the police and Muslim gangs were looking for him. His home had been attacked and badly damaged during the rioting. His brother and sister-in-law were taken to a safe house arranged by Moonjay and Jog. Hedgewar was in a small town called Chandrapur, around three hours south of Nagpur. The hagiographies of the RSS tell us that Hedgewar was so concerned about the violence that had taken place that he refused to listen to his advisors and nonchalantly arrived in Nagpur to support the RSS swayamsevaks in the aftermath.[43] But this does not correlate well with his personality. Hedgewar was a man of consensus. He would always allow RSS workers to influence and shape his whereabouts. After all, he took the advice of the senior leadership team, in the first instance, to relocate himself outside of Nagpur during the clashes.

In all likelihood, what spurred Hedgewar to return to Nagpur at the earliest possible time were the reports he had read; in total, seven Hindu families had lost a loved one, including a young swayamsevak. Well over forty had been seriously injured and hospitalized. The streets were wraithlike. The army had imposed a curfew across the city. Vigilante gangs from both sides were still taking potshots at each other, attacking anyone they could find. One gets the impression that neither Hedgewar nor the likes of Moonjay and the Congress had expected the violence to become so widespread. A brawl was planned for and expected. A message was intended to be sent to the Islamic clerics that they would not be able to intimidate their way to power in Nagpur. Instead, a full-blown riot had taken place, and people had lost their lives. Being over three hours away from events which he had been at the centre would not have sat well with his inner sense of duty.

Hedgewar caught the earliest possible train to Nagpur. He arrived on 10 September around midday to find the city derelict. There was no hustle or bustle. A few people ventured about trying to get hold of essentials like water, medicines and fuel. He failed to find a *tonga* to hitch a ride with.[44] So, he walked across town. A very risky deed considering that the station was located adjacent to a predominantly Muslim neighbourhood, where gangs were out specifically looking for him.[45] He walked the forty minutes to his home, passing by the very neighbourhoods that had seen the epicentre of the fighting. He would have seen the army, who would have stopped him at checkpoints and asked questions of him. He would have seen broken roof tiles, windows and torched buildings as he walked. His brother and sister-in-law were busy cleaning the mess around their house created by the mobs that attacked it. A few locals were cementing damaged plaster caused by all the stones that were pelted. It is hard to say how Sitaram had felt about all this—but one can guess that he was not thrilled.

Swayamsevaks were guarding his home. They were thrilled to see him, and to his surprise, the mood appeared buoyant. He called Anna Sohoni and Martand Jog to his home. They too were charged and enthused to do more. Hedgewar listened. That evening, Hedgewar, with two swayamsevaks by his side, visited Dhundiraj Lehgavkar's home. His final rites had already been concluded, the body cremated, as per Hindu custom, and prayers echoed in his house. Hedgewar met the father and the other men of the house. He consoled them as best as he could. He knew that the price paid was high indeed, and the outcome still was not clear to him. Had it been worth it?

The next morning, he visited the hospital and met all those who were injured. He reassured each one that the Sangh was there to look after them. Many of the wounded were either innocent bystanders attacked by the mob or young men who sought revenge once the tide had turned. Only four swayamsevaks had been injured, and none too severely. Then Hedgewar visited the homes of all those who had been arrested and were in jail pending a trial. He assured families that the Hindu community would stand by their loved ones. To that end, he and the RSS units spent several months raising money to cover the medical expenses of the injured and to fight the court cases of those facing imprisonment.[46]

After a few days, the city had returned to a calm state, and shops began to open. To Hedgewar's surprise, the mood amongst even the business owners had changed. An unsaid, unplanned boycott was in place against all foreign goods and those manufactured or retailed by the Muslim community. The physical fight had now mutated into an economic one. This fight arguably was more painful than the physical losses they had incurred. More than twenty Muslim men had lost their lives, and well over 100 were hospitalized. One mosque and several houses of their leaders were burnt down. And now they faced economic sanctions.

While busying himself with supporting his Hindu community through fundraising, he kept one eye on the Muslim community. He witnessed many Muslim families leave Nagpur. Popular narratives suggest that these families no longer felt protected in a polarized city and feared the majoritarianism that was being propagated by Hindu groups. Even though this may have played a role, there was another phenomenon that was unfolding within the Muslim community. There had always been a schism in Sunni Islam between the Deobandis and the Barelvi movement[47]. The riots had coincidently ruptured a fragile truce between the clerics of the Deobandi and the Barelvi movements. Both wanted a political Islam, but the argument was about 'the how'. Deobandis claimed that Islam had become wayward and had lost itself to the corruptions of the West, and to a lesser degree, by living and integrating with the kuffar (Hindus). For Islam to rise again, it must return to the original teachings of the Prophet. The most antagonistic clerics and the most pious were from this fold.

They would often reside in seminaries and seldom leave the confines of the mosque or madrasa. Unlike the Deobandis, Barelvi clerics, although militant, had the legitimacy of the Sunni masses, which the Deobandis were eager to usurp.[48] The mob that set out to clash with Hindus during the Lakshmi puja were those that followed the Deobandi strand of Sunni Islam, much to the dislike of the Barelvis. This rupture in the Muslim community also played a significant part in quelling clerical aggression towards the Hindu community as their followers had not only become disillusioned but increasingly divided.

When calm returned to the stricken city, not everything went back to normal. In a disorganized ad-hoc manner, many Hindus boycotted purchasing goods and services from anybody in the Muslim community.[49] Within a matter of months, and certainly by 1928, many Muslim traders were unable to sell their wares and were economically forced out of the city. The clerics had miscalculated. What was meant to be just another foray into a Hindu neighbourhood, with a light sprinkling of intimidation, had become a full-blown blowback, and their own position became untenable. Many of the hard-line clerics were also forced to leave the city not by Hindus, who were quite oblivious to the schisms within the Muslim community, but by their own congregations, who had faced the brunt of the hardship caused by their misadventure. The consequence of this series of events is that since 1927, there has never been a religious riot in the city. It is worth noting that in the 2011 census of Nagpur, the Muslim population was around 12 per cent, and on the whole, lived in relative harmony with their neighbours.

Another consequence of the 1927 Nagpur riots was that the RSS, and in particular Hedgewar, became a household name all over Vidarbha and Nagpur. By 1929, there were over 1000 regular swayamsevaks and over fifty daily shakhas.[50] Young men joined in droves, not out of some awakened patriotism but out of necessity and pragmatism. Indian society was in a vortex—it was volatile, uncertain, complicated, with ambiguous forces all interplaying with one another. In this chaos, the RSS had shown itself to be an outfit people could rely on. It had proven itself and showed none of the hot air and arrogance of the political classes. Young men thought they were joining some sort of gymnasium where a fusion of exercise and martial arts was imparted. They were not wrong, per se, but they just hadn't fully grasped the depth of the rabbit hole they were entering.

Hedgewar, having given up public life two years earlier, was now more popular than ever before. Strangers would invite him as a guest of honour for their family functions or religious ceremonies. He would take up as many opportunities as possible. He spent an increasing amount of time during the day meeting people from all walks of life across Nagpur and its suburbs. Hedgewar noticed that people were offering him a one-rupee coin as a parting gift as he left their homes.[51] It was an old, somewhat arcane custom. It was nevertheless a powerful symbol and something Hedgewar knew not to take lightly. It was a gesture one showed to the head of an akhada (gymnasium) as a token of respect and loyalty. Hedgewar would smile courteously, graciously accepting the gesture, and leave. The coin represented that this household was now loyal to the RSS.

People now took shelter under the widening canopy of Hedgewar's creation. Young men were encouraged to attend the daily shakha for training. People went with a plethora of law-and-order issues to the *kar-ya-waha* (the coordinator) of the shakha. The RSS was an organization of strength and a law upon itself. It could get things done, and the more people that joined its shakhas, the more capable it became.

Hedgewar had inadvertently become the Godfather.

ELEVEN: 1928–1930

Values and Leadership

The RSS was growing faster than anyone could have imagined, including Hedgewar. In a society that was anarchic in vast swathes across the countryside and in smaller cities and towns, the RSS provided an umbrella of protection, belonging, pride and, most of all, order for the Hindu community. The RSS could get things done and, by association, stop bad things from happening. The leviathan, although aware, was on the whole incapable of really doing anything significant about it except keep an eye.[1]

Then there was the issue of money—the RSS, like any fledgling organization, needed cash. Yet, Hedgewar was clear that at no cost would the mission of the RSS be swayed by those who gave money. The wealthy often donated generously, only to influence an organization for their own narrow ends. He had no appetite for such things. To navigate through such challenges, the leadership of the RSS decided unanimously to only raise funds from its own—its swayamsevaks [2].

They decided that the movement would actively raise money once a year—during an auspicious occasion in the Hindu calendar called Guru Purnima. Guru is a familiar term to many, but few understand the richness it merits. The word Guru literally means the one who takes us from darkness to light. It can also mean the weighty one. It is carelessly translated as the one who teaches—there is another word for that—an Acharya. The Guru transmits wisdom not only through teaching, though it can be this too, but simply by being. It is akin to the relationship between the rays of the sun on a crisp cold morning and the icicles that it melts. The Guru, like the sun, by just being is enough. Her radiance provides all that is required for one to transform into a more complete human being. The RSS considers the saffron dhwaj as the Guru as it is a reminder of Dharma, the eternal and universal essence of creation; the one banner that has been in Hindu memories for thousands of years and the one symbol that all Hindus can rally behind. It is a symbol of perfection, something which no human being can ever attain. All of this is encapsulated in the term Guru, whereas the word Purnima simply means the night of the full moon.

On the day when the full moon appears, the Guru is to be venerated. Shakhas congregate at their designated locations, and attendees place their offerings to the saffron dhwaj (flag) by placing whatever they can afford at the base of the flagpole. To this day, all over the world, wherever there is a shakha, attendees on Guru Purnima place white envelopes at the base of the flagpole with an undisclosed amount of money dedicated to their inspiration—their Guru. It is a custom of Hindu society that has existed for thousands of years and thrives today all over India and within the Hindu diaspora. To this day, the RSS has no membership fees, and there is never a compulsion to give. One never sees spectacles of swayamsevaks dressing up as superheroes to raise money for their local shakha. A remnant of Hedgewar's personality has inspired the Sangh the world over to live within its means. The RSS has always lived frugally.

On 2 July 1928, at the first Guru Purnima, the RSS raised a trifling eighty-four rupees from its swayamsevaks.[3] Today, the situation is something altogether different in so far as the RSS raises tens of millions of rupees from all over India from millions of swayamsevaks. Indeed, over its history from very lowly beginnings, it now has the financial muscle to build two tower blocks in central Delhi, each tower block being fourteen stories high. [4] Hedgewar's RSS in 1929 was financially still a fledgling. They scrimped, borrowed and raised funds themselves to acquire musical instruments and décor for events, and made their own equipment. Even the uniform was taken in whole from the Congress Seva Dal. The RSS never took donations. It intensely dislikes them. It only accepts offerings, and even then, only from its own swayamsevaks and no one else. Hedgewar was not playing with semantics by distinguishing between a donation and an offering. In Hindu custom, an offering is something that is given without an expectation. It is given to a revered person or idea for the sake of giving. The giver holds no attachment to that which she has given, while the receiver has no compulsion to answer or be held accountable for that offering. Yet, the offering is sacred for both parties and treated as such. The RSS, at Hedgewar's insistence, has always ensured that financial accounts are clear and transparent. Money for Hedgewar, and now for the RSS, is sacred.[5] This principle has certainly held it back on numerous occasions but has been more than compensated by the long arc of history with stability, integrity and instilling a discipline of self-sufficiency.

As numbers swelled in shakhas, new units were started across differing neighbourhoods. His leadership team, especially Anna Sohoni and Martand Jog, were excited by the prospect of such numbers joining. They had the wind in their sails. Hedgewar, however, remained optimistically prudent. He had seen before, on numerous occasions, the fickleness of youth. Great swarms of young people would get excited, join, train and at the first sign of difficulty, would give up and, with a great noisy whimper, return home deflated. He had seen many revolutionary groups rise and disappear in this manner. Hedgewar was insistent on remaining focused on strengthening the Hindu community by way of physical training and character-building programmes. His generals, however, began to have other ideas.

In early 1929, a young man by the name of Shyam Dhadge, who was only twenty years old, and a rising star in the RSS, began organising 'secret' meetings with other impressionable swayamsevaks. These meetings were encouraged by Sohoni and Huddar, both of whom were in Hedgewar's leadership team, to find innovative ways to 'shock and awe' the everyday folk of Nagpur. 'How can we really rile them up?' they would ask. Darker elements were also creeping into their discussions—that of targeting the Muslim community to instil fear in them.[6] Hedgewar would quell such talk immediately and draw their attention to mundane matters of the organization. He would ask, 'Did your shakha start on time, how many attended, how is so-and-so's mother these days, have you been to see her?'[7] These questions were intended to divert the visceral and bigoted nature of some of the conversations that were taking place within certain groups. They also served the purpose of focus. Hedgewar instilled this belief into his young, over-enthusiastic cadre that until and unless everyone did the small things perfectly, there was no point in dreaming up grandiose visions of a liberated, strong Indian society. All this was much to the frustration of Sohoni.

Sohoni was constantly lobbying for a stronger, militant and assertive RSS. He wanted the Sangh to actively attack Muslim clerics and troublesome mosques.[8] He was adamant about attacking the British authorities at every given opportunity. And he wanted the shakha to be more like an akhada, where boys spent more time learning how to fight than anything else. Hedgewar would have none of it! He had been there before. Angry revolutionary talk with dollops of bigotry for flavouring was not what the RSS was about. Kaware, too, sided with Sohoni. For Hedgewar, and he said as much, the mission was to spread the existing model of shakhas across the country and throughout Indian society. Hedgewar was clear that the Sangh was for the masses, and therefore its activities had to remain simple, basic and inclusive. Sohoni persevered out of respect for Hedgewar, but he was finding the whole daily shakha routine bland, and an inadequate response to the call of revolution. In late 1929, Sohoni stopped attending RSS activities.[9] Hedgewar had lost one of his fiercest commanders.

Sohoni was missed but never forgotten. Hedgewar regularly visited him and encouraged an exchange of views. Sohoni had been particularly miffed at the Sangh for allowing kids as young as nine and ten to join the daily shakhas. For him, the RSS was a military organization, one where young men learnt to fight for a revolution and to protect the Hindu community from aggressive forces. Sohoni could not stomach the softness, and the steady approach Hedgewar was instilling in the organization. Sohoni went on to dabble a bit here and there but to no great avail. He was not an organizer and lacked a strategic mind. He opened his own akhada for a while and trained people in martial arts, but eventually, he gave up public work altogether. In later life, he developed a form of paralysis and eventually became bedbound in his sixties. It is worth noting that Sohoni always remained warm towards Hedgewar and the RSS. He never formed any bitterness nor animosity, especially when he realized in later years the tremendous strength and growth of the RSS, an organization that he had been instrumental in establishing.

Bhau Kaware had been a childhood friend and a fellow revolutionary, and now, like Hedgewar, an RSS swayamsevak. Kaware was militant. As with Sohoni, for Kaware, the scope of his vision began and ended with a free India. Nothing else ultimately mattered to him. He was earnest and wore his heart on his sleeve. He was not one to suffer fools gladly. The RSS was a means of achieving that end. But he remained a revolutionary at heart, whereas Hedgewar had changed. The gap in thought between them had widened as the years had gone by, but their friendship remained as close as ever. This is a feature of Hedgewarian thought still emphasized in shakhas everywhere. Never fall out with someone because of their beliefs or ideas; one simply needs to act and allow one's actions to make the points for you. For Hedgewar, every individual was useful, and none were useless—personal beliefs and tastes were not important. Rather, the emphasis fell on the act and the devotion of any individual over the longer term.

Kaware had suddenly fallen ill and began suffering from severe fevers. He died in a village called Hingani sometime in 1928. For Hedgewar, Kaware was a lifelong companion, friend and reliable support. His sudden death had shocked Hedgewar. According to Palkar, after the final rites were performed, Hedgewar was 'inconsolable'.[10] Kaware, unlike Sohoni who had been at the centre of the early Sangh, had been more aloof from the earliest days. He had helped set up several shakhas in the surrounding districts and was always at hand to support the Sangh, but never at its centre. He was, however, a crutch of some sort for Hedgewar. Now, that crutch was no more. Hedgewar had become a little more alone.

In March 1928, Hedgewar introduced the notion of what he called a 'pratigna'—a solemn oath. He took ninety-nine young swayamsevaks up to Starky Point, a small hill with a thick grove at its top.[11] It was a kilometre further on the Nagpur–Amarvati Road from the lake where the young Keshav swam after school on dry, hot summer days. Starkey Point was named after Lieutenant Starkey, whose idea it was to take cannons up to the hilltop during the third Anglo-Maratha war of 1817. From this vantage point, he ordered cannons to be fired on the hapless people of Nagpur. So it is not without some incongruity that Hedgewar chose this site to conduct the Sangh's first oath-taking ceremony. At dusk in the cooling air, with a red sun setting in the west, Hedgewar spoke at length about the purpose of the Sangh. What he said that evening is not clear, but we certainly know the impact upon those who attended. Hedgewar wasn't going to unleash terror on Nagpur like Starkey had, but he was going to unleash another type of power—a power that was perpetual. From the Hedgewarian viewpoint, it was a re-ignition of the age-old tradition within Hindu society of infusing men with a lifelong commitment to upholding Dharma. Hedgewar stood with the saffron flag of the Sangh fluttering behind him. In front was a single line of ninety-nine young men who each in turn repeated the oath and, while doing so, passed through a psychological doorway, which was to change the face of modern India in the decades to come. The oath went something like this:

> 'In the name of Almighty God and our ancestors, I hereby vow that I have become a unit of the Rashtriya swayamsevak Sangh in order to protect

> our sacred Dharma, culture and society and to achieve the all-round development of the Hindu nation. I will do the Sangh's work sincerely with a selfless spirit and with all my body, heart and wealth. I will observe this vow all my life. Bharat Mata ki jai.'[12]

The rendering of the Marathi into English, as done by Chitkara, communicates the essence of the oath while completely lacking the spirit and the nuances of the original. The God that Hedgewar referred to was an impersonal consciousness, not the personal 'saviour' God of Abraham. Furthermore, it is worth noting the emphasis on ancestry. The Hedgewarian prism through which the RSS still operates is one of rootedness to a soil, to kin. One must not confuse this with caste, for the RSS finds caste very distasteful and a blemish on Indian society. The oath highlights that the swayamsevak is an instrument through which service to society can be rendered. The emphasis here is to dissolve the Self into the wider movement of the RSS, in a way that Buddhists may appreciate. According to Jaffrelot, 'the new man must sacrifice his personality to the cause'.[13] It is also worth noting the phrase 'all-round development of the Hindu nation'. The RSS is not a religious outfit spreading the gospel of Hedgewar, but quite the contrary. It vows to build all aspects of a nation—from re-engineering the individual, preserving the family, right the way through to the economic revitalization, environmental protection, to building institutions of law, skill development and much more. No realm is out of bounds for the RSS. The final concluding phrase is also often misinterpreted and muddled in popular discourse. 'Bharat mata ki jai' is a phrase millions of Hindus worldwide can resonate with, without having the words to explain why. The last three words are straightforward enough—victory, glory, or fulfilment to the motherland. It is the feminine divine that Hedgewar invokes. The first word, Bharat, can be vague, perplexing, and impractical. Bharat or Bharata was geographical in nature—but one with a topsoil that had the roots of the Hindu culture seeded within. The term came into recorded history as far back as the first century before the common era.[14] Hedgewar appeals to India's deep past, a time almost forgotten by history, but deeply encoded in the collective memories of Hindu culture. A term that ancient Indians would have used is 'Bharat-varsha'.[15] By invoking the term 'Bharat', and its glory, Hedgewar is identifying what the RSS is fighting for—the protection and revitalization of an ancient culture that was rooted in the soil of ancient India. He is therefore not fighting for a political state; although he did want to see a modern Indian state emerge from the devastation of colonial rule, this was not his raison d'être.

The ninety-nine-strong Hedgewar brigade had taken a life-long vow—which many of those selected that day in March 1928 would go on to fulfil—a few would become the first batch of prachaaraks—lifelong, full-time workers. One amongst them was a young twenty-year-old by the name of Prabhakar Dani, the son of a wealthy landlord, who was sent to Benares Hindu University to spread the RSS network.[16] He remained a prachaarak for many years and expanded the work across central India. Dani's titanic efforts resulted in the emergence of RSS shakhas across Madhya Pradesh, ultimately decades later culminating in a complete overhaul of the political landscape, electing the BJP, the RSS's political child, for twelve years consecutively. He would also go on to play a central role in navigating the RSS through troubled waters during the early years after independence when the movement was outlawed.[17]

Around this time, Hedgewar began to encourage many from this first batch of ordained swayamsevaks to attend prestigious universities for further study. The RSS story suggests that those who came from financially comfortable homes were encouraged to pursue studies as a front to spread shakhas across university campuses.[18] RSS writers have always written such instrumentalist prose to show the single-minded focus of Hedgewar and the complete obedience and sense of purpose from young swayamsevaks. These narratives largely served the interests of the Sangh hierarchy throughout the seventies, eighties and nineties, constantly drawing on these incidents to inspire new young cadres to commit to the organization's mission. On the other side of the spectrum, Indian academics have taken these narratives and depicted a sinister character—an evildoer who essentially sowed the seeds of fascism amongst Hindu youth.[19] Both narratives are inaccurate to varying degrees, although the Indian academic scene very much misses the mark since it has long been maligned by a Marxist reading of history.[20] Hedgewar was a lofty idealist while simultaneously being a complete pragmatist. He had developed an aptitude to reconcile quite contrary views and motives through his unifying acts. RSS writers are correct in noting Hedgewar's far-sighted approach and his sowing the seeds of desh bhakti, but to negate his emphasis on individual flourishing is also equally misleading. Hedgewar was a father figure to many, and he reciprocated that care until his end—he was a father, not a commander. The two motives cannot be separated nor ignored from his personality. To do so would be to obscure reality.

On 27 October 1928, the statue of the great old man of the struggle, Lokmanya Tilak, was installed in Nagpur. To the surprise of many and the visceral anger of Moonjay, the organizing committee led by the Congressman Moreshwar Abhyankar decided to exclude leaders of the Hindu Mahasabha from the proceedings. Moonjay was furious at the petty politics, especially in the light of Tilak being Moonjay's mentor and close friend. Hedgewar, too, was left out as he was widely seen as Moonjay's general and an ardent supporter of the Mahasabha. Hedgewar's reaction was very different from that of his former mentor. He took it in his stride and was delighted that a statue of Tilak was being installed, and to that end, he rallied his swayamsevaks and marched down to the location uninvited. With over a hundred swayamsevaks in uniform, no one was really in any position to stop them. Hedgewar, rather than being confrontational, simply provided support to the organizers and remained courteous throughout. He even gave a ceremonial guard of honour to Dr Mukhtar Ahmed Ansari—a Muslim by faith who had one foot in each camp—Indian National Congress and the Muslim League. Ansari had been given the task of garlanding Tilak's statue at its unveiling. He nervously strode past one hundred swayamsevaks, who held up their fighting bamboo sticks in unison to make an archway for Ansari to walk under as he made his way to the statue.[21] All this was to the bewilderment of Abhyankar. After the speeches were concluded, swayamsevaks stayed behind to clean up the area and were the last to leave. Those who attended, including the Chief of Police, a man named Harbans Singh, sang the praises of the RSS, in particular their sense of duty and discipline.[22]

Was Hedgewar being belligerent? He certainly could be, but that Hedgewar seems to have passed on in 1925. This Hedgewar was far more astute. He firstly demonstrated strength to the organising committee by presenting 100 fully armed and uniformed young men. It was clear to everyone that this was a force in its own right. Furthermore, this strength was overwhelming for the police; hence they were left with no choice but to accept the RSS's presence. Second, Hedgewar could have wielded that strength in any way he so pleased, but he chose dignity and grace, with just a shadow of an underlying threat should anyone dare to resist their presence. And third, the public, who were none the wiser, left deeply impressed, thankful and commended Abhyankar for involving the RSS in this way—all to the inner delight of Hedgewar.

The late 1920s were a time when the RSS was fledgling but growing fast. National leaders took note. The charismatic mayor of Calcutta at the time Subhas Chandra Bose met Hedgewar at a gathering of the Congress, and what was meant to be a ten-minute courtesy 'hello' became a full-blown sixty-minute exchange of thoughts and ideas. Hedgewar, in this private meeting, asked Bose to actively support the RSS, to which the younger man gently refused, stating that he already had other plans well underway.[23] The truth is that Bose, a man much like Nehru and Moonjay, came from the Indian rich. He had a father much like Nehru's, a man patronized by the British, a lawyer who was completely loyal to the Crown. Bose was educated at the best English schools and studied Western philosophy at university. He went on to read further philosophy at Cambridge in 1919 and joined the Indian Civil Service.[24] Bose was also one of Macaulay wayward children—British in mind, housed in an Indian body—his was a pathway to rule independent India as a proxy to British culture and values. Bose was also influenced by a longing to know his own culture and came under the influence of stories about the Hindu sage Ramakrishna and his disciple Vivekananda. Later his wife to be also influenced him to go and seek out a spiritual teacher, much to the annoyance of his father[25]. Bose's worldview was syncretic and was not compatible with Hedgewar's worldview of building a strong Hindu nation to secure real liberty and pluralism. Both agreed on India's ailments—caste prejudice, poverty, illiteracy, the de-industrialization of the country, and Gandhi's problematic leadership. But both believed in different cures and yet could see the merits of each other's proposals. Both had audacious solutions. One might even say complimentary to some extent—but only to an extent. There was still a wide gulf between the two men in thought and deed. Both parted ways—liking each other—but agreeing to disagree.

Bose would return to see Hedgewar ten years later, but the older man was already too unwell to see him, and the two would never meet thereafter. No one quite knows what Bose's motives were in insisting on seeing Hedgewar in 1940, but guesses are that as Bose planned to attack British forces during World War II with his Indian National Army (INA) from the outside, he was seeking help from Hedgewar's RSS to trigger a full-blown revolt from within India at the same time, thereby overwhelming British forces and liberating India.

Throughout 1929, Hedgewar was relentless in his travels. The number of branches continued to grow throughout Maharashtra.[26] As the Hindu society felt increasingly vulnerable, the RSS kept on growing, and their volunteers under the stewardship of Hedgewar became local 'heads'—people who could get things done! The RSS called this working spirit sewa.[27] The sewa spirit ensured that wherever there was a shakha, people could get any assistance they required from the local unit—be it healthcare assistance, protection, financial support for school fees or just having an injustice addressed. As the movement grew, its leadership was under constant surveillance by what was now a bantam state apparatus. Nevertheless, the state was still capable of hangings and life imprisonments in the dark recesses of its empire. Even though the RSS was always on the right side of the law, Hedgewar's revolutionary past was always present in the eyes of the authorities.

In early 1929, the ghost of his revolutionary past had come to haunt Hedgewar. He was no longer a revolutionary—not in spirit nor in action. Back in the early 1920s, Hedgewar had assigned two brothers, now living as wandering vagabonds, to dispose of all the arms and ammunition without drawing any attention. They had done so, but not as thoroughly as they ought to have. Gangaprasad Pandey had been a revolutionary who was now disillusioned and unwell. Word reached Hedgewar that he had arrived in Wardha for medical treatment. His younger brother Anandiprasad was a little more wayward. He carried a firearm with him under his raggedy turban in the off chance that he might be spotted and would have to shoot his way to freedom. He and a friend, a person who has floated out of history, were playing cowboy with the gun. Their hostel was about half a mile from Wardha train station, a busy junction with hundreds of strangers flowing through the area. Several sightings had been made of Anandiprasad and his friend posing and playing with a pistol.

News arrived to Gangaprasad that there had been a robbery by armed men at a nearby town called Hinganghat around 40 kilometres away. The robbery, in broad daylight, had occurred at the station, and the two suspects were seen getting on the train to Wardha. Gangaprasad went into a dreadful frenzy, looking for the firearm. It wasn't where it should have been. As soon as he got hold of his brother, he demanded the pistol back. Naturally the brother and his friend denied any wrongdoing, but to Gangaprasad, it was a surety that these two had wanted some quick cash, and the easiest way was to stick up passengers. Around the same time,

Hedgewar also got news of the robbery. Furthermore, he came to know that cartridges were found at the station and the police were looking for the suspects in Wardha. Hedgewar grew cold. He knew what type of men the two brothers had become. They were poor, scruffy and still angry. It was quite within the realms of possibility that the cartridges could lead back to the brothers, who, under interrogation, could reveal how they got hold of the firearm and reveal the history of the entire revolutionary network. It was an impending disaster for Hedgewar.

He travelled south from Nagpur to Wardha by train that very day. It was a two-hour journey. He went to see Appa Joshi. Hedgewar noted seedy men lurking around his house. Surveillance was in full swing. As Hedgewar entered the house, Joshi knew something was wrong. Both men spoke in hushed whispers and, at nightfall, left the house to make their way to the hostel where the two brothers were staying. Opposite the hostel was an open ground covered with trees. As the two men approached, Hedgewar veered off to cross the road and disappeared into the darkness of the grounds. The stranger tailing them decided to follow Hedgewar. He found a neem tree under which he stood in complete shadow but positioned himself so he could see out onto the street where the hostel was located. He saw his uncle speak to a man who opened the front door. Within a few seconds, he saw Gangaprasad appear. Joshi passed over a note, and after a few more exasperated seconds, he reappeared and handed over a burlap sack. The men clearly exchanged nods, and his uncle was making his way back towards the grounds.

Just as Joshi was about to reach the neem tree where Hedgewar had stood, a hand suddenly grabbed his wrist in an arresting manner. Instinctively, Hedgewar jerked forcefully, freeing his hand from the man's grip. With his instincts now in full drive, he, in turn, took hold of the stranger's hand and pulled him closer. With repeated jabs, he punched the stranger squarely in the face. After several whimpering cries, the man's body went limp, and Hedgewar let the man drop onto the ground. Joshi saw two shadowy figures underneath the designated tree and could clearly make out Hedgewar's large frame pummelling a smaller man. He paused and simply retreated, disappearing into the darkness. Hedgewar, in the meantime, was heard to say to the man on the ground, 'You see, I have nothing in my hands'. He made his way to another friend's home to stay for the night. The next morning, he caught the first train out of Wardha towards Nagpur.

It remains a mystery as to where and how Joshi disposed of the pistol and cartridges. The beaten informant reported what he could to the authorities, and surveillance was increased even further to the point where Govind Charade, a lawyer, accused the police of harassment. He was oblivious to what had happened the previous week and the depth of involvement of Appa Joshi in the revolutionary movement. Nevertheless, he challenged the prosecutor to charge Joshi if they had evidence or stop the open harassment of citizens. The police inspector knew that he had disposed of the firearm and was wrongly convinced that he was behind the robbery too. But, due to a lack of evidence, the case was eventually dropped. Hedgewar was tailed for weeks after the incident, but ultimately, nothing would come of it, and the surveillance was reduced. It was a narrow escape personally for him, but also for the reputation of the RSS. The police would not have wasted any time in implicating the entire RSS network in the dacoity.

Even though Hedgewar was no longer a revolutionary himself, he had great sympathies with those who chose to walk that thorny path. In the late 1920s, between 1928-29, Hedgewar met Shivram Rajguru, the friend and compatriot of the legendary Bhagat Singh, who too had come to see Hedgewar.[28] Rajguru had assassinated a police officer in late 1928 by the name of John Saunders, who had ordered his troops to charge a peaceful demonstration. In doing so, his officers took a heavy hand and beat to death an old political leader—Lala Lajpat Rai. Rai was a major figure in the struggle for freedom and had inspired many young men to join the struggle against the colonialists. Hedgewar had arranged a farmhouse owned by Prabhakar Dani's father well outside of Nagpur as a hiding place for the fugitive.[29] He was instructed to lay low for a while, but Rajguru was desperate to get on a ship and sail out of British India. He left the relative safety of the farmhouse and went to Pune. There, he was swiftly found, arrested and tried. He was sentenced to death and sent to the gallows in 1931. He was barely twenty-two years old.

That summer, the temperatures in Nagpur soared to around 35 degrees centigrade. It was hot and dry. In these conditions, the first RSS training camp was organized. It was a part-gruelling and part-social forty-day marathon.[30] It was called the OTC. Seventeen young men volunteered to join the programme. They were being trained to effectively start new work in different neighbourhoods where the RSS had little or no presence. The days would consist of a 5 a.m. start arriving at Mohite Wada in the run-down basement of the old house. The mornings consisted of tough physical training and exercise, as well as hand-to-hand combat training. The midday sun was too intense to be outdoors, and so the afternoons were spent planning activities, reading, chatting and doing general mischief. The atmosphere was kept jovial and light-hearted. It's unclear how or what they ate, but it seems that most of the participants went home for their midday meals and returned. The evening again would consist of martial training and learning how to take games as instructors. Three times a week the boys would receive an intensive session on Indian history, Hindu culture, analysis and narratives on the causes of civilizational degradation, why caste had to be removed and general knowledge about global affairs. Sessions on character building were compulsory, and stories from the Indian epics were made alive and even acted out during nightly plays. Hedgewar spent all his time with these boys. Others, such as Jog and Sohoni would come and take their specific sessions and leave to go and earn their daily bread. Hedgewar was full-time. He did and thought of nothing else.

In time, these camps grew in size, number and ambition. Today, camp sizes can vary from a few hundred to tens of thousands of participants. Entire micro villages are constructed in large open grounds housing an army of volunteers. Food is cooked on site, and the training, although evolved, is nevertheless still gruelling and relentless. The OTC is now called the Sangh Shiksha Varg, meaning the Sangh Learning Centre. The militarization has been largely removed, and all the combat training has been replaced by softer organizational skills. Hedgewar spent hours mulling over the schema of the OTCs and the atmosphere in which it must be conducted. He strongly felt that without a sense of belonging and an equally deep-rooted purpose, young men would not grow into the citizens modern India required.

By 1929, Hedgewar had become what Scott Atran calls the devoted actor. Atran describes the devoted actor as a person who has psychologically reached a point where their ideas and values are permanently coupled with their outward behaviour. In other words, these are people who live exactly as they believe. If Atran ever met Hedgewar, the latter would be classed as deontic—completely duty-based.[31] Atran's hypothesis of the devoted actor is described as:

> People will become willing to protect morally important or sacred values through costly sacrifice and extreme actions, even being willing to kill

> and die, particularly when such values are embedded in or fused with group identity, becoming intrinsic to "Who I am" and "Who We are."[32]

In other words, the devoted actor has their inner life completely aligned with their outer life, and their sense of 'I' is fused with the group identity to which they have surrendered. Those highly devoted to a cause, such as missionaries, or monks and nuns, maybe even mothers and fathers who have fused their own identity with that of their children, can become devoted actors.[33] The devoted actor is not a person motivated by outcomes but through sacred values. The RSS is completely orientated towards making common folks increasingly more value-focused, ultimately becoming deontic. Hedgewar's life is the fullest expression of the devoted actor, and those of the prachaarak order follow closely behind. The devoted actor(s) can be benign and progressive if married to a set of values that are enlightened. However, it can swing the other way too. Devoted actors can be highly malevolent if the value system they have fused with is 'othering', a case in point could be the Islamism faced by Indian society in the late 1920s. What differentiates the RSS from any other mass Hindu movement is its conscious ability to create thousands of devoted actors, much to the dread of all those who do not understand or agree with its value system. The Indian state, for one, has always feared the RSS for this very reason. The loyalty of the swayamsevaks lies with the RSS, Hindu society at large, and with any organization that lives in accordance with the values of Dharma. Nation-states always view such movements—religious or otherwise—with suspicion and dread because movements like the RSS are capable of wielding a grassroots strength that most politicians can only dream of. The modern Indian State fears the RSS because it has the power to derail and even dethrone any government that it wishes to.

In the late 1920s, Hedgewar's RSS was an enigma for his contemporaries. Was it a force for good or for ill? Was it a force they could harness to propel their own agenda forward? Could Hedgewar be controlled? What was the ultimate objective of the RSS? None of these questions could be clearly answered, and Hedgewar was not interested in answering them. He wanted to let the actions of individual swayamsevaks and the RSS, as a whole, answer in the fullness of time. In acts such as this, one can see that Hedgewar was no longer thinking in an instrumentalist manner but much more like a devoted actor. Everyone from Savarkar to Moonjay tried to harness the RSS for their own ends—namely, to serve the interests of the

Hindu Mahasabha. Hedgewar and the RSS leadership obliged them, but only to an extent. The RSS remained largely apolitical, and it still claims to be, even though people find that hard to believe.

The Congress leadership under Gandhi had become highly suspicious of the RSS. Their suspicion was fuelled by a cocktail of factors, ranging from their utter lack of control over the organization, its swift growth and potency and finally, their complete lack of understanding about the inner drives of the movement. Nehru was principally against the RSS and discouraged anyone in his ranks from engaging with the organization. He even tried to reprimand the man who would become India's second President, Dr Sarvepalli Radhakrishnan, for speaking at an RSS OTC in 1948.[34] Nehru's tone would set a precedent for the animosity between subsequent governments of India and the RSS. Mutual scepticism and fear would reign until the late nineties. However, the seeds of derision began as early as 1929 when the Congress working committee decided to re-orientate their own grassroots volunteer force called the Hindustani Sewa Dal, later named Congress Sewa Dal, to compete with, challenge and diminish the power of the RSS.[35]

Hedgewar was deeply saddened by the decisions of the Congress.[36] Prabhakar Dani and Krishna Mohrir joined several Sewa Dal meetings in Nagpur with the sole intent of reporting their agenda back to Hedgewar. According to these two young men, the Sewa Dal cadres had taken an oath of militancy against RSS shakhas and aimed to shut them down.[37] The RSS took no heed of such rhetoric and simply carried on with their business. Indeed, Hedgewar began to invite ever more dignitaries from the Congress machinery to RSS events.[38] The Hedgewarian approach to such provocations can be summed in a pithy statement often recited by prachaaraks, which is attributed to Hedgewar: 'We do not pull out our teeth when they accidentally bite our own tongue.'[39] The Hedgewarian approach, therefore, is to recognize those within the body politic and those without. These behaviour patterns have deep roots in Hedgewar's childhood when he was memorising the Marathi poetry of Samarth Ramdas. Time would essentially reveal the toothless nature of the Congress Sewa Dal, which was a movement completely in servitude to its political masters in the Congress Working Committee. The RSS, on the other hand, went from strength to strength and dwarfed any other would-be opponent.

One of the principal reasons for the growth of the RSS was Hedgewar's deep penetration into the ailments of the society—namely, the Hindu character. It had become rotten. The entire edifice of the RSS was designed to uplift the individual and build a community based on strength, support and compassion. Organizations such as the Sewa Dal were merely political proxies designed for a narrow end—political power for their masters. Around 1929, in a series of correspondences, Hedgewar refers to the RSS as Sangh (Community) and then as Rashtra (Nation). From the Hedgewarian perspective, a shakha is meant to be a microcosm of the Hindu nation, embodying Dharma and (Hindu) culture. The shakha is meant to be built around responsibility and not positions of power; it is meant to be egalitarian, where individuality is nurtured but in some coherence to the overall service of the nation; to pursue excellence together; self-pride; plural and free from caste, creed and class. The anti-Hedgewarian perspective is that of a terrifying darkness that subsumes all diversity, culture, language, individuality, freedom and everything that attempts to resist it.

The narratives surrounding the RSS for most of its history have been dominated by the nay-sayers, those who see the darkness. This is to be expected, as any Indian institution, including the State, that is rooted in values other than (Hindu) Dharma will feel the heat—literally. Most narratives, before the advent of social media, were tightly controlled by a set of institutions that dominated the public imagination. Yet, for all their intellectual prowess, for millions of common folks globally, the RSS has been experienced as a positive force in their lives. A force which has given them a sense of self-respect and self-pride, a force which has given them the tools to break free and grow past the colonial hangover.

For all its early growth, it was still small but potent. Eyes were on it—the weakening leviathan and those internal forces like the Congress that saw it as a potential threat to their own power grab. Hedgewar was acutely aware of this and insisted on the movement keeping a fairly low profile. The swayamsevaks obviously had other ideas. They wanted to show off their strength and capability. They wanted to do more and faster; the wind was in their sail. To this end, the local cadre wanted to come together to organize a large public event celebrating the coronation of the King, Shivaji—the emblem of Hindu pride. Hedgewar was hesitant. He asked the leadership. They too were hesitant and decided instead to do a smaller gathering and to couple that with an intense two-day planning meeting on 9 and 10 November 1929. The minutes of the meeting show that all attendees were part of the leadership team. These included the military man Martand Jog, the communist Gopal Huddar, the fixer Appa Joshi, the lawyer Vishwanath Kelkar and the rising star Krishna Mohrir, amongst thirty others.

As the Sangh grew, it was becoming increasingly difficult to manage. Each branch was encouraged to operate semi-autonomously. They still are. The Sangh network is a very mature and highly evolved example of a centralized-decentralized system. Branches operate with a significant amount of independence and can vary in style and potency. The central leadership, which was formalized at this meeting in November 1929, took on the responsibility of giving direction to the organization. The central leadership would aim to give some mandatory activities for each branch to execute throughout the year. The execution and its methodology were left to the intuition, capability and leadership of the local branches. As part of the centralized structure, several posts were created in the image of a military force—much like the present-day Salvation Army.[40] The post of 'Sar-sena-pati' was created and given to Martand Jog.[41] It was a fitting post for a military man who had introduced the RSS's unique military-style ritual at the beginning and end of every shakha session. Sarsenapati is the highest-ranking post in the Army. For an organization like the RSS, with its military-style discipline, combat training and nationalism, now to have a 'head of the army' sent waves of trepidation across the society who opposed its presence. It sent out a message that this was a force and a law unto itself, that was building a military strength. Years later, the RSS is still labelled as a paramilitary group, and commentators are obsessed with its military formation. Alongside Jog, Gopal, aka Bala Huddar became the operational head of the RSS.[42]

Even though popular academic commentary would have us believe that the RSS is ruled by a hegemon and all its members are nothing more than anti-intellectual minions mindlessly following orders and completely brainwashed with a fascist ideology—the truth is something else altogether.[43] Evidence to the contrary lies in the RSS archival history. The minutes of the meeting held on 9–10 November 1929 make no mention of these posts being agreed upon. Yet, they were announced apparently spontaneously in the final concluding announcements of the weekend. Furthermore, that evening, completely catching Hedgewar unawares, he was announced as Sara-Sangh-Chalak—literally meaning the highest rank, the one who guides the Sangh (Community). Hedgewar had been announced as the supremo, and he was completely unaware of this post![44]

As Appa Joshi made these announcements to the few hundred swayamsevaks gathered sitting on the floor cross-legged and straight-backed (as is the tradition of the RSS), Hedgewar stood by the side of the saffron flag, almost front and centre of the congregated. He must have looked puzzled and awkward as the announcements were made. Then, Jog, who was the new 'army chief', barked out orders for all to rise and salute the new supremo in the RSS tradition. The salute was followed by a lengthy speech by Kelkar explaining the concept of having a supremo at the head of the organization and why it was necessary. According to those who were present, Kelkar emphasized the point of anointing one leader at the helm as necessary to traverse the upcoming social and political volatility, as well as the need to have strong leadership that can give clear direction to the organization.[45] No sooner had the event concluded, and people began to disperse, Hedgewar went to Joshi and made his displeasure plainly known.[46] 'This decision was not made in consensus, I had not known of these matters, I do not approve it' argued Hedgewar.[47] Joshi's rebuttal was stone-cold and direct, 'For the betterment of our work, we have done what does not please you.'[48]

Hedgewar reluctantly accepted the decision. The supremo 'title' was created, but it seems the RSS, from its inception, has never actually had a hegemon at its helm. The supremo title is glorious and arguably even pompous, but the actual decision-making happens in a decentralized format. Group-level decisions are made in consensus amongst the leadership. The title is a red herring to some extent. It was strange to announce as the head of the movement a man who was not only unaware of it but also actively disagreed with the move. So, who made this bold decision? We know from the notes that there were around thirty sangh-chalaks present; these were elders, well-respected individuals from places where shakhas were present, as well as the core team of Kelkar, Jog, Huddar and Joshi. There seems to have been some sort of agreement reached among these individuals that the movement required a central figure people could look to as being exemplary, as well as a unifying personality. Hedgewar was the obvious choice.

The Hedgewarian perspective is that the Sarsanghchalak, the supremo, is more akin to an elder or father figure rather than a supreme god-like dictator. The father or mother is at the helm of the family and sees themself as part of a unitary whole. In contrast, a dictator would see the organization as her means to achieve her ends, where the individuals committed to the organization are merely tools to be used. A benevolent dictator may indeed treat her people well, and the evil dictator may simply see her people as fodder to be discarded once their utility is over. In both cases, the people are means to another party's ends. There is a strong code of utility at work. The Hedgewarian perspective falls back onto an old Hindu paradigm—quasi tribal and quasi monarchical—the ideal family model. In these structures Hedgewar's utopianism shines through.

Another term to express the Hedgewarian form of leadership is sattvika leadership. It is a model with moral concerns at its core.[49] sattvika leadership focuses on the flourishment of the followers and the collective.[50] In most contemporary conceptions of leadership, the leader is goal orientated. In other words, we focus on achieving things, reaching milestones and getting people to work together to achieve those aims as set by the leadership. The telos is all important. In the sattvika style of leadership, the outward goal is of secondary concern; the people come first. The RSS, all over the world, moves frustratingly slowly. It is a huge movement, and as such, must take into consideration the welfare of the youngest to the eldest, the fittest to the weakest, the most intelligent to the less so and those who are spiritual giants as well as those who are hedonists. All belong to the Sangh, and all contribute to the movement—its speed and direction. The RSS is always happy to scrap projects and short-term goals if it harms or hinders those that belong to the parivaar. It is a unique experiment where millions of people are equally prioritized while moving the whole in a single direction. The direction is not always pointed but rather obtuse, which again frustrates and confuses commentators.

Hedgewarian focus is pointed only on two aspects, which combine to what it calls 'kar-ya-kar-ta nir-man'. The term itself means moulding human beings into responsible, morally oriented citizens. The first aspect is moulding men and women into HEROs—full of Hope, (Self) Efficacy, Resilience and Optimism, what many psychologists call psychological capital.[51] The second aspect, equally important, is psychological empowerment. This is the ability for individuals to be intrinsically task motivated, showing a degree of self-awareness and self-control in relation to one's work and one's role.[52] When these two aspects come together, coupled with a moral orientation towards Dharma, the Sangh produces its ideal workers called karyakartas. The shakha is meant to be a factory for karyakartas. Of course, in reality, the attrition rates are high, many people simply do not last very long in shakhas and the consistency and potency of the movement varies significantly from shakha to shakha and from time to time.

Considering the sattvika leadership of the Sangh, Hedgewar as a hegemon makes little sense. Right from the inception of the role, decisions were made in consensus, with the interests of the movement and all its members considered. Joshi's cold remark to his nephew suggests as much. The minutes of the meeting also indicate that other models were considered, where an executive committee should be at the centre of decision-making. On the whole, this was popular amongst the participants, but given the socio-political turmoil, it was decided that a single point of leadership was required to help navigate the movement through turbulent times.[53] Hedgewar obviously was not in agreement, but the overall sentiments of the group overrode his personal inclinations. Hence, it is unfortunate that a term like 'Ek-cha-lak anu-var-tit-va' was used to describe the role. It literally means there will be only one authority whose direction will be followed unquestioningly—what would later be used to describe the movement as fascist.[54]

In those tumultuous times, before World War II and all its horrors, it seems quite clear that Hedgewar and the early RSS pioneers used the language of the ultra-nationalists of Europe and even to some extent emulated them, not quite realizing what lay ahead and the devastation they would cause in years to come. A blend of naivety and ignorance meant that the outward postures were all anti-colonial and fascist without really any of the malign intent. The acts of the RSS do not align with the outward blustering rhetoric and bicep flexing posturing. The acts are altogether far more conscientious and strategic. Commentators have, naively in turn, and in part conveniently taken the RSS at face value. Added to this is the fact that most commentators have had no access to the inner sanctums of the movement and have assumed a likeness in look and intent to the fascist of Europe.

Hedgewar was a desh bhakt. The RSS was a methodology to create psychologically empowered, devoted actors with plenty of psychological capital. He was creating an apolitical outfit that ironically threatened every political outfit in his time. Hedgewar was moulding a generation of young men who had become disenfranchised from the colonial narratives and wanted something authentically Indian. He was sowing seeds of nation-building by scattering RSS shakhas all over India to reform the Hindu culture, to almost save it from itself. He was putting in practice a solution to rid India of her ills—namely caste, poverty, illiteracy, superstition and sectarianism that was being fuelled by powerful individuals who were vying for power and patronage. He was knowingly harnessing a deep forgotten past to mobilize a Hindu renaissance, wherein he wanted to build a syncretic culture that benefited and learnt from global perspectives but could maintain an inner core that was authentically Indian and Hindu.

His success was his biggest hindrance. In 1930, the Congress announced that it finally demanded the complete independence of India from British rule. Until then, it was divided internally between those who just wanted partial independence and those who wanted complete freedom. The progressives had won. The Congress, with this announcement, re-captured the imagination of the people—albeit briefly.

TWELVE: 1930–1932

Flags and Lies

On 19 December 1929, the Indian National Congress asked the country to struggle for complete independence. Nothing less would do. This was then followed by a brilliant public relations campaign where Jawaharlal Nehru hoisted the proposed Indian flag, the tricolour, on 31 December at Lahore. It captured the Indian imagination. The Indian people had not seen, many had never even imagined, that one day their country would have its own flag. It was a watershed moment. The Congress also urged people across the country to mark 26 January 1930 as Independence Day. The leviathan, and patron of the Congress, was not pleased.

On 21 January 1930, five days before the scheduled date, Hedgewar sent a circular to all the shakhas instructing them to also mark Independence Day. It is a circular that, almost a century later, has created much controversy and continues to fuel the naysayers in their scepticism of the RSS and its real motives. The naysayers claim that the RSS from its earliest days, and Hedgewar's note proves as much, was an anti-national force. The circular Hedgewar wrote was in Marathi, and later it was translated into Hindi. Translated, it reads:

> '…this year the Congress has changed its goal to a demand for complete independence and the Congress working committee has given call for Sunday 26th January 1930 to be observed all over Hindustan as "Independence Day". It is natural that we are filled with joy at such a declaration by the Indian National Congress. Supporting any organisation that keeps such an ideal is our duty … thus every shakha shall on Sunday the 26th of January 1930, in the evening at 6pm, assemble all swayamsevaks at the shakha, and salute the Rashtra Dhwaj meaning

> Bhagwa Dhwaj. A lecture is to be held explaining the importance of everyone taking up independence of the country as their mission. The programme should be concluded by congratulating the Congress for taking up this mission.'[1]

The controversy arises in modern discourse because Hedgewar instructs the RSS to salute the 'Rashtra dhwaj' meaning the civilizational emblem, the saffron dhwaj, and not the new proposed tricolour of India, which is what Nehru had in mind. The precedent was set. For decades hence, the RSS, although respectful of the tri-colour flag, had never hoisted it during Independence Day celebrations, until their man, and their creation came into power—Narendra Modi and the BJP. Instead, the RSS always saluted the saffron flag—the unifying emblem of Dharma, the Guru. For many, this was a brazen show of disunity, and for some, even treasonous. The Congress certainly saw it that way and ever since has labelled the RSS as anti-national and anti-constitutional. These are serious charges by any account, but as far as the RSS was concerned, it simply 'begged the question'.

The loyalty of the RSS has never been towards a nation-state earmarked by modern political boundaries, nor towards the government of the day, but rather to the cultural milieu of India, that is, Hindu Dharma—something which makes the RSS a civilizational force rather than a national force. This also makes the RSS somewhat apolitical and constitutionally neutral. If the Constitution serves the project of rebuilding Indian civilization in a way that makes it capable of flourishing in the modern world, then it is to be protected and championed, but if the constitution fails to represent the people and their civilizational past and future, then it is to be challenged and resisted.

Back in 1930, Hedgewar had no such controversies in mind. He was simply making a point that the people of India were gathered to mark their desire for freedom from colonialism, which for him was Dharma in action, so one ought to support it. Ultimately, for Hedgewar, and later his creation, India matters because it is the birthplace of many, but not all, Dharmic traditions such as Vaishnavism, Shaivism, Buddhism, Sikhism, Jainism and all the other hundreds of religious expressions that constitute Hindu civilization. India was the birthplace of this culture and, therefore, its custodian. Hence, one's salutations, as far as Hedgewar was concerned, should be channelled towards the emblem that represents Dharma and its civilization. For Hedgewar, the tricolour was well-intentioned, but ultimately, without sufficient substance or significant meaning, it was more of a quasi-political emblem that had no definite shape, history or future.

The Congress hoisted the Indian flag with its tricolours, but back then, it was in a different order to what we see today. The flag had three colours—white on top, green in the middle and red at the bottom, with a large cotton spinning wheel in its centre. Even as people celebrated the idea of 'purna swaraj', complete independence, most people around the country were unhappy with the flag proposed. First, it looked terribly like the Bulgarian flag. Second, it was designed on religious grounds—the red represented the Hindu community, the green represented Islam, and the white everyone else—much to the annoyance of everyone else. Consequently, the Congress appointed a seven-person team to investigate what could be appropriate and acceptable to the people of India as their national flag. This team produced a brief in 1931. The brief was signed off by none other than Jawaharlal Nehru, Sardar Patel, a Muslim Moulana named Abul Kalam Azad and four other prominent members of the Congress. They unanimously, albeit reluctantly, concluded that the national flag of India should be a saffron flag, one with an Ashok Chakra located somewhere on it.

> 'Opinion has been unanimous that our National Flag should be of a single colour except for the colour of the device. If there is one colour that is more acceptable to the Indians as a whole, even as it is more distinctive than another, one that is associated with this ancient country by long tradition, it is the kesari or saffron colour. Accordingly, it is felt that the flag should be of the kesari colour except for the colour of the device. That the device should be the charkha is unanimously agreed too.'[2]

Hedgewar was vindicated. It was clearly a non-issue at the time as far as he was concerned. The Indian flag, keeping in line with its ancient past, was the Bhagwa Dwaj, or as the report called it, the kesari or saffron flag. The RSS was already using it. They simply carried on using it for decades since. The question that needs to be asked is why was the Committee's unanimous decision ignored? The answer is Gandhi's dictatorship. Gandhi was always adamant that the tricolour should be used, and he bulldozed the considerations of his own committee and forced his will upon the Congress. India still lives with that historic decision, and although it has come to live with it, there are many tens of millions in modern India who feel that their country has the wrong flag.

As per Hedgewar's circular, shakhas began organizing celebrations across the Sangh network. Large gatherings were organized, 'Vande Mataram' was loudly sung, the Bhagwa Dhwaj was hoisted, poetry was read, and speeches were delivered.[3] The leviathan was annoyed and began its usual intimidation tactics, but to no avail. Local RSS volunteers were pulled onto the side of roads and questioned, searched for weapons and promptly released. This went on for weeks, and the Sangh just took it on the chin, using it as fuel to motivate its own. 26 January is still marked as India's Republic Day, and now, across most RSS centres, one can see the tricolour raised as well as the saffron flag, and there is no sign of state pestering.

With the launch of Gandhi's agitation and the whole country being able to sniff the fragrance of independence, hundreds of swayamsevaks across the RSS network were keen to join the various public protests and disobedience movements. For Hedgewar, all of this was noise and a distraction from the main business of nation-building. Decades later, the naysayers would make much hay out of Hedgewar's notes and letters written around this time. For Hedgewar, India's independence was a matter of when and not an if. According to Palkar, Hedgewar had made it clear that the Sangh would not formally join any agitation, but individuals were free to engage after consideration, having got permission from their local teams.[4] Hedgewar had miscalculated. It proved to be very unpopular, and even after several circulars and in-person meetings, Hedgewar, on the whole, was unable to stop the tide of young swayamsevaks from joining the agitations and risking imprisonment. He knew this was all fuelled by a kind of mania. A few sober young men agreed with Hedgewar and continued the routine work of the RSS without giving too much heed to the euphoria all around them.

Seeing the tide turn quickly against his wishes, Hedgewar pulled in his key leadership team and decided that to prevent so many young, talented men from prison sentences, it would be better if the RSS provided medical support during the agitation. The Sangh created medical units and positioned them in key locations during protests and marches. Medical assistance was provided to hundreds of people in a land where medical support was almost non-existent and very expensive wherever it was available. The RSS was duly noted for providing free medical support, and hundreds of new people became interested in joining this new force. Nevertheless, Hedgewar was inwardly disappointed. Throughout the following weeks and months, hundreds of young men were arrested. Some protesters were being rounded up and sentenced for relatively small durations, often as little as two months, while others were being sentenced far more severely, at times for up to several years in hard labour camps. He was saddened that the Indian youth could be so fickle and roused so easily. He felt that the public at large was being used by India's elite.

Hedgewar was particularly irked by the fact that the Congress had not announced purna swaraj, complete independence, out of a sudden bout of patriotism or some deep-seated realization for freedom as a universal right. To Hedgewar, it appeared as a petty knee-jerk reaction to the withdrawal of dominion status, which had been long promised to India's elite. In 1929, Irwin, the then Viceroy of India, had somewhat tentatively promised the leaders of the Congress that India would be granted dominion status.[5] A year before, in 1928, the National Congress, after much internal feuding between the Associates and Republicans, had voted to pursue dominion status and not complete independence. Hedgewar had fought alongside the Republicans for the latter. Dominion status would mean that India would still be 'loyal to the crown' but would be autonomous on all accounts on the same lines as Canada and Australia.[6] Over that year, Irwin took the case to the British parliament as well as to other colonies. He faced immense opposition to the idea of dominion status being given to India.[7] Canadians and other ethnically white dominions were against non-white countries to be considered equal under the crown[8]. Essentially, on racist grounds, India was denied dominion status. To Hedgewar's mind, it seemed that powerful sections of the Congress decided it was now time to push for complete independence out of a tactical necessity.

Hedgewar was filled with doubts. He read the *Declaration of Purna Swaraj of 1930* and agreed with every paragraph.[9] His doubts arose from two fundamental but subtle differences. The first was that the Congress was an instrumentalist organization, one that was built and behaved in the manner of its colonial masters. To his mind, the Congress was increasingly unrepresentative of the Indian milieu and was led by an English-educated masterly class of men who saw the world from a particular standpoint. Independent India, he feared, would simply remove one set of foreign men who imposed their will upon the people and replace them with another set of men of the same mould, albeit Indian in origin, but British in mind, who would use the same tactics to impose their will upon the people using the same draconian laws to suppress alternative viewpoints and ideas.

The Congress was filled with paternalistic ideas, and the roots of Russian socialism had penetrated its core.

The second was that he simply did not agree with the methodology employed. The focus had to be on strengthening the rich and diverse tapestry of society, which for him meant the Hindu society. The Hindu was fragmented, poor, illiterate, caste conscious and politically disorganized. To Hedgewar's mind, the Congress did not think about these matters seriously enough. What would happen in an independent India where the common citizen is incapable of thriving in a liberal democracy and where the consciousness of society is still built on caste and kin rather than a common idea of nationhood? What would happen to the country if radical clerics from Deobandi and Barelvi mosques up and down the country continued to spout bigoted messages, sowing the seeds of separatism? Indeed, Hedgewar felt that the Congress would take full advantage of the situation and attempt to mould an Indian society built on ideas that were once again foreign to the native culture. Nehru, in 1929, openly declared that he was a 'socialist'.[10] Two years earlier, Nehru was made the honorary president of the Marxist–Leninist League Against Imperialism, and later that year, he visited Moscow for a four-day visit to explore the practical application of socialism and communism.[11] Hedgewar feared a strong, powerful paternalistic socialism—he feared, above all else, Nehru and Gandhi's idea of India.

History, decades hence, has ultimately proven him right. India would be torn into multiple pieces. The weakened British state and the Congress under Nehru and Gandhi's leadership were incapable of fortifying the country against the violence unleashed during partition. Millions died. Many millions more were uprooted. The Congress not only failed to contain Islamic seeds of separatism but went on to fuel the radicalism of Deobandi Islam through appeasement tactics, sidelining moderate Muslim voices who called for unity. Consequently, millions of Hindus became further alienated, and their future remained as uncertain as it was under their invisible white masters. Furthermore, Nehru and Gandhi used the same powers as the colonialists to suppress all forms of dissent, nationalized all heavy industries, the financial sector, and education, and attacked the free press. Communists, capitalists, journalists, and progressives were all rounded up, jailed and, or silenced.[12] The media became the mouthpiece for state-sponsored propaganda.[13] Indeed, for decades, the Indian media was also an agent for Soviet propaganda.[14] India would lose decades under socialism.

Hedgewar did not support the tricolour in 1930 because he was filled with trepidation about the sinister ideas that had seduced India's leaders, and ultimately, had doubts about what this new flag really represented. He was clear, as was the committee that Congress has set up, that the people of India, en masse connected with the kesari flag, which is the saffron flag of the RSS.

By June 1930, Hedgewar had realized that the winds were firmly blowing in favour of the agitations. Even his closest comrades were now getting sucked into the mania of Gandhi's call to boycott specific laws that were deemed to be unjust. Reluctantly, he agreed to join too, much to the delight of his inner team.

Gandhi had coined the term Satyagraha, meaning to hold firmly to the truth. Around this term, he had built up an entire edifice of values, with great emphasis on how one ought to behave while embarking on this struggle for independence:[15]

1. Harbour no anger.
2. Suffer the anger of the opponent.
3. Never retaliate to assaults or punishment; but do not submit, out of fear of punishment or assault, to an order given in anger.
4. Voluntarily submit to arrest or confiscation of your own property.
5. If you are a trustee of property, defend that property (non-violently) from confiscation with your life.
6. Do not curse or swear.
7. Do not insult the opponent.
8. Neither salute nor insult the flag of your opponent or your opponent's leaders.
9. If anyone attempts to insult or assault your opponent, defend your opponent (non-violently) with your life.
10. As a prisoner, behave courteously and obey prison regulations (except any that are contrary to self-respect).
11. As a prisoner, do not ask for special favourable treatment.
12. As a prisoner, do not fast in an attempt to gain conveniences whose deprivation does not involve any injury to your self-respect.
13. Joyfully obey the orders of the leaders of the civil disobedience action.

Gandhi had been long influenced by Thoreau's essay, 'Civil Disobedience'.[16] Like Gandhi, Hedgewar too would have read Thoreau, especially in the light of Emerson, and therefore knew where Gandhi's intellectual ideas stemmed from. Even though Thoreau's ideas were noble in essence, he was never convinced that they would work in practice and certainly did not believe that the Hindu masses were ready for such instruction. Gandhi, on the whole, positioned himself as a militant pacifist—something which Hedgewar abhorred because he felt that these were tools for the weak. Ultimately, Hindu leaders ought to be in the business of capacity building, making the average citizen competent, educated, disciplined, brave and quite able to wield force when necessary. Indeed, at some level, Hedgewar may have even felt that Gandhi used Thoreauvian soil to grow his Gandhian worldview—much to the detriment of Thoreau's work and the Indian people.

After much cajoling and confronting the harsh truth that his entire cadre had been swept up into the call for swarajya, Hedgewar decided to join the Satyagraha of the Central Provinces, led by his old mentor Madhav Aney—the man who had supported him while he was a student. The Central Provinces were particularly eager to break the jungle laws that were enforced in 1917. They essentially transferred the commons of the jungle into the hands of the British.[17] Tens of thousands of tribals and subsistence farmers were effectively barred from using the commons overnight. When their animals meandered into the jungles while grazing, they were confiscated.[18] The satyagraha enabled thousands of people who experienced life without much dignity to find that they had a voice, and all strata of society came together. Animals were let loose. Women walked into the juggles and simply picked up the dried wood for their evening fires. The police would arrive, swinging their bamboo sticks, causing some bruising, and, at times, serious injury to men, women and children; however, they would soon be overrun by protestors. This pattern repeated itself in hundreds of different locations.

The RSS leadership decided that if Hedgewar was to go and participate in the Satyagraha then it was better that someone else become the Sar-sangh-chalak—at the helm of the RSS. In July 1930, it was decided that Dr Paranjape should take over in Hedgewar's absence. Soon after, Hedgewar and a select few left Nagpur to head out towards Yavatmal, a small backwater town of little significance. From here, they would march south towards another small town called Pusad. Rural India in the 1930s was full of small, sleepy towns and villages where things changed very slowly, if at all, where the grip of the leviathan was weakest. Aney had decided to send his three most capable organizers to different locations and march simultaneously, arousing the public to have the courage to break unjust laws. Hedgewar was initially given the responsibility to rouse the people of Pusad, south of Yavatmal, and then march from there north to Dhaman. At some point, everyone knew the police would turn up and arrest the organizer, and a prison sentence would follow. Hedgewar was on a trip that would eventually land him in jail.

RSS folklore is full of interesting stories about how the early prachaaraks, the Hedgewar Brigade, as they are often remembered, managed to turn the fledgling organization that no one took seriously into a behemoth. These are tales of extreme personal hardship and sacrifice, tales of adventure, boldly venturing into the unknown, but above all else, these stories are meant to be exemplary. One of these stories came from Hedgewar's visit to the insignificant town of Pusad. Parmarth, one of his young captains and part of the RSS's first group of prachaaraks, had accompanied Hedgewar to Pusad—it is his rendering of the story that has been passed on for decades.

Every morning at sunrise, Hedgewar would leave his small room, within walking distance from the banks of the river Pus, to meditate. He would wear a traditional white dhoti, and a soft woollen shawl loosely wrapped around his body. He would spend a significant chunk of his morning on the banks listening to birdsong and watching life flow by.

On one such morning, soon after he had finished his meditation, still early enough to feel the moistness in the air, he noticed a young man, clearly identifiable as a Muslim with his skull cap, facial hair and dress. He was leading a cow down the riverbank. To Hedgewar, it must have seemed odd to have seen a young Muslim man in a predominantly Hindu area that people would generally visit for morning prayers and washing. Hedgewar greeted the young man and asked him where he was going. 'To slaughter this cow just a little further along the river,' he casually answered. Hedgewar was quite shocked but could see from the young man's tone and manner that he was doing nothing unusual. Just as Hedgewar was beginning to ask more questions, an older, stern-looking man appeared from the alleyway. He snapped at the young man for standing around talking to strangers and ordered him to keep walking. Hedgewar's mood changed.

Hedgewar made himself visible and apologized to the older man for distracting his young assistant. He pivoted himself, so he was now blocking the way. While stroking the cow, Hedgewar asked the older man if it was true that this cow would be slaughtered. The older man snapped, asking him to get out of the way. Hedgewar stood firm. 'I'd like to buy this cow from you. How much did you pay for it?' he asked.

'Twelve rupees, and the cow is not for sale. Get out of the way!'

'How much will you earn by slaughtering it?' he asked while still stroking the cow.

'Over thirty rupees. You cannot afford it, Brahmin; now get out of the way,' he said scornfully, looking Hedgewar up and down.

With the old Muslim man's raised voice a few more people began to stare. Hedgewar noted how the Hindus stared from a distance as passive bystanders. It dawned on Hedgewar that this man was a butcher.

'I will pay you thirty rupees for this cow; I will save you the trouble of slaughtering her,' he said with a gentle firmness. Hedgewar stared directly at the old man for what must have been only a few seconds. The old man was clearly stunned.

'No. I will not give her to you. I will slaughter her right now,' the old man said, raising the stakes as a direct pushback against Hedgewar's stance. No sooner had he finished speaking, Hedgewar snatched the rope out of the young man's hand and, with an equally raised voice, said, 'I will not let you slaughter this cow, not while I'm alive!' The stakes kept on being raised.

'We will see about that,' the old man said with a little less confidence. He ran off back into the alleyway. Hedgewar stood firmly where he was, with the cow's leash now in his hand. The young man just looked dazed and was far too timid to even look at Hedgewar. Within a few minutes, some elders accompanied the old butcher. These men were Hindu. 'This is the thug,' he shouted, pointing at Hedgewar.

All this time, Parmarth was watching from afar. He was in two minds about whether to go and call the other swayamsevaks to help Hedgewar or simply stand by and enjoy his mentor standing up for what he believed to be just. He was ready to jump in at any given moment, but he was admiring Hedgewar's unflinching nature. Two Hindu elders accompanying the old butcher now spoke, 'Please give the cow back. Don't do this. They have always butchered cows here on the bank of this river. We have all accepted it.'

Hedgewar was somewhat astonished at the meekness and surrendered tone of the man who was clearly a respected figure in the town. Sensing the mood, he lowered his voice and calmly asked, 'Why are they butchering this cow out in the open, in a Hindu area, where we worship, mediate and pray? I have offered to pay him the price he stated for the cow. Why will he not simply let me purchase the cow?'

'You will cause trouble for us. Please hand over the cow,' requested the old man with worn-out eyes.

'Why don't you stick with your duty of care and concentrate on the satyagraha?' shouted a younger, annoyed man, who was also clearly a Hindu, with a large red tilak smeared on his forehead.

While all this was happening, two police constables brushed past Parmarth, walking in the direction of the heated exchange. The police were now on the scene. The stakes now were raised yet another notch. No sooner had the police constables reached the ensuing argument than two more younger menacing-looking Muslim men arrived onto the scene. Now, Parmarth swiftly followed the constables to stand alongside Hedgewar. The constables immediately brandished their bamboo sticks and demanded to know what was happening. Hedgewar towered above both and stated his position. The old butcher snapped at the constables and ordered them to arrest Hedgewar. They did not take too kindly to this. The senior constable threatened to arrest both men on the count of disturbing the peace if they did not resolve this immediately. Hedgewar flared up; his body became large and menacing, eyes suddenly filled with rage, 'I will not let this cow be slaughtered while I am alive. I have offered these men a fair price of their choosing. I suggest they let me purchase this cow.'

The constables looked at the butcher, who had somewhat softened, having lost the will to further up the ante. Hedgewar had won. He knew it. He who dares, wins. The butcher accepted the payment for the cow, and the crowd quickly dispersed. Mildly threatening glances were exchanged between the two sides, but each went their separate way. Hedgewar and Parmarth walked the cow to the nearest animal shelter and handed her over. By sunset, Hedgewar had become the talk of the town. Unbeknown to Hedgewar, he had disturbed and broken a tradition that had been in place for decades. In Pusad, for a very long time, it had become customary for the local Muslim butcher to bring a cow into the Hindu area along the bank of the river Pus and slaughter it out in the open. It was a show of strength and showed which community was ultimately in charge. The old butcher and his assistant were simply carrying out a ritual they had been doing for years. This was the reason why the butcher was not keen on selling the cow, because it was more than a business transaction; it was about which community oversaw the town. It was tribal.

Hedgewar was the first Hindu in decades to have stood up to this barefaced, facetious act of aggression. The grapevine was humming across the town in both the Hindu and Muslim communities. The next evening at the satyagraha event, there were more people than the hall could accommodate, much to the surprise of Hedgewar and his companions. Hundreds of men, women and children packed into the hall to take a glance at the man who had single-handedly stood up to what every Hindu knew were bullying tactics, which inflicted much psychological harm to the community. What surprised people was the sheer daring nature of this man, who was simply willing to fight to death to save a cow in a town that did not mean anything to him, for nothing more than his principles. According to Parmarth, Hedgewar spoke in such fiery prose that night that within weeks of that speech, a new RSS centre was established, and thousands joined the jungle satyagraha.[19]

Buoyed by Hedgewar's actions, those in his company began to see the satyagraha as an opportunity to spread the seeds of the RSS into new towns and villages. They suddenly wanted to do the march in RSS uniform. Hedgewar was not so keen. He had learnt never to be swept away by any euphoric moment. He allowed the discussions amongst his own to go on until the early hours of the morning. The next day, they moved back to Yavatmal, from where they would march north on a ten-hour hike through the jungle villages, rousing up locals. Having reached Yavatmal, Hedgewar finally contributed to the discussion. He was still not keen on the idea, much to the disappointment of Parmarth. Hedgewar's reasoning was clear, at least in his own mind. Having heard the discussions for two days, Hedgewar simply stated that the RSS is not in the business of organising satyagrahas. The RSS has taken on a sacred mission to rebuild Hindu civilization from the sorry state that it finds itself in.[20] It is in the business of rebuilding the character and skills of the average Hindu citizen to be worthy of flourishing. The RSS was there to reform the society—nothing more or nothing less will do. The matter was settled.

The day had arrived when Hedgewar knew he would be in a prison cell by the time it was nightfall. The only thing he did not know was on what charges he would be arrested and how long his sentence might be. It would certainly have been unnerving and somewhat disappointing for him to have to divert his actions from his core mission with the Sangh. The march began on 21 July under the cool morning sun. By noon, the central regions could be hot and dry. The land would be parched and cracked. Nature would be eagerly awaiting the monsoon rains, which, in 1930, were late. By nine in the morning, Hedgewar had reached a village in the Lohara jungles by the name of Ruimandi. At the town hall, which was more akin to a large shack, a meeting was planned. The march had some 3000 people taking part. A swift ceremony had been organized to salute the first flag of India, and hundreds of sickles were provided to every man, woman, and child, who could then walk onto the 'Leviathan's land' and start cutting the grass and foraging the forest. As expected, the police were waiting, and soon after the flag ceremony, the men who oversaw the satyagraha were arrested.

In total, twelve men were arrested, including three swayamsevaks. Parmarth and Joshi were among the arrested. The courts were swift, and sentences were passed down quickly. By midday, Hedgewar had received nine months of imprisonment on two different counts, while most of the other men received four months. Once sentenced, the men were put onto trains and taken to Akola prison. The train line that Hedgewar and his agitators would have taken was decommissioned long ago. The Yavatmal to Murtizapur trainline, as it was known, stopped every half an hour in different towns. To the great annoyance of the police officer in charge, a lowly sergeant, at every stop, a gathering was already planned, and Hedgewar or some other arrested agitator had to say a few words for five minutes before the train would depart. Most of the speeches were delivered by Parmarth, Joshi and Hedgewar. It would have been quite easy for any of the twelve men to escape at any of the stations and disappear into the crowds. No police constable would have dared to pursue them—it would have been a death wish to have done so. Yet, all the agitators played their roles beautifully in accordance with the rules of the satyagraha. The whole affair was scripted, quite civilized and more of a circus than anything else.

At one point during the entertaining train journey, the annoyed sergeant decided that these prisoners were enjoying themselves a little too much and needed to be reminded that they were, after all, criminals who were being taken to prison. To that end, he commanded one of his juniors to handcuff Hedgewar, who was clearly the ringleader. By all accounts, this was a foolhardy thing to have ordered. 'Why?' asked Hedgewar, 'and why now? We have not tried escaping and frankly have no desire to'. The sergeant was flexing his authority and ignored

Hedgewar, and as Indians still do, commanded his lowly private with his eyebrows. Hedgewar stood and looked squarely at the sergeant and threatened to throw him out of the train if he dared to go any further. The poor sergeant was dumbstruck and visibly shaken by his sudden loss of power.

Joshi recognized the seriousness of the situation and knew that Hedgewar was more than capable of simply throwing the poor man off the train. He got up and came in between Hedgewar and the endangered policeman. 'Look, handcuffing this man will not serve you well. Your own commanding officer will see to it that you get reprimanded. Do not do this'.

Suddenly, the sergeant relaxed, his eyes became normalized and he waved his hands towards the private, instructing him to stand down, and simply walked away, sitting back down a few seats away. Hedgewar relaxed, smiled, let out a loud laugh and suggested that he intended to get himself a longer prison sentence. People laughed, albeit cautiously. Joshi nodded in acknowledgement to the sergeant for backing away. Moments later, Hedgewar walked over to the sergeant and offered him some food that had been gifted to the agitators at train stations. The police officers, although surprised by the sudden kindness of a man who moments earlier had threatened to throw them off the train, accepted the gesture, and soon everyone was sharing stories and jokes. The whole atmosphere on that short train ride to Akola prison was something that Parmarth and Joshi never forgot.[21]

By midnight, Hedgewar, as planned, had been processed through the prison system and found himself in a communal cell for the night with all his friends. On 22 July, Hedgewar was pleasantly surprised to find that the Superintendent of the prison was none other than his Irish friend, Ford. Nine years earlier, Hedgewar had become acquainted with Ford at Nagpur prison, and the two men had learnt to respect one another; the Irishman essentially gave Hedgewar a free hand organizing discussions and book clubs and allowed a library to be housed for prisoners. Ford had arranged for all Satyagraha prisoners to be housed separately across three large warehouses near the actual Akola prison. That morning, the twelve men realized they were the first to arrive. They were split into A, B and C groups. Group A meant that you would essentially be living in a simple room but with your own space and sanitation facilities. These rooms were earmarked for India's elite prisoners—this is where the likes of Nehru and Gandhi would have spent their prison time. It was essentially a form of 'hotel arrest' rather than anything physically taxing. Group B prisoners were kept in one of the warehouses, where there was less crowding, some toilet facilities and no real hard labour. This was for the political agitators of the movement. Then there was Group C which really did feel like a prison. Food was poor and intermittent. Warehouses were crowded with insufficient sanitation. Bedding was poor, or non-existent, and often lice infested. Out of the twelve, only Hedgewar was allocated Group B status. The rest went to Group C.

Hedgewar was completely alone for seven days in a small warehouse thirty metres long by twenty metres wide. Eventually, he managed to convince Ford to allow some of the others to move into Group B too. Over the weeks, new prisoners kept on arriving. The situation in Group C was becoming dreadful with overcrowding and tiredness from hard labour. Parmarth was in Group C and became terribly ill with tuberculosis. Hedgewar once again managed to negotiate with Ford to get Parmarth into Group B. Ford saw how Hedgewar day and night nursed Parmarth. Ford and some of the other prisoners helped, while Parmarth's unending coughing and wheezing was enough to take some prisoners over the edge on long, hot nights, and they demanded he be removed. Hedgewar would have none of it. Since he was always ready for fisticuffs, people soon backed down.

Through these nine months, Hedgewar received regular updates from Paranjape about the situation with the RSS shakhas. To his surprise, the shakhas continued to grow, and numbers were constantly increasing. His nine months in prison were by no means filled with arduous labour as far as we can tell, but he did influence many men who came to the prison to rethink and re-orientate themselves towards nation-building rather than just struggling for independence. He was a master communicator and, with all his life experiences, exuded a natural gravitational pull. Many swayamsevaks ended up in prison either in Group B or C. Hedgewar would see them regularly. Around three months into his sentence, a morning shakha was started in the prison compound. Ford allowed it. Hedgewar was a natural leader of men, but he had a style that was unique. He was unassuming. He displayed no ego or caste consciousness. He was caring and generous. Yet, he was powerful physically, and intellectually astute. He expected to be self-sufficient and seldom commanded others.

A case in point, which is often remembered in RSS circles, is that Joshi was put into Group C where conditions were dire. Gandhi had asked all members of the Congress taking part in the Satyagraha not to ask for favours from the State. Joshi kept to those words and never deviated. Even Ford, on occasion, noticed that his frail constitution was struggling with the hardship of Group C and asked him to shift to Group B. Joshi refused. At one point, Ford asked Hedgewar to convince his old friend. Hedgewar spoke to Joshi but never commanded him; instead, he asked him to think about whether he was a Congressman or not. If he was a Congressman, then he ought not to move, but if he was in prison as a swayamsevak then he could and should move. But the decision was his and his alone. Joshi knew he was in prison as a Congressman and not a swayamsevak. He stayed put and bore his hardship.

Months had gone by, and many prisoners were released while many more were sentenced. By December 1930, Hedgewar was suffering from severe migraines and back pain. Prison life began triggering his ailing body with new symptoms. Hedgewar's health had suddenly taken a turn for the worse. He was plagued by migraines, and with little understanding of his symptoms or medicines to help him, he suffered tremendously. Many prisoners were at hand to help him, but it became clear that he had to be released. He was in debilitating pain during those few months in early 1931, and Ford, of his own accord, got permission to have him released early.[22]

He was released on 14 February 1931. By 17 February, he had reached Nagpur by train. He was accompanied throughout by swayamsevaks. Many who saw him in those days were gravely concerned. It is unclear if he too suffered from tuberculosis or some other virus. Conditions in the prison were rife for contracting illness. Whatever it was that Hedgewar suffered from, it had clearly made a visible difference to his posture and presence.[23] He had lost much of his strength; yet after some rest in Akola, he began to show signs of his own personality again. In Nagpur, he was strictly made to rest. His sister-in-law and brother were at hand all day and night. They nursed him back to some level of normal health over the following weeks. A cocktail of herbal remedies and Ayurvedic treatments meant that he was returning to a fitness where he could again resume his self-prescribed duties.

In England at the time, the Labour government had decided to organize round table discussions about how India could be given greater autonomy. The discussions were held in London between November 1930 and January 1931. The Congress led by Gandhi did not attend, but other parties certainly did, including Moonjay representing the

Hindu Mahasabha—the Republican side of the Congress. He was widely condemned amongst the Congress faithful for betraying Gandhi's strict instructions of non-cooperation. The moment Hedgewar had somewhat recuperated, Moonjay was quick to visit, urging him to speed up the work of the RSS. It remains a mystery as to what these two men shared in early 1931, but we do know from Moonjay's papers that the first Round Table Conference was one which had spooked the Hindu Republican.

Over a hundred delegates were invited. Muslim representatives included Muhammed Shafi, the aristocratic co-founder of the Muslim League in 1906; the wealthy brothers Muhammad and Shaukat Ali, who were once supporters of the Congress but had lost faith in Gandhi and now felt that only the Muslim League represented the voices of Muslims; and the man who would go onto play a deft hand, outsmarting Gandhi to bring about the bloody partition of India, a legal expert called Muhammad Ali Jinnah; and finally, the once comptroller of finances of the treasury, Muhammed Ali Hydari, representing the interests of the princely state of Hyderabad. The next contingent consisted of the princes representing their own estates and hereditary rights. These included the Maharaja of Alwar, a man named Jai Singh Prabhakar, who was educated at Mayo School, was charming and erudite, cloned in the image of his masters, and who lived lavishly and was completely in love with all things British including their women; the Maharaja of Bikaner, named Ganga Singh, another Mayo educated man who was the only Indian to be part of the Imperial War Cabinet in World War I, a man who was the archetypal British Indian subject, proud and loyal to the Crown; then there were the Republicans, men like Moonjay and Jayakar, who would become the first vice chancellor of the University of Pune; and Dr Ambedkar, the emerging leader of India's so-called untouchables was also amongst the delegation. All these men travelled together as first-class guests of the British government. Whereas the likes of Moonjay, Ambedkar and Jayakar travelled together, the princes were travelling with a small army of aides and assistants. As many as twelve aides travelled with Ganga Singh. It was a two-week journey from Mumbai to London.

According to Moonjay's diaries, it was clear to him that the Muslim representatives, although differing in backgrounds, were all far more aligned than their Hindu counterparts.[24] He particularly loathed Prabhakar, the Prince of Alwar, who was so yielding and deferential to the Muslim representatives, that he simply ignored the playboy prince. For instance, Moonjay writes,

> A Hindu Raja showing reverence for a bigoted Muslim and none of them thinking of a counterpoise in me is a spectacle which points to the defeatist mentality which all Hindus have developed. They behave like they can't do without Moslems who on their part aspire and conspire to swallow all into themselves from Maharajas to the lowest Hindu in the street.[25]

On 6 October 1930, while Hedgewar was in prison, Moonjay was invited to a private meeting among select Hindu representatives and their Muslim counterparts. The meeting was held in cabin 329 onboard the P&O ship, where five Muslim representatives were present, namely, Jinnah, the Ali brothers, Shafi, and one other who wasn't named. On the Hindu side were seven representatives. We know that Ambedkar, Prabhakar, another aristocratic landowner named Annepu Patro, Tej Sapru, a loyalist to the crown, Jayakar, Moonjay, and one other were present. Patro had initiated these discussions, a man that Moonjay found 'contemptible'.[26] The broad consensus amongst the British was that the best solution for India was a federal system where each state could elect its own members in a state assembly, which in turn would ultimately work in tandem with a federal government in the aftermath of a future British withdrawal.[27] They also proposed separate electorate seats, as well as special guarantees for Muslim 'autonomy' in dealing with sensitive religious issues. Essentially, they had felt that these types of accommodating tactics would be sufficient to avert a full-scale civil war or the need for any actual partition. This could only hold true as long as the British Indian Army remained apolitical and could be relied upon to be hurled into any precarious standoff between Hindus and Muslims.[28]

Moonjay was completely convinced that the Muslims either wanted to establish Muslim rule and fulfil infantile dreams of re-establishing Mughal rule across India, or desired partition to create a separate Muslim state.[29] Most British-educated Hindus, including the princes, were desperate to accommodate the Muslims into federal India under dominion status. This set the tone of the meeting. The Muslim delegation would demand, and the Hindu side would try to accommodate, cajole and appease. The tone and narrative were set by the Muslim agenda, and the Hindu wishes were parked to one side, with everyone's focus on accommodation. To add multiple layers of complexity, Ambedkar was generally sceptical about both sides—the Muslims clearly dreamt of power under some utopian Islamic state, while the Hindu elite composed of Brahmins and princes could also not be trusted to be the representatives of India's majority poor and downtrodden masses.[30] Moonjay experienced on the ship a microcosm of the future of India, with all its social hierarchies, prejudices, divisions and religious tensions.

The Round Table Conference had been generally a failure. Two more attempts would be made, and each time, the discussions would stall. For Moonjay, he became an alarmist from that point onwards. He was convinced that the Hindu society was too fragmented, and her leaders were either devoid of reality or were too busy feathering their own nests, while not reading the motivations of the Muslim community, especially in the light of all the violence that was constantly being deployed throughout India. It appears quite likely that Moonjay came to Hedgewar to plead with him to speed up the work of the RSS and continue with the martial training of young men. In short, either the RSS will have to be the vanguard of the beleaguered Hindu community and be its indomitable force in negotiating a fair settlement, or maybe the leading force in a future civil war for the future of India.

The next day, Hedgewar, against the wishes of his loving sister-in-law, left Nagpur and travelled to Bombay. Although half-fit himself, he went to see Ganesh Savarkar, who was also in very poor health, and his old friend, the youngest of the Savarkars—Narayan. The fiery Vinayak was not there, which is telling of the relationship between Hedgewar and the supposed mastermind of the RSS in popular imagination. The reality was that when Hedgewar really needed to speak to people, he seldom, if at all, went to Vinayak but found much guidance and friendship in his elder and younger brothers. He also went to Vital Patel, the elder brother of the now-famous Sardar Patel. He too was unwell and in hospital.[31] At all these meetings, it is unclear what was discussed, Hedgewar as usual wrote, or said very little in public. What is clear is that his strategy for starting new shakhas and expanding the RSS network changed considerably around this time.

A case in point is his sudden trip to the ancient city of Varanasi, also called Kashi. He had just returned to Nagpur to find an urgent telegram from Ganesh Savarkar to come to Kashi immediately in the light of aggressive intimidation tactics being employed by radical clerics. He wrote back to his friend with the line 'wait, watch, pray and hope'.[32] By 11 March, he had reached Varanasi and went to see Ganesh, who was taking in the fresh air of the city. Much of what Hedgewar did in Varanasi can be gleaned from the letters and biographies of those he met. According to Ganesh Savarkar's biography, Hedgewar stayed in the city until 1 April, a little over two weeks. Hedgewar was there to make 'concrete arrangements for the protection of Hindus in the city'.[33] In that time, he met the vice chancellor and founder of the Benares Hindu University (BHU), an elderly man by the name of Madan Mohan Malaviya. Malaviya was a famous man by his own accounts. Not only did he establish, in 1916, one of the largest learning institutions in Asia, which today has a student population of over 40,000 undergraduates across the arts and humanities, but he was also elected four times to be the President of the Indian Congress. Malaviya opened the door for the RSS to be established at the university and the wider city. Two shakhas were immediately set up, one on campus and the other in the heart of the community.[34]

Tensions were high in Varanasi throughout the 1930s. Fear was rife amongst both communities and radicals, often Deobandi and Barelvi clerics, would dog whistle their congregations every Friday during sermons. The rhetoric ranged from anti-British slogans to setting up a Dar al-Islam in India. One of the key proponents of radical Islam was the founder of Jamaat-e-Islami, a Barelvi cleric, who was vehemently against the partition of India but rather believed that the whole of India could be ruled by Islam.[35] He actively preached Da'wah, the act of calling people to join Islam.[36] He firmly believed that most Indians had to be brought to Islam to preserve national unity. His name was Abul A'la Maududi, an Islamic scholar and jurist, who believed that Islam and power, that is politics, had to go hand in hand; the two could never be separated.[37]

To Malaviya's mind, a moderate by all accounts, the RSS being established on campus would act as a bulwark against the kind of Islam Maududi was preaching. Just as in Nagpur, Hedgewar knew that the RSS was the only real movement within the Hindu society that could resist and even repel the extremism that was being spewed out of mosques and seminaries. Malaviya and Savarkar witnessed for the first time how Hedgewar operated. Both men became convinced that regardless of what one thought of Hedgewar and his views, he was certainly earnest, courageous, loyal to the Hindu cause and above all else, a hugely talented man who could organize. People were willing to be led by him. They also noted how young men who were trained in the RSS shakhas carried themselves with confidence yet with humility and were completely dedicated to a greater mission. They were skilled and capable. At the time, Savarkar oversaw the youth movement of the Hindu Mahasabha with chapters across different parts of Maharashtra and the Central Provinces. His youth were simply not of the same calibre.

Hedgewar and Savarkar sat drinking tea on 23 March. It was a starry night. They sat under the cooling sky, casually talking, wrapped up in their shawls. Savarkar told Hedgewar how unwell he really was; it was fatal, and he remained deeply worried about the future of his countrymen. Earlier that day, three young men had been executed in Lahore by the leviathan. Three men who would capture the nation's imagination—Bhagat Singh and his two friends, Rajguru and Sukhdev. Both men quietly mused and agreed that it was time to stop such young men from dying for their country. It was high time that young people start valuing their lives and look to live to better their society rather than commit such suicidal missions. Then, to Hedgewar's complete astonishment, Savarkar suddenly announced that he wanted his youth organization to merge with the Sangh and for Hedgewar to take over all the chapters.[38] And just like that, the RSS inherited thousands of young men.[39]

Hereafter, Hedgewar travelled extensively. He travelled by every means available to him. He would walk for miles in the blazing midday sun, he would hitch rides on bullock carts and jump onto trains travelling 'cattle class'. Every day, he would visit different towns and villages across Maharashtra and the Central Provinces. His days revolved around finding a few good men who could commit to setting up shakhas in their neighbourhood and be open to being trained. Hedgewar was constantly battling the narrative of the satyagraha, which was in full swing during these months. Hedgewar sent out the likes of Dani, Aptey, Yerkuntwar and Joshi to other parts of the country at various universities to set up shakhas on campus.

Modern naysayers suggest that Hedgewar would stoke up the flames of hatred between Hindus and Muslims wherever he visited. He would effectively sow the seeds of division and then take full advantage when conflict broke out by setting up an RSS shakha there. The reality, as always, is not quite so straightforward. It is true that shakhas seem to have gotten traction wherever Hindu–Muslim tensions were high. It certainly appears to be the case that after Moonjay's visit and his subsequent meetings with the Savarkars, Hedgewar visited these hotbeds of conflict, where conditions were tense, as a priority, mainly because Hindus felt under siege. As part of this siege mentality, he would suggest to the community to come together and set up daily shakhas and begin the martial training of their men. One can imagine that this, in turn, would further spook the Muslims, who would become more susceptible to the extremism of the clerics. The whole situation was unbecoming of a community.

As far as Hedgewar was concerned, he had no time to waste, and pragmatism was the order of the day. Hindu communities up and down the country were being systematically bullied, and were themselves fragmented, and therefore unable to respond appropriately to Muslim aggression—an aggression that was clearly being fanned by clerics. RSS centres sprang up across Vidharba and the Central Provinces. Hedgewar, and his young army of devoted actors, were the only antidote for the Hindu community as far as responding to the challenges posed by extremism and the fragmentation of the Hindu community were concerned.

The strains of leading such a life further created fissures in Hedgewar's health. His migraines and back pains returned. He had little money for medicines and lived off the goodwill of others—much like a mendicant. He stayed wherever someone would put him up for the night, and in new places, he would often sleep on the earth or on the open foyers of small temples. It was a physically taxing life—the life of a prachaarak.

THIRTEEN: 1932–1934

Not Fascist Enough

'All Hindus belong to the same nation, the Hindu nation', said Hedgewar sometime in early 1933 in a letter he wrote to Ganesh Savarkar.[1] Hedgewar was writing to explain the rationale, the vision and the mission of the RSS to the older Savarkar, who had been trying to convince him to attend a large gathering of young nationalists in Lahore. Although Hedgewar was keen to quickly assimilate the newfound youth as a result of the merger between Savarkar's youth movement and the RSS, he, nevertheless, had another large forty-day OTC in the summer of 1933 to plan for. The RSS shakhas were growing, and consequently, the number of those who wanted to be trained as 'officers' was increasing. Twelve attended the OTC in 1927, and several thousand were expected in the summer of 1933. The numbers just kept on rising.

Hedgewar's immense experience in organizing large Congress gatherings was now paying dividends for the RSS. On a shoestring budget, with very basic amenities, the Sangh would create a makeshift tent village on open grounds to house those attending the mammoth forty-day camp. Food was often basic, cooked on-site in makeshift kitchens using firewood as fuel. Sanitation was another problem, where surrounding fields or nearby train lines were used as latrines. Showers were erected using buckets of water, housed on makeshift scaffolding, with pipes running down to cubicles, with drains dug at the end of raised concrete slabs to allow the water to run off. Everything was constructed by volunteers who were also going to be teaching, cooking and cleaning throughout the duration of the camp.

While letters between Savarkar and Hedgewar were being sent to and fro, another meeting of two minds came together for the first time. In 1932, after Hedgewar's lightning foray to Kashi, two RSS centres sprang up, one of them at the university. He had received several letters from those who attended the daily shakha, and in these correspondences, references were being made to lecturers who were showing an interest in this new daily activity. One of the names mentioned on several occasions was that of a young lecturer, someone who had studied marine biology and now taught zoology, who looked more like an ascetic rather than an intellectual. The young lecturer's name was Madhav Golwalkar.

Golwalker was twenty-five years old when he first met Hedgewar in Kashi. The young, tall and slender lecturer was keenly interested in the daily activities of the shakha on campus, although he never participated much and chose to support from the sidelines.[2] Golwalker was learned, composed, austere and above all else, a desh bhakt. He and Prabhakar Dani had become friends. Dani had been sent to Benares Hindu University to not only further his studies but also to run RSS centres. He had taken the oath to become a prachaarak a few years earlier. He was keen for Golwalker to meet Hedgewar and had managed to convince his scraggly friend to make a trip to Nagpur to see the RSS where it was strongest—Nagpur. Golwalker met Hedgewar at his home in early 1933. It remains unknown as to what the two men spoke about, for neither have ever mentioned anything in writing, yet we do know that each man had made a lasting impression on the other. Within a year of that meeting, the young aspiring ascetic would visit Nagpur twice hence, and become the coordinator, or in RSS speak, the karyavah of the Nagpur shakha, which was an important centre for the early RSS as it produced many prachaaraks.[3]

Before the OTC of 1933, in the hot and humid month of May, Hedgewar made a long tiring journey to Karachi upon Savarkar's unyielding insistence. Both men were financially broke, they were also suffering from chronic bad health.[4] It was Savarkar who funded their trip. In a letter between Hedgewar and his uncle, dated 6 May 1933, he shared some of his observations while travelling on the overnight train from Mumbai.

> 'Muslim aggression is rife. I have seen first-hand how Muslim men freely issue threats and then escalate to verbal and even physical abuse. However, when someone stands up to them, they are quick to compromise or even retreat. Unfortunately, the reticent Hindu society only thinks about seeking peace, at all costs, and has completely absorbed the philosophy of ahimsa, and so consequently, only experiences threats and abuse.'[5]

He went on to describe,

> 'In Karnavati too, I only saw Muslim aggression and Hindu cowardice. It was somewhat heartening to see a Gujarati lady stand up for herself against an aggressive Muslim man, but her husband, who stood behind her, possessed no such confidence.'[6]

At the end of the letter, one can feel his astonishment at what he saw,

> 'At Hyderabad station, in Sindh, we felt as if we were in a Muslim country. From Hyderabad to Karachi there were no Hindus in the carriage. We were the only ones.'[7]

Hedgewar's description reveals some interesting insights. Commentators, including RSS ones, give too much emphasis to his fear of the 'other', and not enough to his scathing remarks about his own people. He describes Hindus as meek and constantly seeking peace in the face of threats and abuse. In Hedgewarian thought, ahimsa, the ancient idea of non-harming, something which Gandhi misconstrued as 'non-violence', is only relevant for the strong, for the weak have no choice but to seek peace. In Hedgewar's eyes, the Hindu is not seeking peace out of some high-minded spirituality but out of fear and helplessness. This is why he frames it as 'Hindu cowardice'. Gandhi, from a Hedgewarian perspective, was wrong to promote ahimsa to a weak, terrorized society. Ahimsa was meant to be a principle for those who could actually wield deadly force to obtain their own ends. It was meant to be a means of exercising restraint on the powerful.

He also felt it worthy to highlight and reflect on the difference between Hindu men and women. For Hedgewar, Hindu society was broken. It was patriarchal, and he had witnessed the calamity of a patriarchal culture on women during his days as a medical student. He had seen countless numbers left to suffer or die when medicine could have been administered but wasn't because the only doctors available were men. Hedgewar was clear that Hindu society could only really revitalize itself when its women were also given the same opportunities to flourish, but alas, he recognized that he lived in an age that was still not ready for women's emancipation. Nevertheless, he carried great hope that sooner or later, women would find their own voice on their own terms, where they would play an equal role in rejuvenating the Hindu culture.

These experiences are, much to the detriment, not kept alive in today's RSS. The Sangh faithful very much run off the narrative that 'the Hindu society is under siege'. Popular narratives across academia and the popular press gravitate around the Sangh's persistent caricaturing of Muslims, and to a lesser extent Christians, as vile, malevolent, with the single agenda of converting every Hindu into a Muslim or Christian, and re-shaping modern India into another culturally colonized society. While this type of rendering is absurd and more akin to a conspiracy theory, it is worth noting that in Hedgewarian thought, the Muslim is not the problem; rather she has become the victim of a dangerous ideology that dismembers people from their past, their heritage and connection with ancestral memories, the result of which is alienation of the severest kind.

Hedgewarian thought can be best rendered from Eric Fromm's work on the role of faith in human society. The problem with Islam is that it is totalitarian in nature. It is all-consuming, and as Fromm writes, 'paralyses human forces, and a humanistic faith, which supports the development of reason and love'.[8] From the Hedgewarian perspective, every Indian is a Hindu, yet not every Hindu needs to be an Indian. This is certainly true if one is to see it from the perspective of geography, that is Hindu as a geographical identity, which is now certainly outmoded, but it is also true from the perspective of genetics. Most Indian, Pakistani, Bangladeshi and Sri Lankan Muslims are certainly genetically related to every Hindu. Most Muslims, if allowed to remember, would easily trace their ancestry back to a Hindu lineage.[9] Yet, most Muslims, when polled, claim that their heritage is from Iran or Arabia, when in reality, less than 3 per cent have any genetic connection to the Arabs.[10] This gross deviation from reality caused by a totalitarian religion causes alienation in millions of India's citizens, which, in turn, makes them seek out radical, militant or ultra-conservative expressions of their faith. It is this which Hedgewar was observing en masse in the 1930s.

Today, his devotees have, to a greater or lesser extent, kept with the Hedgewarian perspective, that is that every Muslim is essentially Hindu, at least genetically. They are sons and daughters of the soil. What they lack is rootedness, for they have been uprooted by a totalitarian religion that spawned outside of India and aggressively made its way in. The RSS, even today, is not anti-Muslim; it is anti-Islam, and more precisely, it is 'anti' only a particular type of Islam—the authoritarian, ultra-conservative type that alienates its believers from the wider milieu of Indian society.

Hedgewarian thought is fundamentally not religious. It is only focused on desh bhakti. From the Frommian perspective, the RSS only cares about rootedness, which is the surest way to and a prerequisite of building a society based on reason and love.[11] However, like Marx, who developed the best critique of capitalism but didn't really have anything substantial to say about the solution, Hedgewar comprehensively understood the Islamic challenge better than any of his contemporaries, but had not developed an adequate response, at least not in the 1930s.

These observations give us insight into where the shores of his knowledge had reached. Without an adequate solution for the Islamic challenge to Indian society, he had developed a defensive theory and practice. It essentially meant militarizing the Hindu society by creating a small but elite vanguard of desh bhakts who could hold their own and protect Hindu communities against an ultra-conservative totalitarian foreign religion. To some extent, the RSS, although having tried, is still to develop an adequate response to the challenges that Hedgewar articulated in his time. Hedgewar and his creation spent most of their time and energy on reforming Hindu society, something for which he not only understood the problem, but also had developed a solution that he was rolling out across the country. That process is still under way almost a hundred years hence.

Hedgewar was also clearly astonished at the number of Muslims living in north-west India; it was approximately 70 per cent around this time.[12] It was the first time he had travelled to Karachi. The realization dawned on him at the sheer number of his countrymen who had adopted not just Islam, but were embracing an ultra-conservative Islam, one that was home-grown, Barelvi and Deobandi, which in some very significant ways was uprooting millions of Indians from their own cultural heritage. An overwhelming sense of impending doom submerged his consciousness. He would have asked himself, was it already too late?

He stayed in Karachi for six days. In that time, he came to admire the city and even claimed that it was the 'best city he had seen'.[13] He met all the good and great folks of that city and introduced the concept of the Sangh. Ganesh Savarkar was by his side throughout and encouraged people to attend and hear out Hedgewar's vision. Hindus were a significant minority in this part of the country and so were already accustomed to feeling under siege. Hedgewar noted that Hindu leadership lacked any real organizational skills and could not imagine much beyond conferences and speeches.[14] Over several hours, he patiently explained with practical training and demonstrated what an RSS shakha looks like, why it is daily, and how the work will safeguard the Hindu community in an increasingly anarchic country. People readily embraced it. RSS centres were created shortly after.

While Hedgewar was away in Karachi, his family was terrorized. Mysterious stone pelters would randomly appear at night, smash windows, and disappear back the into shadow. Sitaram, his brother, was not like Hedgewar. He was rather passive, in keeping with the rest of the Hindu society. He and his wife soon moved out of their family home and went to stay with a relative. When Hedgewar returned, he would often make light of the situation:

> '...the stone pelting is only carried out by a community with such habits. I know there are no Hindus in it. When the rains arrive, the pelting stops, and when the rains stop, the pelting starts again. One thing is clear – the stone pelters do not have the guts to come face-to-face with me. Do not worry about it'.[15]

In practice, the Sangh took these threats seriously and organized some level of security around the house over the coming months. The pelting soon stopped.

The Sangh was also increasingly being watched by the British. It was under greater scrutiny between 1932 and 1933 as the organization continued to sprout all over the central regions, Maharashtra, Varanasi and even as far afield as Karachi. Furthermore, the RSS itself was silent on the non-cooperation movement, which was in full swing, yet the British knew that hundreds of its trained swayamsevaks were actively taking part. The Sangh seemed ominous to the State, 'What new curse are you sending us here?', wrote the governor of Mumbai to his counterpart in the Central regions.[16] What made the Sangh even more ill-omened for the British was the fact that its armies of spies and snitches, who were prevalent in every nook and cranny of India's streets, were unable to make sense of what the Sangh was trying to do. Its modus operandi seemed hazy at best and downright perplexing to most Europeans and their brown clones.

Hedgewar heard through the rumour mill that the British were going to start clamping down on all organizations that it thought were subversive, and the RSS was front and centre. Some of Hedgewar's speeches probably unnerved the snitches who were listening at RSS events, and it is well within the realms of possibility that he was at times addressing the British directly, knowing that his words would get back to the colonizer.

> 'A year ago, in 1932 we saw the second instalment of the 1930 civil disobedience movement. Back then, the government feared nationalist organisations and was thinking about declaring them unlawful. I have heard from reliable sources that they (the government) are planning to ban us, as the RSS is by far the most potent force in Nagpur. In the Sangh, we develop discipline and ultimately learn how to live peacefully. I am quite sure that the government would not bring about a curse on themselves by banning us. They would, most certainly, bring about their own downfall if they tried. The day they declare the Sangh unlawful, there will be two hundred shakhas in Nagpur. I say this because I know the capability of our swayamsevaks. Let us imagine that tomorrow, this government decides to make the Sangh unlawful; how will that bring down our demise? I can imagine the physical shakhas having to cease for the time being, but what about the Sangh in our hearts? How can they erase the Sangh that is etched in our hearts? Each swayamsevak is a potential shakha.
>
> If you agree that we can do this if they ban us, then why wait? Let us do it now! This is the thought that many of us have already had, and so we can see sixteen shakhas across Nagpur.'[17]

This short extract from a speech delivered sometime in 1933, recalled by Palkar, was essentially addressing several audiences simultaneously. He was certainly speaking to the state apparatus, as well as his cadre. With the same string of words, he was threatening one group and motivating the other.

The history of all subjugated people, one that is often under-reported, is the history of stooges and snitches. Indian history is no different. For every young man and woman who went to the gallows with fortitude, there were three who profited directly from the deaths of those who struggled for freedom. Take the case of the Chapekar brothers, who upon assassinating a man by the name of Rand, a British plague commissioner, were sold out by their own relatives—the Dravid brothers.[18] Then there was the stooge who was placed by Scotland Yard in 1907 at India House, London, amongst Indian revolutionaries, a man named Kiritkar who leaked sensitive information to his colonial masters until he was found out, and was consequently counteracted by a campaign of misdirection started by Savarkar.[19] We can also take the case of a young man, only seventeen years old, called Basant Biswas who had attempted to assassinate the Viceroy of India in 1914 but was ultimately handed over to the police by his own uncle and then swiftly executed; his immediate family was sent into perpetual penury, while his uncle was made stupendously rich.[20] Then there were the inner workings of the revolutionary outfit called the Ghadar Party, which was snitched on by two fellow Sikhs named Bela and Harman Singh, both of whom worked as informants for British intelligence, resulting in the deaths of many young men who struggled for freedom.[21] There are countless others. Hedgewar would have been acutely aware of the sad fact that a country and millions of her people could only be subjugated through the direct support of collaborators.

He remained vigilant all his life. His writings, on the whole, are mundane, filled with operational jargon and trivial chit-chat, often leading the few historians who have had access to his personal notes to conclude that they are insignificant or not very revealing. Hedgewar never wrote for posterity's sake but rather for his day, fearful of collaborators.

These experiences only motivated him to work harder and faster, to dedicate more time, more of his life force to expanding the Sangh. Ultimately, these experiences cleared whatever haziness there may have been in his reasoning—the RSS must not get involved in 'causes' but must be single-minded in creating a population of worthy individuals who were socially, culturally and politically aware and astute. Everything else will follow from this. To this day, the RSS claims it does 'nothing' in society. It is only interested in running shakhas. The fact that thousands of organizations have spawned independently of the RSS by its own swayamsevaks is the fulfilment of Hedgewarian thought: develop human beings and the rest will naturally take shape.

A few months later, around 28 September 1933, Hedgewar invited his charismatic young 'padavi' Golwalkar to Nagpur to speak at the Vijaya Dashmi celebrations to commemorate Rama's victory over the tyrant king Ravana. This was the flagship event in the Sangh's calendar, where over 1200 swayamsevaks in uniform would attend, completing a route march around central Nagpur and celebrating a festival that is at least several millennia old. Before Golwalkar spoke, Hedgewar went up to inaugurate the event and present his annual report to the public, which was composed of well-wishers, donors, the political elite and families of swayamsevaks.

'…I am pleased to tell you that Sangh work has been welcomed and started in Benaras, Indore, Karachi, Pune, Mumbai, Satara, Kolhapur, and there are many more requests from other places… the mission of Sangh is to protect Dharma, our Culture and the wider society. It saddens me that some people choose to see hatred of others in the protection of our Swadharma, but I do not comprehend why it should be so.'[22]

Hedgewar was clearly aware that the RSS was not only feared by the British and its thousand eyes but also certain strata of Hindu society. The RSS, according to Hedgewar, was being unfairly labelled even as early as 1933 and accused of rousing what the Scottish economists Blyth calls, 'the anger of devils'.[23] He was clearly perplexed by the reaction of certain sections of his own society. What is worthy of note is his use of the term 'Swa' before the Dharma in his speech. Swadharma is a term that describes how one behaves when one is in a natural flow with one's own innate nature or when one is behaving according to societal norms or customs to fulfil a particular responsibility. Hedgewar, in his own manner, was explaining to his audience and the nay-sayers that protecting the Hindu society, even if it means using force at a time of anarchy, is the raison d'être of the RSS. From a Hedgewarian perspective, the RSS is not acting out of hate when it wields force against another but rather carrying out what it's designed to do. One can think of it in the same way that a tiger does not hunt its prey out of any malice towards it but does so out of its very nature. Today, one can often hear prachaaraks use the analogy of the immune system to explain the same point. The immune system attacks foreign objects inside the body not out of hate but out of necessity and design. In some sense, Hedgewar is being explicit with his audience and rather upfront about what the RSS is about. He spells out that one only needs to fear the RSS if one is behaving in a way that is against the grain of desh bhakti and national or civilizational revitalization. The debate that he never addresses is whose desh bhakti? Gandhi had a very different notion of desh bhakti as compared to the RSS—which was right?

In the same speech, he also said,

'...In the Sangh, there is no scope for differentiation based on creed, sect, or caste. Sangh only thinks of rousing the spirit of oneness amongst all Hindus. Since Hindus of all castes and sects seek refuge under the Bhagwa Dhwaj, untouchability has been a non-issue in the Sangh. Therefore, we do not encourage division among Hindus by taking sides on untouchability.'[24]

The RSS, in most popular discourse and academic writings, is described as Brahmanical. In other words, the RSS is described as a caste-based movement, clandestinely maintaining the grotesque inequalities in Hindu society. According to Jaffrelot, the RSS is designed to serve and further ingrain the 'caste inequalities to protect the higher caste of Brahmins'.[25] During Hedgewar's time, the RSS was constantly being asked to join the raging debate of untouchability within Hindu society. It was a grotesque system where an entire stratum of society was effectively expelled from everyday existence and was forced to live in servitude with absolutely no hope of escaping their circumstance. Apologists often argue that untouchability grew out of the desire to segregate those people who worked in unclean environments and were prone to disease and illness, which eventually morphed into discrimination based on an idea of purity.[26] At the pinnacle of prejudice and callousness, in places like Kerala, untouchability had become unapproachability, where certain sections of the society had to cover their mouths when speaking to anyone else to prevent the 'pollution' or 'contamination' of higher castes.[27]

In this context, Hindu society was going through a tremendous revolution when it came to such social evils. There were thousands of men and women from every section of society who were actively working to rid society of such arcane practices. On the other side, many sections of the Brahmin community were resisting these changes. It was a struggle between Brahmin and Brahmin, as much as a struggle between the 'haves' and 'have nots'. Many from both sides had come to Hedgewar and the RSS to actively support their cause. The RSS had frustrated everyone, including Vinayak Savarkar, a Brahmin, who was actively working to remove all forms of caste discrimination. Anybody who had an encounter with the RSS was clear that caste had no future as far as Hedgewarian thought was concerned. Yet, Hedgewar never formally joined any campaign to fight untouchability, which posterity has criticized him for ever since.

Why would Hedgewar not join campaigns that were clearly aligned with the RSS worldview when it came to untouchability? A definite answer is lost to history, but educated guesses can be made by understanding his modus operandi at the time and how the RSS behaves today; after all, much of Hedgewarian thought is encoded into the DNA of the RSS. The RSS was not designed to fight every social ill facing Indian society. Rather, it was designed to build human beings with upright character and the ability to serve society wholeheartedly, who in turn would go out into society and start their own movements or join existing ones. Hundreds of RSS-trained men joined existing movements driving for equality, including Savarkar's own. Many swayamsevaks also joined Ambedkar's mission to eradicate untouchability. Hedgewar and the RSS welcomed such decisions. Yet, Hedgewar never outwardly took sides in public, much to the frustration of his peers. It was to do with his obsession with not causing further divides within an already fragmented society. The RSS would only alienate one side or another if it took sides, and so it never did, yet indirectly supported every major anti-untouchability organization by giving them trained volunteers.

Furthermore, at this time, Gandhi had decided to go on a hunger strike while in his relatively comfortable jail cell. His reason for starting this campaign, which he threatened to do until death, was that the British, at the Round Table Coference in London, had agreed to grant the lower castes and the untouchables separate electorates just like the Muslims. Gandhi was horrified. He was adamant that Hindu society should not be broken up piecemeal and foresaw the disintegration of the country in the years to come. Initially, the leaders of the lower castes ignored Gandhi's threats. Soon, Gandhi was really dying, and pressure fell on Ambedkar to reconsider his position. The pressure came from all sides, including his own. Reluctantly, Ambedkar went to see Gandhi and conceded his position for lower castes to have separate electorates. Gandhi stopped his hunger strike moments later.

Gandhi reciprocated Ambedkar's public back down in the face of his blackmail by changing the name of his *Young India* journal to *Harijan*, meaning the Children of the Divine, which was dedicated to educating the Indian masses on removing the curse of caste and untouchability. He also launched a series of campaigns to publicly condemn all forms of caste prejudice soon after. This was also in the backdrop of Hedgewar's speech that day. He had refused to comment on Gandhi's and Ambedkar's political fight.

The Hedgewarian attitude is one of pragmatism and taking the longer-term view on such matters. In modern times, the Sangh, although vindicated in the sense that it aided the removal of untouchability, was never seen to have done so. As such, the naysayers have continued to brandish Hedgewar and his creation as something that they are definitely not—caste-based. Gandhi, not long after this speech, in 1936, would visit an RSS camp and comment on how egalitarian it was with no signs of caste consciousness or untouchability anywhere. He asked Hedgewar how this had been achieved.[28] Hedgewar and the RSS have certainly left themselves wide open for criticism despite having wholeheartedly fought against the social evil of untouchability.

Returning to his speech in 1933 at the Vijaya Dashmi event, which he concluded by addressing a specific phenomenon,

> '...Outside of Nagpur, I do not see a chasm between the Congress and any other Hindu Organisation. Several Congressmen elsewhere have openly supported the spread of Sangh work. I believe that the differences are not in our respective philosophies but rather in our personalities. My humble request is for everyone present to understand the role of the Sangh, and help it succeed in its mission of nation-building. Sangh has been established to safeguard the Hindu society from mortal danger.'[29]

These words clearly demonstrate the tension that was felt within Nagpur between Congressmen and the RSS. For Hedgewar to speak so candidly in public demonstrates the fault lines between the two. Historically, the Congress has always been the party of the Hindus by default rather than due to any great convergence, and it had become clear that the RSS, although not a rival in the political sense, certainly was a powerful local actor who could not be controlled by the old elites, especially the Advocates. Furthermore, rather inconveniently for Congressmen, the RSS was inclined to support the nationalists. Congress, in their attempt to be the great consolidator of India, ended up alienating large sections of the Hindu community without being able to bring Muslims onside, and even though they were socialist, they were not communists, and so alienated the Communists also. The local Congress leaders viewed the RSS as a threat to what they deemed as the unity of India, that is, between Hindu and

Muslim, and also to themselves. The RSS, if they chose, had the power in Nagpur to overthrow an elected government and push for their own candidates. They failed to believe or even to understand what Hedgewar and the RSS stood for. In this context one can understand Hedgewar's plea from the stage to not see the RSS as a threat to any political party but as a worthwhile partner in nation-building. The naysayers remained unconvinced.

Later that month, Hedgewar and Golwalkar decided to visit several shakhas around Nagpur and surrounding villages. Hedgewar's intention was to show the young professor what the RSS really meant at its epicentre. Alas, as would be the case for years hence, Hedgewar's health collapsed. He was suffering from a severe fever and with what others described as excruciating headaches and back pains. He was unable to travel, and a rather concerned Golwalkar travelled on his own.[30] A Sangh sympathizer and friend by the name of Dr Hardas, who lived down the road, convinced a somewhat stubborn Hedgewar to come and stay with him so he could get some rest and medication. Reluctantly, Hedgewar agreed. According to Hardas, Hedgewar had contracted an infection from drinking contaminated water, which was most likely caused by a sewer that ran past his home. He had suffered for weeks in silence, during which time his lungs had become inflamed, causing severe respiratory problems.[31] Hedgewar was bedridden for several weeks and stayed with his friend for over two months.

During this time, Hedgewar turned his friends' house into his office. There would be a steady stream of visitors throughout the day. While the practising doctor was away, his attendants kept an eye on the sickly but obstinate patient, who often forgot to take his medications and seldom got the rest that was prescribed. He was treated with due courtesy and was in want of nothing. It was something Hedgewar had never got accustomed to. He found it strange to have people all day waiting on him and looking after his every need. Although extremely poorly, Hedgewar was making a steady recovery. During this time, he was constantly writing telegrams to ensure that the work of the Sangh did not slow down. Indeed, during his idle moments, in the early hours of the morning, when his coughing fits would be most acute, Hedgewar concocted new and grander visions for the RSS.

'The Sangh requires 50,000 rupees', he wrote to some of his well-wishers, including the chief editor of the *Mahratta*, a man named Aglay.[32] 'It's time that the Sangh has its own grounds, its own offices, a gymnasium and increased travel expenses to further expand Sangh work,' he wrote.[33] Rs 50,000 at the time was an extraordinary amount of money. Hedgewar was never short of ambition; that much is clear. In today's money, it is equivalent to almost $2,000,000 or Rs 150,000,000. After his experience of Karachi, he had shifted gears and became desperate to see the RSS spread across the country as quickly as possible, viewing it as a bulwark against what he perceived as an impending tsunami of separatism.

On 17 October 1933, Hedgewar called a meeting at the good doctor's house. It was attended by wealthy and well-connected lawyers and businessmen. The meeting did not go as planned. People were hesitant on the grounds that the British were more than capable of simply confiscating any property it liked, and the Sangh would have to spend a lot more money in defending its assets than developing its work. It was a fair argument but not to Hedgewar's liking. 'The entire country has been confiscated, and nobody is worried about that, and we are all worried about an expense of five to ten thousand rupees?' he snapped in a letter. It never occurred to Hedgewar that he was asking for a lot of money and that his deployment strategy was somewhat short-sighted, maybe even naive.[34] For all of his brilliance and financial record keeping, when it came to understanding money, Hedgewar was still out of his depth. He eventually conceded his position and accepted that the RSS could simply do with more funds for operational expenses, which would still allow it to grow nationwide. In late 1933, he managed to raise Rs 700 rupees and acquire two acres of land at Reshimbagh, which in years to come would prove to be a masterful stroke, more out of luck than anything else.

This naivety concerning money still runs deep in some sections of the RSS today. The prachaaraks, who themselves shun personal funds, are often quite unaware when it comes to money for the organization. Occasionally, a swayamsevak would emerge who had a strong grasp of money, taxes and general financial intelligence. On the whole, the organization attracted the working class, who were not particularly known for their financial acumen. Couple this with broadly financially illiterate prachaaraks, and you had an organization that was flying financially blind, or at the very best with partial clarity. One can still find in today's RSS, some prachaaraks who hold the most unrealistic ideas about money, and quite often misconstrued ideas about capitalism and international finance, but because they hold privileged positions within the organization, they are seldom challenged.

Back in December 1932, a circular was released by the government of the Central Provinces, which essentially barred anyone working in the civil service or in any government position, no matter how menial, from joining the RSS. Essentially, the government had classed the RSS as communal and political, and as such, one's impartiality was compromised. [35] Having somewhat recovered from his infection; with a renewed vigour, he confronted the government head-on. The intent of the government was simple—it was to bully, intimidate and obstruct its growth. The strategy of the British was quite correct; their intelligence reports had noted that a significant number of those joining Sangh activities were fairly educated, and many of them held government jobs. This would not be the first or last time that the Indian State would attempt to pin the RSS as communal and then seek to stop those who worked for it from joining. For the RSS, this was a new challenge, not wholly unexpected, but nevertheless troublesome.

A letter from Mumbai's Sanghchalak, the man responsible for the complete oversight of RSS work in the city, and a lawyer named Ganpat Altekar, read,

> 'I do not think that shakha work will run systematically in this area. Even when not related to politics, the government finds every social activity objectionable. Their policy is to keep the 'peace of the grave'. Ordinary gymnasiums have also been declared unlawful.'[36]

Soon after, all the local councils also followed suit, and teachers were barred from joining Sangh activities. The British had finally pulled the trigger on the RSS. Its draconian nature was in full force in the commercial city. Local bureaucrats did not take to the new orders too kindly, not out of any particular love or solidarity with the RSS, but more out of principle. They were going to resist the government from interfering with what they considered to be benign matters. The mood on the street had changed, and Hedgewar planned to take complete advantage of it.

However, in Nagpur, it seemed to have made little difference. People just continued as they were. Many civil servants were RSS-trained men. Had the authorities strictly followed the law and exercised the ban, much of the government's administrative duties would have come to a standstill. In parts of the country where the RSS was still relatively new and unknown, the restrictions had a massive impact. Students feared joining the RSS as it would affect their chances of landing a plum government job afterwards.

As Hedgewar brooded on his wooden swing on the porch of his house late into the night, it dawned on him that there was no way the government could have taken the steps it had without the support of other groups, the most powerful being the Congress. Tensions between the RSS and Congress were heightened year after year as the strength of the Sangh grew, often at the cost of the Congress's local chapters. People could visibly see the difference between the two outfits—one was purely political in nature with a strict hierarchy and a means to a political end, while the other was diffused, highly trained in the same format as a fighting unit, unapologetically Hindu and had shown itself to be the vanguard of the Hindu community when no one else was ready to protect them. It was quite natural, thought Hedgewar, for the Congress to be intimidated by his outfit, but to go as far as to collude with the enemy was something that even Hedgewar couldn't bring himself to believe. Just as these thoughts were percolating in his mind, he received a letter from the newly appointed treasurer and member of the Congress Working Committee, a stupendously wealthy man named Jamnalal Bajaj.

The timing of the letter provided the proof that Hedgewar had needed as to who had been colluding with the British. Hedgewar had worked closely with Bajaj in 1916, when both men were twenty-seven years old, to try and establish the Congress local cadre in Wardha.[37] Bajaj was the adopted son of a very wealthy family who had made their money by working hand in glove with the colonizers. He was conferred the medal Rai Bahadur in 1918 for lending money to British war efforts.[38] It was a medal that he returned in 1921 after joining Gandhi's first non-cooperation movement. He was close to Gandhi. Like the Nehrus, he took the Bajaj family into the struggle, inspired by Gandhi's principles of simple living and complete devotion to removing the ills of caste from Indian society.[39] If Nehru was Gandhi's maverick number two, then Bajaj was his reliable and loyal number three. The rumour mill was making loud noises that Gandhi was even considering moving to Wardha district, to a small village called Segaon, and had vowed not to return to his Sabarmati ashram until India had achieved independence.[40] The lord of the land at Segaon was his trusty number three, who was willing to give three hundred acres of his estate to Gandhi if he decided to move there.

In 1936, two years hence, all of Hedgewar's instincts would be proven right. Gandhi would move to Segaon and rename the entire village with a nonchalant wave of the pen to Sevagram and would live there until his death in 1948, on 300 acres of arable land donated by Bajaj. It was important that if the fakir of the Congress was going to relocate his mission control from Gujarat, in the north-west of the country, to central India, then his had to be the strongest voice. He could not afford to be next door to a rising power that could challenge his or the Congress's authority. Therefore, it was important for the Congress to clear out any weeds from the area, even if that meant collusion with the British. However, not everything would go the way Congress had intended. Hedgewar, although an idealist, was also a pragmatist and immensely resourceful.

Bajaj's letter was full of questions, and what to Hedgewar would have seemed like allegations of working against the interests of the Congress and, ergo, India's independence.[41] The RSS was being framed as anti-national. Narratives were being projected on scant evidence and lots of conjecture. Bajaj, at the same time, wrote to Moonjay, who was the grand old man of the Hindu Mahasabha, which was the breakaway group from the Congress, composed of those men that had wanted India to be completely free from the beginning and who were not in line with the associates, who had been happy to rule under the Crown. Bajaj asked Hedgewar questions about the vision and mission of the Sangh and its views on caste and untouchability. He was most interested in the relationship between the Hindu Mahasabha and the RSS.[42]

Hedgewar could smell a trap. No matter what Hedgewar wrote, he knew that every word could be misconstrued and projected to show whatever it was that the Congress leadership wanted. Hedgewar did write back to Bajaj. It was dull and uninteresting, and certainly did not give the other man what he had wanted. 'It is difficult to give a written response to all your questions. Thus, you could come over for a meeting, at your convenience or permit me to meet you in Wardha', wrote Hedgewar.[43] Bajaj and Hedgewar met on 31 January 1934. Bajaj had travelled to Nagpur. The meeting was long, often tense and frustrating. Bajaj had come with some preconceived ideas, which, in essence, he had to prove, but the evidential words had to come from Hedgewar. Bajaj's preconceptions were that the RSS was just a grassroot army for Moonjay and the Hindu Mahasabha to use for its own ends; the RSS was indifferent when it came to caste and untouchability; the RSS was militant and could be a threat to the future government of India, that is the Congress; the RSS was influenced balefully by Moonjay and Vinayak Savarkar, an alleged influence that took on new life in the light of Moonjay's trip to Italy in 1931, where he met the dictator

Mussolini and was highly impressed by his fascist youth movement[44] and the RSS was undemocratic and inherently anti-Muslim, and therefore would not allow for a united India to exist. None of his preconceptions were proven right. The two men, who had once been friends, parted ways, with only further mistrust.

The irony of the whole matter was that both the Congress and the Hindu Mahasabha wanted to usurp the power of the RSS for their own ends, and both felt dissatisfied with the stance of the RSS. For Moonjay, Hedgewar was like a son. Yet, Hedgewar's creation was mostly unhelpful in supporting the Hindu Mahasabha, which saddened Moonjay to no end. More than that, Hedgewar had his own ideas and seldom agreed with his former mentor about the big questions. While for Congress, the RSS was mute on many issues and was secretly against the vision of India that it had developed. Hedgewar was adamant that the Sangh would navigate itself through the vested interests of both juggernauts, with his first and only priority being not getting squashed by them.

Indeed, what made the likes of Bajaj so distrustful of his old friend was that on the very day, 31 January 1934, Moonjay had concluded a public function organized by the Mahasabha on militarizing the Hindu community in the same way that European societies had. Hedgewar, too, had attended but did not speak; he listened and disagreed with what was being proposed by Moonjay. The evidence arises a few months later. However, to the extent that one relies on perception as much as words and actions, Hedgewar looked complicit in the militancy that Moonjay was espousing. Bajaj was aware of this conference and may have also attended it. His conversation with Hedgewar earlier that morning would have seemed so distant and remote from the desperate rancour of Moonjay.

On 3 March, the Council of the Central Provinces was due to have its quarterly budgetary meeting. Hedgewar was lobbying hard behind the scenes. He personally went out to see councillors and asked them to make a fair representation in the chambers on behalf of the RSS. Between 1 February and 3 March, Hedgewar had managed to convince the District Councils of Akola, Wardha, Umred, Savner, Katol and Bhandara city to all reject the circular to ban their members from participating with the RSS. For thirty days straight, in the rising heat of spring, still suffering from severe headaches and back pain, he travelled day and night, lobbying people, working his networks and leaning into the goodwill he had developed over the years.

To his delight, the Akola district not only led the way in rejecting the circular but wrote their own response and distributed it amongst all the local councils, praising the Sangh for 'overcoming caste discrimination and for training the youth'.[45] On 3 March, the quarterly budgetary session was held. To the surprise of the Home Minister of Wardha, all the representatives had turned up, and even the public viewing galleries were full.[46] Hedgewar too, sat there looking down at the proceedings from his viewing seat. A session that usually lasted half a day went on for three days. Both sides dug their heels in and were unrelenting in the debate chamber. The Home Minister, an associate, was leading the charge in trying to prove the RSS as communal, that is an organization that has hatred towards another community. Charges of fascism and even Nazism were flung about. The onus was on the associates to prove it. In RSS renderings of this event, the government is made to look silly, incoherent and ultimately without substance.[47] In reality, the chamber was charged and polarized, with strong arguments on both sides. The debate continued for three further sittings on 3, 7 and 8 March. The Government was essentially relying on intelligence reports to justify its actions. To Hedgewar's relief, these intelligence dossiers were of poor quality and often fabricated. The Congressmen were desperate to quell all the questioning, but the Councillors were having none of it.

'What is the Government's definition of a communal organization?' came one question from a backbencher.[48] Then came, 'Are there any Muslim organizations that the government recognizes as communal?'[49] These were highly uncomfortable questions. Then a man called Kashi-prasad Pande mockingly asked, 'Is it true that the former Minister of the Central Provinces was the President of the RSS?'[50] This was obviously a deeply embarrassing question to field for the provincial government. A man named Raghavendra Rao was the unfortunate flunky who had been wheeled out to bat the questions. He stumbled and dodged his way through, losing credibility with each answer. His responses were to the effect, 'I have just come to know of this; I will need to check; it surprises me that a former minister was President (of the RSS) when such posts were not allowed to be taken up; I need more time to answer that question'; and so, on it went.[51]

On the other hand, Moonjay's speeches were read out. They were often fiery, emotive and certainly bigoted. Then, his visit to Italy and his praise for fascism were highlighted. Moonjay was positioned as a 'co-founder' of the Sangh, which, of course, was inaccurate, but 'guilt by association' was the main thrust of the attack. The Government also highlighted the military-type behaviour of the RSS and its blatant and well-documented involvement in clashes with Muslim mobs. The relatively small, usually dull chamber was a cauldron of hot boiling egos. Hedgewar watched the proceedings from above. At the breaks, he would walk down the narrow wooden staircase to catch and thank the Councillors who were putting up a surprisingly robust rear-guard action against the circular.

After three days, and when everyone was exhausted, the circular still was not formally withdrawn, but it was implicitly agreed that it would not be enforced. Hedgewar had won his first fight against the British on its own turf. For the Congress, especially for its high command, this was a disaster. Rather than isolate the RSS, they had inadvertently managed to galvanize it. Furthermore, with Gandhi looking to move to Wardha, what would such a strong RSS in this region mean for the credibility of the Congress?

Two months later, on 31 March 1934, Moonjay came to see Hedgewar. They sat sipping chai and nattering on the first floor of Hedgewar's house. This became a meeting that would haunt Hedgewar's image and the RSS for decades to come. Moonjay, regarding the meeting, in his diary wrote,

> 'They should work for the standardisation of Hindu thought throughout India... But the point is that this ideal cannot be brought to effect unless we have our own swaraj with a Hindu as a dictator like Shivaji of old, or Mussolini, or Hitler of present-day Italy or Germany... But this does not mean that we have to sit with folded hands until some such dictator arises in India. We should formulate a scientific scheme and carry on propaganda for it…'[52]

Moonjay had also, back in 1931, after returning from his trip to Italy, addressed the Hindu Mahasabha,

> 'Imitate the youth movements of Germany and the Balilla and Fascist organisations of Italy. I think they are eminently suited for introduction in India, adapting them to suit the special conditions. I have been very much impressed by these movements and I have seen their activities with my own eyes in all details.'[53]

Academics like Casolari, who already have a trajectory of thought, and little, if any direct access to RSS archives, naturally conjecture that 'Is this not reminiscent of the principle of 'obedience to one leader' ('ek chalak anuvartitva') followed by the RSS?'[54] It could not have been possible for her to have known that Hedgewar opposed the idea of one central leader, and was deeply upset by the decision that was made without his involvement. Furthermore, anyone who has studied the RSS closely will know that power is highly diffused, with many checks and balances across its smoky structure. Even Jaffrelot writes that 'there is a sharp distinction between Nazi and fascist ideology on one side and RSS on the other as far as the concept of race and the centrality of the leader are concerned.'[55] Western academics are quick to draw attention to the similarities between Mussolini's Balilla and Hedgewar's RSS, 'they recruited boys from the age of six, up to eighteen: the youths had to attend weekly meetings, where they practised physical exercises, received paramilitary training and performed drills and parades.'[56] This exact description could also describe the military cadets in England at the time, or for that matter, even the Boy Scouts. In fact, Moonjay describes the RSS as being more akin to the Boy Scouts than to the paramilitary outfit he had envisaged. Moonjay himself writes, 'our institution of Rashtriya Swayamsewak Sangh of Nagpur under Dr Hedgewar is of this kind, though quite independently conceived.'[57] Hedgewar's inspiration was much closer to home, it was the British military. He admired the very power that was used to enslave his own people. The influence of Mussolini's fascism and Nazism on the RSS are the fantasies of those with the darkest imagination—western academics and their ill-informed and sometimes colonized Indian counterparts. The darker the fantasy, the more they can justify themselves to themselves and others.

Moonjay wanted Hedgewar and the RSS to help him develop military academies like those he had seen in England, France and Italy. He felt that Indian society had to militarize and re-cultivate its martial spirit. Hedgewar listened but ultimately never actively supported the endeavour. Moonjay eventually became frustrated and set off on his own. The fundamental difference between the two men was that Moonjay believed that some men were born to rule, and those men should be concentrated on, nurtured and militarized. Hedgewar was far more egalitarian and believed that every individual, the basic unit of society, had to be transformed. He was sceptical of elite men and their capability, as well as their character. Hedgewar was ultimately a Republican; he believed in the power of the masses to hold the powerful to account, but only if the masses themselves were capable of doing so. Unlike many others who were impatient to see change, Hedgewar was adamant about staying the course. The RSS was for the masses and must transform the common man to make him capable of meaningfully contributing to the process of nation-building. Hedgewar was bottom-up, whereas Moonjay was top-down. Furthermore, for Moonjay, Hedgewar's mission was too far-fetched.

At the grand age of sixty-three, the old man went on to set up the Bhonsala Military School in Nasik in 1937 with ninety students and was funded in large part by those whom it was meant to serve—India's elite royal houses, who were swayed by Moonjay's vision. The academy was designed to give martial training to the next generation of Hindu men and women who would join the ranks of the Indian Armed Forces. Today, there are two such schools, one in Nasik and another in Nagpur. The schools are privately funded and, on the whole, have produced stellar results in terms of imparting an education that breeds confidence, intelligence and a sense of duty in young people. Interestingly, history likes to twist and turn, but the arc is always towards that which is sustainable. Today, the education society that Moonjay set up in 1935, which runs these two schools, is firmly managed, supported and developed by RSS-trained men and women. The schools are part and parcel of what is broadly called the Sangh Parivar.

The confluence of several forces in the mid-thirties gave rise to three strands of thought, which today provide the mainstream narrative about the RSS and the reason for it largely being treated as a pariah by the international community. In any power vacuum, those who fight to set the trajectory of a society inevitably get to a point where the disagreements become up close and personal, where long-distance sniper rifles are replaced by hand-to-hand combat and bayonets; it becomes bloody, messy and completely chaotic. The 1930s were when the differing forces trying to shape the trajectory of an ancient society came in close contact and were prepared to use any form of skulduggery available to them to get what they wanted—power.

'RSS is fascist' is the first and most cited claim. The evidence, when cited, usually comes from Moonjay's rhetoric and behaviour. In the thirties, Moonjay was already in his sixties. His idealism was well behind him, and his diary reveals the large knot of pessimism that had lodged deep inside his psyche. He was angry, bitter and overwhelmed by a sense that his countrymen were quite hopeless. The deeper his pessimism became, the more venomous his rhetoric. His anger transformed into bigotry. His frustrations led to short-temperedness. His hopelessness sadly led him to clutch at immediate solutions, and he readily found anti-colonial propaganda in Italy and Germany. This, coupled with the fact that everyone thought Moonjay and Hedgewar had co-founded the RSS, meant that it was easy to discredit the RSS through association. There can be little doubt that Moonjay and Hedgewar were like father and son; and Hedgewar's development, in large parts, was shaped by the older man. However, it is an overstatement to say that Moonjay directly influenced the RSS or that it was even partially built in his image. The facts speak for themselves.

Had Hedgewar been fascist, that is, had he actually been an ultra-nationalist, he would have created far more mayhem for the authorities than he did. A case in point is that in 1927, when the RSS acted to protect the Hindu population of Nagpur from the Muslim militias sent out by radical clerics dreaming of a theological state, he could have quite easily taken that opportunity to be far more aggressive in order to have caused a complete exodus of Muslims out of Nagpur. He did no such thing. Indeed, when the general Hindu population began to freely riot, he told his swayamsevaks to stand down and only protect temples and Hindu neighbourhoods from being counterattacked.[58]

Then there were the likes of Vinayak Savarkar, who had always felt that the RSS was too soft. Even members of the RSS leadership became disenchanted with Hedgewarian thinking for being too mild and for not doing enough to attack Muslim neighbourhoods. These men were bordering on fascist. A case in point is Gopal Huddar, the radical revolutionary who wanted the RSS to fight an armed resistance against the British.[59] The truth is that the RSS has always been more akin to a centrist reforming movement, whereas those who were on the fascist right of the spectrum found the RSS far too mild-natured and without much revolutionary gusto. Nathuram Godse, the man who assassinated Gandhi in 1948, was one of those men who 'grew up' and received training at RSS shakhas, but found the organization too mild and impotent to stop the disintegration of India, and so he found a home with Vinayak Sarvarkar's Hindu Mahasabha.[60] Here, too, he did not get the satisfaction he was looking for and ultimately went alone to commit one of the most heinous assassinations of the twentieth century.

The real reason for the RSS being labelled as fascist was because it was never going to buy into the idea of India that Nehru's Congress had envisaged, that of a non-aligned, socialist, secular and Soviet-like industrialized nation, where democracy consisted of only one party to rule them all. Sardar Patel, the man who now has a 182-metre-tall statue in Gujarat commissioned by Prime Minister Narendra Modi, who was a prachaarak of the RSS, had expressed his concerns as far back as 1948. In a letter to the head of the Hindu Mahasabha, Shyam Prashad Mukherjee, he writes,

> 'There is no doubt in my mind that the extreme section of the Hindu Mahasabha was involved in the conspiracy [to kill Gandhi]. The activities of the RSS constituted a clear threat to the existence of the Government and the State. Our reports show that those activities, despite the ban, have not died down. Indeed, as time has marched on, the RSS circles are becoming more defiant and are indulging in their subversive activities in an increasing measure.'[61]

Patel's concern was primarily that the RSS was capable and, indeed, planning on overthrowing the new government. They were subversive to the idea of India which Nehru and the Congress had adopted. This was an ideological battle, where the Congress saw themselves as India and India as belonging to the Congress. It is worth noting that Patel demarcates between the extreme forces of Vinayak Savarkar's Hindu Mahasabha and the RSS.

By fusing the idea of nation and state into one entity with a 'sleight of hand', it became impossible for anyone to oppose the Congress without themselves falling prey to the charge of being anti-national and subversive. For Hedgewar, the state was temporary and artificial, a means to an end; it was a foundational piece, but nevertheless, a single piece in the wider jigsaw of the nation. The nation was constructed through the forces of history, and a tattered Hindu culture was all that remained of a once vibrant Hindu civilization. The state was responsible for safeguarding that culture, through which a new modern civilization could be built. In the Hedgewarian worldview, democracy, although deeply flawed, was still arguably the best story in town. However, he knew that for it to have a chance the leadership had to be composed of desh bhakts and not men and women who had ideas of India that were foreign, such as Russian or European socialism, or Communism, which was hostile towards the culture of the land. This is where the second charge against Hedgewar arises—that he wanted to create a theological Hindu State.

These narratives naturally flow out of the previous sleight of hand. Hedgewar was a Republican, in that his single-minded motive at this time in his life was to strengthen and reform the Hindu society, so that a democratic state could be held accountable, and a civilizational state could be installed. However, he was a realist, which ironically made him sound pessimistic about society when, in actual fact, he was a complete optimist. For Hedgewar, the state should be answerable to the people, and he was deeply worried that it would be the reverse in Nehru's socialist utopian vision. Furthermore, he was concerned that such a fragmented and weak Hindu society, and a state that was, at best, openly indifferent and, at worst, hostile to Hindu culture, with Nehru at its helm, openly being uninterested in it, could only mean further subjugation for the Hindu society. The white masters would leave and be replaced by their brown counterparts who had equally confused ideas about identity and secularism.

From a Hedgewarian perspective, Hindu culture is inherently diverse and plural, and therefore, a civilizational state would need to be in its image, that is secular in the truest sense. Once again, it is worth repeating that during the thirties, Hedgewar was curbing the extremists on the fringes of his movement while openly challenging the Advocates and their misconceptions of what India and Hindu society was and should be. In Hedgewarian thought, Hindu culture could not have a theological basis because it has no dogma or single creed it can be pinned down to. Hindu culture is a composition of a myriad of creeds, beliefs and practices, so many that it becomes meaningless to start arguing about which is the right way. In Hedgewar's weltanschauung, any creed is acceptable, but only on the condition that it is rooted and loyal to the soil. The creed was of secondary importance, but an affinity as sons and daughters of the soil became paramount. The strange dichotomy in western narratives—secular India versus a Hindu India—completely misses the point, as no such dichotomy exists;[62] there is no Hindu state as a religious entity; for Hindu *is* secular from the Hedgewarian standpoint. The RSS keeps in complete alignment with this subtle but potent thought even today.

The RSS, as far as Hedgewar was concerned, had little to say, or do, as regards to minority religions in India, so long as they towed a nationalist line of thought. The reality is that the Church is generally pointed towards Rome, London or Salt Lake City in the USA. Whereas Islam is pointed strictly towards Mecca. Indeed, both religions, which are exclusivist in nature, struggle to deal with the diversity of Hindu society at large and find it blasphemous to have any reverence for the soil, as that would be a form of crude idolatry. Here, the two world views collide and, thus far, have not been reconciled.

The third narrative spawns from the association with the Hindu Mahasabha, which was a platform for majoritarianism, something that Hedgewar could never accept. In the Hedgewarian perspective, the entire society must be bound and unified in their efforts of nation-building, whereas for Vinayak Savarkar's Mahasabha, a new India had to safeguard the majority and defeat the 'aggression of Islam'.[63] The current narrative suggests that (Vinayak) Savarkar was the architect of the RSS, and as they were majoritarian in nature, then ergo, the RSS must be designed to safeguard only the Hindu population and drive out or re-convert the Muslim population. The truth is that Hedgewar, throughout the thirties, attempted to distance himself from the Mahasabha, and although he respected Savarkar, he never particularly liked the man and kept him as far away as possible from the RSS. Moonjay writes,

> 'The RSS and Dr Hedgewar are developing a mentality of isolation and separateness from Hindu Mahasabha and its activities and becoming almost an actual opposition.'[64]

Moonjay also makes it clear that he was taken to task whenever he overstepped the mark during his speeches and how, ultimately, he withdrew from active interest in the RSS. In a journal entry from 1932, he writes,

> 'In the morning, Dr Hedgewar and Martand Jog turned up. Jog took me to task for yesterday's speech. He quoted them as saying, "People blame us and our Sangh… They say it is the Sangh that provides [a] platform to Dr Moonjay in Nagpur. I was disillusioned; the cat was out of the bag… this protest from Jog, which assumes that I want to have a platform for myself at the cost of the prestige and reputation of the Sangh and that I cannot get such a platform without their help and support, opened my eyes. I wish the Sangh all prosperity and good luck but henceforward I will cease to take a personal interest in it…'[65]

Even the charge of Moonjay being the 'holy ghost' of the RSS is a work of fiction by those that it serves best. The argument was settled as far back as 1934 at the debate in the chambers of the Central Legislative Council, where Kolte, a barrister and a councillor, stated, 'So far as I know, Dr Moonjay is neither the founder nor the moving spirit of the RSS'.[66] The Mahratta newspaper, in its editorial on 7 March 1934 mocked the government,

'From where has Home Minister (Raghvendra) Rao acquired this information (that Moonjay is commander-in-chief of the RSS)? We declare... on the basis of the information that we have, and we collected that Dr Moonjay does not have any remotest relation with the formation, activates or the leadership of the RSS. Is it academically and intellectually moral to use Moonjay to ridicule the RSS?'[67]

The RSS as being a proxy, or the grassroots army, for the Hindu Mahasabha, is a myth, and it is time that it be put to rest. Images of Moonjay and Savarkar tightly colluding together in darkened basements, plotting to use the RSS to overthrow the British and massacre minorities, are dark imaginings, initially spawned from the dying Leviathan and then the Congressmen in whose interest it was to keep the nightmare alive. Western academics have continued to use these narratives and have constructed myopic models to understand the motivations of the RSS and have completely misinterpreted the phenomenon. Without understanding the subtleties of the RSS, it is not possible to fully grasp Hindu revivalism throughout the world.

FOURTEEN: 1934–1936

Between Saffron and Silence

In the winter months of 1934, two RSS OTCs were taking place simultaneously. The first was in Nagpur, where Martand Jog was in charge, and the second, where approximately 1500 swayamsevaks had gathered, was in Wardha and was led by Appa Joshi. The grounds of the camp belonged to Jamnalal Bajaj, who, at the beginning of 1934, had gone to see Hedgewar with a series of questions about what the Sangh stood for and to ascertain what type of movement the RSS would be in a new India. He had known Hedgewar personally, having worked together in 1916 for the Congress. Bajaj was trying to understand who was behind the RSS; was it just a muscular expression of the Hindu Mahasabha, which had broken away from the Congress? Hedgewar, as had become his way, was fairly candid and told him the RSS way and why he could not align fully with the Congress or the Mahasabha. Bajaj was dissatisfied with the answers. Both men were of the same age, and though at different ends of the spectrum socio-economically, and in world views, they both nevertheless respected each other. Bajaj's actions indicate as much in so far as he made his vast estate available to the RSS[1].

Directly opposite the grounds where the RSS was constructing its camp lay a vast swath of land also owned by Bajaj, which he had donated to Gandhi's ashram. As soon as the ashram was somewhat ready to be occupied, Gandhi, unilaterally, as often was his way, decided to rename the entire village from Segaon to Sewagram. Gandhi had arrived and was settling into his new ashram when the camp was in full swing. It was hard not to notice. Gandhi stayed in a large manor house opposite the camp a few hundred metres away. He saw what would have looked like a military regiment setting up camp opposite. The RSS OTCs were notoriously like

British military training camps, with the subtle but unmissable difference being that at the centre of the grounds would be a tall pole on top of which fluttered the bhagwa dhwaj (saffron flag).

The inauguration of the camp was held on 22 December 1934. Gandhi and his entourage were invited but failed to show. At the inauguration, the RSS's marching band would have been on full display and probably could have been heard throughout Bajaj's massive estate. Hundreds of people had gathered, with many local dignitaries present to inaugurate the forty-day camp. Gandhi observed from afar. He had obviously seen enough for his interest to be piqued. The very next day, Gandhi's personal secretary, and lifelong follower, sent a note to Joshi. It read,

> 'As your camp is close to the ashram, it has drawn the attention of Mahatmaji's. He wishes to pay a visit to the camp, even though he is extremely busy. Please let us know what time would be convenient for you. It will be appreciated if you could come over to the ashram to fix the time.'[2]

There is much to glean from such notes. The man who had written it was Mahadev Desai. He was far more than Gandhi's personal secretary; he was more of a chief of staff, everything happened through him. He was Gandhi's loyal administrator who rose before his 'master' daily and slept long after the aged man had fallen asleep.[3] He knew everything that was to be known and tightly controlled who got to see Gandhi and, more importantly, who didn't. He, in some way, was the gatekeeper to the most powerful man in India at the time. He diligently kept a daily diary between 1917 till his death in 1942, chronicling the life of Gandhi. Guha notes that it was Desai who acted as Gandhi's 'alter ego', who would write down the words by which the world would remember his esteemed master.[4]

Gandhi knew he was in the business of making history, and it was important for him to be remembered as his devotees saw him—as a maha-atma. Maha can be translated as simply 'great', but the term atma requires rendering. A lazy translation is 'soul', but this would be a great disservice to the term and to what Gandhi had in mind for himself. The term atma etymologically comes from the Sanskrit term breath or essence. In other words, maha-atma means the great essence, which in Indian culture is akin to a divine being, often attributed to the devas of Hindu culture.

Gandhi had been sculpting his image for posterity right from the get-go, positioning himself as a saint, or enlightened being, more akin to a saviour who had arisen in the east, with a universal message of non-violence, which incidentally was a poor rendering of the Hindu conception of non-harming. Around the thirties, many men and their followers in India were trying to pass themselves off as 'saviours from the east'—Besant's Theosophical Society was grooming Krishnamurti; Mirra Alfassa, who was trying to build a cult around Aurobindo in Pondicherry and here we have Desai trying to do something similar around Gandhi. He was by far the most successful.

The invitation to Gandhi for the inauguration of the camp would have arrived on Desai's desk. Did he ignore it? Did he advise Gandhi to not attend such a public gathering? Or was it that, as Gandhi would have us believe, he knew nothing about the camp and the RSS until it just so happened to be taking place at the same time as his arrival at his new ashram? History will not tell us the secret thoughts of men, but we can conjecture.

Joshi, the head man at the camp, did as requested, and immediately marched out to see Gandhi, where he was met by Desai. Desai was a tall man of medium build with a small moustache and thinning hair, who wore round spectacles, similar in style to his master. 'Good-looking' and 'well spoken', he received Joshi's note.[5] The note read, 'Whenever you can come to the camp, we shall be ready to welcome you.'[6] Desai informed the enthusiastic Joshi, who had remained a Congress worker while also devoting much of his time to the Sangh, that Gandhi was maintaining silence and so will write you a note. A few moments later, Desai returned with a note claiming to be from the Mahatma stating, 'Tomorrow the 25th early morning at 0600 hours, I shall visit the camp. I can spend an hour and a half with you.'[7] Joshi took leave and returned to the camp. He was probably feeling elated at the thought of Gandhi's visit.

That night, preparations were made. Swayamsevaks, many of whom would have been thrilled at the thought of meeting Gandhi, the godman and international celebrity, practised well into the evening to demonstrate their martial skills; exhibitions were tidied up, and the grounds swept clean. At exactly six in the morning, Gandhi could be seen walking in his customary way, slightly hunched, with his walking stick and white robes, coming towards the camp. Behind him walked his familiar entourage—Desai walked a few feet behind with his customary diary in hand. To the right of him was an English lady by the name of Madeleine Slade, who liked to be called Mira-behn, which meant sister Mira. Gandhi had named her after the famous Mirabai, a household name across India, who was a sixteenth-century Hindu mystic and wrote mesmerizing poetry and devotional songs dedicated to Krishna. Slade was the daughter of an aristocratic English family. She had come to India after hearing about Gandhi in England, when a friend had described 'Gandhi as another Christ and as the greatest figure of the twentieth century'[8]. Like many European women looking for their Christ, Slade ventured forth. Then trailing the Mahatma's disciples was Bajaj, who was the money man and power broker and who, in turn, led a small contingent of servants and clerks.

Joshi received the Congress leader at the arched entrance of the camp. They were all greeted, and a customary red tilak would have been smeared on their foreheads, and then they would have been led inside. The first place Gandhi would have been taken to is the Bhagwa Dhwaj, as is the RSS way, in the centre of the ground. Here, Gandhi, with the arranged RSS troops in line and uniform, saluted their Guru.[9] Following the salute, Gandhi saw the Sangh's marching band and 1500 uniformed young men march past in complete unison. It would have felt like a military parade to the bystanders. Even the music was taken directly from British military instruments. It is not clear how Gandhi and his devotees would have felt at seeing this kind of strength and organization, but one can imagine they would have been somewhat unnerved.

According to Palkar, 'Mahatmaji placed his hand on Appaji's shoulders and said, "I am extremely pleased. I have never seen a more impressive sight in the whole of the country.'[10] This line should be taken with a pinch of salt as it comes out of Palkar's hagiography, but nevertheless, it does communicate somewhat how Gandhi may have felt having seen how the swayamsevaks lived. Gandhi visited the kitchens, breakfast areas and sleeping quarters, and he personally interacted with swayamsevaks, asking them all sorts of questions. He was surprised to find that most of the young men did not know the caste or class of men they were sitting next to, nor did they care, and said as much to Gandhi, who, according to Sinha, would have been charmed by the occasion.[11] Men from all strata of society lived, ate and trained together. RSS camps are still executed with the same Hedgewarian spirit of equality and brotherhood. Gandhi also noted that there were no images of deities; the usual pantheon of the Hindu Gods and Goddesses were visibly absent. The only imagery that he found was an image of India personified as a mother goddess—an image that still pervades the Sangh world.

Gandhi, as reported in his journal called the *Harijan*, on 28 September 1947, just months before his assassination, visited an RSS-run relief camp in Delhi for the thousands of refugees flooding in from the newly created 'Land of the Pure', where Islamic aggression went unabated. Here, Gandhi remarked, 'he had been very impressed by their discipline, complete absence of untouchability and rigorous simplicity'.[12] He was referring to the visit he had made in 1934. This visit has always been seen with embarrassment and equal annoyance by the naysayers, as it went against the narrative of the RSS as being bigoted, prejudiced and a hater of the divinity that was Gandhi. As with life, history too has a way of seeping out from the edges, no matter how tightly one tries to seal it from others, to reveal a nuanced truth over time. Such imaginations, as the one Congress had been projecting, ought to be bested over the coming decades.

According to Palkar, Gandhi asked Joshi who the founder of the RSS was. This incident is portrayed as if the name Hedgewar was something new to Gandhi.[13] Both seem tenuous at best. Firstly, it beggars belief that such a well-informed man who managed his diary like a military five-star general appears at a 1500-strong 'military' training camp completely unaware as to where he was going and clueless as to who was behind it all. Furthermore, it is astounding that a man like Desai who controlled every movement of the Mahatma would not have known who founded the RSS, and what it stood for. Furthermore, Bajaj was with him, the man who had given the land to the RSS and knew Hedgewar personally for almost twenty years. Even he had apparently not said a word to Gandhi. Was Gandhi simply testing Joshi and trying to covertly verify his information?

Having discovered Hedgewar, Gandhi asked Joshi if he could meet 'this Hedgewar fellow who has removed untouchability.'[14] Hedgewar was due to arrive at the camp the following day unaware that the great man himself was visiting the RSS camp. The next day, Hedgewar arrived at the camp after all the fanfare consisting of speeches and marching bands from the train station to the camp—it was a hero's welcome. He was met upon arrival by a starstruck Joshi, who exclaimed what had happened the previous morning and that Gandhi wanted a personal audience with him. Hedgewar, who up to that point had never met Gandhi but had crossed paths with the great leader on many occasions at Congress gatherings, simply took it in his stride. Hedgewar was once in the upper middle tiers of the Congress, whereas Gandhi was its overlord, for whom the younger upstart would have just been one of thousands.

As requested, Hedgewar, Joshi and an older man named Anna Bopatkar, who was the chief guest at the camp, and was associated with Gandhi, all turned up at eight in the evening. The sun had set, and the air had cooled. It was 26 December 1934 and Gandhi's new manor was well-lit and looked regal. Desai greeted them at the door and took them up the flight of stairs to Gandhi's lounge. Gandhi was waiting at the door, leading the way inside, and ushering everyone to sit. He had Hedgewar sit next to him on the cushions placed on the floor. Once all the niceties were out of the way, and water was served, the room settled with Desai, Madeleine Slade and a man called Swami Anand sitting on one side of Gandhi, and Hedgewar, Joshi and Bopatkar on the other. The conversation is said to have lasted an hour before Hedgewar rose to take his leave, allowing the old leader to rest. The tone throughout the conversation was awkward and prickly; cleavages were highlighted without ever explicitly being dwelt on. Gandhi was the inquisitor, and Hedgewar the inquisitee.

> In Hindi, Gandhi said, *'You must know by now that I visited the camp yesterday'*.
>
> *'It is our good fortune'*, responded Hedgewar, just lowering his gaze as a mark of courtesy. *'If I had known about your plans'*, momentarily glancing at Desai, *'I would have made sure that I was there to greet you.'*
>
> In a very un-conciliatory tone, Gandhi explained, *'In a way, it was good that you were not there. I was able to interact freely with many of your swayamsevaks, and I learned a great many things.'*
>
> To Hedgewar this would have come across as a jibe, suggesting that had Hedgewar been there, he would have been restricted from free interaction, and would not have learnt as much as he had done without him. Gandhi treated Hedgewar as the lesser man, letting him know, through what wasn't said but implied, that 'I may have got to know more than you would have liked!'

Sensing Hedgewar's loss of face, Gandhi, the communicator par excellence added respectfully, *'Doctor, I am extremely pleased at several aspects of the camp like the number of men taking part, the discipline I witnessed, the character of these men, the cleanliness of the camp, and that all men were equals.'* Thus, he managed to put the bigger man at ease.

After some complimentary comments, Gandhi dove into what he really wanted to know—money matters. *'Tell me Doctor, how do you fund all your activities? I heard yesterday that you provide meals for just two or three annas. How is this possible? We spend much more —why is that?'* he asked, looking around at Desai with raised eyebrows as if asking him, but only rhetorically. It was one of those loaded questions with a healthy dollop of cynicism layered on top for effect. An anna was a currency now not in use; it was equivalent to one-sixteenth of a rupee in British India.

Before Hedgewar could utter a sound, Bopatkar made his entrance into the conversation, *'Your expenses Bapu'*, leaning in towards Gandhi, and using a respectful nickname for the Mahatma, which meant father in rustic Hindi, *'are much higher because of the way you live. You may like to believe that you and the Congress live frugally; you like to call it a "parnakuti", but yours has all the princely amenities'*, he answered while gesturing to the shocked audience, encouraging them to look around where they were having this conversation.

Bopatkar used a specific term that Gandhi used in public to describe where he lived, in a parnakuti, which literally meant a hut made from sticks, branches, leaves and mud. It was a pure Gandhian phrase thrown right back at him. Desai was visibly shocked at the directness and glanced over to his master, catching his eye momentarily, before Gandhi let out a brittle laugh to diffuse the situation, and to show that he took it in jest. Bopatkar, in all likeliness, jumped into the fray out of a paternalistic feeling towards Hedgewar and to shield him from the mocking inquisition that Gandhi was conducting. Even though the younger man could not give his due response out of respect and decorum, the older man clearly thought his seniority in age would trump Gandhi into submission. He was right. As soon as Gandhi's brittle laughter ended, Bopatkar was off again, *'You see, I was the Chief guest today, and all I got was daal and roti, what every man ate. There are no distinctions in the Sangh. If you follow the equality as practised here [in the Sangh], your expenses will also come down to a few annas,'* he said while making eye contact with all three including a muted Gandhi, whose displeasure was growing. He wasn't finished, it was as if he had found the perfect moment to let loose and really tell Gandhi what he thought about his frugality. *'It seems you'*, now squarely looking at Gandhi, *'want aristocratic facilities while bearing no expenses. Tell me how is that possible? Not even the doctor can help you with this,'* he finished off while pointing at an inwardly satisfied but quiet Hedgewar.

At that moment, Gandhi's English disciple leaned in to indiscreetly show the time. Everybody got the message, but Hedgewar was the first to react. Hedgewar immediately got up and looked down at the frail master and suggested *'it must be time for you to end your day, I will take my leave.'*

'No, no,' Gandhi protested, gesturing to the giant to be seated once again. *'You can be seated. I can stay awake for at least another half an hour,'* he said clearly wanting to continue the exchange. Completely ignoring everything that had just been said, Gandhi changed the direction and mood of the conversation by asking Hedgewar about his past. *'Doctor'*, he began once again, *'I came to know that you were part of the Congress for a long time, tell me why you never started an organisation like this within a popular movement like the Congress?'* he asked inquisitively. Then, before Hedgewar could give a response, came another jibe, *'why did you make a separate organisation for no reason?'*

Hedgewar, sensing the situation, took a moment, and answered, *'I did try and start a movement such as this within the Congress back at the 1920 Nagpur Conference. Back then I was the secretary, and my dear friend Doctor Paranjape was in charge of all the volunteers. We both tried, but we could not do much. So, we started independently.'*

'Then why did it fail in the Congress?' Gandhi chirped back. *'Was it money related matters?'* he asked, coming back to what seemed like a favourite topic for the renunciate.

'No, not at all,' answered Hedgewar, trying to find the right words, *'there was no paucity of funds. I know that most things become easier with money,*

but things seldom succeed just because of money. I think the problem was . . . ', still thinking of the right words to say, but seemingly his vocabulary was abandoning him that night. '*The problem here was one of inner spirit*', he said finally, seemingly pleased with the answer.

'*Do you mean to say that people of good inner spirit were not in the Congress or are still not there?*' he said with the tone of a prosecutor cross-examining the lead suspect.

Hedgewar knew that this was not at all going in the right direction. While trying to find his footing again, he said, '*That is not what I meant*', taking a subtle breath and buying some time to rediscover his runaway vocabulary. '*The Congress, of course, has good people*' now raising his eyes to meet Gandhi's', '*but it is a question of organizational mindset. The mindset of the Congress, I believe . . .* ' he said just as Gandhi leaned in, indicating his complete attentiveness and looking for the slightest slip-up to pounce on. '*. . . is that it wants to win politically. Every program of the Congress is designed to achieve that singular end. Volunteers are needed to complete tasks by following the instructions of those higher up the chain of command. The Congress, as far as I can tell, does not believe trained volunteers can solve problems themselves without top-down command. The idea of a volunteer [within the Congress] seems to be one of free labour for arranging meetings and conferences.*' Hedgewar had found his vocabulary again and was beginning to assert himself. '*I do not believe that people can be nurtured and trained in a way that will contribute to the all-round development of the country for years to come with such a mindset. That is why I do not think this work is possible within the Congress,*' he signed off.

For the first time, Gandhi was taken in somewhat by what Hedgewar had said. There was a momentary silence as people absorbed what had just been shared when he launched into another question, '*Tell me, Doctor*', indicating another pejorative, slightly condescending tone, '*What do you mean by this term you use "swayamsevak"?*'

Hedgewar had found his mojo and was now confidently batting on a safe wicket. '*swayamsevaks are those men who offer a significant part of their life to the development of the nation. These men are leaders,*' he said with emphasis to land the point. He continued, '*Our purpose is to create such men. The RSS does not differentiate between the leader and a swayamsevak, for all men inside the movement are swayamsevaks first. A deep and sincere feeling of brotherhood is created through which a sense of equality is achieved, without harbouring any distinctions, as you would have noted yesterday,'* he said, looking at Gandhi, expecting an acknowledgement of some sort. None was forthcoming. *'This is our secret,'* exuding confidence, *'. . . this is how the Sangh has grown in such a short amount of time and with such meagre resources.'*

Gandhi was nodding as if accepting what was being said while also pensive. *'This is incredibly good,'* he commended, what seemed to be with sincerity, *'. . . the nation, I am sure, will benefit from the success of your endeavours.'* Then, just as things were swinging in the right direction, Gandhi once again snipped at the upstart sitting next to him, *'I have heard that your work is particularly effective in Wardha. I am sure this must have been possible only with the generous support of people like Jamnalal.'*

This, once again, calls into question the integrity of Gandhi's line of questioning. Everyone in that room knew that Jamnalal was the big financial fish. Everyone present, in some sense, was grateful for the generosity of men with such deep pockets, but why would Gandhi need to ask such a question when clearly, he was in the know as to how the RSS had been supported by his devotee? Was it that Gandhi was, in some sense, letting Hedgewar know that he could turn the financial taps off in Wardha if he so chose?

'We do not take financial help from anyone,' stated a slightly frustrated Hedgewar.

'Then how do you finance the expenses of such a large organization?' came back the renunciate.

'RSS volunteers make an offering to our Guru, the Bhagwa Dhwaj, what they can afford once a year. These men, all together, shoulder the burden of running the Sangh,' Hedgewar replied, losing faith in the merit of the conversation.

'What!' bellowed a childlike Gandhi, cutting Hedgewar off. *'That is unheard of; you do not take money from anyone else?'* There was a tone of incredulity in his voice.

'We definitely accept financial help from the community, from whoever wants to give, but we have decided to keep the Sangh self-reliant,' he clarified with a sober tone. *'There are times when people give us piles of cash when we have not asked for it,'* stated Hedgewar, now layering it on richly, to probably annoy the Mahatma.

'This work must be consuming much of your time,' he asked quizzically, still referring to raising money. *'Then tell me, how do you find the time to run a medical practice?'*

'I do not have a medical practice, and nor am I employed in any economic activity,' Hedgewar retorted, getting bored with Gandhi's incessant money-related questions. But his ordeals were not quite over yet.

'Then how do you manage your family?' the older man asked.

'I do not have a family, I am not married, and as such, have no responsibilities of that kind.'

Gandhi was clearly taken aback. Gandhi was *the* image of a renunciate, the man who had nothing, and gave everything he had, his entire life force to a noble existence. It dawned on him at that moment that here was a man who *really* was a renunciate, a man with nothing and, therefore, nothing to lose. Hedgewar was the real deal. A man living on the breadline, who, if he chose, could run a medical practice and be wealthy. Gandhi, for all his obsession with money, and maybe because of it, was a man who held the idea of renunciation as the highest virtue. Indeed, his autobiography *My Experiments with Truth* extols his endeavours in attempting to live like a hermit while being in the midst of the world. In front of him was an unassuming man who was just that.

'So...you are not married,' said Gandhi, almost muttering to himself, his mind awash with a new reality. *'This is why you have achieved so much in such little time.'*

Hedgewar was exhausted with the aged Mahatma, *'I have taken much of your time. With your blessings, I am sure everything will be achieved,'* he said, bringing his hands together the way Indians greet and lowering his head in respect of his elder. *'Please allow me to take leave now,'* he asked rhetorically.

Hedgewar got up, having sat cross-legged for almost ninety minutes with lower back pain and stiff legs. The Mahatma, too, slowly got up, with some assistance from Desai and Slade. Gandhi walked all three guests to the door of his room and made a final comment, somewhat sincerely it seems, *'Doctor, you will surely succeed in your chosen mission on the strength of your character and the unflinching faith in your work.'* [15]

Hedgewar turned, lowered his head in respect, and walked down the stairs to leave Gandhi's new manor house. The two men would never meet again, but Gandhi would recollect this meeting almost ten years later when he visited a refugee centre run by the RSS during the partition.

This was how Palkar recorded the only interaction between two pioneers of modern Indian history. At present, there are no public records from Desai's diary about this interaction, but much of his work has yet to be translated into English.

Each man was in the process of making that history. One was already famous and had international acclaim, while the other was lowly in comparison. We can be quite certain that not even the Gandharvas, from Hindu lore, would have placed a bet on lowly Hedgewar going on to build a movement that would dwarf the Mahatma's in less than a century. Gandhi today arguably remains the most famous uninfluential man in the world, while Hedgewar is still unknown, whose legacy is shaping the lives of millions across India and many more around the world. Gandhi's story, as he wanted it to be projected, has been dominant in Western and Indian imagination alike. Still, as declassified letters are revealed, and letters once systematically kept out of circulation by Nehru come into public scrutiny, the Gandhi story may well transform the Mahatma back into just an atma.

> 'I feel that the Vidarbha tour was not conducive for my health. Since my return, I have had a mild fever all the time, and I feel severely weak. There is no cough, but the lungs feel weak. Thus, despite my strong desire to visit Kanpur, I had to cancel the trip.'[16]

Hedgewar wrote in a letter in early 1935 to his uncle Moreshwar, not long after his meeting with Gandhi. Hedgewar's health was failing; his pains were episodic, both in frequency and potency. In another letter he wrote in April 1935, after the OTC that year, he wrote candidly to his brother Sitaram,

> 'We left for Sangli; there was enough space to sleep on the train. But in the attempt to reserve the spot, I sprained my lower back. The sprain would not reduce the whole night. In the morning, a reception was organized at the Sangli station, but I could neither sit up nor stand without incurring tremendous pain. The train reached Sangli at six in the morning. I am referring to the same Sangli shakha whose brilliance we have been hearing of. swayamsevaks were in full uniform and stood ready in formation on the platform. Several prominent individuals of the city had also come.
>
> Somehow, I bore the pain in my back, not letting anyone know of it. I got down at the station and went through the rigmarole of an elaborate but well-intentioned welcome ceremony. Having left the station, we were then presented with a parade at the Shakha grounds. With great difficulty, I managed to sit through that program. The pain had become unbearable. It became impossible to even sit or stand by afternoon, and we had to cancel the program in the evening.
>
> I am bedridden due to the pain. But thankfully, I have no fever or any other problem. I have nevertheless been constantly meeting swayamsevaks and other prominent personalities at Shri Kashinath Rao Limaye's place. My incapacity, it seems, has been beneficial to Sangli, as I am now stationary for almost a week. The people in Sangli are jovial and have labelled my condition the "talking illness".'[17, 18]

His letters, during this period, reveal his personal struggles due to a failing constitution. It also reveals his vulnerability and how dependent he was on the goodwill and care of others. In turn, it also clearly demonstrates that people were keen to have him around and that he had deep, meaningful relations with a great many people. People were willing to put him up, take care of him during his bouts of illness, fund his medical treatment and allow him to turn a portion of their house into offices because the man never stopped working.

Hedgewar was now forty-six years old. His skin had darkened considerably from his younger days, and his large, heavy Nietzschean moustache was completely white. He was still tall and broad, but over the years, he had become considerably heavier. His exercise regime had ended a decade earlier, and his wrestling practice had stopped over fifteen years earlier. Hedgewar was relentlessly travelling like a mendicant—living on alms that were given, in houses where he was a guest. Such a lifestyle is not conducive to achieving good health. His poor health was the direct consequence of his missionary zeal to spread the work of the Sangh to every nook and cranny of India. 'The end of days' spirit had enveloped him, much like the early Christian saints who had believed the world was close to its end. When people work with such time-bound zeal, all other considerations become inconsequential. Eventually the body begins to fail, and the pain caused through its demise is turned into ever greater fuel to complete one's mission.

We can understand the Hedgewarian mindset and the mindset of many prachaaraks when we think about the rationale of love through penance in Christianity.[19] The logic goes something like this: the call of the Hindu life is Dharma—its greatest commandment. The precept of Dharma is two-fold: mastery of oneself and serving society. One's capability is developed through serving one's fellow human beings. In other words, we will live in Dharma when we serve life, and the society exists so that the Hindu can develop herself through service. True service is delivered when one has developed the capability to love, which in turn means one's ability to make a total gift of self to another, to give oneself away fully. But of course, one cannot give what one does not possess, and therefore the Hindu calling for mastery is central, so that it can be given away through love to the society. Mastery is achieved when one devotes oneself, that is becomes a devoted actor and pursues self-denial and penance. The highest form of self-denial and penance is achieved in asceticism. Ergo Dharma is achieved through the journey of service (Sewa), through which character is developed (Sanskaar), which then develops mastery in the world, only to be given away in love for thy neighbour. When this is achieved, a harmonious society is developed (Sangathan). Today, the RSS and its foreign progeny, the Hindu swayamsevak Sangh (HSS), has these exact words in their motto: sewa, meaning selfless service; sanskaar, meaning a virtuous character; and sangathan, the state of society when it is homogenous in Dharma (while retaining all its diversity and expressions).[20]

Seen in this light, Hedgewar was practising asceticism. He used his pain as fuel to further entrench his commitment to the practice of sewa. Sewa done in this way leads to Dharma—the force that sustains, or the truth. Through the act of sewa he was able to lose himself completely in the service of others. This is often elaborated in speeches made by senior prachaaraks of the order. They will use words such as 'prem-bhav' meaning the spirit of love, noting it should be the catalyst of all those working in the Sangh. 'Tyaag', is another favourite term that is often carelessly translated as sacrifice, often by RSS men. It means something more akin to being in a state of mind where one has no desire to sacrifice, and so one is fully immersed in their work—that is sewa. And another favourite in developed countries is the phrase 'saadaa jeevan', which means simple living. A common message delivered in the prachaarak order is to live 'materially one step behind society' and 'one step ahead in thought and character'. In other words, live minimalistically, and consume as little as possible, while remaining in touch with the common person one is working with, or serving. Likewise, in thought and character, the swayamsevak is to set an example of behaviour for others to emulate. This is the RSS culture that comes out of Hedgewarian thought and action.

By 2 May, Hedgewar was back on his feet—just about. His back pain had subsided. Nevertheless, he knew his health was getting worse. He was due to deliver a speech just before his departure from Sangli, almost seven hundred miles away from Nagpur. He had owed his presence to the swayamsevaks of Sangli, who had been expecting to meet him almost ten days earlier. Even though it was a long hot journey back, Hedgewar spoke at length on the need for strength and the fallacy of Gandhian non-violence.

> '...self-defence is a duty. Not being violent is a great virtue; however, that does not mean one should simply capitulate in the face of aggression and violence. That would be suicidal. This idea is causing great harm to the Hindu society. We must challenge this.'[21]

He then revealed something that still informs modern Indian discourse, the question of other non-Indian religions, and their proselytising natures.

> 'Initially, all the inhabitants of Hindustan were Hindu. Today, we are 250,000,000 strong. But, about 100,000,000 have taken refuge in an alien

religion, one that is not of this land. Those who have converted are not outsiders; they are Hindu by blood.

This shows the degradation of our society. We need to have faith in the inherent viability of our culture and nurture it back to strength to command the awe and respect of the world once more. Only with strength can we establish the principles of Dharma, the principles of truth and non-harming. Only the strong can practise the principle of non-harming.'[22]

Speeches like this are often used as evidence against Hedgewarian thought. They are presented as bigoted, angry and militant. Indeed, taken as a standalone comment, which is exactly how it is presented in modern discourse, Hedgewar comes across grossly ill-informed and angry, encouraging Hindus into militancy.[23] The reality is that throughout the twenties and thirties, as the British retreated, the vacuum left caused civil strife, predominantly caused by the dreams of wayward Islamic clerics.[24] These clerics were simultaneously causing fright amongst their congregation about a Hindu India emerging after the British leave, where Muslims would be persecuted, while also fuelling an alternative narrative of re-establishing Dar al-Islam in India by evoking ideas of Muslim natural rights to rule.[25] In the Islamic narratives of the 1920s, India only existed from the time of the Arab conquests, and so it was believed that India rightfully belonged to the Muslims. Much of this narrative was spread from the 1860s from an Islamic seminary at Deoband in Northern India.[26]

For Hedgewar to be understood, and therefore his creation, one must take into account the prism of Islamism, which often led to Muslim aggression throughout the country, resulting in skirmishes and full-blown riots where thousands were killed—or forced to migrate.[27] From a Hedgewarian perspective, the Islamists were hell-bent on riling up Muslims, mostly from a lower socio-economic stratum of society, who, until the early 1900s were largely fragmented and peaceful.[28] In this regard, he calls the audience to reject Gandhi's utopianism of non-violence in the face of militant separatist aggression. For Hedgewar, peace can only be achieved from a position of strength, not too dissimilar to the strategy of the USA when it comes to geopolitical stability—it is America's overwhelming strength that keeps the world relatively peaceful.[29] At a camp in Pune in 1935, Hedgewar practically said as much,

> 'We must create such a situation [in the country] that nobody can dare dream of perpetrating atrocities on the Hindu society. The fact that there are still fanatics [referring to Islamists] who are affronted by Hindu worship and decide to go rioting shows that we are very weak today'.[30]

It is clear to see that the Hedgewarian position is to build up such strength that it becomes a deterrent for others to even think about using force while remaining engaged and non-threatening to others. The fear, somewhat acknowledged by Hedgewar through his instructions to the RSS vanguard at times of strife, was that 'peace through strength' could easily become 'peace through threat' and then 'peace through war'.[31]

His speech reveals that he had absorbed Vinayak Savarkar's idea of 'Hindu as a geographical identity', even though he never accepted the man himself.[32] Interestingly, the RSS today sees the term Hindu as referring to a cultural phenomenon, one that is universal in nature and, therefore, not bound by ethnicity, geography or creed. The RSS is not even attached to the beliefs of its own founder.

When this speech was delivered, India's population hovered around 300,000,000, of which two-thirds were Hindu and about a third Muslim.[33] Hedgewar was clearly well-informed about the demographics of his country. He further alluded to the fact that most of the Muslims were recent converts who had taken 'refuge' in Islam. His selection of words clearly lays bare his mind. For Hedgewar, the problem lay with the Hindu society with all its poverty, prejudices and social stratification. To escape such prejudice, people, mostly the poor, were enticed to convert in their search for equality. Hedgewar, as does the RSS today, does not see Muslims as outsiders but as neglected insiders. The belief still persists that once Hindu society is reformed and all its outdated ideas ejected from the cultural milieu, Muslims will naturally rediscover the creed and traditions of their ancestors, and rejoin the civilizational march of Hindu society. From the Hedgewarian perspective, Muslims are part and parcel of the Indian story, and therefore, there is no question of treating them as 'others'. In fact, many RSS chiefs have openly said that 'Indian Muslims are Hindu'—in both the geographical and genetic sense.[34] On the issue of genetics, Hedgewar, and the RSS are correct, at least from the limited research that has thus far been completed, that Hindus and Indian Muslims are largely genetically related, they are of the same ancestry.[35]

At this gathering of RSS men at Sangli, a rare picture was taken of Hedgewar. The forty-six-year-old generally refrained from pictures being taken. But on this occasion, he was somehow cajoled into it. The picture reveals him wearing the uniform of an officer in the British Indian Army. He has an austere, and intense look about him as he sits on a photographer's chair with a baton in hand. The picture gives away the fact that he is seriously overweight, and that the leather strap that ran across his chest was ill-fitting. He was in knee-length khaki shorts and matching socks that stopped just below the knee. The picture elaborates on the idiosyncrasies of the early RSS and how they saw themselves, namely as a military protectorate of the Hindu population. By today's standards, the picture makes Hedgewar and the RSS look somewhat out-dated and from an age best forgotten. Interestingly, the man who took the photograph revealed to Palkar a decade hence that Hedgewar had explicitly instructed for the picture never to be published and for the negative to be destroyed.[36]

Having left Sangli in May, he made his way back to Nagpur, zigzagging across Maharashtra, visiting people and places, including the OTC held in an emerging city called Akola. By the time he arrived back in Nagpur, it was 24 May. He arrived at the train station early that morning where he witnessed a commotion on the platform. People were clearly excited about something, and he soon saw black clouds of smoke rising into the air from around a mile away. Joshi was pleased to inform him that the central offices of the police department had caught fire, and the whole building was likely to be destroyed. Nearly all of Hedgewar's police records were destroyed in that fire much to his satisfaction.[37] A weary Hedgewar, reached home only to discover a pile of letters for him to read and respond to. His brother and sister-in-law would help him organize his endless correspondences, which were increasingly fuelling his already intense sense that the country was falling apart.

A wealthy businessman, Padmaraj Jain, who had come from Bengal, was the chief guest at the Nagpur OTC that year. Before his departure from the OTC, he had left a letter for Hedgewar, where he stressed the importance of the RSS spreading to the outer posts of Northwest India and Uttar Pradesh. This is where Hindus were most at threat, because these were the epicentres of militant separatism fuelled by Islamism. He also received letters that read, 'The condition of Hindu society is very fragile. I wish to stay with you to learn the skill of community defence. Another person shall accompany me.'[38] On another occasion, people even invited him to spend a year, expenses paid, in the Punjab to build up RSS strength. He responded to these requests by sending his brigade of prachaaraks to such places. Parmarth, Aptey and Yerkuntwar were sent out under the guise of being students.[39]

Around this time, Hedgewar made it a point to speak in Hindi and he began to noticeably speak less in his native tongue, Marathi. He did this to encourage the rest of his swayamsevaks to start learning Hindi and other Indian languages such as Bengali, Tamil, Telugu, Punjabi and the like. He was clear that if the RSS was to be truly national, then it must have speakers of every language spoken in India.[40] Hedgewar also never seemed to emphasise paperwork and documentation to codify Sangh work and training. Instead, his prachaaraks were the medium through which work could be spread and standardized. Furthermore, his annual OTCs were specifically designed to bring some coherence and symmetry to the work. In October 1935, he and a select few travelled as far as Sindh in north-western India, today part of Pakistan, to discuss how the shakhas ought to be engineered.

During these discussions, Golwalkar was also constantly in touch with Hedgewar. The young zoologist had completed his one-year conversion Law course as Hedgewar had advised. He had also been the man in charge at the OTC held at Akola earlier that year, and he was coming along swiftly in his understanding of the Sangh. Yet, Golwalkar was constantly haunted by his desire to take up formal renunciation and become a monk in the Ramakrishna Order. He would suddenly and frequently drop everything and disappear to a monastery for weeks on end. Then suddenly, he would reappear and carry on for a few more months and then wander off again. Hedgewar was worried by this tendency and knew that Golwalker could only be truly relied on once this desire for monkhood abated. Hedgewar re-emphasized that renunciation ought not to mean disappearance from the world to live as a recluse, devoid of a sense of reality. Rather, for Hedgewar renunciation could also happen while being in the midst of material concerns for one's countrymen, and the welfare of humanity.[41] Hedgewar's words appeared to be falling on deaf ears.

In December 1935, the Hindu Mahasabha conference was held at Pune. Thousands had attended, and over five hundred swayamsevaks were present to support the logistics of the conference, which only further fuelled the narrative that the Sangh was a proxy for the increasingly hysterical Mahasabha. Hedgewar was unwell again. He was immobile this time, having got a deep gash on one of his legs. He missed most of the conference and only attended on 28 December. Two days later, on 30 December, over 500 swayamsevaks took out a route march through Pune city centre, where Padmaraj Jain and Moonjay spoke at its zenith. Hedgewar was noticeably unwell and did not speak. He was constantly in excruciating pain, which at times made him completely bed bound. He had many well-wishers, and many were willing to put him up and support his rehabilitation with medication and other healthcare costs. Hedgewar ignored most offers of support that came his way. We only get an insight into his state of mind in an exchange of letters with an elder called Chitlay. 'Neither do you reply nor do you come to Akola for rest,' wrote the older man, after having already tried on several occasions to support Hedgewar.[42] 'I cannot leave Nagpur until I have raised some funds that are desperately needed by the Sangh, but my health is deteriorating so much so that I cannot go and fundraise. I do not see what I can do,' he replied a few days later.[43]

Responding to the sorry state of the Sangh's treasury and Hedgewar's inability at that time to fundraise, Chitlay reached out to the businessman Jain in Bengal. Jain was happy to financially support the Sangh directly. Chitlay immediately wrote to Hedgewar to say as much but was only met with silence. Then, at a meeting held around this time, where Jain, Chitlay and Hedgewar were present, the issue of the Sangh's finances was brought up. Chitlay publicly called upon Jain to support the RSS, to which Jain was all too happy to do so, but Hedgewar piped in, much to the annoyance of Chitlay, and the surprise of Jain, 'Jain ji,' said Hedgewar, 'in order to strengthen Sangh work in Bengal please send as many young men to our OTC as possible. Money is of secondary importance.'[44] Hedgewar openly but politely seemed to devalue the offer of money that he so badly needed for the Sangh.

> Chitlay, not one to be outdone, said, 'Please do not listen to our Doctor ji. You can see for yourself the dire need for money, so please just donate it and to make the good doctor happy, send a few young men to the OTC too.'

> Hedgewar was having none of it, and was reported to push back, 'Chitlay ji, you know I respect you immensely, but try and see that if Jain's heart

and spirit are devoted to Sangh work, then why do we need to worry about money?'[45]

Jain was apparently smiling throughout. Chitlay was visibly annoyed and frustrated by Hedgewar. He muttered to himself just loud enough for people to hear, 'Look, here was a golden opportunity I had created to get some much-needed money for the Sangh, and he just squandered it away.' [46]

It is unclear if Jain ever financially contributed to the Sangh at that time, but it does show Hedgewar's idealism. Why was Hedgewar so reluctant to openly accept, and be grateful for the funds that he so badly needed? There are two answers and either could be equally true. The first was that Jain was ultimately a Mahasabha leader, and to accept money from him would most certainly have come with a quid-pro-quo attitude. For Hedgewar, who wanted the RSS to be kept at arm's length from the Mahasabha, this money could be dangerous. The second reason is the Sangh attitude to money—it only ever raises money from its own. Those individuals who are willing to make an offering and never think of it as a transaction are welcome to give. An offering was sacred to Hedgewar, whereas a donation was simple utility. If Jain was a swayamsevak then the money becomes an offering, and would be welcome, but if he saw it as someone on the outside helping the Sangh, then it was not welcome. The RSS, although a behemoth today, still operates in this fashion—it usually never has enough money for what it wants to accomplish.

In June 1935, Hedgewar had come to know about a pamphlet that articulated in its fullness Hedgewar's nightmare. The pamphlet was titled *Now Or Never; Are We To Live Or Perish Forever*? It was written by a student at Emmanuel College, Cambridge.[47] His name was Choudhry Rahmat Ali. He was born in Punjab in 1897 to wealthy parents. In 1931, he found himself at Cambridge, having taught for several years at various colleges in India. Ali embodied a fusion of British education, Islamic ideology and Nazi influences.[48] He had evolved into an articulate, confused separatist who believed that Islam's days in an independent India were numbered unless a separate Islamic state could be formed. He is largely credited with the term 'Pakistan', which means the 'land of the pure', by using the first letters of the major territories of North-west India and the 'tan' from Baluchistan.[49] In 1933, he had lobbied his philosophical mentor, a man named Muhammad Iqbal, to stop the Muslim League from agreeing to the idea of a unified India.[50] He ultimately departed from Iqbal as his own ideas became more extreme and paranoid. A year later, in 1934, he went to see Jinnah in London, the man who would take most of the credit for the creation of Pakistan, with his leaflet of dread. 'My dear boys, don't be in a hurry; let the waters flow, and they will find their own level,' responded the aristocrat Jinnah.[51]

When Hedgewar saw the leaflet in late 1935, he was horrified by the sheer ambition displayed by the extreme factions of the Muslim League, represented by men like Ali. The leaflet clearly showed a map of India carved up into many separate pieces of territory marking out the Muslim ones. The northwest territories of Baluchistan, Punjab, North-West Frontier Province (NWFP), Kashmir and Sindh were all formed into one state called Pakistan. Then, in the East, all of Bengal and the northeastern territories were packaged up into Bangistan, Kerala was turned into Malpistan, which would have brought the memories of the 1921 massacre of Hindus in that region back to the fore and the middle of the country from Hyderabad to Aurangabad, including swaths of Wardha and Vidarbha, was turned into an Islamic state called Osmanistan.[52] The Indian subcontinent was renamed Dinia, an anagram of India with the position of 'd' changed. For many, these were the darkest imaginings of a mad extremist, and not many took him seriously, including his once mentor.[53] But not Hedgewar; he did not take such imaginings lightly.

Everything Ali stood for, including his Nazism, much of which was memorized verbatim, was abhorrent to Hedgewar—there was simply no reconciliation with such men and their ideas. Ali claimed in the leaflet that there was a clear and present danger to Muslims across a new Hindu India. In Hedgewar's mind, all he could sense was what lay in store for all those non-Muslims, the impure, in these Islamic States. Wherever he spoke, he would bring up Ali's vision of a Pakistan, and an Indian subcontinent named Dinia, in efforts to try and motivate people to step forward and establish RSS centres in their respective areas.[54] As events would prove to show over the next decade and a half, Hedgewar was generally reading the unfolding of history correctly. Hedgewar became increasingly less interested in independence, but more in unifying India for a post-colonial world. Ali, for his part, would see his dream of Pakistan manifest but would criticize Jinnah for accepting such a small part of India. He would return from England in 1948 to a newly created Pakistan, only for his Nazism and dangerous Islamism to be rejected. The first Prime Minister of the land of the Pure would send Ali into exile and confiscate everything he owned, leaving him 'destitute, forlorn and lonely' at the time of his death in 1951.[55]

A political vortex was created throughout the thirties, leading up to independence where the maddening rhetoric of the Hindu Mahasabha would fuel the radical Islamist clerics, who, in turn, would create not just political pressure, but violence on the streets, which would further fuel the maddening rhetoric of the saffron brigade, releasing the anger of devils on both sides. The more violence that the Islamists instigated, the harder the rhetoric of the Hindu Mahasabha became. Hedgewar watched the madness unfold before him, and no matter how much he tried, he was helpless against the forces of history. As the violence ramped up, the only show in town that could be relied on to protect life, liberty, and property (for the Hindu community) was the RSS. There was a fully developed tapestry of Islamists up and down the country, urging the Muslim poor to rise and protect themselves against the invisible enemy of a hegemonic Hindu society. On the Hindu side, only the RSS was consistently capable of repelling any acts of aggression by Muslim vigilantes. Indian history, for the best part of a hundred years, has disproportionately highlighted the transgressions of the Hindus, while negationists have wiped out Islamist aggression.

In October 1936, Hedgewar received word that his young padawan, the zoologist turned lawyer, had suddenly left, but this time leaving a note indicating that he had decided to take formal renunciation into the Ramakrishna Order in an ashram at Sargachi, Bengal. Hedgewar felt a deep sense of loss.[56] Ever since Golwalkar had returned to Nagpur and taken over as General Coordinator of the Nagpur shakha and the OTCs, which flourished under his care, Hedgewar was convinced of his leadership material. His departure certainly would not have come as a shock to Hedgewar. He had become aware of Golwaker's propensity for monkhood. Nevertheless, Golwaker's absence would have depressed him to no end. He would have certainly sat outside on his porch late into the moist monsoon night, brooding—the Sangh needed leadership, it required funds and his society was desperately falling short of what was required of it to face the challenges of separatism and extremism. In that darkness, he was at a loss as to what one does with a society where its best and brightest young men were either anglophiles or desired escape from the world to pursue monkhood. He often reflected on the genius of Aurobindo Ghosh and how different the Congress would have been had he taken over its leadership instead of Gandhi. But alas, he was broken by the hanging of Khudiram Bose, a seventeen-year-old boy, and chose to escape the cruelty of oppression and the fight against it for a life of contemplation and writing. The same, he feared, had happened to Golwalkar.

FIFTEEN: 1936–1938

The Vanguard

India faced huge law and order problems. Justice was out of reach for the common man and woman. The only way one could ensure their own security was if they belonged to a wider identity—a caste, tribe, clan or some political outfit that, in turn, could wield influence. Protection and safety could only be ensured through association.

For women, this problem was insufferable, as they were a further step removed from influence and justice—after all, it was a man's world. Women, generally, were absent from any form of institutional influence and were completely dependent on the whims and talents of their husbands, brothers or fathers.[1] There were always exceptions, but the general position of women in Indian society meant that they were even more vulnerable to the dark forces of injustice. Most women bore their lot quietly.

Hedgewar had always been sensitive to the plight of women, largely influenced by Moonjay and later by his own experiences as a medical student. He was acutely aware that his nation-building project could never flourish without the wholesale reformation of the status of women in Hindu society. It is worth noting that the British, after much resistance, had granted universal suffrage to women in Britain in 1918, but did not grant the same rights to women in the wider empire, including India. Instead, it was the Hindu principalities that were the first to grant such suffrage to women, most notably the Kingdom of Travancore (1920), Jhalawar State (1920) and Rajkot (1923).[2] Although movements dedicated to reforming Indian society were sprouting across the country, most of them were regional, small and consequently had limited reach. The sheer scale and challenge of reforming a society that had been in freefall for several centuries was a mammoth task, and one in which there were comparatively few organizations that were by women, for women. This changed in 1936.

Lakshmi Kelkar came to visit an unwell Hedgewar at his home in Mahal, Nagpur. She was thirty-one years old, stupendously rich and a widow. She was the third wife, and the youngest, married at the tender age of fourteen to a merchant named Purshottam Kelkar, who had died of tuberculosis four years earlier.[3] She came to ask Hedgewar what many today ask the RSS: 'Why aren't women involved in your work?'[4] Over multiple meetings spanning several months, Hedgewar and Lakshmi came to an understanding that she would start a women's movement along the same lines as the RSS, but it would be operationally and financially independent. Hedgewar was initially uninterested.[5] However, Lakshmi was not one to be put off. She soon persuaded Hedgewar, who was clear and adamant that the RSS was not ready to start involving women in its work. The society was simply not ready to see men and women work in tandem for social reform. He may have been equally hesitant due to the timing—the RSS found itself at a precarious moment with his own failing health, the sudden disappearance of one of its leaders and a desperate shortage of cash. The compromise reached was that Joshi—one of Hedgewar's captains—was ready to train Lakshmi on how the RSS operated, while Lakshmi would independently build her movement and begin to repair the status of, and opportunities for women.

Being a widow in India in 1936 was not easy. Society was plagued with superstition. Customs prohibited widows from remarrying, and they often encountered many forms of indignities and discrimination.[6] Lakshmi was, to some extent, incubated from these indignities because she came from a stratum of society that was generally progressive. She was born in 1905 in Mahal, Nagpur, the same neighbourhood as Hedgewar. Even though her late husband was an anglophile and generally aloof to the struggle for freedom, he was wealthy, and therefore, through association, Lakshmi came to socialize with women who were materially comfortable and relatively educated.[7] Endless afternoons were frittered away playing bridge, where she would attempt to cajole her contemporaries into reading nationalist literature and magazines. She is said to have convinced many women to donate their gold for the freedom struggle after Gandhi had made Wardha his base.

Women in the 1930s were only educated until the age of eleven, and being able to read and write meant being educated. They were often married off in their teens. Lakshmi, too, was married young and had her first child, a boy, at fifteen. In quick succession, she had a daughter and another son by the time she was twenty years old. Her anglophilic husband was at least seventeen years older than her and clearly enjoyed women; after all, he had three wives and multiple children with each. Having been widowed by twenty-seven and having lost her daughter also to tuberculosis, she found herself to be a woman who, on the one hand, was cut off from the pursuits of further love and marriage while on the other, had gained control of a sizable empire by way of land and property. With money and time now on her hands and having been exposed to the struggle for freedom from an early age, her gaze turned towards higher ends. Lakshmi used her privilege for something much grander than those around her could have imagined. She would devote the rest of her life to inspiring thousands of women across the length and breadth of India to do the same—rebuild Hindu society from the ground up.

On 26 October 1936, on the day of Vijaya Dashami, Lakshmi founded the Rashtra Sevika Samiti. After eighty years of existence, Lakshmi's RSS is one of the largest women's organizations in the world, led by women for women. Lakshmi died in 1978, leaving behind an established women's organization that has hundreds of centres across India and a volunteer force in the tens of thousands. Today, the samiti runs over 900 charity outfits, addressing issues ranging from domestic violence in homes to supporting the elderly and sick.[8]

In popular academic imagination, Lakshmi's RSS was simply a rouse to keep women largely confined to the home; according to Tyagi,

> 'Confining women to the role of the homemaker and working specifically in the private sphere, most of the wives/daughters of RSS members go on to join its parallel women's organisation, the Rashtra Sevika Samiti. Thus, the Samiti becomes a space where women are given a chance to step outside the binds of the home and yet remain under the larger ideological framework of the RSS.'[9]

These narratives can be extensively found throughout academia and have become tropes that have been regurgitated and cited so often that an echo chamber has been created amongst writers while completely missing the actuality of the role of women. Contemporary academia generally relegates the role of stay-at-home mothers to something less than those who are 'in the world', earning their keep and competing shoulder to shoulder with their male counterparts.[10] Lakshmi's RSS from day one understood, quite rightly, that for Hindu women to play a meaningful role in the process of nation building, they would need to address the role of 'motherhood', what in RSS parlance is called 'Matritva' (Ma-trit-va). Coupled with this idea of motherhood is the development of responsibility (kar-trit-va) and leadership (net-rit-va). All three concepts are intertwined and become manifest in Lakshmi's identification of the ideal Hindu woman.

While the early Samiti was a force for radical change and worked tirelessly to unshackle women from being lowly housewives to active participants in shaping society, modern criticisms of the Samiti are the exact opposite. 'The Samiti is out of touch,' is often a charge that can be heard amongst India's aspirational young women, who feel that Lakshmi's RSS has nothing much to offer them. For years, the Samiti was teaching its volunteers that wearing jeans and make-up is not Hindu.[11] This type of conservatism has meant that an organization that was once radical and forward-thinking has now become labelled as out of touch, conservative and orthodox.

Back in the 1930s, as Lakshmi prepared to train under Joshi's supervision, Hedgewar, driven by both his own sense of duty and the needs of the RSS, undertook a thirteen-day journey starting on 13 November 1936, despite being seriously unwell. Hedgewar wrote to Joshi, 'I suffer from fever every day. My head throbs with pain, and I feel a severe weakness in the body'.[12] Like many prachaaraks today, who in some serious sense, embody the life of Hedgewar, he too always put the feelings of his fellow swayamsevaks above the needs of his own health. Hedgewar was insistent on visiting the homes of the most ordinary swayamsevaks for dinner to show solidarity. What might look like a small point in case was rather a big deal in a caste-ridden society, where even entering the home of someone beneath you in the caste pecking order meant something close to sacrilege. In Hindu culture, even today, it is customary to serve a rich meal when someone of significance visits. For the ordinary man or woman, it was highly unusual for someone like Hedgewar—a regional celebrity, Godfather and mendicant rolled into one—to pay a visit. It was a big deal. To that end, every house he attended prepared rich meals full of ghee, butter, spices and fats, a diet that Hedgewar needed to avoid. Even when others, who were accompanying him would urge caution, he would often ignore them and simply have the meal that was prepared.[13] This tendency is quite an oddity by today's standards, but in India, and in Indian culture more generally, 'food is an identity marker of caste, class, family, kinship, tribe affiliation, lineage, religiosity, ethnicity, and increasingly, of secular group identification'.[14] Consequently, prachaaraks, mostly from India, who travel across Europe and the United States, continue to uphold the Hedgewarian 'truth' even though none of these dietary markers play much of a role in the Hindu diaspora. It has become a fetishization amongst prachaaraks and many Sangh families that host prachaaraks, each fuelling the other into something unsavoury.

Even though the RSS was struggling for funds, Hedgewar travelled over 500 kilometres by motor car.[15] In those days, to travel by motor car was only for the splendidly privileged and wealthy. There were some 13,000 cars in India around the mid-twenties, and by 1936, that number may well have quadrupled, but with a population of nearly 350,000,000, cars were a serious fascination, and certainly not one of those things that one travelled in to remain inconspicuous.[16] Whatever image Hedgewar wanted to create in those days, it was certainly not simplicity or that of a medicant. He was the chief of an organization that everyone needed to pay attention to, and when his motor carriage rolled into town, people stared and took note.

Today, the RSS installs a thick shiny veneer on Hedgewar as being solely ideologically driven, but he was complex and subtle, was more than capable of playing realpolitik and was aware of how to draw attention by a show of strength—in this case, driving around in a motor carriage. Of course, there is another possible explanation for the expensive mode of transport. In all likelihood, it was Moonjay's car, which he had lent to Hedgewar out of concern for his deteriorating health. Indian public transport is difficult to navigate even today in rural India, so one can imagine how difficult it must have been for an ageing Hedgewar who was increasingly unwell to be travelling. It may have been out of compassion that Moonjay made his car available. Whichever may have been the case, it was certainly true that the perception of the chief of the RSS was that of a godfather rather than a simple, humble social worker.

As the year ended, he attended the Sangh's winter training camp at a small town called Chanda in Maharashtra. Here, he gave a speech on the last day of a twenty-day camp, which became rather famous and is often cited in RSS literature. In this speech, he was quick to point out to the assembled audience that the Sangh's reach had spread as far as Karachi in the West and Bengal to the East.[17] He clearly asserted that over 25,000 young men were being trained to serve the emerging nation, which gives us an inkling as to the scale of Hedgewar's vanguard.[18] Considering that the RSS boasts some 6,000,000 swayamsevaks today, Hedgewar's force was minuscule by comparison—yet likely far more potent per capita. In this speech, he also wanted to answer critiques of the Sangh, those Hindus who felt uneasy about the modus operandi of this new rapidly expanding movement. A staunchly Hindu outfit that had not an ounce of religious dogma or caste consciousness, an outfit not interested in politics or state power and a man at the helm who generally craved anonymity, except when he drove in motor carriages. The movement did not resemble anything that was around at the time, and yet seemed to mimic, in part, many contemporary movements. The secrecy and ambiguity of the RSS, coupled with its rapid rise, made people uneasy—even those who were benefiting from this emerging power. These things caused angst—which by all accounts seemed to be something that Hedgewar was not only aware of but continued to fuel.

Hedgewar made a play for those Hindus who criticized the Sangh, such as Gandhi, who expressed his concerns over the new movement for not practising ahimsa. Hedgewar was annoyed on two fronts—first, that Gandhi had misconstrued a sacred aspect of Hindu philosophy, and second, for criticizing those probably in greater sync with the term ahimsa than he was. Hedgewar's critique stemmed from the same Churchillian concerns, or better still Chanakyan insight that 'only the strong can promote peace', and since the Hindu society was largely weak, poverty-stricken and backward, it had no business preaching restraint to the tyrannized, while side-stepping the very powers that were exploiting it.[19] 'The goal of the Sangh', he went on, 'was to build a strong society, one that could wield force if necessary, through which it could maintain a lasting peace'.[20]

The exterior of the Sangh was that of a paramilitary outfit, and the interior was absent of prayers, religious rituals and symbols while claiming to be a vanguard of Dharma. All of which had left the public confused. Hedgewar was unapologetic. He claimed that the Hindu society lacked men and women of capacity, and hence, no great endeavour could be taken. The first task was to empower the individual through skills and character formation. Only when the individual has the capacity to protect his or her home and earn his keep can one pursue the outwardly religious practices so accustomed to being Hindu. The Sangh, by developing the individual, was serving Dharma. Indeed, he further emphasized that those who claim to be religious and the custodians of Hindu traditions by rigidly following rituals and religious worship by chanting the mantras, but neglect the well-being of society, are the ones who are out of step with Dharma.[21] He went on to spell out that the fault squarely lay with the Hindus—past and present—for the pitiful state they found themselves in.

The wizardry of Hedgewar lay in his ability to simultaneously criticize almost everything about being Hindu while inspiring complete devotion to its renaissance. It is a difficult line to walk, but the RSS continues to walk it even today. The RSS is often at the helm of radical societal reform, while maintaining the image of orthodoxy.

Throughout 1937, Hedgewar travelled extensively across the country, visiting shakhas wherever he went. The average number of swayamsevaks in shakhas swelled into the hundreds. An ever-increasing portion of the Hindu citizenry saw the RSS as the only place of respite and protection in the wake of lawlessness and extremism. Hedgewar was aware that there were forces released upon the Indian landscape that he had to harness in order to protect Hindu life and liberty. With the slow and steady retreat of the British administration and amidst the anarchy throughout the land, a peculiar form of Islamic revivalism was taking root amongst the Muslims. This strange Muslim revivalism was at the heart of the intolerant stance of imams from mosques across the country who suddenly were unable to bear the music of Hindu festivities or prayers, having lived side-by-side with Hindus for centuries. Islam in India has had a long history of intertwining religion with politics, consistently seeking a distinct identity alongside a separate political dominion.[22] According to Rafiq Zakaria, had Muslims been informed and educated about their religious and social past, had they any memories of their ancestors, they would not have been so susceptible to the fundamentalism that was released by conservative clerics such as Shah Waliullah or Ahmad Barelvi.[23] Contrary to popular belief that it was the British who had whispered into the Muslim ear that it would be intolerable for them to live under the rule of their once former subjects, the Hindus, it was Sayyid Ahmed Khan who time and again convinced the British that 'being a descendant of high Mogul officials, he emotionally could not accept that Muslims should be ruled by their former subjects. He also feared that Hindu rule would result in the imposition of an Aryan culture on the Muslim Persio-Arabic civilisation'.[24] It is somewhat ironic to think that most Muslims in India today, apart from reciting the Quran in Arabic with little to no understanding of what they are reciting, are all genetically related to their Hindu brethren, and culturally share more in common with their Hindu neighbours than they do with the Arabs of Arabia.

There is a strong correlation between the rise of Muslim intolerance towards Hindus in their search for a separate identity, and the rise of the RSS throughout India. In many states, with the will of Gandhi's Congress and Muslim outfits such as the Muslim League, the British administration banned the RSS, including Rajasthan and Kolhapur, where, in the latter, RSS was renamed 'Rajaram swayamsevak Sangh' and grew even faster.[25] New shakhas would be spontaneously formed, calling themselves branches of the RSS. In many circumstances, Hedgewar would come to know about these ad hoc shakhas months after they were formed, or when men would suddenly appear at joint training sessions alongside existing established units. The reality was that, as Hindu society became increasingly fearful, their only chance of receiving justice and protection came from the RSS. Hedgewar, almost unbeknown to him, was becoming tremendously powerful by the day. In 1937, at Pune, Hedgewar initiated the longest and biggest public march after the training camp held there. Thousands of men in uniform armed with bamboo sticks and knives, led by a marching band with the British bugle being played in very similar tunes to the military, gave immense confidence and pride to hundreds of Hindu families who otherwise felt vulnerable and exposed, while simultaneously frightening those that opposed this force—the clerics, socialists, communists, Gandhi's Congress and many conservative Hindus. The RSS still does this procession through any Indian street where it holds its training camps. It is a pure show of strength—and even though it does not pack the punch it would have done in Hedgewar's time, it still is a sight to intimidate naysayers.

Throughout 1937, Hedgewar was focused on developing the prachaarak order—men who took oaths, lived by a code and dedicated their lives to developing the Sangh in order to rebuild a broken civilization. In the late 1920s, there were eighteen prachaaraks concentrated around Nagpur; in 1930, sixty, and in 1933, there were 125 travelling across Northern India.[26] Baba Aptay and Paramarth were his two most competent lieutenants and helped Hedgewar coordinate the work of the order.[27] They travelled relentlessly all year round and certainly never by motor carriage. Theirs was a life more in keeping with the oaths of the order—that of simplicity and humility.

Vasant Oak, a twenty-three-year-old young graduate from a middle-class background, had taken his oath in early 1937. He was sent to Delhi. Oak would go on to become part of the Hedgewar brigade, a band of brothers who would give their entire lives for the order and play pivotal roles in shaping the tapestry of modern Indian society. He would find himself in the eye of the storm soon after Gandhi's assassination. He was imprisoned shortly after, only to be released and become a founding member of Jana Sangh—RSS's first attempt at creating a political party. He rubbed shoulders with and influenced other well-known Indian giants such as Shyama Prasad Mukherjee, who is the poster boy for the ruling Bhartiya Janta Party (BJP) and an influence on the incumbent Prime Minister Narendra Modi—also, one of the order. His name is now almost forgotten, even amongst the Sangh faithful.

Then, at the same time, two brothers came through the ranks of the RSS, also from Nagpur, Murlidar and Madhukar Deoras.[28] The brothers came from a well-established large family of ten children and were eighth and ninth in the pecking order. Murlidar was the youngest. He and his older brother took oaths to join the order in the same year.[29] Murlidhar came to be known as Bhaurao, which literally meant brother. Murlidhar was political and a phenomenal organizer, considering he was only twenty years old when he was sent to Lucknow in Uttar Pradesh, India's most populous state.

He went on to build strong relations with the Indian Jewish community and was an open advocate for a Jewish homeland to be established, and for an independent India to recognize the state of Israel in 1947.[30] Nehru disagreed, and India failed to build ties with Israel to appease its conservative clerical voter base. All that changed when the BJP came to power first in 1999 and then in 2014. Today, India has a strong relationship with the Jewish state and is considered a close ally by Prime Minister Modi. Murlidhar's visionary ideas percolate India's foreign policy today.[31]

He was also one of the key organizers behind the Ram Mandir agitation, which no political figure would touch at the time; to do so would make you an instant pariah.[32] Murlidar took on the role of the proverbial pariah for decades, never wavering in his pursuit of justice and truth. In 2024, one of the largest Hindu temples in the world was opened in Ayodhya, at the birthplace of Rama, where a disused mosque from the sixteenth century had stood, built on top of an older Hindu temple.[33] After much controversy and vilification, the courts ruled in favour of a temple to be built. Murlidhar's legacy was consecrated in stone when the Ram Temple was built, but hardly anyone will know about his influence.

Then there was his brother, two years his senior, Madhukar Deoras, commonly known as Balasaheb in RSS parlance. Bala is another name for Shiva, one of the three most important deities in the Hindu pantheon. Madhukar was sent to Bengal, to the East, which by the 1930s was no longer the nest of revolutionary movements but nevertheless had become the epicentre of the battle for Hindu India versus Muslim India. Having established a relatively small network of shakhas, he returned to Nagpur. He became the editor of an RSS newspaper called *Tarun Bharat*. He and his younger brother would then fall out of favour with Golwalkar and become inactive for four years. Golwalkar was insistent that the Sangh must stay true to its core mission of grassroots social work, whereas the brothers were adamant that the time had come for the RSS to enter politics and take on a more activist role. In the late fifties he would return to the Order, and by the early sixties, he had become the general secretary of the RSS. After Golwalkar's death, Madhukar became the RSS's third chief. All these forces were set in motion by Hedgewar in 1937, and the Hedgewar brigade was clear that it was their mentor and guide who had the foresight to trigger this chain reaction.

By this time, the prachaaraks worked with three aims in mind. The first was to develop shakhas everywhere, where individuals could be gathered and trained. Second, to build a community of like-minded individuals who were equally capable and motivated for the project of nation-building. Third, was to act. To bring the group with a collective strength to add meaningful value to the wider society and initiate the projects for nation-building. Swayamsevaks, in their thousands, came to be known for their character traits—charity, courage, honour, purposefulness and honesty. Even their darker elements, their ability to fight, to intimidate and be judge and jury, all became add-ons by joining the Sangh.

Around thirty prachaaraks today operate all over the world and they still have the same modus operandi, namely, to contribute meaningfully to society. They usually start working within the Hindu community but gradually look to initiate projects that will strengthen the wider community. Prachaaraks in the USA will think about how to contribute to American life; prachaaraks in mainland Europe will think about how they can add value to European nations, all the while continuously spreading Dharma through action. The martial spirit of Hedgewar is all but gone from shakhas outside of India and they are more cultural centres of play, learning and a safe space for Hindus. Back in 1937, we can be quite sure that Hedgewar could not have dreamt that one day his order of prachaaraks would be working with the same missionary zeal across the world from Japan to Colombia, and swayamsevaks would be composed of every nation, ethnicity and language—with many women at the helm of the Sangh.[34]

Then, suddenly, two things shifted in Hedgewar's favour. The first was money. It had become increasingly tight. The Sangh was growing quickly, and the resources required to sustain the growth were always on Hedgewar's mind. Then, in late 1937, he met a regal-looking man, someone who looked like a movie star, with the presence and authority of a British officer but with the rootedness of a villager. That man was Jugal Kishore Birla, the eldest son and heir to the Birla corporation. The Birlas were spectacularly rich, having made their money from the opium, silver and spice trades.[35] Next to the Tatas, they were one of the wealthiest families in Asia, and his father Baldeo had the patronage of the British. By the 1930s, the Birlas had built countless temples, schools and colleges. They were also huge supporters of Gandhi's movement for a unified India. Hedgewar met Jugal Birla in Delhi at his palatial home, which is now the Gandhi Museum, located on Tees January Marg (meaning 30 January Road). The house today stands to mark Gandhi's death. Today, according to Forbes, the Birlas are worth $15,000,000,000, making them one of the wealthiest families in the world.

Hedgewar spent some sixty minutes with Jugal. We have no details of this meeting. Neither of them has ever mentioned it. All we know is that upon Hedgewar taking leave, Jugal offered a measly Rs 500 rupees as a contribution, which Hedgewar turned down, saying in typical Hedgewarian speak, 'We would rather have you than your money'.[36] Rs 500 in the late thirties would amount to Rs 60,000 in today's money—which would not get an organization the scale of the RSS very far. It is quite unclear what happened next, but suddenly, Hedgewar stopped fretting about money and began addressing other issues. His concern for funds evaporated. Maybe Birla made another anonymous donation that was much more significant. We know that Birla was in the Gandhian camp, and his moralizing master would have been deeply unimpressed had he openly supported the Sangh. Far better to snub the Sangh publicly and do something altogether different privately. Many wealthy families chose to support the rising sun quietly without upsetting the applecart. They either supported the Sangh because they were ideologically convinced, which in the 1930s would have been most unlikely, or they were won over by Hedgewarian wit and charm, or they were simply hedging their bets as to who would be best to keep oiled to win favour in some distant unseen future. Money follows power, but some early-stage money also follows rising powers, and the Sangh was categorically the latter.

Meanwhile, in Nagpur, the prodigal son had returned.

Golwalkar had taken flight twelve months earlier without telling anyone, much to the annoyance of the senior leadership and to the angst of Hedgewar. To leave the Sangh, as the coordinator (karyawaha) of Nagpur shakha in such a manner was, in effect, the same as absconding from your regiment at a time when you are expected to be leading your troops. But in classic Hedgewarian style, instead of reprimanding Golwalkar, he embraced him and simply ignored his misdemeanour.[37] Golwalkar stayed with his parents during the early months of his return.

Golwalkar was now thirty-one; he had already committed himself to a life of service and renunciation with Vivekananda's Ramakrishna Order, but it remains unclear whether he had also taken the pracharaak oaths at this time. He had left the Sangh a year previously to go and serve an old and frail Swami. The term Swami is honourific and is attributed to anyone who has joined a monastic order; it literally means the 'one who knows herself'. Swami Akhandananda was a peer of the famous Swami Vivekananda, and a direct disciple of the mystic Ramakrishna, after whom the Order is named. The Swami had been instrumental in spreading charitable works throughout India and had inspired thousands of people to serve their fellow man. Golwakar spent his entire year taking care of Akhandananda, as the old Swami gradually deteriorated and awaited death.[38] On 7 February 1937, the Swami passed, but just a few weeks earlier, he instructed the younger man to leave the ashram and return to Nagpur and continue his service there.[39] The Swami's message had left Golwalkar completely perturbed and in a state of anxiety.

Had Golwalkar been rejected by the Ramakrishna Order? Had he displeased Akhandananda, or had he thought that Golwalkar was not up to the task after all? Even if Akhandananda meant well and had foreseen a different purpose for Golwalkar, he certainly hadn't made it clear. A confused and somewhat depressed Golwalkar returned to Nagpur after many months, meandering through the countryside, trying to make sense of his life and purpose. Upon arrival in Nagpur, Hedgewar gave him no immediate responsibility. Instead, Golwalkar shadowed Hedgewar throughout the day and attended meetings simply to listen.[40] Golwalkar had no better ideas of his own, and the prospect of staying home with parents who would only exacerbate his anxiety left him with little option. For much of 1937, Golwalkar travelled alongside Hedgewar. They spent days together at a time, talking long into the late hours, and would often sit on Hedgewar's brooding swing on his porch. During these months, Golwalkar clawed his way out of depression and began to see Hedgewar not merely as a social or political leader but as a saint. He began to see Hedgewar as a man who knew himself, a man with all the qualities of a Swami but with no title, no initiation into monasticism but who was a man who lived an impeccably monastic existence. It was in one of these late-night conversations long into the cool early hours of the morning that Hedgewar explained to him that Dharma, the very essence of life itself, could only be protected when we nurtured better human beings. Until the common Indian man and woman exhibited better qualities, there was no hope of serving Dharma, and therefore, reforming the human being was the most sacred task before them. By transforming human beings, they became individuals of a higher order capable of practicing Dharma. When enough human beings are transformed, they build communities in flow with Dharma, and when enough communities are built, an entire nation arises. This was the task Hedgewar had set himself. Upon seeing and hearing Hedgewar with new eyes and ears, Golwalkar surrendered.

SIXTEEN: 1938–1939

Wars and Visions

Walter Benjamin once wrote that 'even the dead will not be safe from the enemy if he is victorious'.[1] Benjamin was warning us that history is written and left blank by the victors as it suits them. The medieval church in Europe created vast volumes of martyrdom stories, starting with the Golden Legend, a collection of gruesome tales about how perfectly pious Christians were tortured and killed by bloodthirsty Romans. Then let us consider that those who inherited India from the British, namely, Nehru and the Congress, had decided that Hedgewar be best forgotten and his creation brandished as a scourge on society. The problem is that both sets of tales are untrue. In reality, the Romans were far from bloodthirsty and the Christians far from reasonable. And this book is an attempt to redress this wrong as far as Hedgewar is concerned. The blank that was left now must be filled.

Hedgewar was increasingly convinced that the reign of the British was swiftly coming to an end. 'War', he said, 'was brewing in the West'.[2] He had foreseen that if the Crown went to war, then it would most likely lose, or at least become so weak that a new Imperial power would rise, one that would dismantle the empire—namely the United States. He was also acutely aware that Nehru and his Congress chums were also increasingly coming under the sway of Communist Russia. Several Congress leaders, along with Nehru, had started to visit Russia from as early as 1927. Hedgewar, who was already familiar with Laski's work, also knew that the radical Marxist thinker and teacher from the London School of Economics (LSE) had been a significant influence on his contemporary.[3] Laski was as red as it gets. He was an open advocate of Stalin's execution of Marxist ideology and would later in life regret his exuberance.[4] Hedgewar knew that India's political class was being kept on a string, or maybe many strings, where the puppeteers increasingly sat in Moscow and not London. The RSS, therefore, was building a force for an imminent threat on three separate fronts—the first coming from within, namely, the strife between tribes, clans and castes that were Hindu; the second, from the belligerent Muslim clerics and their political elite and now from the so-called Red bloc, disguised in Congress colours and Gandhian robes.

Hedgewar's behaviour during these times reveals his mindset. He was clearly expecting a fight and a looming emergency. He would arrive at various towns where RSS shakhas existed and issue a command for an assembly of all the swayamsevaks in full uniform, ready for instruction within two hours.[5] The local coordinators would scramble to assemble the volunteers, most of whom were working married men. When coordinators would appeal to his better senses that they needed at least six hours to assemble the men, he would rebuke them, citing the orderliness and commitment of the British forces. He wanted to test the men to determine whether they were ready and committed to serve at any given notice.

There may have been something else going on, too. Hedgewar was constantly suffering from fevers, chronic back pain and migraines. At one of these moments, at a particularly low point, two visitors came to see him while he was resting in a remote village called Deolali, on the outskirts of Nasik. He was staying in a rather posh comfortable bungalow on the Dhondy Road, which was slightly out of the village towards the West, facing southwards. This region is idyllic even today, and back in 1939, it was lusher, with constant rain and fertile soil, where the magnificent fire trees bloomed. Known in India as the gulmohar trees, they produced a stunning red and orange flower and kept the soil cool even in the midst of summer. A constant breeze swept through the rolling tree-covered hills, which made it a popular destination for the rich, and the military. The bungalow had a veranda in front where Hedgewar, Golwalkar and Telang would spend most of their time. Neem trees covered the grounds of the grand house, which had been rented by a wealthy benefactor who was genuinely concerned for Hedgewar's health. His name was Ghatay. Golwalkar and Telang were to look after Hedgewar, who was increasingly unable to look after himself.[6]

The two men that suddenly arrived were known. The first was one of Hedgewar's very own, Huddar, the radical communist who had felt that the RSS was too soft and not at the sharp end of things. The other was a man named Vasant Sanjgiri. Both men were messengers for Subhas Chandra Bose. Bose wanted to meet Hedgewar, and rather urgently at that. The Congress leader had resigned from his presidency after falling out with Gandhi in April 1939 and immediately created an organization, or faction, within the existing party called the All India Forward Bloc. It was meant to bring together all the hard-left elements into unison to execute a plan to attack the British all over India. War was brewing in Europe, and Bose had wanted to launch a full-scale uprising at the same time.[7] It was the perfect time for a bold and dastardly coup d'état against the British, but alas, Bose had grown exasperated with Gandhi. The old man of the Congress wanted to do the exact opposite. He wanted to show full one hundred percent solidarity with the Leviathan during its weakest moment. Indeed, he gave his full commitment to the British that India and her poor, wretched people were at their disposal. Bose was in Nagpur for the All-India Forward Bloc's first conference and had publicly labelled Gandhi 'as the best policeman the Britishers had in India'.[8] It was the first rallying call of the Forward Bloc. The fact that Nagpur was chosen as its launchpad tells us much about the nature of the city. Nagpur and the wider Vidarbha region had become a hotbed of ideas and political movements. Gandhi, Hedgewar and Savarkar had already set up camp there, and now Bose had arrived. Huddar was chosen because, like Bose, he was a militant communist who was always prepared to do what it took and held the responsibility for organizing the Nagpur event.

Hedgewar was lukewarm to the idea of an immediate uprising. He was in favour of the principle and the timing, but he was also a realist. He knew that the people were simply not ready, and Bose, for all his confidence and reputation, in fact, had very few committed men. Hedgewar saw Bose's hidden intention from the get-go. Bose, under his rhetoric of a free India, thought that he could induce Hedgewar to let him wield the power of the Sangh, which would become his 'force qui combat l'oppression' inside the country, and he would build up a force on the outside with the help of his comrades in the Soviet Union, Germany and Japan.

Hedgewar had a lot of time for Bose as a leader and as a person, but they were at complete odds when it came to their visions of India. This is a fact that the RSS seldom dwells on these days. The RSS has co-opted Bose's legacy for themselves. His attempts to free India from the outside by raising an army of Indian soldiers taken prisoners of war (PoWs) in German and Japanese camps, is eulogized, and is told and retold to every swayamsevak, who should remember, celebrate and even emulate Bose's heroics. Yet, history tells us that Bose's vision for a future independent India was more akin to a Nehruvian dream than a Hedgewarian vision. Bose was a committed communist. What is more; he was not in favour of democracy because he felt that the Indian people were not ready for it. The country needed a strong, benevolent dictatorship to bring it to an even kilter with other global powers before transitioning into a socialist democracy.[9]

Apart from such conjecture, what we do know is that when Huddar and Sanjgiri visited Hedgewar, he was simply too unwell to entertain the discussion for any great length of time. After thirty minutes, the two men, who could clearly see that Hedgewar was in no state for lengthy discussions, took their leave. On 12 July, four days later, Huddar wrote to Hedgewar, offering some more dates to come and see Bose in Mumbai.[10] Hedgewar declined. His ill health was the reason given.

We will never know with certainty why Hedgewar was keen to make the shakhas battle-ready for any sudden eventuality, but Bose's plans may have had something to do with it. Furthermore, it could also have been his expectation of the upcoming chaos that would be unleashed if, and when, Britain lost the war. His health may have also played into it.

Between April and July 1939, he was severely unwell, to the point of being unable to walk and experiencing bouts of unconsciousness; not that surprising when considering that his body temperature soared well past forty degrees. Golwalkar, through his letters, describes how his mentor and Guru drifted into unconsciousness and started spewing broken sentences and words, showcasing the inner recesses of his consciousness. Golwalkar was at his bedside throughout the ordeal and was well equipped to do so, having just served Swami Akhandananda during his final days. According to Golwalkar's testimony, Hedgewar was uttering his innermost anxieties; he was essentially, psychologically speaking, naked. According to these testimonies, during these times of extreme pain and vulnerability, Hedgewar would reveal his inner workings, which, too, were only ever concerned with the struggle.[11] He would spew out a variety of things from more mundane concerns about letters or responses, to more macro worries such as the communist or Islamic threat to his people, and occasionally, Hedgewar would reveal his deep memories about his days as a militant revolutionary in Bengal. Golwalkar makes it a point for posterity's sake that Hedgewar never once unknowingly uttered a bad word against anyone. Not a single piece of memory was lusty, or angry and hateful.[12]

Eventually, by late July, his health somewhat improved. The fevers, unbearable migraines and bouts of unconsciousness had stopped but had left him severely weakened. swayamsevaks decided to move him closer to Nasik city, where it was easier for locals to come and take care of him and support the two men who were his constant carers. They moved into a simple abode, somewhere near NH60, the Mumbai–Agra Road. In 1939, this would have been a simple road built for animal traffic with the occasional truck or motor carriage. Soon the number of visitors began ramping up, and Hedgewar would stay up every night well past midnight, something that doctors were desperate for him not to do. At one time, Golwalkar tells us that doctors began putting pressure on him to ensure that Hedgewar got more sleep. On one occasion, these doctors stayed behind to see what he was up to every night. As the evening rolled on, they discovered the nature of these visitors and the types of conversations that were happening, and why his visitors had to come under the cover of darkness.[13] The doctors never pressed their wish thereafter. Along with visitors, letters were pouring in from across India and Golwalkar was charged with penning a response to each one after consulting the chief.

In August that year, Hedgewar was taken to Mumbai to meet some seasoned medical professionals to see if they could diagnose the health condition he was suffering from. Several reputed doctors gave him the once over but could not diagnose him. In a letter dated 22 August 1939, Hedgewar writes, 'The opinion of the doctors in Bombay is the same as those in Nagpur. X-rays and Electro-Cardiographs have revealed nothing.'[14] Hedgewar, by 6 August, had arrived in Nagpur to discover that one of his major patrons had died. A wealthy man by the name of Tattulay was a significant donor to the RSS and by today's standard, quite the brute. He enjoyed hunting; his house was full of stuffed animals, a habit that he had picked up from his white masters, and he was known to especially show off his animal rugs to anyone who would entertain such frivolity. By modern standards, he was the antithesis of what modern swayamsevaks could ever accept, but in 1939 Hedgewar would simply dismiss such shows of pomp as immature. When he was offered the animal fur to wrap around on cold nights while staying with Tattulay, he would politely decline and wrap his simple shawl around his body instead, much to the annoyance of his colleagues, who were easily seduced by the pomp. Although a loss for Hedgewar, he seems to have been too weak to truly grasp the gravity of Tattulay's death. Even base emotions require some magnitude of well-being, something which Hedgewar was now in short supply of.

Later that year, at a public gathering, Golwakar was formally announced as sarkaryawaha, or in normal parlance, Chief Coordinator of the RSS. Many would have been surprised by this sudden and impulsive decision by Hedgewar, especially in the light of the younger man's tendencies to disappear. Many within the experienced ranks of the order, men such as Parmarth or Joshi, would have certainly raised an eyebrow or two. Evidently, Hedgewar, too, had fostered his own doubts about Golwalkar's preparedness, having not given him any responsibility upon his return. However, it appears that after having spent the best part of a month together, initially in travel and then in care, their interaction and Golwalkar's earnestness had obviously convinced him that a certain amount of rootedness had now taken hold within his protege.[15] Furthermore, there was another calculation at play. Golwalkar was effectively a non-political player. He was a nobody when it came to local, regional or national politics. What was most favourable was that Golwalkar was far removed from the endless bickering of old men in the Hindu Mahasabha.[16] He had no desire for political office and, therefore, could never be seduced by the alluring spirits of Peitho and Suadela, in the modern guise as power and money. The RSS and the Sabha were close but different. Equilibrium was kept mainly thanks to the relationship between Moonjay and Hedgewar.

One of Hedgewar's biggest anxieties was Vinayak Savarkar—a charismatic and intelligent man, perhaps even a polymath by some accounts, but deeply emotive and divisive. Savarkar held a Hobbesian-like worldview, where violence and brutality were part and parcel of what it meant to be human, while also fusing the darkest aspects of Nietzschean thought when he writes about every nation's 'will to power' and the need for perpetual war against the outsiders. Hedgewar could never accept such ideas; they were antithetical to Dharma. In India today, Savarkar is completely dehumanized—either worshipped or loathed. The truth is that he was human, and like many gifted people, he suffered from inner contradictions, bouts of intense melancholy and was highly irritable and quick to temper. He was an abrasive atheist and never suffered fools. A personality like Savarkar could never have any significant influence on Golwalkar. Savarkar was a seasoned political nationalist, a man who had been severely tortured and scarred by the British, whereas Golwalkar was spiritual first and foremost, a renunciate who had no desire for the limelight and was more akin to a cultural nationalist. By making Golwalkar the chief coordinator, Hedgewar had knowingly built a buffer between the Hindu Mahasabha and the RSS, thereby taking it further away from having any meaningful influence on the government of independent India.

Then on 1 September 1939, Hitler's Germany invaded Poland and triggered World War II. Of course, the term 'second world war', according to Reynolds, was only coined in 1942 and has all the hallmarks of Eurocentrism.[17] For Hedgewar and his contemporaries, Hitler's misadventures and Hirohito's imperial dreams caused a cataclysmic rupture across South Asia, from Afghanistan to Myanmar, and from Tibet to Sri Lanka—what in Hedgewarian terms was civilizational Bharat. Wars and civil strife raged from the mid-1940s through to 1971, when India liberated East Pakistan, today's Bangladesh, from the tyranny of military generals from West Pakistan.[18] From the Indian perspective, thirty years of instability and chaos reigned. Borders continuously changed. Mass migrations of tens of millions of people changed entire landscapes. Ethnic, religious and tribal conflicts raged everywhere, from Malaya to Afghanistan. Interweaving with these conflicts were economic interests, such as the rubber and tin from Myanmar and Malaya, the sheer scale of human labour required to reclaim South-East Asia from Japan and coal and timber from the Eastern jungles of India.[19] With so many variables and interests at play, the great retreat of the British had started, and in its wake would be bloody conflict, as Hedgewar had envisaged much to his distress. His people were simply not ready in body, mind nor spirit.

No sooner had the war started that Hedgewar received a letter from Golwalkar, who was in Punjab attending the OTC. While there, he came to know about the Khaksar movement, an organization with the same kind of ethos, discipline and martial spirit as the RSS but with an Islamic heart. Khaksar, in Persian, means 'from dust', emphasizing the humility of the movement and its focus on service and upliftment of the downtrodden and poor.[20] Like the RSS, it was in the business of nation-building, except theirs was that of a unified Islamic India.[21] Even their uniform resembled, almost uncannily, that of the RSS. The uninitiated could be forgiven for mixing the two entities up. Started in 1931, six years after the RSS, in Lahore, by its eighth year, some commentators reckoned that it had an active membership of 4,000,000 members.[22] Even though this is likely to be a vastly exaggerated number, it still points towards the fact that the RSS had a competitor that was occupying somewhat of a similar modus operandi, with equal, if not greater, success, but with a completely polar vision. These two movements were antithetical to one another. A serious clash was destined to happen sooner or later, especially now that the RSS had reached the 'home-turf' of the Khaksars—the Punjab.

An eyewitness account described the Khaksars thus:

> 'My eyes were opened by a unique experience in Lahore in the Punjab. My car was stopped one afternoon in a main street of Lahore by a band of uniformed men armed with sharp spades. No policeman was present to stop them and regulate the traffic. They were Khaksars under the leadership of a Moslem who, according to a public statement made later by the late Premier of Punjab, owned his inspiration to Nazi sources. There were thirty to forty thousand Khaksars in the Punjab and some of the adjacent provinces and States.'[23]

Their inspiration was a mathematician and, by all accounts, a man of great talent—Inayatullah Khan Mashriqi. His family were late converts to Islam and came from Hindu Rajput stock. He came from an established family with deep roots, where his forebears served the Mughal courts and then the British. Through his father's connections, he had come into contact with and was greatly influenced by the likes of Jamal al-Din al-Afghani, Sayyid Ahmad Khan and Shibli Nomani. Afghani, in particular, was a radical. A man whose ideas come to life in the work and life of Mashriqi. Afghani hated the British and yet admired their science and technological advances. He was a committed Muslim with a deep desire for reform within Islam. He was bigoted towards non-Muslims, especially Hindus, but felt that for India to free itself from the shackles of colonialism, Muslims had to work closely with and even co-opt Hindus into a Muslim movement. The Khaksars were also a threat to Jinnah's two-nation theory, from both an ideological standpoint and as a private army that could really disrupt things if the British ever left. Later that same year, during a gathering of the All India Muslim League, where they were discussing the creation of Pakistan, the Khaksars, armed to the hilt, marched out to disrupt the proceedings. According to reports, some forty Khaksars were killed in clashes with the police, and a statewide ban was made on the group.[24]

Golwalkar makes clear that the Sangh was somewhat nervous about the Khaksars and their militancy in Punjab and how the statewide ban on the RSS would affect their own work. Hedgewar, in his response, advises him to carry on confidently expanding the Sangh throughout Punjab. In the thirties and forties, throughout India, there were countless quasi-paramilitary outfits, one for every political or religious movement. These organizations, much like the early RSS, were laboratories where, within their own microcosms, ideas about the nation, the state, citizenship and political participation were articulated and enacted.[25] Many of these groups attracted those individuals who felt marginalised, vulnerable or threatened during the general retreat of the British after World War I. The RSS attracted a huge portion of marginalized Hindus who came from the lower-middle and middle-class communities. The RSS gave its swayamsevaks the opportunity to buy into and further shape their own popular political imagination, where they could construct their own political identity and aspirations. These imaginations were often created through lived experiences of actual threats, violence and intimidation. Historical forces, cultural traditions and the social and economic conditions of the people fuelled the narratives that came from these groups, including the RSS.[26]

What separates the RSS then from all these other quasi-paramilitary groups belonging to some political or religious group? It was Hedgewar himself. Whereas the Hindustani Seva Dal, founded in 1924, and from whom the RSS cheekily took its own uniforms, was not only a militant arm of the Congress but ultimately was fused fully into the party at the behest of Gandhi, for Hedgewar, the RSS was not a tool for any Hindu religious or political group, nor was it a form of an umbrella organization; rather it was focused exclusively on the goal of nation-building—not politically, but culturally. The RSS, unlike all the other groups that ebbed for a while and then eventually disappeared or lost steam, continued to grow into the behemoth it is today because it was rooted in cultural nationalism. It was only interested in its own ideas, which were indeed political in nature, but they were rooted firmly in the native culture of the land and her people. The RSS would use political outfits as one of its arms and not vice versa, as had been the case with all the others. The Khaksars, for their part, ultimately lost their way soon after 1947 and the creation of Pakistan. Most of its members felt content with a Muslim land carved out of India and lost their appetite for a unified India built on an Islamic ideology.

Hedgewar's installation of Golwalkar as the National Coordinator of the RSS was brilliant and hugely fortuitous because it kept the RSS firmly rooted in cultural nationalism and not seduced by some short-term pursuit of political power like so many of its contemporaries.

Another way to frame the difference between Hedgewar's RSS and its contemporaries was that his order of prachaaraks was more akin to the friars of the medieval church—men who were single-minded on a humanitarian mission, not a narrow political one. It was the prachaarak order that truly set the RSS apart from all the others. At the core of the RSS is a deep spirituality that is often overlooked or completely unseen by modern commentators.

Golwalkar's impact was puissant. Hedgewar had struck a wedge between the Hindu Mahasabha and the RSS. In 1939, the editor of *Vande Mataram*, the leading publication of the Sabha, published a series of twelve articles in which he called out Hedgewar directly, labelling him as 'stubborn, ambitious, and vainglorious'.[27] The Sabha's main gripe with Hedgewar was that he was being non-compliant to the wishes and whims of the political outfit, much to the displeasure of its leadership, especially Vinayak Savarkar. The main charge levelled against him was of dividing the Hindu power base instead of uniting it. None of the Hindu Mahasabha leaders stepped forward to defend him, including Moonjay. Only an old, unwell and tired Ganesh Savarkar publicly defended Hedgewar at the time. The grassroots across Maharashtra were, however, miffed at such slander. Hundreds of letters were sent to the editor to encourage him to rethink his position but to no avail. Late in 1939, another article appeared, making the displeasure even more explicit with an indirect mention of the problem at hand, namely Golwalkar.

> 'No doubt, you have done a yeoman service to the Hindu society by establishing the Rashtriya swayamsevak Sangh. But what can be said, if one who has built an oasis for weary travellers himself lets loose ferocious creatures into the pond from where the weary quench their thirst? You are doing exactly this and doing so deliberately. Therefore, we implore you, please desist. If you persist in your presence course, historians of the Hindu society will not even deem you worthy of mention.'[28]

What exactly is the editor of *Vande Mataram* saying here? Who is this ferocious animal who is subverting the purpose of the oasis that is the RSS as far as the Sabha is concerned? Who had recently been introduced into this pool—we can guess it for ourselves. Hedgewar was being warned. He ought not to lose sight of who the real power brokers of history were, while simultaneously appealing to Hedgewar's sense of self-interest—his legacy. This was an amateurish mistake by the editor, for anyone who knew Hedgewar would have known that appealing to his own self-interest was like appealing to a lion's self-interest to eat grass. A non-starter. Hedgewar dismissed such articles and continued to push forward with his agenda. Interestingly, the Hedgewarian practice of 'doing not doing' paid dividends, as the very same editor who wrote all these letters a year later would publish an entire book compiling all of Hedgewar's speeches.

On 22 October, Golwalkar addressed an audience composed of the senior rung of Mahasabha leaders including Moonjay. The *Mahratta* reported,

> 'The Sangh today completes fourteen years and is stepping into the fifteenth. We are now progressing towards some maturity. There is much to do (for the Nation), but the Sangh has chosen only one. We are here to organize the Hindu society. We have consciously chosen to avoid all other activities that carry the label of "politics", in the sense that the Sangh does not align itself with any political party or organisation. We have to work according to our mission, and our mission only. We must work without confusion.'[29]

It is little wonder that the editor of *Vande Mataram* was so visceral towards Golwalkar in his article, calling on Hedgewar to intervene and stop this wedge from widening further. It appears that the RSS and Hedgewar were clear from day one that the RSS was what it was—a movement rooted in cultural nationalism with no desire to sully its plans with the politics of the day. The Mahasabha, however, appears never to have quite understood these plans and seems to have dismissed them as mere rhetoric and posturing. Every time a Hindu Mahasabha bigwig was appointed in a ceremonial position within the RSS's local infrastructure (as sanghchalaks), the Sabha leadership naturally felt that their men were in control of the local RSS infrastructure. Often, these men were rich and locally influential—the RSS made them their own. When push came to shove, the sanghchalaks naturally put the interests of the Sangh first, much to the horror and anger of the Sabha.

In September, a month earlier, the Mahasabha, having gotten the message from Hedgewar, decided to set up its own quasi-paramilitary outfit poorly named the Hindu Militia.[30] Moonjay, the everlasting bridge between the RSS and the Sabha, tried to engage Hedgewar and encouraged him to attend the inaugural meeting of the Militia. Hedgewar's letter dated 30 September 1939 is stark:

> You know my health is poor, and does not allow me to travel, and therefore I shall not be coming to Poona on October 8th as you requested. Even if you propose to hold the meeting in Nagpur, I shall be unable to attend, as there is a meeting of Sangh officers planned on the same day, which I will attend, health permitting. I urge you to refrain from associating my name with this "Hindu Militia" anywhere![31]

Moonjay, as was his tendency towards his adopted son, ignored Hedgewar's request to keep his name out of it and, at the launch event, added Hedgewar's name to the leadership team. This was later retracted at the younger man's insistence. Countless attempts to start an alternative movement to the RSS were started, and quickly disappeared. After the Hindu Militia, there was the Ram Sena (Ram's Army), then the Hindu Rashtra Dal, Shakti Dal, Hindu Sewa Dal, and finally the infamous Nathuram Godse's Hindu Rashtra Sena—all of which were attempts to undermine the RSS and establish a rival parallel organization under the helm of the Sabha.[32] All failed. Once again, what all of these poor attempts fundamentally lacked was 'spiritus', the rootedness of culture and spirituality that was at the heart of the RSS. These are all telltale signs of the power and steadiness of the prachaarak order, an order of devoted actors rooted in cultural and spiritual nationalism. This was an aspect of the Sangh that even Moonjay never grasped. His protégé had far outgrown him in vision and practice.

While this toing and froing was underway, Hedgewar received another note of a completely different kind. The note read, 'I am dying. Instead of offering my life to the development of the nation, I have instead been forced to sacrifice my body at the altar of this godforsaken disease. Yours Narayan Karvai'.[33] By the time Hedgewar read the terrible news, Narayan from the Raipur shakha was already dead. Hedgewar himself was suffering tremendously and knew himself to be approaching the end sooner rather than later. It remains unclear how or what Hedgewar said in reply to his family, but we can be quite certain that a local prachaarak and swayamsevaks would have visited his home and paid their respects to his grieving mother and father. Hedgewar would have most certainly spent his time addressing the welfare of such families than the politicking of nitwits at the Hindu Mahasabha.

Many revolutionaries, new and old, wanted to come and visit Hedgewar to rally the RSS for an impending uprising. Revolution. Revolt. War. At the helm of this misadventure was Subhas Chandra Bose. He had reignited the burnt-out passions of old revolutionaries scattered across northern India. In modern Indian narratives, Bose is seen as a son of the soil, a patriot, a revolutionary, a strategist and a man above reproach. Alas, history is cruel, and rightly so to those who would shun her away when her truth is unpalatable. Bose was not only a hardened communist and a fascist, but he also inadvertently led thousands of young men and women to their deaths through his immense capacity to inspire and lead. He had managed to influence people of all ranks, from Lakshmi Sehgal—the famous head of the Indian National Army's all-women unit at one end, and to the other, a lowly subordinate named Perumal who until 2020 lived in a rundown Tamil district part of Yangon in Myanmar.[34]

The average swayamsevak today would know almost nothing meaningful about Bose apart from his adventures and glamorized patriotism. Only positive images exist in the minds of Indians today. Yet, Hedgewar and then Golwalkar, along with the entire Sangh leadership, stayed clear of Bose's plans—why? Could it have been that Bose had a darker side that many in the upper echelons of the Congress party were well aware of, including Gandhi, Nehru and even Hedgewar? Was this the reason that Gandhi effectively out-witted Bose for the presidency of the Congress earlier that year?

What we do know is that Bose kept the wrong type of friends. Bose showed immense solidarity with the Axis—Japan, Italy and Germany. He made a widely publicized visit to Nanjing in Japanese-occupied China in 1943, knowing full well that in 1937, something like 3,00,000 Chinese were massacred by the Japanese army over a six-week period during the infamous 'Rape of Nanjing'.[35] Then we know that through his charm and charisma, he managed to network his way to the top of the Nazi regime, where he was already in close communication with Ribbentrop, Himmler and Goebbels.[36] Bose's biggest flaw, and one that Hedgewar saw and the RSS stayed clear of, was that he was a man who was prepared to go to any length for his desired end. A man who wrongly believed that the end justifies the means. It almost never does.

As 1939 rolled on and the news of the war filtered into Hedgewar's room through radio, telegrams and visitors, his mind increasingly began to mute out such noise, maybe for the first time in his life. Instead, he began to ponder and brood, as was his way, on the hereafter and what the future leadership of the Sangh would look like. His end was nigh, and it was time to face it.

SEVENTEEN: 1940

Last Stand

Hedgewar tried remaining steadfast and emotionally steady as his body fell into a tailspin of poor health and sickness. Many of his closest friends tried to convince him to leave Nagpur and head out to a secluded natural reserve for rest and recuperation. After initially resisting their calls, he eventually agreed and headed out to the hot water springs at Rajgir in Bihar on 31 January 1940.[1] Rajgir was one thousand two hundred kilometres away from Nagpur. It would take over twenty-four hours by train. Rather unusually, Hedgewar asked his ardent stewards to accompany him. They were Appa Joshi, Babu Indurkar, Tatya Telang and Baba Kayani.[2] Golwalkar, too, was expected but declined the offer due to impending work for the upcoming OTC due to be held in Pune later that year. The four men were insistent that they travel on the second-class carriage, where they were assured a place to sit and some peace. Hedgewar's response was as expected, 'No. The RSS does not have the funds,' he said, 'to offer us such luxury.' Third class it was for all of them. [3]

Passengers in the third-class carriages were poor, and the conditions were often basic. The seats were wooden, with no padding or cushions. Passengers had to sit on benches the entire time, often for hours on end and, in the case of Hedgewar, for days. The carriages were overcrowded, sweaty and smelly. The smell of human perspiration, the sign of hard labour coupled with little to no opportunity to bathe, and the pheromones of domesticated animals—often goats and chickens—would all fuse to create an insufferable environment. Sitting next to the window or hanging out of the doorway was considered premium travel. Carriages were dirty and unsanitary, and there was always the risk of disease. There were no toilets in the third-class carriages, and passengers had to wait until the train stopped and use the facilities at the stations, which were also dirty and unhygienic. To travel in this way was never considered lightly; it was quite the ordeal.

Along the route, we know the train stopped at several towns and cities—where the entire carriage would empty, look for some space to do their bodily business and then return back in time to grab a seat near a window. For Hedgewar and his merry men every station meant visitors, swayamsevaks waiting patiently to see the man himself arrive. In the smaller towns, Hedgewar would often dish out whatever food they had brought along with them to the swayamsevaks at the station. This would have been a powerful gesture and one that people would have taken note of and respected deeply. They finally disembarked at Gaya, in Bihar, some two hours away from the hot water springs, to stay with Krishna-Vallabh Singh.[4] Even today, Gaya is not much of a town. However, just eight kilometres away lies a small village called Bodh Gaya, where the Buddha attained enlightenment. The tree under which he meditated still remains alive and is worshipped by millions of people each year. Hedgewar knew where he was and visited this hallowed place to take 'darshan', meaning to take light, knowledge or blessings from a source. For Hedgewar, this site was more than just a historically sacred place, it was rather a treasure trove of memory for millions of people; this, he felt, was a place from which his cultural nationalism ought to spring forth.

Cultural nationalism draws inspiration from shared culture, language and history to create a sense of national identity.[5] For Hedgewar, this naturally meant promoting and celebrating important cultural sites and monuments, such as Bodh Gaya, that are emblematic of India's history and identity. Therefore, even today, the RSS proactively promotes and highlights any historical site or monument that is in any way rooted in the religions or cultural practices of India. The RSS today disowns the Taj Mahal—why? The answer is clear—it is the symbol of the 'other', the outsider, the tyrant and the oppressor—no inspiring cultural memories there. However, the temples of Ajanta or Ellora are quite different; these are sites that speak to the Indian mind and remind it of its deep past, indigenous religions and culture, a past before Islam and Christianity wreaked havoc on these lands. Hence, these are to be promoted.

Meanwhile, Nehru's political nationalism, and likewise the modern-day Congress Party's nationalism, is devoid of such historicity and narratives. For them, the emphasis is on capturing the state and its apparatus through which a union can be forged—one built on modernity, industrialization and some weird sense of secularism which, in India, is as dysfunctional as it can get. For Nehru, the Taj Mahal is important because it represents supreme state power, as does the Red Fort. But not for the RSS. This all goes back to Hedgewarian cultural nationalism. So, it is no surprise then that Hedgewar inaugurated several shakhas in Gaya and its surroundings.

On 6 February 1940, they made their way to the hot water springs in Krishna-Vallabh's motor car. Hedgewar was simply unable to bear the pains caused by the uneven roads and travel by bullock cart, or an early version of a tuk-tuk, called a tum-tum. During the two-hour drive, which was in relative comfort, Palkar tells us that Hedgewar spoke at length about the psyche of someone rooted in cultural nationalism, or what he would have called 'Rashtriyata'.[6] He gave the analogy of birds and their relationship with an orchard. 'The birds enjoy the orchard so long as it gives them fruit, juicy worms in the fertile soil and a place to build their nests. If ever the orchard no longer suits their purpose, they will simply fly away and look for some other place. This, he said, 'is not Rashtriyata.''[7] As he spoke in raspy tones, his listeners could clearly make out the strain he was under. Rashtriyata, is when a person is completely fused with the idea of his or her nation, an unconditional oneness is achieved. The birds, when they realize that there is no 'them' without the garden, their very identity and well-being is interlocked with the garden; only then would the spirit of Rashtriyata arise. The birds would realize that they are part and parcel of an eco-system and that the garden was as much theirs as they belonged to the garden. The Sangh, for Hedgewar, was the college that was constructed to build this spirit of devotion in the hearts of citizens, a spirit that notes there is no dignified self-identity without the dignity of the nation.[8] It was the physical manifestation of 'desh bhakti', devotion to the very soil upon which one lived.

Hedgewar and his comrades were surrounded by history—Bodh Gaya to the South-east; the ruins of the Haryanka dynasty all across southern Rajgiri, a kingdom some two thousand five hundred years old; then to the mountain ranges where the Jain monk Mahavir lived and did penance to find enlightenment; to where the mythical kingdom of King Jarasandh was located on the hills overlooking the small town—a kingdom recorded in the epic Mahabharata, a story that is at least 5000 years old. Hedgewar was immersed in history, and it was the kind of history he was fighting for, the kind of history that was to fuel his brand of cultural nationalism.

In the West, we often fail to recognize that India has a living tradition that predates any other living culture in the world. Songs are still sung that would have been sung at the time of the Buddha, and mantras are recited at millions of homes that would have sounded the same around 1500 BCE, and festivals are celebrated that belong to a primordial past. The RSS's prachaarak order is still deeply rooted in this history and aims to ensure that India's renewed freedom not only lasts but also rebuilds on this civilizational heritage.

Ram Jain, a local businessman, rented a four-bedroom house with a large lounge for meetings and a beautiful veranda looking out towards the lush green hills. The hot springs were about a kilometre away. Every morning at four-thirty, Joshi and Hedgewar would make their way to the springs by tum-tum while the others walked. The short, bumpy trip up the hill proved to be an exhausting experience for Hedgewar on some days. There was a small temple complex surrounding the hot springs. Situated at the foot of Vaibhava hill, he had to climb thirty-five steps to arrive at seven hot springs, all with holy significance for Buddhists, Jains and Hindus at large. It wouldn't be ludicrous to say that this place was for Hindus what Lourdes is to Christendom. Among the seven pools, Hedgewar was encouraged to bathe in Brahmakund, which, according to local folklore, was the most potent in healing. Brahmakund has a consistent temperature of 45 degrees. Today the spring is housed inside a temple complex, but in Hedgewar's time it would have been directly under the morning sky. The air temperature would have been cool and moist. The water would have been hot and steamy. Hedgewar and Joshi would see the sun rise while bathing, concentrating on their breath, and feel the air warm with the first rays of the sun. It would have been quiet, with only a few people dedicated enough to trudge up the hill at that hour. Those that did make the effort were met with an orchestral delight—birdsong from the Indian silverbill and the magpie robin. In these few moments, Hedgewar could afford to lose himself in the present, freeing him from a lifetime of self-imposed poverty and struggle. While Hedgewar continued to bathe under a small waterfall of hot spring water massaging his back, Joshi would make his way to the temple deity and begin a long series of mantras.[9] It would be almost seven in the morning, well past sunrise, when the two men would leave their sanctuary.

At the house, Hedgewar would rest. He slept. He arose for brunch at around ten. He read and slept some more until three in the afternoon. He would walk around the gardens often in silence. After his afternoon chai, he began his day and re-engaged with the world. He was unable to walk for long or sit and would often spend a great number of hours lying in bed as others around him made calls, wrote telegrams and went about the town meeting locals. In these days, Hedgewar spent much time reading and talking about the teachings of Samarth Ramdas, the seventeenth century renunciate from Maharashtra who wrote a book called the *Dasbodh,* meaning advice or guidance for a disciple.[10] Often late into the evening, Hedgewar would speak out loud about his musings and churnings, and what he had read that day from the *Dasbodh*. Those around him listened, questioned and absorbed what they could from the dying mind of a man who was quite capable of living in the spiritual and the physical realms simultaneously. In such moments, Hedgewar would infuse the RSS leadership with deep insights into the civilizational wisdom they were so dedicated to protecting and promoting.

The *Dasbodh* is composed of over 7500 verses, what in Marathi are called ovya. Each ovya is four lines long. Composed in rhythm and rhyme, it is poetry of the highest order. Chapters are titled 'Signs of Fools', 'Nine Stages of Communion', 'Attributes and Forms', 'Prudence and Renunciation', 'In Search of Providence', 'On Teaching' and 'Understanding the complete-whole' just to name a few. The verses elucidate practical steps to live a fulfilled life and touch on things from commerce and trade, sex and love, family and rearing children, politics to metaphysics and epistemology.

Dasbodh is not a book that we can easily read today. In its English translation, the first to be lost is the rhythm and rhyme, followed by the spirit of the text with its tone and sprinkling of rascality, followed by the nuance of words and the potency of the analogies. Nevertheless, we can still gather something from the text that kept Hedgewar returning to it repeatedly throughout his life. He would spend hours discussing and elucidating specific ovyas that he felt were instrumental for RSS office bearers to understand. He saw the *Dasbodh* as an instruction manual of some sort, one that would help instil the fundamentals of how prachaaraks ought to behave and, thereby, the way the organization should approach future challenges and opportunities.

Some of the ovyas describe the qualities of fools, that is those who only think about their own interests, forsaking the common good. This is not too dissimilar to the meaning of the word *idiṓtēs,* which is idiot in Greek, the man who only pertains to himself. Fools, says Ramdas, come in two guises. The first and obvious ones are the uneducated, the uncouth and those who are thuggish. The second are those that are learned, who are couth but lack even the basic adherence to common sense, and in this context, stray from that which is virtuous. He describes at length the qualities of the virtuous, the noble and the truly learned.[11]

Other ovyas go into great detail about identifying the signs of virtue and noble character and those who suffer from mental afflictions and are prone to suffering. It is as much a work of psychology as it is philosophy, and it is layered with religious language that one must untangle before getting to the nectar of the text. There is a small section in there about death and dying.

> 'Death is the only definite thing in this world. Everyone is coming closer to death by every passing moment. Death accompanies us right from our birth. One does not know what is in store in one's future. At the destined time one has to die, there is no tomorrow for death.
>
> ...Even the celestial beings must die when their time has come.
>
> One should therefore have no illusions about death. Rather one should always remember this fact and utilise whatever little time remains for doing actions in accordance with Dharma. One should think that death can take my body, but it cannot touch my good deeds, which will be remembered by posterity.'[12]

We can only wonder how this last paragraph would have touched Hedgewar as his body suffered and wilted. The RSS was his legacy; it was his life, and he knew that it must continue to be a force for the resurrection of an ancient civilization, his civilization.

Over chai, Joshi would try to get as much of a download as possible from Hedgewar's past. For his part, Hedgewar obliged. Sitting up with his back resting against a wall of pillows, covered by a woollen shawl, protecting his broken body from the cold winter air, he revealed how he managed to evade capture and arrest during his time as a revolutionary in Calcutta. According to Palkar, who interviewed an aged Joshi, Hedgewar evaded capture by never writing anything down nor speaking on the telephone.

Every meeting was face-to-face, and every detail was memorized. Joshi joyfully remembered how Hedgewar went on to remember addresses, passwords and locations. He remembered in great detail how to make a handmade bomb with the power to blow up walls. He remembered the art of fighting and how revolutionaries were seen with dread by the public as well as the authorities.[13] Reliving these memories for Hedgewar was cathartic.

One night, news came in that some hooligans had broken into a local Buddhist shrine and had claimed it as an Islamic site to mark the death of a Muslim fakir. Only one monk of Japanese descent stood up to the thugs and was badly beaten for doing so. These kinds of tactics, often encouraged by the clerics, were on the rise as a means of capturing land, using a combination of violence and the law, first to grab, and then to retain their claims. As expected, no one else opposed the forcible takeover. Hedgewar suggested that Rajgir needed a shakha. Soon, locals found out that the strong man of the Sangh was in their sleepy village and came to visit Hedgewar. As usual, people complained. As they moaned, Hedgewar would listen with Telang and Joshi on either side. People came in a similar vein as they would to visit a Godfather, 'Oh please Godfather, please do this one favour for us, and I will be indebted to you . . . '. Everything from 'my cow was stolen', to 'our shrines are being desecrated', and 'our daughters are being harassed'. Hedgewar was silent. After the emotive deluge was over, he told them that it was ultimately their responsibility to look after themselves and that there was no one else they could rely on. He explained why the establishment of a shakha was important, and the training and support that could be afforded by the Sangh, but ultimately it required the braves of the village to step forward. After a few of these meetings, Joshi and Telang began training some men of the village in how to run and organize a shakha.

During this time, Hedgewar was in constant touch with Golwalkar via telegram. On 17 February 1940, he wrote tongue-in-cheek, 'There is a great deal of improvement in Joshi's and Telang's health. My health, however, has seen little change.'[14] Then Inurkar, who was also there, wrote on 23 February,

> '... the environment here does not seem to have had any impact on Doctor ji's health. The locals feel that it will take several weeks before he might start responding to the treatment.'[15]

Things were clearly not improving, and Hedgewar was getting itchy feet, a compulsion to move on. As his health worsened, his desire to get things done grew. On 6 March, he left for Nagpur even though many appealed to his self-interest to remain and continue his treatment and rest. Golwakar travelled some 300 kilometres to Jabalpur by motor carriage to pick them up. Travel by train was proving too difficult for Hedgewar, and the others were concerned that his pain was exacerbated by the dire conditions of the train carriage. His health was in rapid decline, and people began to visibly notice. Increasingly, he needed constant care, round the clock, from bathing to dressing and morning and evening massages. Having attended a few public events in Nagpur, Hedgewar was cajoled into going back to Rajgir to continue his treatment.

He returned to Rajgir on 31 March with a single question on his mind: how many trained swayamsevaks would it require to rebuild this nation after the British left and to deter any attempts at a quick takeover from outside forces? His answer was simple. In a letter addressed to Golwalkar, he wrote,

> 'To make the Sangh truly a vanguard, I place this idea for your perusal. Over the next three years (1940-42), the number of swayamsevaks in uniform should be one percent of the population in rural areas and three percent of the population in urban areas. If each one of us thinks about it thoroughly and then acts with energy and enthusiasm, I am sure we would complete this work in three years. I pray Providence supports our work and blesses us with success.'[16]

This simple line, written for a specific setting and context, continues to be the rule of thumb with which every swayamsevak in the RSS still operates. In large swathes of the country, Hedgewar's percent rule is still a long way off. It was a euphemism at best for him to give a three-year timeline to achieve such high numbers. Considering that Hedgewar was a pragmatist, this kind of unrealistic aim begins to show his absence of mind as his illness began its final ascent to conquering and taking his life.

At Rajgir, his health began to show some improvement. His fevers had abated somewhat, and he was able to concentrate and write during the day. His back pain had become manageable, and even though he was on painkillers, he was able enough to start working all day and late into the evening. During one of his better days, Hedgewar took the opportunity to visit Nalanda—the site of the ancient university of the same name, destroyed by Muhammad Bakhtiyar Khalji around 1200 CE.[17] It was one of the world's largest and oldest residential centres of learning, and science, commerce, language, art, philosophy and religion were all taught there under the umbrella of Buddhism from 427 CE. It was located at a place where the Buddha was said to have taught sitting within a mango grove around 600 years earlier. It was ancient history, which from a Hedgewarian perspective had ended with the Islamic invasion of the region, when thousands of monks were slaughtered, and the great libraries, the storehouses of ancient Indian knowledge systems, were once and forever burnt to ashes.[18] In the Hindu narrative, it is often recollected that the fires of Nalanda burned for three months, as thousands of books and bodies burned. Hedgewar wrote in anguish about his visit, 'If only there were historians who were sons of the soil, who had studied the history of this place, to give every visitor the right perspective.'[19] Hedgewar was pointing to the fact that the 'sons of the soil' had all but forgotten this history, and ruins lay there, as if tombstones of unknown and forgotten ancestors that no one had claimed. Everyone knew it was their history but were too uneducated and wretched to own it. These are sources of the cultural nationalism that Hedgewar's long shadow, the RSS, not only draws on for inspiration but are also rejuvenating a popular interest amongst aspiring Indians.

Three weeks had passed, and with a recovering Hedgewar, the group decided it was time to return to Nagpur. They reached Nagpur on 20 April after spending several days meandering around visiting shakhas at Gaya, Kashi, Prayag and Jabalpur. Three days later, the OTC at Pune, which was to last twenty days, had started. For the first time, the military commands were all given in Sanskrit rather than English. Golwalkar's influence was beginning to tell. To this day, all over the world, where the Sangh has its reach, many instructions are given in Sanskrit. Often, the first time most swayamsevaks would have uttered Sanskrit terms is when barking out orders of *daksha* (attention) or *aarama* (at ease). Golwalkar's aim was to unify all Hindus through the 'mother of all languages', and this has largely worked, apart from Tamil-speaking regions.

Hedgewar reached the camp at Pune on 27 April, and although his health appeared to be better, he was largely an observer, silently taking it all in. Over 800 participants from over 100 different towns and villages were taking instruction. Even though Hedgewar was, on the whole, passive in action, his presence was felt everywhere. Everyone wanted to catch a glimpse of the Godfather, the man at the helm, the one who was going to do something extraordinary. Wherever Hedgewar went, folks were energized and wanted to put on a show. Hedgewar, in turn, made it a point to visit and speak with as many swayamsevaks as possible. In a hierarchical, caste-ridden society, Hedgewar was a breath of fresh air for many down the pecking order. Hedgewar oozed equity—both in presence and action. In a private note to Joshi, he commented that the daily shakha was having its due effect on the minds of swayamsevaks in so far as there was a distinct sense of self-confidence and a desire to further the mission.[20]

Although fragile in health, he managed to give four lectures, each an hour long, over the course of the training. Palkar, in his book, sums up the essence and themes covered in these talks, which revolved around cultural nationalism. Hedgewar made clear that Indians, on the whole, had to accept that it was their lack of 'Rashtriyata' that led to a vacuum of sorts in their collective consciousness—a complete lack of a common national identity. For Hedgewar, the entire Indian edifice was flawed because of this inherent problem. This, he said, could not be fixed by simply gaining independence and gaining control of the State apparatus. Newspapers and speeches could not solve such deep-rooted civilizational problems. The solution, he would iterate, was the individual who, in the first instance, had to discard his false consciousness and adopt cultural nationalism as the guiding principle upon which to lead his life—a life of personal development and growth. This individual glory and success had to be anchored in the overall aspirations of society. 'Society first' was the mantra he espoused. Taken by itself, this may seem antithetical to liberty and individualism, but then this would be straw manning Hedgewarian thought.

Popular tropes against Hedgewar and his creation often rest on the relationship between the individual and a fascist state, where the individual is sacrificed for the sake of the state or group. Another version of this is that the individual is important so long as the purpose of the state is being served. The individual has little to no intrinsic value. Both approaches to understanding Hedgewar and the RSS are wrong because this premise is wrong. Hedgewar was not a fascist, nor was he a cultural chauvinist. Nevertheless, some may rightly say that elements of the RSS in its one-hundred-year history have certainly been chauvinistic, if not fascist. Opponents often quote the RSS leadership as saying that 'India is a Hindu nation', or 'India's role in the world is that of a Vishwa Guru'—a world teacher, as examples of chauvinism.

Lao Tzu, the Daoist philosopher, might be able to help us out of the fly bottle when he writes:

> 'When we see beauty, then ugliness exists.
> High and low rest on each other.
> First and last follow each other.
> Heavy is the root of light.
> What is, and what is not create each other.'[21]

Much in the same way, for Hedgewar the truth of the world is that there is no individual without society, and vice versa. Both are complementary, and both help the other exist. A reductionist or an 'othering' framework will not do—it cannot be that the individual is in any way separate from society. Thatcher, much like Hedgewar, was poorly interpreted and misunderstood when she said in an interview in 1987,

> 'I think we have been through a period when too many people have been given to understand that when they have a problem it is government's job to cope with it. I have a problem; I'll get a grant. I'm homeless, the government must house me. They are casting their problems on society. And, you know, there is no such thing as society. There are individual men and women and there are families. And no governments can do anything except through people, and people must look to themselves first. It is our duty to look after ourselves and then, also, to look after our neighbours. People have got their entitlements too much in mind, without the obligations. There is no such thing as an entitlement unless someone has first met an obligation.'[22]

Hedgewar may not have used the same expression as Thatcher, but he certainly would have been in complete agreement with her sentiments. The RSS is a deeply individualistic organization, while concurrently being hell-bent on disciplining the individual into becoming socially orientated. Hedgewar's focus was on the individual to first, and foremost, fulfil her obligation towards society and nation, only then to secure individual rights.

To understand the Hedgewarian mind one must dissolve the subject-object relationship between the individual and society. Had Thatcher ever met him, she may have labelled him a progressive conservative.

Hedgewar also punctuated his speeches with the fact that the RSS had grown rapidly only due to the commitments made by every person. Each individual was important. Their personal commitment was the fuel that was driving this extraordinary growth.[23] He highlighted the need to give even more time to the work of nation-building, and how reading newspapers and rhetoric alone was not going to be enough. 'Action over words', is a mantra still very much in vogue within RSS circles. Hedgewar said as much in a speech later that year at a conclave of all active swayamsevaks held in a small school hall in Pune's Nutan Marathi Primary. In this speech, he urged his vanguard not to let a difference in ideology or viewpoints be the reason to 'other' anyone. Hedgewar spoke for sixty minutes, slowly, softly and with long pauses, probably caused by a combination of pain and thoughtfulness. He was more akin to a softly spoken pastor than the hot-blooded political agitator he had been most of his life. He spoke about the need to work together, collaboratively, patiently and with affection for people and the work. He called out organizations that actively worked to undermine the RSS, and still called them 'ours'.[24] 'A worker of the RSS', he said, 'ought not to work from a place of hatred'.[25] These words are probably lost on many amongst the RSS ranks in modern India, and yet they are as relevant as ever. The Sangh would do well to revitalize them.

He spoke at length about the need for character formation through playing games and why it was so central to the work of the RSS. Hedgewar understood more than most that character is formed in a child's early years. 'Only through games could so much be achieved', he stressed.[26] 'Our young need to be cared for, they need role models, and only through love and belonging can future generations form characters that are noble in spirit and upright in character'.[27] According to the Centre for Parenting Education, 'role models are people who influence others by serving as examples. They are often admired by the people who emulate them. Through their perceived personal qualities, behaviours, or achievements, they can inspire others to strive and develop without providing any direct instruction.'[28] Hedgewar elaborated on the necessity and honour of nurturing the next generation through love and care. Indian men of his day, and even today in large parts, felt emasculated by looking after and playing with young children in their daily shakhas instead of doing manly things like fighting, attending protests and being tough and burly. Many questioned why they were made to play games every morning at the shakha with small children and teenagers. Those who conducted the shakha were made aware of the power and importance of nurturing personalities through playing games. Nevertheless, the doubts were endless, and coordinators spent much of their time convincing newcomers and observers as to why the system was important.

It is interesting that in his final days, Hedgewar stressed such things to his growing cadre. To many at the time, including the likes of Nehru, Savarkar and, to a lesser degree, Moonjay, playing with children was simply a baffling way to channel the energy and time of so many young men. To maintain a wholesome atmosphere in the Sangh was Hedgewar's utmost priority. He knew, just as so many parenting coaches today stress, the magic of raising strong individuals who can navigate life and contribute meaningfully to society lies in their role models. The Sangh builds role models. This is the secret sauce of the Sangh and the entire shakha system. It was something that Golwalkar implicitly understood and would militantly focus on for forty years.

As the camp was approaching its zenith, on 11 May 1940, Vinayak Savarkar, Hedgewar's inspiration and the one who caused him constant consternation arrived. He had been invited to give the final speech at a gathering of the core leadership and its prachaaraks. The meeting had all but finished, where Hedgewar, along with his seniormost devoted actors, had already given the messages that they had intended. All that remained was the ceremonial final keynote speech. According to RSS hagiographies and folklore, Savarkar showered praise on their leader.

> 'The condition of the Hindu Rashtra is fragile. The RSS is our only hope. The Sangh is doing what great nations must do.... Organisation is the path to go from weakness to strength. Thus, please have complete faith in your leader. I have headed several agitations all my life. None of them fully succeeded. Hence, I wish to stress again that only this organisation can cause the resurgence of the Hindu Rashtra'.[29]

We can be fairly safe in our assumption that it would have been highly unlikely that these were Savarkar's actual words or, indeed, even a rephrasing of them. What he said at that meeting is lost. What we do know is that only a few months before, in November 1939, Savarkar and leaders of the Mahasabha directly attacked the RSS and Hedgewar personally for being 'neutral' on matters that were paramount to Hindu revitalization and ousting the British.[30] We also know that Savarkar had endlessly tried to use the RSS to become the ground force for the Hindu Mahasabha. Savarkar and Moonjay had tried on several occasions to launch their own 'paramilitary' outfit, one that was more akin to their own wishes and whims. Nothing had worked. The RSS, and Hedgewar in particular, was nothing but a source of frustration. That is not to say that the two men did not respect one another. Nor did any man doubt the intent of the other. It was their methodologies that were the source of their friction.

Whatever was said is lost. The fact that Hedgewar, even after all the angst between the two men, had invited Savarkar to give the concluding remarks at the most important RSS meeting of the year shows two things: first, the immense respect they held for one another, and second, that Hedgewar was constantly trying to find the balance between staying close to the Hindu Mahasabha, while simultaneously keeping a healthy distance. This technique is something the RSS still applies. Any religious, political or social leader that is to be respected and engaged but kept at an arms distance, or to be brought closer due to their pre-existing distance, is invited to give keynotes at major Sangh gatherings. The leader is given all the pomp and ceremony they require, while ordinary swayamsevaks sit on the floor in straight lines, earnestly listening and thinking that the leader in front has all but endorsed their work. It becomes a win-win for all concerned. This was ultimately an attempt by Hedgewar to end what Sampath calls a fratricidal animosity.[31]

The next day, on 12 May, after Golwalkar had completed his speech as Chief Coordinator, Hedgewar was given two hours to speak. He spoke at the Nutan Marathi Vidyalay, one of the oldest schools in Pune, founded in 1883.[32] The auditorium would have been full, with people standing and sitting wherever they could find space. Hundreds of invitees had packed into the auditorium. Hedgewar spoke slowly and remained seated. People could see that he was clearly unwell. Joshi remained by his side throughout. Golwalkar sat on the podium next to him. This was a speech not meant for public consumption, but rather for RSS cadres and its leadership.

Hedgewar's penultimate speech, unbeknown to him at the time, reveals the deepest aspects of his philosophy about the methodology of the Sangh. He would have simultaneously been speaking to his cadre at one end and to Golwalkar and his prachaaraks at the other. His principal thrust remained on the character development of every individual while simultaneously focusing on the need to work with and bring onboard the entire spectrum of society for the purposes of nation-building. At the root of his message was compassion. He urged his swayamsevaks to work with an affection for all those around them, especially those who were of different mind, thought and ambition. He called for the need to recognize that all those who work with and for the Congress, the communists and the Hindu Mahasabha are all 'our own'.[33] He spoke at length about why all forms of hatred have no place in the minds and hearts of swayamsevaks. Having a different opinion or a political viewpoint does not mean we should not work together. He pushed further, 'The Sangh is not only to work with people who agree with us, but we must work closely with those that do not see the world as we do'.[34] Hedgewar spent some time focusing on the relationship between the strength of an organization and how the public-at-large feels about the organization.[35]

The latest person to hold the position Hedgewar once held is Mohan Bhagwat, who in 2022 expanded the same philosophy in a speech in which he said, 'there is no need to look for a Shivling in every mosque,' referring to the call by the extreme right Hindu lobby for all mosques built on destroyed Hindu temples to be given back.[36] Bhagwat has also publicly called Muslims part and parcel of Indian society.[37] The RSS leadership still attempts to quietly work with all those who differ with it in mood and spirit. Across modern India, once hardliners of the Communist Party are now turning towards the RSS for a multitude of reasons, but the underlying cause is the RSS's spirit of absorbing a wide spectrum of ideas and personalities into its mission of nation-building.[38] The RSS is vehemently against identity politics and political tribalism—a statement that may bring many commentators to snigger and raise an eyebrow or two. The popular narrative over decades has been exactly the opposite, that the RSS is fundamentally divisive and tribal. Academics the world over have narrated that the RSS has been divisive and that many of its members are inherently chauvinistic and demonstrate a fascist tendency. This may well be the case at various points in its one-hundred-year history, and certainly, one can find chauvinistic individuals as part of the organization, but the latent or inherent philosophy of the RSS, articulated, as well as demonstrated by Hedgewar, is one of encompassing a broad church of ideas, temperaments and backgrounds, all underpinned by the single desire for nation-building.

According to Palkar, Hedgewar, in the same speech, made it clear that 'our work is not reactionary. We are not organizing to battle or to defeat anyone. We do not organize because of the existence of threats, but rather we organize so that threats may never come into existence.'[39] If there was a line that sums up the RSS attitude to challenges it is this one. The RSS behaves as it does because it is the vanguard of modern India. It was designed from the off to fulfil that role. In many respects, it has succeeded. Those who would like to see India in any other form than its civilizational one would need to confront and defeat the Sangh first. Arguably, Nehru's Congress has been trying to do exactly that, but it continues to fail.

The next day Hedgewar had arranged to return to Nagpur where the next OTC camp was due to commence. Upon leaving Pune, he asked the local head of the Sangh to organize a full-blown inspection of the shakha in uniform at the train station just before his departure. Two long lines of 100 swayamsevaks lined up in full uniform. Hedgewar choreographed the scene for himself to walk in between the column of men to his carriage. Upon entering his carriage, Hedgewar turned, raised his cane and mustered just enough energy to give a final farewell to his unit in Pune. That would be the last time he would see any of them.

Upon entering the carriage, the train soon left the station. An exhausted Hedgewar fell into his seat and into a deep slumber. It is worth contemplating what exactly Hedgewar was trying to achieve by holding such performances in public spaces. For any bystander, it would have seen a sight to behold. Only royalty or some British, white-skinned General would have got such an honorary send-off. Here was what appeared to be the military or the police, sending off an Indian man who was in civilian clothing. Who was he? He must be important! He must be powerful! On closer inspection, people would have noticed that this had nothing to do with the British military, because all the orders were barked out in Sanskrit. Was this an indigenous army being formed? How do I find out about it? How do I join it? How do I become as confident and stout as these young men in full uniform? It would have been a sight that would have captured the Indian imagination. A stooge or a real police officer looking at the spectacle would have immediately reported it. Intimidating would be how many police constables described the early Sangh. There is little doubt left as to why, only two years later (1942), the British Secret Police wrote a report for the highest authorities of the Raj about the RSS.

In this secret report, Hedgewar's RSS is described in the following manner:

> '...regard the Rashtriya Swayam Sevak Sangh as a harbourage of considerable potential danger. Alliance with the Hindu Maha Sabha, extending in degree to the latter's control, is not doubted, although this has not been proved. The Sangh has been described as the Hindu answer to the Khasksars; it is anti-British; it has shown signs of pro-Japanese bias; in its organisation and behaviour Fascist tendencies are obvious.
>
> Provinces are concerned about the rapid increase in the strength of the Sangh. There is no doubt of its growing appeal to Hindu youth, but the reasons for this are not clearly defined in what is known regarding the organisation. So far, the Sangh has not provoked authority, indeed the impression clings that it has been careful to avoid conflict. It is felt that the true purpose of its being lies in the future and that the revelation will be to the accompaniment of disorder.'[40]

The report spells out each member of the Sangh leadership and provides an insight into the contents of their speeches given at an OTC held in Pune in 1942. The description of the Sangh as 'a harbourage of considerable potential danger' is telling. The Sangh is clearly a paramilitary force, but to whom does it pose a threat? The answer is the British State, the authors of the report. For any state to function and maintain a semblance of law and order, violence must be monopolized by the state's apparatus. Here was an organization that was clearly capable of wielding significant force but had not done so to date. Everyone at this time was on a war footing, and it is quite understandable that the authorities were on edge with regards to any movement that was against British rule and could wield deadly force. Furthermore, the fear was also made explicit that this organization was gathering strength for some moment in the future. At this unknown moment it could unleash its true purpose with the 'accompaniment of disorder'. The authorities were not too wrong on the whole.

The RSS was not plucking up to fight the British; indeed, that would have been a poor use of its strength. Rather, it was gearing up for any eventuality where it would be called upon to protect the Hindu society from any external or internal new threat, such as the Khaskars or a newly formed Pakistan. In 1940, Hedgewar was clearly demonstrating this latent force through performances in public spaces. He created rituals where guards of honour and victory parades with thousands of men in uniform would dazzle the lay public. These were all performances to inspire one's own, while instilling caution and fear in the other. Almost eighty-five years later, these performances still go on in India.

Much is now made of the men dressed in funny-looking shorts and black caps, holding bamboo sticks and marching in unison. When the West gazes at these performances, they see an arcane bygone past that brought nothing but suffering and war to Europe. They see images of Mussolini's Opera Nazionale Balilla and Hitler's Nazi Youth. Most Indians are completely oblivious to this European history and how it seeped into the Indian nationalist imagination during the struggle. In this regard, Hedgewar was evidently not just all about desh bhakti; there was also a far more sophisticated sense of showmanship in him. He was acutely aware of the kind of performances required to nudge both the masses and the authorities to believe what he wanted them to believe. As the Indian state has matured and increasingly swung towards a civilizational footing since 2014, these performances have become benign and are now more for show. In Hedgewar's Sangh, these performances were more potent.

The image he was creating of the Sangh was having its due effect. People from as far away as Bengal would travel into Nagpur to see him for a few brief hours to request that he create RSS shakhas in their district or town. One such case was Dr Shyama Prasad Mukherjee, who was a Congressman and a member of the Savarkar–Moonjay Hindu Mahasabha. He went on to become a member of Nehru's first cabinet in Independent India. He was of elite stock. The son of a high court judge and a medical doctor. He, too, was highly educated, well-to-do and immensely influential in Bengal. He had come to see Hedgewar to inform him of the 'calamity' that was unfolding there and requested that the RSS prioritize Bengal. Mukherjee had been spooked by the elections of 1937, three years earlier, when suddenly large swathes of constituencies in East Bengal came to be represented by Muslims. Even though the largest party was the Indian National Congress, with fifty-four seats out of 250, Gandhi essentially refused to form the government.[41]

Why was this such a calamity for Mukherjee? The answer lies in understanding the complex relationship between class, caste and religion.

Historically, the British ruled at the end of a bayonet and deputized upper caste land-owning Hindus to administer the state. A few sections of the Hindu community were rich and educated. They owned the lion's share of land. Vast numbers of low-caste Hindus, and those who had converted to Islam over hundreds of years to escape the drudgery of caste, found themselves electing many members from their own communities.[42] The democratic process effectively brought to the surface the underlying rifts in Bengali society. It was not just about Hindu versus Muslim. It was equally about rich versus poor, landowners versus landless. It was also about envy and a time for retribution.

As Mukherjee narrated his tale of woes, Hedgewar listened quietly and in considerable pain. Mukherjee asked Hedgewar to allow the RSS to enter Bengali politics. Next to him sat Golwalkar and Joshi, also patiently listening and keeping half an eye on Hedgewar. Upon hearing Mukherjee's request, Hedgewar was categorical in his response—'No!'[43] Even though a lot is made out in the RSS hagiographies about the plight of the Hindus in Bengal after 1937, the reality is something altogether different and far more complex. Hedgewar was no fool. He was aware of the decrepit state of Hindus in Bengal under the existing jajmani system. It was a system of exploitation of the poor landless labourers. He also knew that it had to be elite Hindus who led the charge in the very reform that would undermine their self-interest for the betterment of the nation. He was acutely aware that Gandhi had just inadvertently handed Bengal over to a separatist by the name of Fazlul Haq. Haq was known to Hedgewar. Both had been in the Congress around the same time. Haq was a socialist and wanted to desperately reform the land act, empowering the landless poor, while curtailing the power of the Hindu zamindars. Ultimately, he knew that if he played his cards right, he would be able to get a mandate from the Muslim majority in East Bengal to break away from India and join a future Pakistan.

Hedgewar slowly and patiently told Mukherjee the RSS way. 'The problem with Bengal, Punjab and every other part of India is that the Hindu majority are poor, riddled with caste consciousness, uneducated, exploited and without any sense of nationhood. Consequently, they are disorganized.'[44] An increasingly disappointed Mukherjee was then told, ' . . . so long as the root cause is not dealt with, no reactionary solution will work.'[45] Even with a dampened mood, Mukherjee was taken in by what Hedgewar said. The solution Hedgewar suggested was compelling.

Hedgewar told Mukherjee, 'Wholesale rejection and annihilation of caste! Once Hindus reject caste, only then a greater consciousness of fraternity and equality could arise wrapped in a sense of nationhood.'[46] This was the essence of the Hedgewarian notion of desh bhakti.

Mukherjee soon left, but not with the outcome he had wanted; yet something in him had shifted. Not long after, Mukherjee would dedicate himself to understanding the Sangh better and would become a lifelong admirer and defender of the movement. He grew close to Golwalkar, who in turn quietly encouraged him to start a Hindu party in independent India called the Jana Sangh (People's Community/Party), which was the precursor to the modern Bharatiya Janta Party (BJP), the world's largest and most successful political outfit in the twenty-first century. Hedgewarian seeds have become entire epistemological forests with their own biodiversity of theories that are driving modern Indian discourse.

The OTC in Nagpur had started. Two weeks in, and Hedgewar was still too unwell to visit. His health was in serious decline. Fevers ran as high as 40 degrees Celsius; he was effectively incapable of doing anything by himself. He continuously shivered, sweated and, at times, became delusional. His head throbbed endlessly. Usually, in healthy adults, if a fever such as this runs for three days, they are told to rush to hospital. Hedgewar had this for over two weeks. Doctors came and went. Nothing seemed to work. At one level, Hedgewar was barely lucid and was bedridden for most of his days. On the occasional day when his fever would subside and open a window of clarity, Hedgewar would complain about not being at the OTC. However, the doctors would not allow him to leave the house. Those who attended the OTC would sneakily disobey orders and rush over at any opportunity to get a glimpse of the Godfather. Many were reprimanded, but Hedgewar would insist on leniency, 'it is after all not their fault that I am unwell and unable to speak with them', he would say.[47] When Hedgewar was unwell, everyone worried; when he was somewhat cognisant, he was stubborn and almost petulant in his behaviour. He was insisting on meeting his swayamsevaks.[48] Eventually, Golwalkar caved in. He arranged for a private gathering of all the participants who had attended the third year of the OTC. These individuals were the ones who were deemed to be most dedicated, and many of them were potential prachaaraks.

Hedgewar was finally allowed to leave the confines of his room. He was brought over to the venue where almost 1000 hardened swayamsevaks gathered, many of them delaying their return home. After listening to a few first-hand experiences from those who completed the gruelling forty-day camp, Hedgewar was invited to speak, sitting on a chair, with microphones brought in especially for him. His final speech, short as it was, was written in full and can be found in many of the hagiographies of the Sangh. His core message was one of fraternity and the inner quality of an RSS swayamsevak—nothing that he hadn't said a million times before. But sprinkled into this speech were further glimpses into the Hedgewarian mind. In a sunken tone, he told his audience that 'the final redemption of the Hindu society will happen only through the Sangh'.[49] Hedgewar was making it clear as to what he thought was the final aim of the Sangh—to improve and revitalize the Hindu society. To what end, one might well ask. 'With all your efforts, Sangh will rapidly expand its work, and a day will come when the entirety of Bharat will appear to be one with us.'[50]

Many commentators have interpreted this line with the presumption that Hedgewar was essentially a fascist. This line is often referenced to show the ultimate goal of the Sangh—namely, to take over the state and assert its will upon the nation. The oneness Hedgewar refers to is not of a fascist takeover, where individual interests are subordinated to the perceived good of the nation, led by a dictator and a natural social hierarchy. These are all the things that would sum up a 1984 dystopia. This is not how Hedgewar lived. Even though he continuously used a language that was steeped in anti-colonial rhetoric often inspired by revolutionary fascist movements in Europe, he never believed in a social hierarchy, nor did he believe that the individual was to be sacrificed for the betterment of some greater good. Rather, it seems that Hedgewar wanted to empower the individual, to form stronger bonds of kinship and ultimately to serve one's neighbour. Indeed, Hedgewar was criticized constantly by Hindu fascists and the Hindu ultra-right. The RSS was too soft, not revolutionary enough, nor radical enough—he even lost some of his best men because they refused to toe the milder, middle way that Hedgewar insisted on. In all probability Hedgewar may have simply meant that a time would come when the Indian public would not only be sympathetic towards the RSS, but agree with its ultimate aim—rashtriyata.

Soon after the speech, Hedgewar was taken to Mayo Hospital in Nagpur, a premier medical institute of its time. Doctors gave him a complete once-over and took X-rays to ascertain the root cause of his pains. Nothing was revealed. Painkillers were prescribed, and Hedgewar was insistent on returning home. A wealthy friend, benefactor and staunch supporter of the RSS, a man named Babasaheb Ghatate, insisted that Hedgewar be sent to his home, where there was more space, better facilities and cleaner conditions. Hedgewar obliged. His pain, however, only increased. He remained restless. He had poor sleep, continuous headaches and relentless back pain. He was neither able to sit, sleep or walk. On the darkest nights, he would be delirious and would mutter a random, incoherent jumble of words and sentences. Occasionally, according to Palkar, who interviewed Joshi, who was there throughout trying to take care of Hedgewar, the broken, but much respected head of the RSS would reveal his inner fears. 'We are at war, and yet we are not ready,' Hedgewar would mutter.[51]

By 12 June, in a letter Golwalkar wrote to Mukherjee, he wrote, 'Doctor ji's health is deteriorating rapidly. He cannot focus on any issue at this time, and it is impossible for us to contemplate on any important matters right now.'[52] This tells us that Hedgewar's illness had reached its zenith. Seven days later, around 19 June, a night that Hedgewar did not sleep and was in insufferable pain, was when Subhas Chandra Bose was in town. On the 20th, he arrived at the house unannounced. Hedgewar was fleeting in and out of consciousness, and it was difficult to tell if he was asleep or simply unconscious. Bose had come especially to see him. A year before, he had wanted to meet in Mumbai, but Hedgewar politely declined to meet, giving his health as a reason. Bose was in Nagpur for the first convention of his new Forward Bloc, a hard fascist communist movement—yet another breakaway from the Congress. As Bose entered the room, he found Hedgewar still, eyes closed, clearly unwell. Joshi was sat in a chair by his bedside. After a few minutes and some polite conversation, Bose left. According to Joshi's testimony, after a few moments, Hedgewar awoke, but Bose had already left.

Subhas Chandra Bose and Hedgewar never met. Six months later, in January 1941, Bose would escape house arrest and flee to Manchuria, China, heading towards the Soviet Union. Bose went on to lead what became known as the Indian National Army (INA) in 1943, a collection of captured British Indian soldiers who were returned to Bose's custody to fight against the British under Japanese command. The INA, as is the popular belief, was not actually founded by Bose but by a man named Mohan Singh, who had managed to convince the Japanese to release captured Indian soldiers into his care. At its peak, Bose led 3,50,000 men and women, composed of trained soldiers and volunteers, into battle. The Japanese provided arms and munitions for the INA. The plan was ultimately to take back Delhi, entering through the east from the Burmese border.

Since Bose and Hedgewar never actually met, we can only conjecture what the purpose of Bose's visit may have been. We can fathom a guess. Bose, in all probability, wanted the RSS to rise and attack British positions while the INA would attack the British forces from the east. An uprising in the interior and a fighting force from without would give the best chances to defeat the British forces and free India. According to some historians, the INA was never able to defeat the British due to their lack of equipment and formal training.[53] But we already know that Hedgewar, in all likeliness, would have never entertained such an idea.

Later that evening, Hedgewar's blood pressure became dangerously high. He was suffering from idiopathic intracranial hypertension. A doctor by the name of Hardas suggested that there was no option but to try a lumbar puncture in the hope of removing some of the excess fluid from the spine to help reduce pressure on the brain. Reading Hardas's face, Hedgewar realized the seriousness of what was being proposed. After a few moments to reflect, he called in Golwalkar and some of his other captains. In a soft tone, he told Golwalkar to take over the Sangh if he failed to recover from this procedure. A somewhat shocked Golwalkar quietly took a seat at the side of the bed.

Three experienced doctors were present to perform the procedure. Dr Hardas led the way, supported by a slightly older balding man named Dr Cholkar and a Dr Tatwavadi, who wore thick rounded spectacles and was the youngest of the three. Hedgewar lay on his front topless. The three men gathered around him, murmuring words that were only audible to them. The room, with its high ceilings, wooden beams and dimly lit walls, suddenly became much smaller for Joshi as he stood watching the doctors plan the incision. The procedure lasted only a few minutes but felt like an agonizing eternity. The pain was so excruciating for Hedgewar that Golwalkar remembers he ground his teeth so hard and clutched his face, trying to suppress his agony. A sharp, tight pain would have shot through Hedgewar's legs as the needle touched his nerves in the spine. With little to no anaesthetic given, the pain would have been unbearable. After a few minutes, the ordeal was over, and plenty of fluid was removed. Yet, the high blood pressure remained. In their desperation, the doctors decided to take blood, thereby releasing the pressure on the brain. This too didn't work. Hedgewar was exhausted. He fell into an unconscious state.

By two in the early hours, Hedgewar was not getting better. His blood pressure was still too high. He remained mostly unconscious, breathing heavily. By early morning, as the sun rose, Hedgewar's grimacing face had relaxed. The doctors concluded the end was near, because he remained unconscious and had a dangerously high blood pressure. After a momentary silence in the room, Golwalkar quietly but authoritatively asked Joshi to make the calls to get the leadership of the Sangh over to the house immediately. By nine that morning, the key leadership who were in Nagpur had assembled. Outside the house swayamsevaks and friends began to gather under a grey sky. After a warm night, the morning was surprisingly cool. People stood in quiet whispers. Anxious. Waiting. Everyone kept an eye on Hedgewar, a man who had changed the life of every man in that room. Then, at nine twenty-five in the morning, Hedgewar's head fell to the side, and two minutes later, he stopped breathing.

EIGHTEEN

Postscript: Long Shadow

'He was soon borne away by the waves and lost in darkness and distance.'[1]

Hedgewar was dead. The large airy room must have suddenly felt much smaller. With both palms clasped, and a bowed head, Golwalkar led the small silent group in prayer. After a few deep breadths he opened his eyes, looked at Parmanand Joshi and instructed him to put into action the plan. Joshi and Dani both left the room and actioned what they had sat down and planned a few weeks earlier should Hedgewar die. In no time at all, the key people were informed by telegram. Dani briefed a few swayamsevaks to rush over to Reshimbag, a private garden and grounds, to arrange Hedgewar's final rites and cremation. It was to be held that same day. Reshimbag was almost five kilometres away, and a good twenty-minute bike ride. After some initial back-and-forth with the local authorities, the permissions for the grounds were secured for the funeral. Several local schools gave permission for young swayamsevaks to take the day off to attend Hedgewar's final rites. Local shakha coordinators across the Vidarbha district were informed, and as per the plan, hundreds of swayamsevaks and well-wishers started their journey to pay homage to their godfather.

Within hours, hundreds of men and women had gathered outside Ghatate's house. People waited to line the Dharampeth Road, a leafy suburb of Nagpur, with anxious expectation for further news. Hedgewar's brother and uncle had both arrived in the early hours and sat across the bed where Hedgewar's broken body lay. Flowers were placed at his feet. Moonjay was informed, who was in Nasik at the time, almost six-hundred and fifty kilometres away. His telegram read, 'Doctor ji's untimely death has been a great setback. His demise is a national calamity.'[2] Vinayak Savarkar, too, soon after sent a telegram. It read, 'Doctor Hedgewar is no more. May Hedgewar be immortal. Hedgewar is no more. May Sangh be immortal.'[3]

By three in the afternoon, the greying sky had caved in, and a heavy downpour drenched the crowds. The procession was planned for five o'clock and would take over two hours to reach the designated cremation grounds. The route would start at Dharampeth, where Golwalkar would lead the procession alongside Sitaram, his wife and another relative, the patriarch of the Hedgewar family, a man named Tatya. On either side of the casket walked Joshi and Dani, orchestrating the procession. A select honour guard was assigned to carry the makeshift wooden casket, and swayamsevaks would take turns in carrying Hedgewar's heavy frame. Those involved in the procession were in uniform, with prachaaraks in white clothing. Just before the procession was to begin, the rain eased off and soon stopped altogether. The clouds dispersed and a weak sun broke through. Along the route the wealthy laid floral wreaths, while the common man and woman threw petals as the casket passed, and the poor simply said a prayer. Thousands made their way to Reshimbag. The Bhagwa Dhwaj fluttered in front of the procession, held high by a young swayamsevak. At the grounds the pyre was readied with scented oils and hundreds of incense sticks. Thousands of men and women sang the Sangh prarthna in an echoey ground. Their collective voice carried much further than the confines of the grounds. Tatya, the old Hedgewar, lit the pyre, as Golwalkar stood just behind him, and quietly watched the flames grow and dance in the mild-mannered wind. The sun was setting. By the time the flames had truly taken to the pyre, it was dusk, and in the quiet of a darkening sky the RSS leadership watched on as their Godfather, their mentor and inspiration journeyed into the hereafter.

As the minutes and hours passed, people gradually left Reshimbag. As they departed, people were sure to pay due respect to Golwalkar, a new godfather, the man at the helm. Only the inner core of the Sangh and the select honour guard were left to watch the night consume a day marked by sadness, and above all uncertainty. It was for Golwalkar and his order of prachaaraks to steer the Sangh through this uncertainty. At this time, the RSS was still somewhat fragile, with only semi-formed roots. It was Hedgewar's will that secured the RSS externally, and its cohesion internally. He was now gone. For Golwalkar, who was only thirty-five years old, and looked more akin to a medicant than the godfather, the future would have looked daunting. He contemplated on the immediate challenges that he was going to face from within, and from without.

Golwalkar would remain as head of the RSS until his death in June 1973, totalling thirty-three years at its helm. In this time, he would rudder Hedgewar's creation to new vistas and reorientate the entire organization. Golwalkar may have looked like a renunciate, but he marshalled the RSS much like a General. Under his leadership, the RSS ballooned in size and influence. He reorganized the Sangh and disbanded the military units much to the disgust of many senior RSS swayamsevaks.[4] He openly advocated for Hindus to not fret about independence, and rather called for reform of the Hindu society from within, and to be wary of internal threats.[5] He would inspire thousands of young men to become prachaaraks and in an attempt to consolidate his position within the Sangh, he took the power of the local Sangh chalaks (local Presidents) away by creating a new post of Pranth prachaaraks in their stead. In the early days of his leadership, many senior experienced workers and prachaaraks quit—they were confused by Golwalkar and his intentions. He severed all ties with Savarkar and the Hindu Mahasabha.[6] The extreme right, bigoted side of the Sangh would split from the main core and form other militant organizations such as the one Nathuram Godse created: the Hindu Rashtra Dal in 1943 and would be responsible for the assassination of Gandhi in 1948.[7]

Between India's independence in 1947, and 1955, the RSS, although still relatively small, was deeply involved in shaping a newly formed India. Golwalkar was late to the realization that partition would eventually happen, but his prachaaraks in the Punjab and Sindh were some of the first to realize that violence was about to erupt. The RSS went onto play a significant role in humanitarian efforts to support the stranded Sikh and Hindu communities throughout the regions that later became Pakistan.[8] Most historians agree that around 1,000,000 people died, and over 14,000,000 were displaced during partition.[9] All types of people, rich and poor, Muslim and Hindu, upper caste and lower caste—all lost their lands, properties, and ancestral homes with the swift pen of a few British bureaucrats who had been instructed to leave India permanently with a deal or no deal by June 1948.[10] Instead 'the master of disaster', Lord Mountbatten, popularly known as Dickie, a naval officer was put in charge of the negotiations, who in his haste to please the folks back home, sped up the process without really understanding the context or the magnitude of his decisions.[11] Nehru, too, along with the entire Congress leadership, was blindsided by the violence that ensued.

Soon after Gandhi's assassination in 1948, the Congress leadership, would use the opportunity to clip the wings of the RSS. Although found not guilty by multiple courts and rulings, Golwalkar and the RSS were only allowed to operate after having pledged allegiance to the constitution of India. The Sangh would continue to have a problem with the tricolour of India for decades hence and felt that the real representation of the civilizational nation lay in the words Bharat, and the Bhagwa Dhwaj (saffron flag). The Indian State continued to fear and loathe the RSS in equal measure for decades, and seldom trusted Golwalkar and his prachaarak order.

In 1954, RSS swayamsevaks led a battle that liberated Dadra, Nagar Haveli and Daman from Portuguese rule, which had endured since 1783. Acts of such valour endeared the RSS to many Indians, while unsettling politicians, intensifying their efforts to curb the RSS's ability to challenge the state's monopoly on force. Throughout this period, Jawaharlal Nehru, until his death in 1964, harboured concerns about the RSS's leader—a lean, bearded science graduate who asserted India's primacy as a Hindu nation since as early as 1938. In hindsight, it becomes evident that Golwalkar differed significantly from Hedgewar. While Golwalkar excelled in organizational prowess and expanded the RSS into a cohesive national force, his occasionally myopic viewpoints, as exemplified in controversial statements, painted him as a perceived zealot and ideological risk to modern India. However, these statements were later revealed to be a misattributed translation of Ganesh Savarkar's work, '*Rashtra Meemansa*', which Golwalkar had translated for internal discussions among swayamsevaks without initially crediting Savarkar.

Upon Golwalkar's passing in 1973, Madhukar Dattatraya Deoras, also known as Balasaheb, assumed leadership. Despite philosophical differences with Golwalkar, both leaders adhered to the prachaarak order's oaths, underscoring their commitment to Hedgewar's vision. Shortly thereafter, in June 1975, Indira Gandhi declared a national emergency, suspending democracy and banning the RSS. It was under Deoras's leadership that the RSS mobilized to resist authoritarianism and restore democratic norms, a movement in which figures like Narendra Modi, then a prachaarak, played pivotal roles, covertly organizing and mobilizing the RSS network.

Contrary to misconceptions, the RSS transcends rigid ideologies, lacking a formal economic, political or theological doctrine. Instead, it navigates societal shifts, oscillating between spiritual introspection and progressive reform, advocating both free-market principles and state intervention as circumstances dictate. Its decentralized structure comprises autonomous shakhas, each responding independently to local needs while unified by a shared commitment to the saffron flag and the principles of the prachaarak order, originally envisioned by Hedgewar and adapted over decades.

Engaging with the RSS transcends mere political discourse—it necessitates a nuanced understanding of its historical evolution, organizational ethos and societal contributions. As India continues to evolve, the RSS stands as a testament whether one likes it, or not, to resilience, adaptability and a call for inclusive dialogue and collaborative action toward a prosperous India.

All of this spawns out of Hedgewar's genius.

In the labyrinthine complexities of India's societal fabric, one cannot overlook the RSS, an entity as vast and influential as the land it calls home. Revered by some, contentious to others, the RSS transcends mere ideology; it embodies a formidable force shaping India's socio-political landscape. In the pursuit of India's flourishing, the RSS emerges as an undeniable protagonist. Its grassroots influence spans communities, echoing through temples and town squares alike. To ignore the RSS is to turn a blind eye to the pulse of millions who find solace in its cultural ethos and organizational prowess. For India to stride confidently into its future, understanding and engaging with the RSS becomes imperative. While opinions on the RSS may diverge sharply, its footprint in India is indelible. From social initiatives to educational outreach, the RSS leaves an imprint that cannot be erased. Its commitment to nation-building, though debated in approach, resonates deeply with those who see it as a guardian of traditional values and a bulwark against perceived threats.

To envision a thriving India demands a nuanced dialogue—one that confronts complexities with empathy and engages divergent perspectives with openness. Whether viewed as a stabilizing force or a polarizing entity, the RSS compels attention, its sway extending beyond political rhetoric to the very heartbeats of communities across India. For each stakeholder in India's future, be it citizen, scholar or statesman, embracing the challenge of engaging with the RSS is a call to navigate through differences towards a shared understanding. In this diverse tapestry of beliefs and aspirations, the RSS occupies a pivotal role, urging us to transcend biases and forge paths of mutual respect and dialogue.

Thus, as India continues its journey of evolution and growth, acknowledging and engaging with the RSS emerges not merely as a choice, but as an imperative for fostering inclusive progress. In this pursuit, each of us, regardless of personal inclination, must heed the call to comprehend and engage with the RSS—because India's flourishing demands nothing less than a collective embrace of its intricate realities.

The RSS makes a million decisions daily, and every decision will divide. While the RSS has always claimed it is for unity, it knows that its very essence is divisive. It is the raw nature of leadership that it confronts. It is at the epicentre of everything. To know modern India, one must get a handle on the RSS; and to do that, one must start at the source—Hedgewar.

The Unseen Architect

In Nagpur's dawn, where shadows grew,
A steadfast soul the morning knew.
Orphaned young, yet burning bright,
He walked the path from dark to light.

Through nights of toil, through silent strife,
He shaped a creed, devoted life.
A scholar's mind, a rebel's flame,
He rose, though few would know his name.

With dharma's torch, he lit the way,
Where fractured hopes in silence lay.
To bind the land, he laid his plan,
A vision vast, a humble man.

Through sacrifice, his truth took hold,
A tale of courage, yet untold.
No crown he wore, no wealth he gained,
Yet in his cause, pure faith remained.

But time moves fast, and visions wane,
When roots grow weak beneath the strain.
A century nears, its judgment cast—
Will dreams hold firm or fade at last?

To every soul who calls this home,
The future rests in hands alone.
Revisit him, his words, his fire,
Or watch his legacy expire.

If duty wanes, the roots will fall,
His house will crumble, lose it all.
Yet steadfast hearts his flame sustain,
To guard his truth through loss and pain.

Through steadfast hearts, his dream takes flight,
A flame sustained in darkest night.
So hold his vision, fierce and high,
Or watch it falter, dim, and die.

Acknowledgements

To begin with, I must confess that my perpetual complaints about the quality of RSS literature in English—filled with hyperbole and lacking depth—somehow reached the RSS leadership. Imagine my surprise when I was summoned by Dr Ram Vaidya, a prachaarak of the RSS, who threw down the gauntlet and challenged me to write something better. With no access or resources, I naturally balked. Yet, in a twist straight out of a Bollywood thriller, Dr Vaidya promised me access to the private archives in Nagpur, India. I was stunned and sceptical. Who, outside the organization, had ever been granted such privilege? Yet, a few months later, there I was, meeting the keeper of the archives, Milind Oak.

Milind was a rock of support during those first three years of archival research and translation. His patience, kindness and openness made the whole process not only tolerable but enjoyable. He was a sage in the dusty halls of history, guiding me through the labyrinthine records with an ease that belied the complexity of the task.

Dr Ram Vaidya, my silent sentinel, deserves immense gratitude. His presence was a constant, his involvement subtle yet profound. He granted me complete freedom to explore, question and navigate through the streams of historical clues that led to the answers I sought. Remarkably, he never once objected to my analysis, even when I adopted a critical tone or humanized Hedgewar to a degree that might have made many RSS members uncomfortable.

Drishti Mae, my pillar of support, was always there, urging me to push on, especially during the dark and opaque moments. She delighted in correcting my grammar with a glee that was both endearing and exasperating. Her insights helped shape the mood and overarching message of this book. She witnessed my transformation from a sceptic to an ardent admirer of Hedgewar's legacy, her confidence in me unwavering.

Hinesh Shah, a true scholar and friend, deserves heartfelt thanks. He meticulously read every word, corrected every diacritic and sorted out my references with the precision of a master craftsman. His deep knowledge of Islamic history and languages was invaluable in understanding the seismic shifts after World War II.

The late Dr Anil Nene, a journalist, poet and dear friend, tirelessly translated the entire Palkar biography of Hedgewar from Marathi into English. His efforts were pivotal in shaping this book, and it is a bittersweet reality that he will not witness its launch. His contribution was immeasurable.

Premanka Goswami at Penguin Books deserves a special mention for nursing a fledgling author through the tumultuous publishing journey. His trust and recognition of Hedgewar's significance for modern India ensured this book saw the light of day.

Ravi Mishra, the director at the Nehru Memorial Museum and Library in Delhi, was instrumental in providing access to microfilms on Hedgewar, shedding light on his inner life. His assistance was crucial.

Lastly, to my family, who sacrificed too much. They saw little of me for eight years, as I was ensconced in writing, reading or playing detective. Yet, without a hint of irritation or lack of support, they let me get on with it, proving that patience and love are indeed virtues in abundance in our household.

Please forgive me if I have not mentioned anyone who has helped in some shape or form in making this biography possible. Thank you all for making this journey not just possible but profoundly enriching.

Notes

Introduction

1 *prachaaraks* and *prachaarikas* are the men and women who dedicate themselves in spreading the work of the RSS with missionary zeal across India and beyond.

2 Christophe Jaffrelot, *The Hindu Nationalist Movement in India*, Columbia University Press, 1996, New York, p.51

3 Prabhat Patnaik, 'Fascism of Our Times', *Social Scientist*, Issue 21 (3/4), p. 69–77.

4 Rudyard Kipling, *The Disciple*, Limits and Renewals, 1932

5 Winston Churchill, "The Russian Enigma," BBC Radio Broadcast, October 1, 1939, accessed January 18, 2025, https://winstonchurchill.org/resources/quotes/russia-2/.

Chapter 1: Roots

1 H. V. Seshadri, *Dr Hedgewar, The Epoch-Maker*, Sahitya Sindhu, Bangalore, 1981

2 J. D. B Gribble, *History of the Deccan*, Rupa Publications India, 2002.

3 In Sanskrit, the term Śāstrī (शास्त्री) is derived from 'śāstra' (शास्त्र), meaning "sacred or authoritative book," combined with the suffix "-ī," indicating a person associated with or proficient in a particular field. Therefore, "Śāstrī" refers to a scholar or teacher well-versed in the śāstras, encompassing various fields of knowledge such as law, philosophy or sacred scriptures.

4 K. P. Menon, 'History of Kerala: Written in the form of notes on Visscher's letters from Malabar', *Manohar Publishers*, 1924.

5 Tipu Sultan, 'Select letters of Tippoo Sultan to various public functionaries', *London*, 1811, p. 228; Prabhu, 1999, p. 223.

6 Justine M. Cordwell and Ronald A. Schwarz, 'The fabrics of culture: the anthropology of clothing and adornment', *Walter de Gruyter*, 1979, pp. 144–145.
7 ibid.
8 Thomas R. Trautman, 'Chapter 4', *British Indophobia, Aryans and British India*, Berkeley, *University of California Press*, 1997, pp. 99–130.
9 'Selections from Educational Records, Part I (1781-1839)', *Delhi, National Archives of India*, edited by H. Sharp, 1920.
10 John Gaylor, 'Sons of John Company: Indian and Pakistan armies 1903-1991', *Spellmount*, 1992.
11 ibid.
12 James Hough, 'The history of Christianity in India', *R.B. Seeley and W. Burnside*, London, 1845.
13 Stephen Legg, 'Governing prostitution in Colonial Delhi: from cantonment regulations to international hygiene', *Social History*, vol. 34, *Routledge*, 2009.
14 Kamaldeo Narain Singh, 'Urban development in India', *Abhinav Publications*, 1978.
15 'The Census of British India of 1871-72', *Journal of the Statistical Society of London*, 39, no. 2, 1876, pp. 411–416.
16 N. H. Palkar, *Dr Keshav Baliram Hedgewar – a Biography*, Lokhit Prakashan, Lucknow, 2014.
17 H. V. Seshadri, *Dr Hedgewar, The Epoch-Maker*, *Sahitya Sindhu*, Bangalore, 1981.
18 ibid.
19 Aaron O'Neil, 'Child Mortality in India 1880-2020', *Statista*, June 2021, https://www.statista.com/statistics/1041861/india-all-time-child-mortality-rate/#:~:text=Child%20mortality%20in%20India%201880%2D2020&text=From%201900%20until%20today%2C%20the,under%20four%20percent%20in%202020.
20 N. H. Palkar, *Dr Keshav Baliram Hedgewar – a Biography*, Lokhit Prakashan, Lucknow, 2014.
21 Geraldine Pinch, *Egyptian Mythology: A Guide to the Gods, Goddesses, and Traditions of Ancient Egypt*, Oxford University Press, 2004, p. 124.
22 Margo De Mello, *Animals and Society: An Introduction to Human-animal Studies*, Columbia University Press, 2012, p. 314.
23 Chakori was a game where two or more people raced while spinning a circular tube or wheel with a stick.
24 N. H. Palkar, *Dr Keshav Baliram Hedgewar – a Biography*, Lokhit Prakashan, Lucknow, 2014.
25 Will Durant, *A Case for India*, Simon & Schuster, New York, 1930.
26 Shashi Tharoor, *An Era of Darkness*, Aleph Book Company, 2016.

27 Ibid.
28 H. V. Seshadri, *Dr Hedgewar, The Epoch-Maker*, Sahitya Sindhu, Bangalore, 1981.
29 ibid.
30 N. H. Palkar, *Dr Keshav Baliram Hedgewar – a Biography*, Lokhit Prakashan, Lucknow, 2014.
31 'Mumbai airport named Chhatrapati Shivaji International receives its name from the great Hindu King', Scroll.in, 30 August 2018, https://scroll.in/latest/892591/mumbai-airport-renamed-chhatrapati-shivaji-maharaj-international-airport?utm
32 N. S. Takahav, *The Life of Shivaji Maharaj*, Manoranjan Press, Bombay, 1921.
33 George Macartney, *An Account of Ireland in 1773 by a Late Chief Secretary of that Kingdom*, p.55, cited in Kenny, Kevin, *Ireland and the British Empire*, Oxford University Press, 2006.
34 Shashi Tharoor, 'Britain does owe reparations', 14 July 2015, Oxford Union Debate, Oxford
35 Dinyar Patel, 'India and the Last Jubilee Queen', *The Hindu*, 16 June 2012, http://www.thehindu.com/opinion/lead/india-and-the-last-jubilee-queen/article3533400.ece, accessed 18 July 2018.
36 Dinyar Patel, 'Victoria's Diamond Jubilee: Jashan at Wadia Atash Behram, 20 June 1897', *Dinyar Patel's Blog*, 18 June 2012, https://dinyarpatel.com/2012/06/18/victorias-diamond-jubilee-jashan-at-wadia-atash-behram-20-june-1897/.
37 'Central Museum Nagpur pictures', *Nation Next*, 20 January 2025, https://nationnext.in/central-museum-nagpur-pictures/
After the independence, in 1948, these statues were dislodged from these places and thrown in the Ambazari lake by the citizens. Thirty-eight years later, in 1986, when the water level decreased in the lake, these statues came to the fore. They were then taken in custody by Department of Archaeology and Museums and were installed at Nagpur's Central Museum where they still stand today.
38 Dinyar Patel, 'India and the Last Jubilee Queen', *The Hindu*, 16 June 2012, http://www.thehindu.com/opinion/lead/india-and-the-last-jubilee-queen/article3533400.ece, accessed 18 July 2018.
39 Samuel K. Cohn, *The Black Death Transformed: Disease and Culture in Early Renaissance Europe*, Arnold Publications, 2003.
40 *Imperial Gazetteer of India, Vol. III* (1907), *The Indian Empire, Economic* (Chapter X: Famine, pp. 475–502), Published under the authority of His Majesty's Secretary of State for India in Council, Oxford at the Clarendon Press. Pp. 490, 1 map, 552.
41 Dinyar Patel, 'India and the last jubilee queen', *The Hindu*, 16 June 2012, http://www.thehindu.com/opinion/lead/india-and-the-last-jubilee-queen/article3533400.ece, accessed 18 July 2018.

42 Dinyar Patel and S. R. Mehrotra, *Dadabhai Naoroji: Selected Private Papers*, Oxford University Press, 2012.
43 The term Weltanschauung is a German noun that translates directly to "worldview" in English. It refers to a comprehensive conception or apprehension of the world from a specific standpoint. In essence, it encompasses the fundamental cognitive orientation of an individual or society, including their beliefs, values, and philosophies about life and the universe.
Merriam-Webster Dictionary
44 Hyndman became fascinated by Karl Marx's *Das Capital*, which he read in a French translation during his voyage to America in 1880. After returning to England, he invited Marx and his youngest daughter Eleanor ('Tussy') to dinner and told them that he considered reviving the Chartist movement. (Tsuzuki 33) Hyndman did not share Marx's belief in the inevitability of popular revolution. Instead, he preferred gradual constitutional transformation because he genuinely had faith in the parliamentary road to socialism.
45 Ibid.
46 Ibid.
47 Myron J. Echenberg, *Plague Ports: The Global Urban Impact of Bubonic Plague, 1894–1901*, New York: New York University Press, 2007, pp. 66–68.
48 N. H. Palkar, *Dr Keshav Baliram Hedgewar – a Biography*, Lokhit Prakashan, Lucknow, 2014.
49 ibid.
50 ibid
51 Vaze (pronounced VAH-zay)
52 N. H. Palkar, *Dr Keshav Baliram Hedgewar – a Biography*, Lokhit Prakashan, Lucknow, 2014.
53 ibid.
54 'Public Health Reports (1896-1970)', *Sage Publications*, Vol. 19, No. 47, 18 November 1904.
55 N. H. Palkar, *Dr Keshav Baliram Hedgewar – a Biography*, Lokhit Prakashan, Lucknow, 2014.
56 'Report on Plague Investigations in India', *Advisory Committee for Plague Investigations in India*, Cambridge University Press, 1911, p. 519-520.
57 Friedrich Nietzsche, *The Will to Power*, Penguin Classics, 2017, p. 481.

Chapter 2: Fire and Famine

1 Shashi Tharoor, *Inglorious Empire: What the British Did to India*, C Hurst & Co Publishers, 2017.
2 ibid

3 Shashi Tharoor, *Inglorious Empire: What the British Did to India*, C Hurst & Co Publishers, 2017.
4 Dinyar Patel, 'How British Let One Million Indians Die in Famine', BBC News, 11 June 2016, www.bbc.co.uk/news/world-asia-india-36339524, accessed April 2019.
5 Raju A. Deva, *A fight for Swaraj*, 2000, The *Hindu*, 22nd July 2000.
6 John H. Bodley, *Cultural Anthropology: Tribes, States, and the Global System*, Altamira Press, 2011, p. 314.
7 Kista C. Reddy, *Impact of Water Harvesting on the Environment of Telangana During the 20th Century*, Dept. of History, Osmania University, 2015, http://shodhganga.inflibnet.ac.in/bitstream/10603/176277/8/08_chapter_2.pdf, p. 23.
8 ibid
9 Romeo Vitelli, 'When a child loses a parent', *Psychology Today*, 4th February 2018, accessed March 2020, www.psychologytoday.com/gb/blog/media-spotlight/201802/when-child-loses-parent.
10 Virgie Townsend, 'How the death of a parent affects a child', *Vice.com*, 23 April 2018, accessed March 2020, https://tonic.vice.com/en_us/article/a3y9g4/how-the-death-of-a-parent-affects-a-child.
11 Jane Hirsfield, 'My doubt', *Poem a Day*, Academy of American Poets, 2016.
12 N. H. Palkar, *Dr Keshav Baliram Hedgewar – a Biography*, Lokhit Prakashan, Lucknow, 2014.
13 Rakesh Sinha, *Dr Keshav Baliram Hedgewar*, English version, Ministry of Information and Broadcasting, 2015, p. 6.
14 H. S. Sardesai, *Shivaji, the Great Maratha*, Cosmo Publications, 2002, p. 506.
15 Setu Pagadi, *Chhatrapati Shivaji*, Continental Prakashan, 2004, p. 39.
16 Rakesh Sinha, *Dr Keshav Baliram Hedgewar*, English version, Ministry of Information and Broadcasting, 2015, p. 8.
17 A. D. Athawale, *Manobodh Vivran* (8th ed.), Shree Radhadamodar Pratisthan, Pune, 2008.
18 ibid.
19 François-Marie Arouet (Voltaire), 'Patrie,' *Dictionnaire philosophique*, sec. iii (1764) (S.H. transl.),
20 John Hutchinson, *Dynamics of Cultural Nationalism: The Gaelic Revival and the creation of the Irish State*, Routledge, 1987
21 ibid
22 Ibid
23 Alp Yenin, 'Pan-Islamism (Ottoman Empire),' *International Encyclopaedia of the First World War*, 14 April 2020, https://encyclopedia.1914-1918-

online.net/article/pan-islamism_ottoman_empire, accessed August 2022.

24 Rakesh Sinha, *Dr Keshav Baliram Hedgewar*, Ministry of Information and Broadcasting, 2015.

25 N.H. Palkar, *Dr Keshav Baliram Hedgewar – A Biography*, Lokhit Prakashan, Lucknow, 2014.

26 Moonjay (popularly written as Moonjay)

27 H. K. Mokashi, 'Dr. B.S. Moonjay, Upholder of Hindu Cause and Champion of Military Training,' Central Hindu Military Education Society, 2012.

28 ibid

29 ibid

30 N.H. Palkar, *Dr Keshav Baliram Hedgewar – A Biography*, Lokhit Prakashan, Lucknow, 2014.

31 A.K. Bhagwat, and G.P. Pradhan, Lokhmanya *Tilak – A Biography*, Jaico Publishing, 1956.

32 Ross Bassett, *The Technological Indian*, Harvard University Press, 2016 p. 57.

33 N.H. Palkar, *Dr Keshav Baliram Hedgewar – a Biography*, Lokhit Prakashan, Lucknow, 2014.

34 ibid

35 Ross Bassett, *The Technological Indian*, Harvard University Press, 2016, p. 58.

36 N. H. Palkar, *Dr Keshav Baliram Hedgewar – a Biography*, Lokhit Prakashan, Lucknow, 2014.

37 ibid.

38 Gurpreet Singh, 'Racism, the RSS, and Narendra Modi's efforts to turn India into a Hindu nation', The Georgia Straight, 5 March 2017, https://www.straight.com/news/877876/gurpreet-singh-racism-rss-and-narendra-modis-efforts-turn-india-hindu-nation, accessed October 2019.

39 Christophe Jaffrelot *The Hindu Nationalist Movement in India*, Columbia University Press, 1996, p.33.

40 Theodore Parker *Ten Sermons on Religion, Justice and the Conscience*, Crosby Nichols and Company, 1853.

41 Kautilya, better known as Vishnu Gupta, lived in the 4th BCE and wrote a political treatise often compared to *The Prince* by Machiavelli.

42 June Purvis, 'Letter bombs and IEDs: Were the suffragettes terrorists?', Sky News.com, 6 February 2018, https://news.sky.com/story/women-would-have-got-the-vote-earlier-if-not-for-suffragette-terrorists-11227772, accessed April 2019.

43 Winston Churchill expressed this sentiment to the Soviet Ambassador, Ivan Mikhailovich Maisky, in 1942, saying: 'Eventually, the Moslems will become

master, because they are warriors, while the Hindus are windbags. Yes, windbags! Oh, of course, when it comes to fine speeches, skilfully balanced resolutions and legalistic castles in the air, the Hindus are real experts! They're in their element! When it comes to business, when something must be decided on quickly, implemented, executed—here the Hindoos say "pass". Here they immediately reveal their internal flabbiness.' Quoted from *The Indian Spy: The True Story of the Most Remarkable Secret Agent of World War II*, Aleph Book Company, 2017.

44 Barbara and Thomas Metcalf, *A Concise History of Modern India (PDF)*, Cambridge University Press, 2006.

45 Hermann Kulke and Dietmar Rothermund, *A History of India (PDF)*, 4th ed., Routledge, p. 280.

46 Craig Baxter, *Bangladesh: From a Nation to a State*, Westview Press, 1997, p. 39.

47 Christophe Jaffrelot, *The Hindu Nationalist Movement in India*, Columbia University Press, 1996.

48 Richard Sisson and Stanley A. Wolpert, *Congress and Indian Nationalism: The Pre-independence Phase*, University of California Press, 1988, pp. 22–23.

49 William Wedderburn, *Allan Octavian Hume: Father of the Indian National Congress*, T. Fisher Unwin, London, 1913.

50 Dadabhai is a loving expression, which translates roughly as 'dear older brother.'

51 B. L. Grover and Alka Mehta, *A New Look at Modern Indian History (From 1707 to The Modern Times)*, S. Chand Publishing, 2018, p. 330.

52 N. H. Palkar, *Dr Keshav Baliram Hedgewar – A Biography*, Lokhit Prakashan, Lucknow, 2014.

53 Barbara and Thomas Metcalf, *A Concise History of Modern India (PDF)*, 2nd ed., Cambridge University Press, 2006, pp. 136–137.

54 S. S, Ikram, *Sir Sayyid Ahmad Khan: Muslim Scholar*, Encyclopædia Britannica, retrieved 30 July 2015.

55 N. H. Palkar, *Dr Keshav Baliram Hedgewar – A Biography*, Lokhit Prakashan, Lucknow, 2014.

56 ibid.

57 Ibid.

58 ibid.

59 ibid.

60 ibid.

61 ibid.

62 Ibid.

63 Herbert Hope Risley, *The Study of Ethnology in India*, *The Journal of the Anthropological Institute of Great Britain and Ireland*, Royal Anthropological Institute of Great Britain and Ireland, 1891.
64 N. H. Palkar, *Dr Keshav Baliram Hedgewar – A Biography*, Lokhit Prakashan, Lucknow, 2014.
65 ibid.
66 Rakesh Sinha, *Dr Keshav Baliram Hedgewar*, 2015, English version, Ministry of Information and Broadcasting, p. 11.
67 N. H. Palkar, *Dr Keshav Baliram Hedgewar – A Biography*, Lokhit Prakashan, Lucknow, 2014.
68 *An eyewitness account of a classmate, Ganesh Govind Awade*, Maharashtra, 28 July 1940.

Chapter 3: Expulsion and Revolution

1 N. H. Palkar, *Dr Keshav Baliram Hedgewar – A Biography*, Lokhit Prakashan, Lucknow, 2014.
2 Rakesh Sinha, *Dr Keshav Baliram Hedgewar*, 2015, English version, Ministry of Information and Broadcasting, p. 13.
3 N. H. Palkar, *Dr Keshav Baliram Hedgewar – A Biography*, Lokhit Prakashan, Lucknow, 2014.
4 Ibid.
5 ibid.
6 ibid.
7 ibid.
8 ibid.
9 S. N. Sen, *History of the Freedom Movement in India (1857–1947)*, New Age Publishers, 1997, New Delhi, p. 354.
10 N. H. Palkar, *Dr Keshav Baliram Hedgewar – A Biography*, Lokhit Prakashan, Lucknow, 2014.
11 Ibid.
12 Ibid.
13 Ibid.
14 R. Harris, 'Vivekananda, Sarah Farmer, and global spiritual transformations in the fin de siècle', *Journal of Global History*, Vol. 14, 2019, p. 179–198.
15 N. H. Palkar, *Dr Keshav Baliram Hedgewar – a Biography*, Lokhit Prakashan, Lucknow, 2014.
16 S. Shabbir, *History of Educational Development in Vidarbha, 1882–1923*, Northern Book Centre, 2005.
17 Ibid.

18 J. H. Hutton, 'Census of India 1931', *Archive.org*, British Government of India, August 2018, [link].
19 Ibid.
20 Ibid.
21 Rakesh Sinha, *Dr Keshav Baliram Hedgewar*, Ministry of Information and Broadcasting, English version, 2015, p.14.
22 Shashi Tharoor, *An Era of Darkness*, Aleph Book Company, Delhi, 2016, p. 216.
23 Paul Monroe, *Paul Monroe's Encyclopaedia of History of Education*, Vol. 1, Genesis Publishing, 2000.
24 Pintu Kumar, *Buddhist Learning in South Asia: Education, Religion, and Culture at the Ancient Sri Nalanda Mahavihara*, Lexington Books, 7 May 2018, p. 13.
25 Will Durant, *The Case for India*, Simon and Schuster, 1930, pp. 31–35.
26 BA (F) stood for Bachelor of Arts Degree, and the (F) stood for fail, to indicate that the candidate was learned enough to reach higher education but did not pass out with a degree.
27 Shashi Tharoor, *An Era of Darkness*, Aleph Book Company, Delhi, 2016, p. 223.
28 N. H. Palkar, *Dr Keshav Baliram Hedgewar – A Biography*, Lokhit Prakashan, Lucknow, 2014.
29 ibid.
30 ibid.
31 ibid.
32 Rakesh Sinha, *Dr Keshav Baliram Hedgewar*, Ministry of Information and Broadcasting, 2015, English version, p. 14.
33 H. V. Seshadri, *Dr Hedgewar, The Epoch-Maker*, Sahitya Sindhu, Bangalore, 1981.

Chapter 4: Into the Beehive

1 Rakesh Sinha, *Dr Keshav Baliram Hedgewar*, 2015, English version, Ministry of Information and Broadcasting, p. 14.
2 Alex Wolfers, 'Spiritual violence and the divine revolution of Sri Aurobindo Ghosh', *University of Cambridge*, 29 October 2015, https://www.cam.ac.uk/research/features/spiritual-violence-and-the-divine-revolution-of-sri-aurobindo-ghosh.
3 Aurobindo Ghose *Tales of a Prison Life*, 1997, English version, Aurobindo Ashram, PDF.
4 Halday (popularly written as Halde)
5 H. V. Seshadri, *Dr Hedgewar: The Epoch-Maker*, 1981, Sahitya Sindhu, Bangalore.
6 A. Ghoshal (2020) Howrah Bridge: icon of a 330-year-old city in India – part I: history, planning and design. Proceedings of the Institution of Civil

Engineers – Engineering History and Heritage 173(3): 117–128, https://doi.org/10.1680/jenhh.19.00017

7 N. H. Palkar, *Dr Keshav Baliram Hedgewar – A Biography*, 2014, Lokhit Prakashan, Lucknow.

8 Aravind Ganachari, *Nationalism and Social Reform in the Colonial Situation*, 2005, Kalpaz Publications, Delhi.

9 Cul-de-sac is a French expression that translates to 'bottom of the sack'. In English, it refers to a street or passage closed at one end, commonly known as a dead-end street.

10 N. H. Palkar, *Dr Keshav Baliram Hedgewar – A Biography*, 2014, Lokhit Prakashan, Lucknow.

11 Ibid.

12 M.N. Srinivas, *Class, caste and gender*, 2017, Sage Publications, New Delhi, p.161-162

13 Rakesh Sinha, *Dr Keshav Baliram Hedgewar*, 2015, English version, Ministry of Information and Broadcasting, p.18

14 Jogesh Chandra Chatterjee, *In Search of Freedom*, 1958, Paresh Chaiterjee Press, Calcutta, p.21

15 ibid, p.22

16 'The Riots in Calcutta', *The Mercury*, 15 December 1910, Trove.

17 'The Riots in Calcutta', *The Mercury*, 15 December 1910, Trove.

18 Bipal Kumar Jana, *Impact of Climate Change on Natural Resource Management*, 2010, Springer Publications, p. 468.

19 H. V. Seshadri, *Dr Hedgewar: The Epoch-Maker*, 1981, Sahitya Sindhu, Bangalore.

20 Eric Neumayer and Thomas Plumper, 'Annals of Association of American Geographers', Vol. 97, No. 3 (Sept. 2007), pp. 551-566.

21 M. G. Agrawal, *Freedom Fighters of India*, Gyan Publishing House, 2008, India, p. 106.

22 H. V. Seshadri, *Dr Hedgewar, The Epoch-Maker*, Sahitya Sindhu, Bangalore, 1981.

23 'Hindu-Muslim Tension', *Mahatma Gandhi Foundation*, n.d., https://www.mkgandhi.org/g_communal/chap02.php.

24 John Keegan, *The First World War*, Vintage, London, 2000, p. 8.

25 Harriet Sherwood, 'Indians in the trenches: voices of the forgotten army are finally to be heard', *Guardian Newspaper*, 2018

26 Gary S. Messinger, *British Propaganda and the State in the First World War*, Manchester University Press, 1992.

27 N.H. Palkar, *Dr Keshav Baliram Hedgewar – a Biography*, Lokhit Prakashan, Lucknow, 2014.

28 Rakesh Sinha, *Dr Keshav Baliram Hedgewar*, Ministry of Information and Broadcasting, 2015, English version, p. 21.

Chapter 5: Guns and Inner storms

1 'British Indians: a remarkable story of success', *The Telegraph*, 2015, https://www.telegraph.co.uk/news/worldnews/asia/india/11981677/British-Indians-a-remarkable-story-of-success.html.
2 Rakesh Sinha, *Dr Keshav Baliram Hedgewar*, Ministry of Information and Broadcasting, 2015, English version.
3 Ira Klein, 'Death in India 1871 – 1921', *Journal of Asian Studies*, Vol. XXXII, No. 4, 1973.
4 H. V. Seshadri, *Dr Hedgewar-The Epoch-Maker*, Sahitya Sindhu, Bangalore, 1981.
5 N. H. Palkar, *Dr Keshav Baliram Hedgewar – a Biography*, Lokhit Prakashan, Lucknow, 2014.
6 Ibid.
7 Vivekvani, 'Vedanta in its Application to Indian Life, 2019', https://vivekavani.com/vedanta-application-indian-life-vivekananda/
8 Lucy Carroll, *Law, Custom and Statutory Social Reform: The Hindu Widows' Remarriage Act of 1856, Women and Social Reform in Modern India: A Reader*, Indiana University Press, 2018, pp. 78–80.
9 *Moonjay Papers*, File No. 5, 1918-19, Nehru Memorial Museum and Library, New Delhi.
10 Rakesh Sinha, *Dr Keshav Baliram Hedgewar*, English version, Ministry of Information and Broadcasting, 2015
11 Satbir Singh, 'A Critical Analysis of Lucknow Pact', *JETIR*, December 2018, Volume 5, Issue 12.
12 Spencer Laven, 'The Kanpur Mosque Incident of 1913: The North Indian Muslim Press and Its Reaction to Community Crisis,' *Journal of the American* Academy of Religion, Vol. 42, No. 2, 1974, pp. 263–279.
13 'Lucknow Pact', *Encyclopaedia Britannica*, n.d., https://www.britannica.com/event/Lucknow-Pact.
14 Kawre (pronounced Kaw-ray)
15 Rakesh Sinha, *Dr Keshav Baliram Hedgewar, English version*, Ministry of Information and Broadcasting, 2015.
16 Zamindars were landlords often with peasantry as part of their land.
17 Rakesh Sinha, *Dr Keshav Baliram Hedgewar, English version*, Ministry of Information and Broadcasting, 2015.
18 In the context of Indian society, the term jāti (जाति) refers to a group of people sharing a common profession, geographic origin or lineage. It is often translated as "sub-caste" and denotes thousands of distinct communities within the broader social hierarchy. Each jāti typically has its own customs, traditions and social rules, including practices like endogamy (marriage

within the same group). The concept of jāti is complex and varies significantly across different regions and communities in India.

Chapter 6: Seeds of Division

1 K. N. Panikkar, *Against Lord and State: Religion and Peasant Uprisings in Malabar 1836 – 1921*, Oxford University Press, 1989.
2 P. P. Razak Abdul, 'Colonialism and Community Formation in Malabar: A Study of Muslims of Malabar,' Unpublished PhD thesis, Dept. of History, University of Calicut, 2013.
3 E. Roland Miller, *Mappila Muslim Culture*, State University of New York Press, Albany, 2015.5
4 Sanjay Subrahmanyam, *The Portuguese Empire in Asia, 1500-1700: A Political and Economic History*, John Wiley & Sons, 2012.
5 Laurent Murawiec, *The Mind of Jihad*, Cambridge University Press, New York, 2008.
6 Tom Holland, *In the Shadow of the Sword*, Abacus, London, 2013.
7 Erik J. Zürcher, *Turkey: A Modern History*, I.B. Tauris, 3rd edition, 2004.
8 Mansoor Moaddel, *Nationalism, and Fundamentalism: Episode and Discourse*, Chicago University Press, 2005.
9 Edward Curtis, *Encyclopaedia of Muslim-American History*, Infobase Publishing, 2010, p. 499.
10 J. Turner, *Religious Ideology and the Roots of the Global Jihad: Salafi Jihadism and International Order*, Springer, 2014.
11 The term Salafiyya is derived from the Arabic word "Salaf," referring to the "pious predecessors," specifically the first three generations of Muslims. The Salafiyya movement advocates for a return to the practices and beliefs of these early Muslims, emphasizing adherence to the original teachings of Islam as found in the Qur'an and Sunnah, and rejecting later innovations (bid'ah).
12 Shadee El Masry, 'The Salafis in America,' *Journal of Muslim Minority Affairs*, Koninklijke Brill NV, Leiden: Routledge Publishers, 2010.
13 Mohammed M. Hafez, *Suicide Bombers in Iraq: The Strategy and Ideology of Martyrdom*, US Institute of Peace Press, 2017.
14 Babasaheb Ambedkar, *Writings and Speeches*, Vol. 8, Thacker and Co., Bombay, 1940.
15 Robert L. Hardgrave, *The Mappilla Rebellion, 1921: Peasant Revolt in Malabar* (PDF), Modern Asian Studies, Cambridge University Press, 1977
16 ibid.
17 Babasaheb Ambedkar, *Writings and Speeches, Vol. 8*, Thacker and Co., Bombay, 1940.

18 K. K. N. Kurup, *The Malabar Rebellion - An Analysis of the Impact*, Proceedings of the Indian History Congress, Indian History Congress, 1996.

19 O. P. Salahudheen, *Anti-European Struggle by the Mappilas of Malabar 1498 - 1921*, retrieved 2019.

20 Diwan Bahadur Gopalan Nair, *Moplah Rebellion 1921*, Norman Printing Bureau, 1923.

21 Ibid.

22 ibid.

23 ibid.

24 Babasaheb Ambedkar, *Writings and Speeches*, Vol. 8, Thacker and Co., Bombay, 1940.

25 ibid.

26 Manu S. Pillai, 'The Mapilla rebellion of Malabar', Live Mint (online), 7th Sept 2018

27 V. Ajmal, 'Deccan Herald', *Deccan Herald*, 25th October 2018, accessed July 2020 https://www.deccanherald.com/specials/after-97-years-forgotten-699719.html

28 ibid.

29 Babasaheb Ambedkar, *Pakistan or the Partition of India*, Ch. 7, Thacker and Co., Bombay, 1940.

30 ibid.

31 H. K. Mokashi, 'Dr B.S. Moonjay', *Central Hindu Military Education Society*, Nashik, India, 2000, p. 69.

32 ibid.

33 ibid., p. 70.

34 Jyotirmani Vatakkayil, 'The Servants of India Society in Modern Kerala History', *Proceedings of the Indian History Congress*, vol. 67, 2006, pp. 464–69, http://www.jstor.org/stable/44147965.

35 N. H. Palkar, *Dr Keshav Baliram Hedgewar – A Biography*, Lokhit Prakashan, Lucknow, 2014.

36 Ranbir Vohra, *The Making of India: A Historical Survey*, 2nd ed., Armonk, New York, 2001.

37 Nigel Collett, *The Butcher of Amritsar: General Reginald Dyer*, A&C Black, 2006.

38 N. H. Palkar, *Dr Keshav Baliram Hedgewar – A Biography*, Lokhit Prakashan, Lucknow, 2014.

39 Moonjay Papers, 'Hedgewar to Moonjay', 24th Feb. 1919, Nehru Memorial Museum and Library, New Delhi.

40 Moonjay Papers, *Personal Diary*, Nehru Memorial Museum and Library, New Delhi.

41 N.H. Palkar, *Dr Keshav Baliram Hedgewar – A Biography*, Lokhit Prakashan, Lucknow, 2014.
42 Moonjay Papers, 'Hedgewar to Moonjay', *Nehru Memorial Museum and Library*, New Delhi, 24th Feb. 1919.
43 ibid.
44 H. K. Mokashi, *Dr B.S. Moonjay*, Central Hindu Military Education Society, Nashik, India, 2000,
45 ibid.
46 Ibid, p. 69.
47 ibid.
48 M. K. Gandhi, *An Autobiography*, Penguin Books, London, 2001.
49 ibid.
50 ibid.
51 Moonjay Papers, 'Ghosh to Moonjay', *Nehru Memorial Museum and Library*, New Delhi, 30th Aug. 1920.
52 'Tharoor apologises for his 'cattle class' remark', The *Economic Times*, 18 September 2009, accessed November 2019, https://economictimes.indiatimes.com/news/politics-and-nation/tharoor-apologises-for-his-cattle-class-remark/articleshow/5025961.cms.
53 'Ghosh to Moonjay', *Moonjay Papers, Nehru Memorial Museum and Library*, New Delhi, 30th Aug., 1920.
54 ibid.
55 Aurobindo Ghosh, 'Bande Mataram: Political Writings and Speeches 1890–1908', *The Complete Works of Sri Aurobindo*, Volumes 6–7, *Sri Aurobindo Ashram*, Pondicherry, 2002, p. 1182.
56 'Bande Mataram: Political Writings and Speeches 1890–1908', *The Complete Works of Sri Aurobindo*, Volumes 6–7, Sri Aurobindo Ashram, Pondicherry, 2002, p. 1183.
57 P. Rajeswar Rao, 'Colossus of Salem', *The Great Indian Patriots*, Volume 1, Mittal Publications, 1991, p. 194–198.
58 'Indian Review', *Madras*, January 1921, p. 36–37.
59 Rakesh Sinha, *Dr Keshav Baliram Hedgewar*, Ministry of Information and Broadcasting, 2015.
60 Jawaharlal Nehru, *Towards Freedom*, The Bodley Head Ltd., 1936.

Chapter 7: Shackled Freedom

1 N.H. Palkar, *Dr Keshav Baliram Hedgewar – a Biography*, Lokhit Prakashan, Lucknow, 2014.
2 Now called Mumbai.

3 N.H. Palkar, *Dr Keshav Baliram Hedgewar – a Biography*, Lokhit Prakashan, 2014.
4 ibid
5 Bobday (often spelt as Bobde)
6 Rakesh Sinha, *Dr Keshav Baliram Hedgewar*, Ministry of Information and Broadcasting, 2015.
7 ibid.
8 Rakesh Sinha, *Dr Keshav Baliram Hedgewar*, Ministry of Information and Broadcasting, 2015.
9 'Dr Hedgewar Yancha Khatla', *The Mahratta*, June 29th, 1921, p. 4.
10 Rakesh Sinha, *Dr Keshav Baliram Hedgewar*, Ministry of Information and Broadcasting, 2015.
11 H.V. Seshadri, *Dr Hedgewar, The Epoch-Maker*, Sahitya Sindhu, 1981.
12 N.H. Palkar, *Dr Keshav Baliram Hedgewar – a Biography*, Lokhit Prakashan, Lucknow, 2014.
13 Stephen E. Atkins, *Encyclopedia of Modern Worldwide Extremists and Extremist Groups, Greenwood Publishing*, 2004, p. 264.
14 N.H. Palkar, *Dr Keshav Baliram Hedgewar – a Biography*, Lokhit Prakashan, Lucknow, 2014.
15 ibid, 2014.
16 He would have delivered this speech in Marathi.
17 *The Mahratta*, National archives, August 24, 1921
18 'Kautilya's Arthasastra,' *Mysore Printing and Publishing House*, 1960, sixth edition, pp. 247-265.
19 ibid
20 ibid
21 *Indian Prison: A Sociological Enquiry*, Jainendra Press, 1979, p. 23.
22 Michel Foucault, *Discipline and Punish*, Penguin Books, London, 1991, p.121
23 Franklin E. Zimring, and Gordon Hawkins, quoted in *The Scale of Imprisonment*, University of Chicago Press, Chicago, 1991, p.51
24 'The Second Enclosure Movement and the Construction of the Public Domain,' *Law and Contemporary Problems*, Winter/Spring, Vol. 66:33, p. 35, http://www.law.duke.edu.
25 Herbert Risley, *The People of India*, Forgotten Books, London, 2019.
26 David Skuy, 'Macaulay and the Indian Penal Code of 1862', *Modern Asian Studies*, 32 (1998), pp. 513, 526–530.
27 'Indian Prison System under British Rule', *Racolblegal*, https://racolblegal.com/indian-prison-system-under-british-rule/#_ftnref16.
28 H. V. Seshadri, *Dr Hedgewar, The Epoch-Maker*, Sahitya Sindhu, Bangalore, 1981.

29 Sacred threads were worn by Brahmin boys to mark their coming of age to take on religious duties. Hedgewar's parents would have garlanded him after the ceremony, and he would have worn the janeu throughout his life.
30 Rakesh Sinha, *Dr Keshav Baliram Hedgewar*, English version, Ministry of Information and Broadcasting, 2015.
31 ibid
32 H. V. Seshadri, *Dr Hedgewar, The Epoch-Maker*, Sahitya Sindhu, Bangalore, 1981.
33 ibid
34 Jawaharlal Nehru, *The Discovery of India*, Penguin Books, Delhi, India, 2010.
35 ibid, p.239
36 Ibid, p.240
37 Om Prakash Misra, *Economic Thought of Gandhi and Nehru: A Comparative Analysis*, M.D. Publications, New York, 1995, pp. 49–65.
38 Arun R. Kumbhare, *Women of India: Their Status Since the Vedic Times*, iUniverse, 2009, p. 80.
39 Richard M. Eaton, *India in the Persianate Age 1000-1765*, University of California Press, 2019.
40 Rafath Begam, *Secularism in Political Ideas of Pandit Jawaharlal Nehru*, University of Hyderabad, 2011.
41 'Simply Extraordinary', *VSK Telangana Archives*, n.d., https://archives.vsktelangana.org/simply-extraordinary.

Chapter 8: Crossroads

1 *Mahratta*, 12th July 1922, p. 5.
2 B. R. Nanda, *The Nehrus: Motilal and Jawaharlal*, John Day, New York, 1963.
3 Luv Puri, *The Past and Future of Deobandi Islam*, CTC Sentinel, West Point, New York, 2009
4 Jawad Syed, Edwina Pio and Tahir Zaidi, *Faith-Based Violence and Deobandi Militancy in Pakistan*, Palgrave Macmillan, London, p. 139.
5 Palkar, N.H., *Dr Keshav Baliram Hedgewar – A Biography*, Lokhit Prakashan, Lucknow, 2014.
6 Kipling, Rudyard, *IF – and Other Poems*, Michael O'Mara, New Edition, 2016.
7 '*Mahratta*', 19th July 1922, p. 11.
8 N. H. Palkar, *Dr Keshav Baliram Hedgewar – A Biography*, Lokhit Prakashan, Lucknow, 2014.
9 ibid
10 In the *Star Wars* universe, a Padawan is an apprentice Jedi undergoing training under a Jedi Knight or Master. The etymology of "Padawan" is not

definitively established. Some sources suggest it was coined by *Star Wars* creator George Lucas, possibly inspired by the Sanskrit word 'upadhyaya', meaning 'teacher'.

11 Rakesh Sinha, *Dr Keshav Baliram Hedgewar*, English version, Ministry of Information and Broadcasting, 2015.

12 'Mahratta', 20th December 1922, p. 4.

13 Basheer Nafi, 'The Abolition of the Caliphate: Causes and Consequences', *The Different Aspects of Islamic Culture*, vol. 6, pt. I: *Islam in the World Today, Retrospective of the Evolution of Islam and the Muslim World*, UNESCO, 2016, pp. 183–192.

14 Raj Kumar Trivedi, *Proceedings of the Indian History Congress*, vol. 42, Indian History Congress, 1981, pp. 458–467.

15 Mushirul Hasan, 'Religion and Politics: The Ulama and the Khilafat Movement', *Economic and Political Weekly*, vol. 16, no. 20, Economic and Political Weekly, 1981, pp. 903–905.

16 K. A. Karandikar, *Islam in India's Transition to Modernity*, Praeger, New Delhi, 1971.

17 Seddon, Mohammad Siddique, 'Constructing Identities of "Difference" and "Resistance": The Politics of Being Muslim and British', *Social Semiotics*, 2010, pp. 557–571, http://www.columbia.edu/itc/mealac/pritchett/00ambedkar/ambedkar_partition/307b.html#n07.

18 'Young India – A Weekly Journal', ed. Gandhi, M.K., Gandhi Heritage Portal, [10 December 1939], www.gandhiheritageportal.org/journals-by-gandhiji/young-india

19 In Islamic terminology, kufr (رفك) refers to the act of disbelief or rejection of the fundamental tenets of Islam. The term originates from the Arabic root "kafara," meaning "to cover" or "to conceal." In a religious context, it signifies the denial or concealment of the truth of Islam. There are various forms of kufr, including:

- Kufr al-'Inaad (Disbelief out of stubbornness): This occurs when an individual acknowledges the truth of Islam but refuses to accept it due to arrogance or obstinacy.
- Kufr al-Inkaar (Disbelief out of denial): This form involves outright denial of the truth, even when it is presented clearly.
- Kufr al-Nifaaq (Disbelief out of hypocrisy): This pertains to those who outwardly profess belief in Islam but internally reject it.
- Kufr al-Juhood (Disbelief out of rejection): This type is characterized by rejecting or concealing the truth despite knowing it, often due to envy or hatred.

20 Ali, Abdul, *Proceedings of the Indian History Congress*, Vol. 43, Indian History Congress, [1982], pp. 726-739

21 Usually, a shrine to mark the death of a Sufi saint, but often *mazars* and *dargahs* are built randomly all over India, and Sunni Muslims consider such practices as idolatry.
22 Idol in Hebrew has a pejorative meaning to mean false image. The Hindu murti is not an image of God but a personification in the same way that Jesus is the personification of the one God.
23 V. R. Karandikar, *Architects of the RSS*, Snehal Prakashan, Pune, 1999.
24 H. V. Seshadri, *Dr Hedgewar, The Epoch-Maker*, Sahitya Sindhu, Bangalore, 1981.
25 ibid
26 Ahmed Aijaz, *Lineages of the Present*, Verso, 2002.
27 'Biography of Babarao Savarkar', *Savarkar.org*, [date], https://savarkar.org/en/pdfs/babarao-savarkar-v003.pdf
28 H. V. Seshadri, *Dr Hedgewar, The Epoch-Maker*, Sahitya Sindhu, Bangalore, 1981.
*Veer Savarkar was sentenced to prison at the Andaman Islands in 1911, and therefore in 1923, he would have been in prison for twelve years, not fourteen.
29 Tacitus, *Agricola*, translated by Duane Reed Stuart, The Macmillan Company, New York, 1909.
30 Richard, Warren, 'Tacitus and Nationalism in Nineteenth-Century Art', *Durham Theses*, Durham University, 2014.
31 Rakesh Sinha, *Dr Keshav Baliram Hedgewar*, English version, Ministry of Information and Broadcasting, 2015].
32 'Report on Indian Newspapers of CP&Berar, No.3, 1924', *National Archives of India*, New Delhi
33 N.H. Palkar, *Dr Keshav Baliram Hedgewar – a Biography*, Lokhit Prakashan, Lucknow, 2014
34 ibid.
35 ibid.
36 Elizabeth Berg, *The Year of Pleasures*, Arrow Publishing, London, 2007.
37 N.H. Palkar, *Dr Keshav Baliram Hedgewar – a Biography*, Lokhit Prakashan, Lucknow, 2014.
38 ibid
39 H.V. Seshadri, *Dr Hedgewar, The Epoch-Maker*, Sahitya Sindhu, Bangalore, 1981.

Chapter 9: It Begins

1 Hindutva is a complex and contested term. Hindutva means Hinduness, or the essence of what it means to be Hindu. Outside of India, Hindutva has

become the outward expression of Hinduness. Hindutva is largely benign, something which covers outward display of symbols, and public festivals. Hindutva, for Hedgewar would have been much more potent, and more akin to Hindu nationalism, it would have been Sarvarkar's Hindutva.

2 Chetan Bhatt and Mukta Parita, 'Hindutva in the West: Mapping the Antinomies of Diaspora Nationalism', *Ethnic and Racial Studies*, 2000
3 V.R. Karandikar, *Architects of RSS*, Snehal Prakashan, Pune, 1999.
4 Vikram Sampath, *Savarkar: Echoes from a Forgotten Past, 1883–1924*, Viking Penguin, 2019.
5 Vinayak Savarkar, *Hindutva*, Pandit Bakhle, Mumbai, 1999.
6 ibid.
7 ibid.
8 ibid.
9 ibid.
10 Shashi Tharoor, *The Hindu Way*, Rupa Publications, Delhi, 2019.
11 Vivekanand Jha, 'Caste, Untouchability and Social Justice: Early North Indian Perspective', *Social Scientist*, 25, no. 11/12 (1997), 19–30, https://doi.org/10.2307/3517591.
12 Karl Popper, *The Open Society and Its Enemies*, Routledge, 2012, 1945.
13 Inspired from Kahlil Gibran's *The Prophet*, 'On Children'.
14 Others included Raghunathan Baande, Bapu Bhedi, Anna Vaidya, Krishna Mohril, Narhar Palekar, Anna Gaikwad, Devghare, Babu Telang, Balasaheb Aathalye, and Anna Sohoni
15 J. Nandakumar, *Hindutva for the Changing Times*, Indus Scrolls Press, 2019.
16 ibid.
17 Christophe Jaffrelot, *The Hindu Nationalist Movement in India*, Columbia University Press, 1998, https://carnegieendowment.org/2020/02/03/i-could-not-be-hindu-is-unique-testimony-to-sangh-s-casteism-pub-81000.
18 Robert Rotberg, *When States Fail: Causes and Consequences*, Princeton University Press, 2013.
19 Muhammad Naeem Qureshi, 'The Khalifat Movement in India, 1919–1924', Doctoral thesis, University of London, School of Oriental and African Studies, 1973.
20 Bidyut Chakrabarty, *Communism in India: events, processes and ideologies*, Oxford University Press, 2014.
21 Register 2, RSS archives, Nagpur
22 N.H. Palkar, *Dr Keshav Baliram Hedgewar – a Biography*, Lokhit Prakashan, Lucknow, 2014.
23 'Rashtriya swayamsevak Sangh Annual Report 2018', *Arise Bharat*, March 2018, archived from the original on 2 April 2019.

24 N.H. Palkar, *Dr Keshav Baliram Hedgewar – a Biography*, Lokhit Prakashan, Lucknow, 2014.
25 Ibid.
26 H.V. Seshadri, *Dr Hedgewar, The Epoch-Maker*, Sahitya Sindhu, Bangalore, 1981.
27 Tapan Basu and Tanika Sarkar, *Khaki Shorts and Saffron Flags: Critique of the Hindu Right*, Sangam Books Ltd., 1993.
28 ibid.
29 H.V. Seshadri, *Dr Hedgewar, The Epoch-Maker*, Sahitya Sindhu, Bangalore, 1981.
30 Ibid.
31 N.H. Palkar, *Dr Keshav Baliram Hedgewar – a Biography*, Lokhit Prakashan, Lucknow, 2014.
32 H.V. Seshadri, *Dr Hedgewar, The Epoch-Maker*, Sahitya Sindhu, Bangalore, 1981.
33 ibid.

Chapter 10: The Godfather

1 'Central issues of American Foreign Policy', *Foreign Relations of the United States 1969–1976, Vol. 1*, Dept. of State, United States of America, 1969, accessed Sept. 2023, https://history.state.gov/historicaldocuments/frus1969-76v01/d4.
2 *Dr Keshav Baliram Hedgewar – a Biography*, Lokhit Prakashan, Palkar, N.H., Lucknow, 2014.
3 N.H. Palkar, *Dr Keshav Baliram Hedgewar – a Biography*, Lokhit Prakashan, Lucknow, 2014.
4 Ibid.
5 The name means the one who attains bliss through reasoned belief.
6 "Who was Swami Shraddhananda who fell to bullets in 1926', *Indian Express archives*, December 28th, 2019. https://indianexpress.com/article/explained/explained-who-was-swami-shraddhanand-who-fell-to-bullets-in-december-1926-6188039/
7 'The collect work of Mahatma Gandhi', *Young India*, Vol. 32, 30th December 1926, p.473–475.
8 Ibid.
9 Ibid.
10 Ibid.
11 Bernard Lewis, *The Middle East, a Brief History of the Last 2000 Years*, Touchstone Books, 1995, p. 229.

12 David Hardiman, *Gandhi in His Time and Ours*, Orient Blackswan, 2003, p. 165–166.
13 N.H. Palkar, *Dr Keshav Baliram Hedgewar – A Biography*, Lokhit Prakashan, Lucknow, 2014.
14 H.V. Seshadri, *Dr Hedgewar, The Epoch-Maker*, Sahitya Sindhu, Bangalore, 1981.
15 ibid
16 ibid
17 H.V. Seshadri, *Dr Hedgewar, The Epoch-Maker*, Sahitya Sindhu, Bangalore, 1981.
18 V.R. Karandikar, *Architects of RSS*, Snehal Prakashan, Pune, 1999.
19 Vikas Putter, 'The False Narrative of Brahminical Patriarchy', *TFIpost*, 21 November 2018, https://tfipost.com/2018/11/hindu-patriarchy-01/ (accessed July 2023).
20 See Chapter 2, p.7
21 Christophe Jaffrelot, *The Hindu Nationalist Movement and Indian Politics*, C. Hurst & Co. Publishers, 1996.
22 N.H. Palkar, *Dr Keshav Baliram Hedgewar – A Biography*, Lokhit Prakashan, Lucknow, 2014.
23 B.R. Ambedkar, *Pakistan or the Partition of India*, 3rd ed., Thacker & Co. Publishers, 1940, Mumbai.
24 N.H. Palkar, *Dr Keshav Baliram Hedgewar – A Biography*, Lokhit Prakashan, Lucknow, 2014.
25 Zaheen Shah, *Shah: Tajul Auliya, Volume II*, Taj Publication, 1971, p. 221.
26 N.H. Palkar, *Dr Keshav Baliram Hedgewar – A Biography*, Lokhit Prakashan, Lucknow, 2014.
27 H.V. Seshadri, *Dr Hedgewar, The Epoch-Maker*, Sahitya Sindhu, Bangalore, 1981.
28 N.H. Palkar, *Dr Keshav Baliram Hedgewar – A Biography*, Lokhit Prakashan, Lucknow, 2014.
29 ibid.
30 V.R. Karandikar, *Architects of RSS*, Snehal Prakashan, Pune, 1999.
31 N.H. Palkar, *Dr Keshav Baliram Hedgewar – A Biography*, Lokhit Prakashan, Lucknow, 2014.
32 ibid.
33 V.R. Karandikar, *Architects of RSS*, Snehal Prakashan, Pune, 1999.
34 Ibid.
35 A. Edgar Guest, *The Proof of Worth, Collected Verse*, 3rd Edition, Chicago Reilly & Lee, 1936.

36 N.H. Palkar, *Dr Keshav Baliram Hedgewar – A Biography*, Lokhit Prakashan, Lucknow, 2014.
37 '25 Dead, 180 Injured in Creed Riots in India', *The New York Times*, 8 September 1927, retrieved 10 January 2009.
38 Alyssa Ayres and Philip Oldenburg, *India Briefing: Quickening the Pace of Change*, M.E. Sharpe, 2002.
39 ibid
40 N.H. Palkar, *Dr Keshav Baliram Hedgewar – a Biography*, Lokhit Prakashan, Lucknow, 2014.
41 '25 dead, 180 injured in creed riots in India', *The New York Times*, 8 September 1927, Retrieved 10 January 2009.
42 B.R. Ambedkar, *Pakistan or the Partition of India*, 3rd ed., Thacker & Co. Publishers, 1940, Mumbai.
43 H.V. Seshadri, *Dr Hedgewar, The Epoch-Maker*, Sahitya Sindhu, Bangalore, 1981.
44 A tonga was a horse pulled cart that was often used as a taxi.
45 V.R. Karandikar, *Architects of RSS*, Snehal Prakashan, Pune, 1999.
46 N.H. Palkar, *Dr Keshav Baliram Hedgewar – a Biography*, Lokhit Prakashan, Lucknow, 2014.
47 William Kesler Jackson, *A Subcontinent's Sunni Schism: The Deobandi-Barelvi Rivalry and the Creation of Modern South Asia*, Maxwell School of Citizenship and Public Affairs, Syracuse University, 2013
48 ibid
49 V.R. Karandikar, *Architects of RSS*, Snehal Prakashan, Pune, 1999
50 N.H. Palkar, *Dr Keshav Baliram Hedgewar – a Biography*, Lokhit Prakashan, Lucknow, 2014.
51 Ibid.

Chapter 11: Values and Leadership

1 'Secret Report on the Rastriya swayamsevak Sangh (1942)', National Archives of India (Delhi), Identifier: PR_002025315, File No: 28/8, p.62.swayamsevak
2 N.H. Palkar, *Dr Keshav Baliram Hedgewar – a Biography*, Lokhit Prakashan, Lucknow, 2014.
3 Bidyut Chakraborty and Bhuwan Jha, *Hindu Nationalism in India: Ideology and Politics*, Routledge, 2019.
4 Its central offices, literally a campus in New Delhi, were under construction at the time of writing this book (2021).
5 H.V. Seshadri, Dr Hedgewar, *The Epoch-Maker*, Sahitya Sindhu, Bangalore, 1981.

6 V.R. Karandikar, *Architects of RSS*, Snehal Prakashan, Pune, 1999.

7 Nagpur archives

8 Martin E. Marty and Scott R. Appleby, *Fundamentalisms and the State: Remaking Polities, Economies, and Militance*, University of Chicago Press, 1996.

9 N.H. Palkar, *Dr Keshav Baliram Hedgewar – a Biography*, Lokhit Prakashan, Lucknow, 2014.

10 ibid.

11 H.V. Seshadri, Dr Hedgewar, *The Epoch-Maker*, Sahitya Sindhu, Bangalore, 1981.

12 M.G. Chitkara, *Rashtriya swayamsevak Sangh: National Upsurge*, APH Publishing, 2004.

13 Christophe Jaffrelot, *The Hindu Nationalist Movement in India*, Columbia University Press, New York, 1996.

14 Dwijendra Narayan Jha, *Rethinking Hindu Identity*, 1st edition, Routledge, 2009.

15 F.F. Pargiter, *Ancient Indian Historical Tradition*, Motilal Banarsidass, Delhi, 1922.

16 Christophe Jaffrelot, *The Hindu Nationalist Movement in India*, Columbia University Press, New York, 1996.

17 Ibid.

18 H.V. Seshadri, *Dr Hedgewar, The Epoch-Maker*, Sahitya Sindhu, Bangalore, 1981.

19 S.M. Nazmuz Sakib, 'Sprouting fascism or nationalism in India', *APSA*, 2021, 10.33774/apsa-2021-wbn4w.

20 T.B. Bottomore, *A Dictionary of Marxist Thought*, Harvard University Press, Cambridge Massachusetts, 1983.

21 N.H. Palkar, *Dr Keshav Baliram Hedgewar – A Biography*, Lokhit Prakashan, Lucknow, 2014.

22 Ibid.

23 H.V. Seshadri, *Dr Hedgewar, The Epoch-Maker*, Sahitya Sindhu, Bangalore, 1981.

24 Romain Hayes, *Subhas Chandra Bose in Nazi Germany: Politics, Intelligence and Propaganda 1941-1943*, Oxford University Press, 2011.

25 Leonard A. Gordon, *Brothers Against the Raj: A Biography of Indian Nationalists Sarat and Subhas Chandra Bose*, Columbia University Press, 1990.

26 W. Anderson, 'The Rashtriya swayamsevak Sangh: III: Participation in Politics', *Economic and Political Weekly*, 7(13), 1972, p. 673–682swayamsevak.

27 H.V. Seshadri, *Dr Hedgewar, The Epoch-Maker*, Sahitya Sindhu, Bangalore, 1981.
28 N.H. Palkar, *Dr Keshav Baliram Hedgewar – a Biography*, Lokhit Prakashan, Lucknow, 2014
29 Ibid.
30 V.R. Karandikar, *Architects of RSS*, Snehal Prakashan, Pune, 1999
31 Scott Atran, *The Devoted Actor, Current Anthropology*, Vol. 57, Supplement 13, June 2016.
32 ibid
33 ibid
34 'Letter from J. Nehru to Dr S. Radhakrishnan', *Radhakrishnan Archives*, Radhakrishnan Papers, Chennai, 22 January 1948.
35 Gyanendra Pandey, *The Ascendancy of the Congress in Uttar Pradesh: Class, Community and Nation in Northern India*, 1920-1940, Anthem Press, London, 2002.
36 H.V. Seshadri, *Dr Hedgewar, The Epoch-Maker*, Sahitya Sindhu, Bangalore, 1981.
37 N.H. Palkar, *Dr Keshav Baliram Hedgewar – a Biography*, Lokhit Prakashan, Lucknow, 2014.
38 Arun Anand, *The Saffron Surge: the untold story of the RSS leadership*, Prabhat Prakashan, 2020.
39 Ibid.
40 Salvation Army Doctrine Council, *The Salvation Army Handbook of Doctrine*, Salvation Army, 2010.
41 Christophe Jaffrelot, *The Hindu Nationalist movement in India*, Columbia University Press, New York, 1996.
42 H.V. Seshadri, *Dr Hedgewar, The Epoch-Maker, Sahitya Sindhu*, Bangalore, 1981.
43 Vidyadhar Date, 'The deep roots of the RSS's anti-intellectualism and its disregard for dissent', *The Wire Magazine*, 2018.
44 N.H. Palkar, *Dr Keshav Baliram Hedgewar – a Biography*, Lokhit Prakashan, Lucknow, 2014.
45 ibid.
46 Ibid.
47 Ibid.
48 Ibid.
49 Alok Kumar, 'Sattvika Leadership', *Journal of Business Ethics*, Vol. 142, No.1, Springer, 2017, p.117-138
50 Ibid.
51 Fatih Cetin and Nejat Basim, 'Organizational Psychological Capital: A Scale Adaptation Study', *Amme Idaresi Dergisi*, vol. 45, p. 121–137, 2012.

52 S. E. Seibert, G. Wang and S. H. Courtright, 'Antecedents and Consequences of Psychological and Team Empowerment in Organizations: A Meta-Analytic Review', *Journal of Applied Psychology*, Vol. 96.5, 2011, p. 981–1003.
53 V.R. Karandikar, *Architects of RSS*, Snehal Prakashan, Pune, 1999
54 Sanjeev Kelkar, *The Lost Years of the RSS*, Sage Publishing, Delhi, 2011

Chapter 12: Flags and Lies

1 N.H. Palkar, *Dr Keshav Baliram Hedgewar – a Biography*, Lokhit Prakashan, Lucknow, 2014
2 Indian National Congress, 'Report of the National Flag Committee', *published by Jairamdas Doulatram*, Ahmedabad, 1931.
3 N.H. Palkar, *Dr Keshav Baliram Hedgewar – a Biography*, Lokhit Prakashan, Lucknow, 2014
4 Ibid.
5 'Irwin Declaration, Lord Irwin, 1929, 31st October 1929', www.constitutionofindia.net/historical_constitutions/irwin_declaration__lord_irwin__1929__31st%20October%201929.
6 Rohit De, 'Between Midnight and Republic: Theory and Practice of India's Dominion Status', *International Journal of Constitutional Law*, Volume 17, Issue 4, October 2019, p. 1213–1234.
7 Ibid.
8 Ibid.
9 'Declaration of Purna Swaraj, Indian National Congress, 1930, 26th January 1930', www.constitutionofindia.net/historical_constitutions/declaration_of_purna_swaraj__indian_national_congress__1930__26th%20January%201930.
10 M. Louro, *Comrades against Imperialism: Nehru, India, and Interwar Internationalism (Global and International History)*, Cambridge, Cambridge University Press, 2018.
11 Ibid.
12 Elizabeth Kolsky, 'The Colonial Rule of Law and the Legal Regime of Exception: Frontier 'Fanaticism' and State Violence in British India', *The American Historical Review*, vol. 120, no. 4, 2015, p. 1218–46..
13 Shalini Sharma, '"Yeh Azaadi Jhooti Hai!": The Shaping of the Opposition in the First Year of the Congress Raj', *Modern Asian Studies*, vol. 48, no. 5, 2014, pp. 1358–88.
14 Mary Catherine French, '"Reporting Socialism: Soviet Journalism and the Journalists' Union, 1955–1966" (2014)', *Publicly Accessible Penn Dissertations*, 1277, p. 253.

15 M.K. Gandhi, 'Some Rules of Satyagraha', *Young India (Navajivan)*, 23 February 1930, (The Collected Works of Mahatma Gandhi vol. 48, p. 340).
16 George Hendrick, 'The Influence of Thoreau's "Civil Disobedience" on Gandhi's Satyagraha', *The New England Quarterly*, Vol. 29, No. 4, 1956, p. 462–471.
17 Anil Kumar Pandey, 'Forest Satyagraha in Dhamtari Tahsil in Central Provinces', *Proceedings of the Indian History Congress*, vol. 59, 1998, p. 490–95.
18 ibid
19 N.H. Palkar, *Dr Keshav Baliram Hedgewar – a Biography*, Lokhit Prakashan, Lucknow, 2014
20 ibid
21 N.H. Palkar, *Dr Keshav Baliram Hedgewar – a Biography*, Lokhit Prakashan, Lucknow, 2014.
22 ibid.
23 Ibid.
24 Stephen Legg, 'Political lives at sea: working and socialising to and from the India Round Table Conference in London, 1930-1932,' *Journal of Historical Geography*, vol. 68, 2020, pp. 21-32.
25 Delhi, Nehru Memorial Museum and Library, Moonjay papers, Moonjay/1, 11th Oct 1930.MoonjayMoonjay
26 Stephen Legg, 'Political lives at sea: working and socialising to and from the India Round Table Conference in London, 1930-1932,' *Journal of Historical Geography*, vol. 68, 2020, pp. 21-32.
27 'Muslim separatism,' *Encyclopaedia Britannica*, https://www.britannica.com/place/India/Muslim-separatism, accessed June 2022.
28 'Muslim separatism,' *Encyclopaedia Britannica*, accessed June 2022, https://www.britannica.com/place/India/Muslim-separatism
29 Delhi, Nehru Memorial Museum and Library, Moonjay papers, Moonjay/1, 7th Oct 1930MoonjayMoonjay
30 Stephen Legg, 'Political lives at sea: working and socialising to and from the India Round Table Conference in London, 1930-1932,' *Journal of Historical Geography*, vol. 68, 2020, p. 21–32
31 N.H. Palkar, *Dr Keshav Baliram Hedgewar – a Biography*, Lokhit Prakashan, Lucknow, 2014.
32 ibid
33 Sunita Deshpande, *Biography of Ganesh Damodar Savarkar*, Global Vision Publishing House, Delhi, 2021.
34 N.H. Palkar, *Dr Keshav Baliram Hedgewar – a Biography*, Lokhit Prakashan, Lucknow, 2014

35 Charles J. Adams, 'Maududi and the Islamic State,' *Voices of Resurgent Islam*, Oxford University Press, 1983.
36 ibid
37 Seyyed Vali Reza Nasr, *Mawdudi and the making of Islamic Revivalism*, Oxford University Press, 1996
38 N.H. Palkar, *Dr Keshav Baliram Hedgewar – a Biography*, Lokhit Prakashan, Lucknow, 2014.
39 H.V. Seshadri, *Dr Hedgewar, The Epoch-Maker*, Sahitya Sindhu, Bangalore, 1981.

Chapter 13: Not Fascist Enough

1 Seshadri, H.V., *Dr Hedgewar, The Epoch-Maker*, Sahitya Sindhu, Bangalore, 1981.
2 Andersen, Walter, and Damle, Sridhar, *The Brotherhood in Saffron: The Rashtriya swayamsevak Sangh and Hindu Revivalism*, Avalon Publishing, University of Michigan, 1987.swayamsevak
3 N.H. Palkar, *Dr Keshav Baliram Hedgewar – a Biography*, Lokhit Prakashan, Lucknow, 2014
4 ibid
5 'Nagpur,' *Dr Hedgewar Bhavan*, Hedgewar Archives, 6th May 1933, translated from Marathi.
6 ibid
7 ibid
8 Dietrich, Jan, 'The Religious Understanding of Erich Fromm,' published in *Fromm-Forum*, Tuebingen, No. 3/1999, p. 28–29.
9 Eaaswarkhanth, M., Dubey, B., Meganathan, P., et al., 'Diverse genetic origin of Indian Muslims: evidence from autosomal STR loci,' *J Hum Genet*, vol. 54, 2009, p. 340–348.
10 Ibid.
11 Fromm, Erich, *The Sane Society*, Holt Paperbacks, Reissue edition, 1990.
12 Khan, Rahimdad, *Molai, Shedai, Janet ul Sindh*, 3rd edition, Sindhi Adbi Board, 1993, p. 2.
13 'Nagpur,' *Dr Hedgewar Bhavan*, Hedgewar Archives, 6th May 1933, translated from Marathi.
14 N.H. Palkar, *Dr Keshav Baliram Hedgewar – a Biography*, Lokhit Prakashan, Lucknow, 2014.
15 'Nagpur,' *Dr Hedgewar Bhavan*, Hedgewar Archives, 8th June 1933, translated from Marathi.

16 N.H. Palkar, *Dr Keshav Baliram Hedgewar – a Biography*, Lokhit Prakashan, Lucknow, 2014.
17 ibid
18 Chapekar, Damodar, *Autobiography of Damodar Hari Chapekar*, Bombay Police Abstracts of 1910, p. 50–107.
19 Popplewell, Richard J., *Intelligence and Imperial Defence: British Intelligence and the Defence of the Indian Empire 1904-1924*, Frank Cass, London, 1995.
20 Anand, Anita, *The Patient Assassin: A True Tale of Massacre*, revenge and the Raj, Simon & Schuster, 2019
21 Nayar, Kamala Elizabeth, *The Sikh Diaspora in Vancouver: Three Generations Amid Tradition, Modernity, and Multiculturalism*, University of Toronto Press, 2004.
22 N.H. Palkar, *Dr Keshav Baliram Hedgewar – a Biography*, Lokhit Prakashan, Lucknow, 2014
23 Lonergan, Erik, Blyth, Mark, *Angrynomics*, Agenda Publishing, 2020
24 Ibid.
25 Jaffrelot, Christophe, *Hindu Nationalism: A Reader*, Princeton University Press, 2007
26 Jaiswal, Suvira, 'Some Recent Theories of the Origin of Untouchability: A Historiographical Assessment,' *Proceedings of the Indian History Congress*, 1978.
27 Balakrishnan, A., 'Social Evils in Kerala Society: Its Evolution and Practice,' *Journal of East-West Thought*, December 2020, p. 37–48.
28 *Delhi*, Nehru Memorial Museum and Library, 'Harijan,' Gandhi, M.K., 28th Sept 1947.
29 N.H. Palkar, *Dr Keshav Baliram Hedgewar – a Biography*, Lokhit Prakashan, Lucknow, 2014.
30 Seshadri, H.V., *Dr Hedgewar, The Epoch-Maker*, Sahitya Sindhu, Bangalore, 1981
31 Seshadri, H.V., *Dr Hedgewar, The Epoch-Maker*, Sahitya Sindhu, Bangalore, 1981
32 Nagpur, Dr Hedgewar Bhavan, Hedgewar archives, 20th September 1933, translated from Marathi
33 ibid
34 'Nagpur,' *Dr Hedgewar Bhavan*, Hedgewar Archives, 22nd October 1933, translated from Marathi.
35 Ankit, Rakesh, 'How the Ban on the RSS Was Lifted,' Economic and Political Weekly, vol. 47, no. 16, 2012, p. 71–78.
36 'Nagpur,' *Dr Hedgewar Bhavan*, Hedgewar Archives, March 1933, translated from Marathi.

37 Sinha, Rakesh, *Builders of Modern India: Dr Keshav Baliram Hedgewar,* Publications Division, Ministry of Information and Broadcasting, Govt. of India, 2017.

38 Narayan, Shriman, *Jamnalal Bajaj: Gandhiji's 'Fifth Son',* Ministry of Information and Broadcasting, Govt. of India, 1974.

39 Ibid.

40 Ibid.

41 N.H. Palkar, *Dr Keshav Baliram Hedgewar – a Biography,* Lokhit Prakashan, Lucknow, 2014

42 Ibid.

43 Sinha, Rakesh, *Builders of Modern India: Dr Keshav Baliram Hedgewar,* Publications Division, Ministry of Information and Broadcasting, Govt. of India, 2017.

44 Casolari, Marzia, 'Hindutva's Foreign Tie-Up in the 1930s: Archival Evidence,' *Economic and Political Weekly,* vol. 35, no. 4, 2000, p. 218–228.

45 Sinha, Rakesh, *Builders of Modern India: Dr Keshav Baliram Hedgewar,* Publications Division, Ministry of Information and Broadcasting, Govt. of India, 2017.

46 N.H. Palkar, *Dr Keshav Baliram Hedgewar – A Biography,* Lokhit Prakashan, Lucknow, 2014.

47 Seshadri, H.V., *Dr Hedgewar, The Epoch-Maker,* Sahitya Sindhu, Bangalore, 1981.

48 N.H. Palkar, *Dr Keshav Baliram Hedgewar – A Biography,* Lokhit Prakashan, Lucknow, 2014.

49 Ibid.

50 Ibid.

51 Sinha, Rakesh, *Builders of Modern India: Dr Keshav Baliram Hedgewar,* Publications Division, Ministry of Information and Broadcasting, Govt. of India, 2017.

52 Casolari, Marzia, 'Hindutva's Foreign Tie-Up in the 1930s: Archival Evidence,' *Economic and Political Weekly,* vol. 35, no. 4, 2000, p. 218–228.

53 Ibid.

54 Ibid.

55 Jaffrelot, Christophe, *Hindu Nationalism: A Reader,* Princeton University Press, 2007.

56 Casolari, Marzia, 'Hindutva's Foreign Tie-Up in the 1930s: Archival Evidence,' *Economic and Political Weekly,* vol. 35, no. 4, 2000, p. 218–228.

57 Delhi, *Nehru Memorial Museum and Library,* Moonjay papers, Moonjay/1, 31st March 1934

58 N.H. Palkar, *Dr Keshav Baliram Hedgewar – a Biography,* Lokhit Prakashan, Lucknow, 2014

59 'Gopal Mukund Huddar: An Indian Volunteer in the IBS', *Alba Volunteer*, 8 August 2016, https://albavolunteer.org/2016/08/gopal-mukund-huddar-an-indian-volunteer-in-the-ibs/.
60 Punyani, Ram, *Gandhi's assassination – Godse and the RSS connection*, Centre for Study of Society and Secularism, Mumbai, 2000.
61 Patel, Sardar, ed. Durga Das, *Sardar Patel's correspondence 1945–1950*, Vol. VI, Navajivan Publishing House, 1973, p. 323.
62 Carothers, Thomas, O'Donohue, Andrew, *'Political Polarisation in South and South-East Asia: Old Divisions, New Dangers', Carnegie Endowment for International Peace*, 2020.
63 Treanor, Tom, *'One Damn Thing After Another', Kessinger Legacy Reprints*, 2010.
64 Delhi, *Nehru Memorial Museum and Library, Moonjay Papers*, Moonjay/1, 2nd June 1938
65 Delhi, *Nehru Memorial Museum and Library, Moonjay Papers*, Moonjay/2, 14th Febuary 1932
66 Delhi, *Nehru Memorial Museum and Library, Moonjay Papers*, Moonjay/10, 10th January 1933.MoonjayMoonjay
67 Delhi, *National Archives of India, Mahratta Daily*, 7th March 1934.

Chapter 14: Between Saffron and Silence

1 N.H. Palkar, *'Dr Keshav Baliram Hedgewar – A Biography'*, Lokhit Prakashan, Lucknow, 2014.
2 Sinha, Rakesh, *'Builders of Modern India: Dr Keshav Baliram Hedgewar', Publications Division, Ministry of Information and Broadcasting, Govt. of India*, 2017.
3 Guha, Ramachandra, *'A Tribute to the Greatest Gandhian', Scoll.in*, 15th August 2021, accessed 16th July 2022.
4 Ibid.
5 *Mirabehn, The Spirit's Pilgrimage, Great Rivers Books*, 1st edition, Utah, 1995.
6 N.H. Palkar, *'Dr Keshav Baliram Hedgewar – A Biography'*, Lokhit Prakashan, Lucknow, 2014.
7 Ibid.
8 Lindley, Mark, *'Mirabehn, Gandhi and Beethoven', Journal Sarvodaya Talisman*, vol. 1, Madurai, 2000.
9 N.H. Palkar, *'Dr Keshav Baliram Hedgewar – A Biography'*, Lokhit Prakashan, Lucknow, 2014.
10 N.H. Palkar, 'Dr Keshav Baliram Hedgewar – a Biography', Lokhit Prakashan, Lucknow, 2014.

11 Sinha, Rakesh, 'Builders of modern India: Dr Keshav Baliram Hedgewar', *Publications Division, Ministry of Information and Broadcasting, Govt. of India*, 2017.
12 Delhi, Nehru Memorial Museum and Library, 'Harijan', *Gandhi, M.K.*, 28th Sept 1947.
13 N.H. Palkar, 'Dr Keshav Baliram Hedgewar – a Biography', Lokhit Prakashan, Lucknow, 2014.
14 N.H. Palkar, 'Dr Keshav Baliram Hedgewar – a Biography', Lokhit Prakashan, Lucknow, 2014.
15 N.H. Palkar, 'Dr Keshav Baliram Hedgewar – a Biography', Lokhit Prakashan, Lucknow, 2014.
16 Nagpur, 'Dr Hedgewar Bhavan', *Hedgewar Archives*, translated from Marathi.
17 Ibid.
18 N.H. Palkar, 'Dr Keshav Baliram Hedgewar – a Biography', Lokhit Prakashan, Lucknow, 2014.
19 Bianchini, Davide A., 'Penance and Mortification', *Religious Vocation*, http://www.religious-vocation.com/penance_and_mortification.html#.Yta7TXZBzSI, accessed 19 July 2022.
20 'Hindu Swayam Sevak Sangh UK', https://hssuk.org/sanskaar-sewa-sangathan/
21 N.H. Palkar, 'Dr Keshav Baliram Hedgewar – a Biography', Lokhit Prakashan, Lucknow, 2014.
22 Ibid.
23 Curran, Jean A., 'The RSS: Militant Hinduism', *Far Eastern Survey* 19, no. 10, 1950, p. 93–98.
24 Saberwal, Satish, 'On the Making of Muslims in India Historically', *Sociological Bulletin* 55, no. 2, 2006, p. 237–266.
25 Ibid.
26 Ibid.
27 Ambedkar, B.R., *Pakistan or the Partition of India, Samayak Prakashan*, 2013.
28 Saberwal, Satish, 'On the Making of Muslims in India Historically', *Sociological Bulletin* 55, no. 2, 2006, p. 237–266.
29 Wood, Houston, *Invitation to Peace Studies*, Oxford University Press, 2015, p.24–25
30 N.H. Palkar, *Dr Keshav Baliram Hedgewar – a Biography*, Lokhit Prakashan, Lucknow, 2014
31 George, Jim, 'Leo Strauss, Neoconservatism and US Foreign Policy: Esoteric Nihilism and the Bush Doctrine', *International Politics, Palgrave Macmillan*, 2005, vol. 42, p. 174–202

32 Savarkar, Vinayak Damodar, *Hindutva, Hindi Sahitya Sadan*, 2003
33 Ambedkar, BR., *Pakistan or the partition of India, Samayak Prakashan*, 2013
34 Ashraf, Ajaz, 'What Muslim intelligentsia doesn't get about Bhagwat and the RSS', *News Click*, 5th August 2021, https://www.newsclick.in/What-Muslim-Intelligentsia-Doesn%E2%80%99t-Get-About-Bhagwat-RSS, accessed 21st July 2022.
35 Eaaswarkhanth, M., Dubey, B., Meganathan, P. et al., 'Diverse genetic origin of Indian Muslims: evidence from autosomal STR loci', *J Hum Genet* 54, 2009, p. 340–348.
36 N.H. Palkar, *Dr Keshav Baliram Hedgewar – a Biography*, Lokhit Prakashan, Lucknow, 2014
37 N.H. Palkar, *Dr Keshav Baliram Hedgewar – a Biography*, Lokhit Prakashan, Lucknow, 2014
38 Nagpur, Dr Hedgewar Bhavan, *Hedgewar Archives*, letter dated 12th May 1935, translated from Hindi.
39 N.H. Pal*kar, Dr Keshav Baliram Hedgewar – a Biography*, Lokhit Prakashan, Lucknow, 2014
40 ibid
41 N.H. Palkar, *Dr Keshav Baliram Hedgewar – a Biography*, Lokhit Prakashan, Lucknow, 2014
42 Nagpur, Dr Hedgewar Bhavan, *Hedgewar Archives*, letter dated 13th January 1936, translated from Marathi.
43 N.H. Palkar, *Dr Keshav Baliram Hedgewar – a Biography*, Lokhit Prakashan, Lucknow, 2014
44 Lele, N.V., 'Valued heart over money', *HSSworld.org*, http://www.hssworld.org/doctorji/lele_narrations/96.htm.
45 Ibid.
46 Ibid.
47 Malik, Rashida, *Iqbal: The Spiritual Father of Pakistan*, Sang-e-Meel Publications, 2003.
48 Ikram, S.M., *Indian Muslims and the Partition of India*, Atlantic Publishers & Distributors, 1995, pp. 177–178.
49 Wolpert, Stanley A., *Jinnah of Pakistan*, Oxford University Press, New York, 1984.
50 Hiro, Dilip, *The Longest August: The Unflinching Rivalry Between India and Pakistan*, Public Affairs, 2015, p.69
51 Ibid.
52 Ali, Choudhry Rahmat, *Now or Never: Are We to Live or Perish Forever?*, Pakistan National Movement, 1933.
53 Aziz, Khursheed Kamal, *Rahmat Ali: A Biography*, Steiner Verlag Wiesbaden, 1987.

54 N.H. Palkar, *Dr Keshav Baliram Hedgewar – A Biography*, Lokhit Prakashan, Lucknow, 2014.

55 Kamran, Tahir, *Chaudhary Rahmat Ali and His Political Imagination: Pak Plan and the Continent of Dinia*, Cambridge University Press, 2017, pp. 82–108.

56 Anderson, Walter K., Damle, Sridhar D., *The Brotherhood in Saffron: The Rashtriya swayamsevak Sangh and Hindu Revivalism*, Vistaar Publications, Delhi, 1987.swayamsevak

Chapter 15: The Vanguard

1 Southard, Barbara, *Colonial Politics and Women's Rights: Women Suffrage Campaigns in Bengal, British India in the 1920s, Modern Asian Studies*, Cambridge, Cambridge University Press, 1993, pp. 397–439.

2 Ansari, Sarah, Gould, William, *Boundaries of Belonging: Localities, Citizenship and Rights in India and Pakistan*, Cambridge University Press, 2019.

3 Vekaria, Reena, *A Life Sketch of Vandaneeya Mausiji*, Published by Hindu Sevika Samiti (UK), 2020.

4 N.H. Palkar, *Dr Keshav Baliram Hedgewar – a Biography*, Lokhit Prakashan, Lucknow, 2014

5 N.H. Palkar, *Dr Keshav Baliram Hedgewar – a Biography*, Lokhit Prakashan, Lucknow, 2014

6 Bhattacharyya, Rituparna, and Singh, Suman, *Exclusion (and Seclusion): Geographies of Disowned Widows of India, GeoJournal* 83, no. 4, 2018, pp. 757–774.

7 Vekaria, Reena, *A Life Sketch of Vandaneeya Mausiji*, Published by Hindu Sevika Samiti (UK), 2020.

8 Jaffrelot, Christophe, *The Sangh Parivar: A Reader, Critical Issues in Indian Politics*, Oxford University Press, 2005, pp. 445.

9 Tyagi, Aastha, 2014, 'Vasudeva Kutumb?: Membership and Recruitment in the Rashtriya Sevika Samiti', *Sub-Versions: A Journal of Emerging Research in Media and Cultural Studies*, Vol. 2, Issue 2.

10 Pradhan, Aishwariya, 2022, 'Why are stay-at-home moms looked down upon?', *We Are Restless*, 04/02/2022, accessed 25/12/2022.

11 The Wire Staff, 12/06/2017, 'Swords, knives and motherhood: Lessons from an RSS women's camp', *The Wire*, https://thewire.in/gender/rss-womens-wing-motherhood, accessed January 2022.

12 N.H. Palkar, *Dr Keshav Baliram Hedgewar – a Biography*, Lokhit Prakashan, Lucknow, 2014

13 Ibid.

14 Srinivas, Tulsai, 2011, 'Exploring Indian culture through food', *Education About Asia*, Vol. 16, Issue 3.

15 N.H. Palkar, *Dr Keshav Baliram Hedgewar – a Biography*, Lokhit Prakashan, Lucknow, 2014
16 Muthiah, S. & Gopalan, K.N., *Moving India on Wheels: The Story of Ashok Leyland*, Ashok Leyland Ltd, 2008.
17 N.H. Palkar, *Dr Keshav Baliram Hedgewar – a Biography*, Lokhit Prakashan, Lucknow, 2014
18 ibid
19 Churchill, Winston, 1946, 'Sinews of Peace (Iron Curtain Speech)', *National Churchill Museum* [online], https://www.nationalchurchillmuseum.org/sinews-of-peace-iron-curtain-speech.html, accessed 17/01/2022.
20 N.H. Palkar, *Dr Keshav Baliram Hedgewar – a Biography*, Lokhit Prakashan, Lucknow, 2014
21 Ibid.
22 Mehta, Ashoka & Patwardhan, Achyut, *The Communal Triangle in India*, Kitabistan Publishers, 1942, p. 123
23 Zakaria, Rafiq, *Indian Muslims: Where Have They Gone Wrong?*, Popular Prakashan Press, 2004.
24 Baig, M.R.A., *The Muslim Dilemma in India*, Vikas Publishing House, 1974, pp. 51-52.
25 N.H. Palkar, *Dr Keshav Baliram Hedgewar – A Biography*, Lokhit Prakashan, Lucknow, 2014.
26 Jeffrelot, Christophe, *The Hindu Nationalist Movement in India*, Columbia University Press, New York, 1996, pp. 65-66.
27 Seshadri, H.V., *Dr Hedgewar: The Epoch-maker*, Sahitya Sindhu, Bangalore, 1981
28 N.H. Palkar, *Dr Keshav Baliram Hedgewar – a Biography*, Lokhit Prakashan, Lucknow, 2014
29 Seshadri, H.V., *Dr Hedgewar: The Epoch-maker*, Sahitya Sindhu, Bangalore, 1981
30 Mahajan, Anilesh S., 5th July 2017, 'Israel is everything the RSS wants India to be, Modi is making it happen', *DailyO* [online], www.dailyo.in/politics/modi-rss-israel-india-muslim-world-benjamin-netanyahu-18179, accessed January 2022
31 Ibid.
32 Naqvi, Saeed, 27th August 2016, '"I want every Muslim to live here in peace": A Conversation with the RSS Ideologue Bhaurao Deoras', *The Caravan* [online], https://caravanmagazine.in/vantage/1990-conversation-rss-bhaurao-deoras-naqvi, accessed January 2022.
33 Sharma, A.K., 1992, 'Ayodhya and Rama', *Puratattva: Archaeological Survey of India*, Vol. 23, pp. 35-40.

34 Personal interviews with swayamsevaks outside of India, mainly in the UK and USA (Vishwa Vibhag)
35 Herdeck, Margaret & Piramal, Gita, *India's Industrialists*, Lynne Rienner Publishers, 1985, p. 62.
36 Seshadri, H.V., *Dr Hedgewar: The Epoch-maker*, Sahitya Sindhu, Bangalore, 1981
37 Seshadri, H.V., *Dr Hedgewar: The Epoch-maker*, Sahitya Sindhu, Bangalore, 1981
38 N.H. Palkar, *Dr Keshav Baliram Hedgewar – a Biography*, Lokhit Prakashan, Lucknow, 2014
39 Goyal, Des Raj, *Rashtriya swayamsevak Sangh*, Radha Krishna Prakashan, Delhi, 1979, p. 78.swayamsevak
40 Anderson, W., Damle, Sridhar D., *The Brotherhood in Saffron: The Rashtriya swayamsevak Sangh and Hindu revivalism*, Westview Press, 1987.swayamsevak

Chapter 16: Wars and Visions

1 Lowy, Michael, *Fire Alarm: Reading Walter Benjamin's On the Concept of History*, Verso, New York, 2005, p. 25.
2 N.H. Palkar, *Dr Keshav Baliram Hedgewar – a Biography*, Lokhit Prakashan, Lucknow, 2014
3 Laski, Harold, 'A Life on the Left', *The Free Library*, Washington Monthly Company, 1993, accessed 8th February 2023, https://www.thefreelibrary.com/Harold+Laski%3a+A+Life+on+the+Left.-a014687963.
4 Gordon, Michael R., *Conflict and Consensus in Labour's Foreign Policy 1914–1965*, Stanford University Press, 1969, p. 157.
5 Seshadri, H.V., *Dr Hedgewar: The Epoch-maker*, Sahitya Sindhu, Bangalore, 1981.
6 N.H. Palkar, *Dr Keshav Baliram Hedgewar – a Biography*, Lokhit Prakashan, Lucknow, 2014
7 Ghosh, Asok, A short history of the All India Forward Bloc, Lokmat Printers Pvt Ltd., Kolkata, 2001, p.32-34
8 Bose, Subhas C., *The Indian Struggle: 1920-1942*, Oxford University Press, 1998
9 Bose, Subhas C., *The Indian Struggle: 1920-1942*, Oxford University Press, 1998
10 N.H. Palkar, *Dr Keshav Baliram Hedgewar – a Biography*, Lokhit Prakashan, Lucknow, 2014
11 ibid
12 ibid

13 N.H. Palkar, *Dr Keshav Baliram Hedgewar – a Biography*, Lokhit Prakashan, Lucknow, 2014
14 Ibid.
15 N.H. Palkar, *Dr Keshav Baliram Hedgewar – a Biography*, Lokhit Prakashan, Lucknow, 2014
16 Singh, Rajesh, *Portraits of Hindutva: from Harappa to Ayodhya*, Rupa Publications, 2018
17 Reynolds, David, 'The Origins of the Two "World Wars"; Historical Discourse and International Politics', *Journal of Contemporary History*, Issue 38, Vol. 1, 2003, pp. 29–44.
18 Bayly, C.A., 'The Nation Within: British India at War 1939–1945', Raileigh Lecture on History, *Proceedings of the British Academy*, Vol. 125, 2004, pp. 265–285.
19 Dorschner, Jon, 'World War Two Provides the Indo/British Breaking Point', *American Diplomacy*, 2017, accessed March 2023, https://americandiplomacy.web.unc.edu/2017/01/world-war-two-provides-the-indo-british-breaking-point/.
20 Jackson, Roy, 'Mawlana Mawdudi and Political Islam: Authority and the Islamic State', *Taylor & Francis*, 2011, p. 60.
21 Ibid.
22 Ibid.
23 Rao, Shiva B., 'After the War in India', *Pacific Affairs*, Vol. 18, Issue 2, 1945, pp. 169–179.
24 Raza, Ali, Roy, Franziska, 'Paramilitary Organisations in Interwar India', *South Asia: Journal of South Asian Studies*, Issue 38, Vol. 4, pp. 671–689.
25 Ibid.
26 Ibid.
27 Sinha, Rakesh, *Dr. Keshav Baliram Hedgewar*, Publications Division, Ministry of Information and Broadcasting, 2015.
28 Ibid.
29 Ibid.
30 Ibid.
31 Seshadri, H.V., *Dr Hedgewar: The Epoch-maker*, Sahitya Sindhu, Bangalore, 1981
32 Sinha, Rakesh, *Dr. Keshav Baliram Hedgewar*, Publications Division, Ministry of Information and Broadcasting, 2015
33 N.H. Palkar, *Dr Keshav Baliram Hedgewar – a Biography*, Lokhit Prakashan, Lucknow, 2014
34 Balakrishnan, Uday, 'Subhas Chandra Bose – a flawed hero', *The Hindu*, 4th Sept 2020, accessed: March 2023, www.thehindubusinessline.com/opinion/subhas-chandra-bose-a-flawed-hero/article32525573.ece.

35 Hayes, Romain, *Subhas Chandra Bose in Nazi Germany: Politics, Intelligence and Propaganda 1941-1943*, Random House India, 2011.
36 Ibid.

Chapter 17: Last Stand

1 N.H. Palkar, *Dr Keshav Baliram Hedgewar – a Biography*, Lokhit Prakashan, Lucknow, 2014
2 Ibid.
3 Ibid.
4 Ibid.
5 Hutchinson, John, and Smith, Anthony, *Nationalism*, Oxford University Press, 1995
6 N.H. Palkar, *Dr Keshav Baliram Hedgewar – a Biography*, Lokhit Prakashan, Lucknow, 2014
7 Ibid.
8 Ibid.
9 Ibid.
10 N.H. Palkar, *Dr Keshav Baliram Hedgewar – a Biography*, Lokhit Prakashan, Lucknow, 2014
11 Ramdas, Samartha, *Dasbodh: Spiritual instruction for a servant (of Divinity)*, Sadguru Publishers, 2010
12 Ramdas, Samartha, *Dasbodh: Spiritual instruction for a servant (of Divinity)*, Sadguru Publishers, 2010
13 N.H. Palkar, *Dr Keshav Baliram Hedgewar – a Biography*, Lokhit Prakashan, Lucknow, 2014
14 N.H. Palkar, *Dr Keshav Baliram Hedgewar – a Biography*, Lokhit Prakashan, Lucknow, 2014
15 Ibid.
16 Ibid.
17 Pinkney, Andrea M., 'Looking West to India: Asian education, intra-Asian renaissance, and the Nalanda revival', *Modern Asian Studies*, Cambridge University Press, 2014, Vol. 49, Issue 1, p. 111–p. 149
18 Basham, A. L., *The Wonder That Was India: A Survey of the History and Culture of the Indian Sub-continent Before the Coming of the Muslims*, London: Picador, 1954.
19 N.H. Palkar, *Dr Keshav Baliram Hedgewar – a Biography*, Lokhit Prakashan, Lucknow, 2014
20 Ibid.
21 Tzu, Lao, (translated by Lau, D.C.), *Tao Te Ching*, Penguin Classics, 2003.

22 Thatcher, Margaret, 'Interview for *Woman's Own*', *Thatcher Archive* (THCR 5/2/262): COI transcript, accessed 20th May 2023, https://www.margaretthatcher.org/document/106689.
23 N.H. Pal*kar, Dr Keshav Baliram Hedgewar – a Biography*, Lokhit Prakashan, Lucknow, 2014
24 Ibid.
25 Ibid.
26 Ibid.
27 Ibid.
28 Krisbergh, Audrey, 'Role Model: The Promise and the Peril', *Centre for Parenting Education*, 2006, accessed 2022, https://centerforparentingeducation.org/library-of-articles/focus-parents/role-model-promise-peril/
29 N.H. Palkar, *Dr Keshav Baliram Hedgewar – a Biography*, Lokhit Prakashan, Lucknow, 2014
30 *Mahratta*; November 3rd,1939
31 Sampath, Vikram, Savarkar: *A Contested Legacy 1924-1966*, Penguin India, 2021
32 Taksal, Vinod, 'A Maha Festival for Ganesh', *The Times of India*, 9th September 2002, accessed July 2022.
33 Sinha, Rakesh, *Dr. Keshav Baliram Hedgewar*, Publications Division, Ministry of Information and Broadcasting, 2015.
34 Seshadri, *H.V., Dr Hedgewar: The Epoch-maker*, Sahitya Sindhu, Bangalore, 1981
35 Ibid.
36 Arya, Shishir, 'RSS Chief Mohan Bhagwat: Why Look for a Shivling in Every Mosque', *The Times of India*, 3rd June 2022, accessed January 2023.
37 HT News Desk, 'Islam Is Safe in India… Forget Foreign Connections: RSS Chief Mohan Bhagwat', *Hindustan Times*, June 2023, accessed August 2023.
38 Parth, MN., 'Why Ex-Communists Are Joining Modi's BJP in India's West Bengal', *Al Jazeera News*, 11th April 2021, accessed June 2023.
39 N.H. Palkar, *Dr Keshav Baliram Hedgewar – a Biography*, Lokhit Prakashan, Lucknow, 2014
40 *Delhi*, Nehru Memorial Museum and Library, 'Intelligence Bureau Report', 1942.
41 Chatterji, Joya, *Bengal Divided: Hindu Communalism and Partition, 1932–1947*, Cambridge University Press, p. 230.
42 Eaton, Richard, *The Rise of Islam and the Bengal Frontier 1204 to 1760*, University of California Press, 1996.
43 Seshadri, H.V., *Dr Hedgewar: The Epoch-maker*, Sahitya Sindhu, Bangalore, 1981

44 N.H. Palkar, *Dr Keshav Baliram Hedgewar – a Biography*, Lokhit Prakashan, Lucknow, 2014
45 Ibid.
46 Ibid.
47 Ibid.
48 Ibid.
49 Ibid.
50 Ibid.
51 Ibid.
52 Ibid.
53 Fay, Peter W., *The Forgotten Army: India's Armed Struggle for Independence, 1942–1945*, University of Michigan Press, 1993.

Chapter 18: Postscript: Long Shadow

1 Shelly, Mary, *Frankenstein*, Penguin, 2003
2 N.H. Palkar, *Dr Keshav Baliram Hedgewar – a Biography*, Lokhit Prakashan, Lucknow, 2014
3 ibid
4 Anderson, Walter K., Damle, Sridhar D., *The Brotherhood in Saffron: The Rashtriya swayamsevak Sangh and Hindu Revivalism*, Vistaar Publications, 1987.swayamsevak
5 Goyal, Des Raj, *Rashtriya swayamsevak Sangh*, Radha Krishna Prakashan, Delhi, 1979.swayamsevak
6 Goyal, Des Raj, *Rashtriya swayamsevak Sangh*, Radha Krishna Prakashan, Delhi, 1979.swayamsevak
7 Ibid.
8 Andersen, Walter, 'The Rashtriya swayamsevak Sangh: II: Who Represents the Hindus?', *Economic and Political Weekly*, vol. 7, no. 12, 1972, pp. 633–40, JSTOR, http://www.jstor.org/stable/4361149, accessed 23rd March 2024. swayamsevak
9 Von Tunzelmann, Alex, 'Who Is to Blame for Partition?', *The New York Times*, 18th August 2017, https://www.nytimes.com/2017/08/18/opinion/india-pakistan-partition-imperial-britain.html, accessed 20th March 2024.
10 Ibid.
11 Ibid.

Scan QR code to access the
Penguin Random House India website